THE INTERNATIONAL BOOK OF
COMICS

Denis Gifford

Crescent Books
New York

ACKNOWLEDGMENTS

All the comics reproduced in this book come from the author's own private collection, and are reproduced as historic illustrations to the text. Grateful acknowledgement is made to the original publishers and their artists, without whose contribution this book would not have been possible. Full copyright is acknowledged and quoted in the captions to the illustrations, credited according to the original copyright or publication data as printed in the comics. Any omission or incorrect information should be notified to the author and publisher, who will be pleased to amend in any future edition of this book.

Jacket: A selection of Special Editions: *Beano* No.1000 © 16 September 1961 D.C. Thomson; *Mad* No.1 © October 1952 E.C. Comics; *Tiger Tim's Weekly Jubilee Number* © 4 May 1935 Amalgamated Press; *Lone Ranger Silver Anniversary Issue* © April 1958 Dell Publishing; *Walt Disney's Comics and Stories, 25th Anniversary Issue* © September 1965 Walt Disney Productions/Gold Key; *The Amazing Spider-Man* No.100 © September 1971 Marvel Comics; *The Crypt of Terror* No.1 (No.17) © April 1950 E.C. Comics; *Film Fun* No.1000 © 18 March 1939 Amalgamated Press; *Captain America* No.100 © April 1968 Marvel Comics; *Eagle Coronation Number* © 29 May 1953 Hulton Press; *Superman* No.100 © September 1955 National Periodicals.

Back: *Popeye 50th Anniversary Number* © March 1979 King Features/Gold Key; *Wonder Woman* No.300 © February 1983 D.C. Comics; *Hotspur* No.1000 © 16 December 1978 D.C. Thomson; *Flash Gordon* No.1 © October 1950 King Features/Harvey; *Girl Birthday Number* © 2 November 1955 Hulton Press; *Tom Mix Comics* No.1 © September 1940 Ralston; *Comic Cuts* No.3000 © 1 August 1953 Amalgamated Press; *The Spirit* No.1 © October 1966 Harvey Publications; *Tiger Silver Jubilee Issue* © 22 September 1979 IPC; *Tarzan of the Apes* No.100 © 1975 Top Sellers; *Battle Picture Weekly* No.100 © 29 January 1977 IPC; *Radio Fun* No.1000 © 7 December 1957 Amalgamated Press; *Incredible Hulk* No.1 (No.102) © April 1962 Marvel Comics; *Lion 20th Birthday Issue* © 26 February 1972 Amalgamated Press; *Dandy* No.2000 © 22 March 1980 D.C. Thomson; *Batman* No.100 © June 1956 National Periodicals; *Captain Marvel Adventures* No.100 © September 1949 Fawcett Publications; *Archie's Joke Book* No.100 © May 1968 Archie Publications.

Endpapers: Panels and strip headings selected from comics © Amalgamated Press.

Half Title: Ally Sloper drawn by W. G. Baxter (1885).

Title Spread: Selection of comics from around the world: Russia, France, Australia, Spain, Holland, India, Finland, Germany, China, Mexico, Jugoslavia, Italy, Hong Kong, Brazil, Greece, Japan, Canada, Saudi-Arabia.

First English edition published by
Deans International Publishing
52–54 Southwark Street, London SE1 1UA
A division of The Hamlyn Publishing Group Limited
London · New York · Sydney · Toronto

This 1984 edition is published by Crescent Books
Distributed by Crown Publishers, Inc.

ISBN 0-517-439271
Library of Congress Catalog Number: 84-70949
h g f e d c b a

Printed in Italy

CONTENTS

(continued overleaf)

INTRODUCTION:
A World of Comics

1984 may have been George Orwell's year to you, but to me it was Ally Sloper's! A century since No.1 of *Ally Sloper's Half-Holiday* first came out with its eight packed pages of strips and cartoons, the world's first weekly comic to feature a regular cartoon character. Surely Sloper, with his bashed-in brolly and matching nose deserves a bit of a knees-up: he certainly fathered more fun than George and his Big Brother!

So to Ally Sloper, F.O.M. (Friend of Man), I dedicate this sumptuous yet superficial rummage through my collection of comics, provided he doesn't mind sharing the dedication with my Auntie Florrie. Can it really be over half of this comic century ago that my Auntie came round one Friday night with a copy of *Puck* rolled up in her macintosh pocket? And every Friday after that until I was old enough to run round to the corner shop with two pennies in my hand, big boy enough to buy my own. It was then that I really discovered the world of comics, for, for the price of one twopenny *Puck*, I was delighted to find I could buy a penny *Chips* and a penny *Jester*! The pink pranks of "Weary Willie and Tired Tim" and the blue doings of "Basil and Bert" were much more my meat than the full colour fun of "Jingle's Jolly Circus". Soon every penny pocket money went on comics: they lasted longer than any gobstopper, and besides, sometimes they gave away free sweets if you were lucky! Comics piled up on the chair beside my bed, then shared space with the coal in the cupboard under the stairs. I can still see the black stripes down the spines where a careless coalman wiped his sack, although my original comic pile has long been gone, thanks to my mum getting a patriotic urge while I was evacuated ...

My childhood is signposted by comics: the day in 1936 I rushed out to buy No.1 of *Mickey Mouse Weekly*, its radiant photogravure colours shining out to put every other comic in the shade. The day in 1937 I bought No.1 of *The Dandy*, and blew the Grand Free Express Whistle all the way home. I recall an old lady and her house in Dulwich purely because it was there I bought No.1 of *The Beano* in 1938. The wonder of seeing my wireless favourite Big-Hearted Arthur in No.1 of *Radio Fun*, and the joy of buying No.1 of *The Knockout* in 1939, and munching my way through the Grand Free Tuck Hamper, a packet of six different kinds of cheap sweets! No.1 of *Happy Days*, the finest comic of a Golden Age, and the dreadful shock when the final issue announced that it was combining with *Chicks' Own*, a hyphenated comic I had given up in scorn at the grand old age of five!

American comics, too, were my equal delight. These came in two varieties: huge, mysterious coloured comics stapled into wrappers and sold at twopence a time on street corners in Peckham (mysterious because I could never understand why comics should have such strange titles as *The New York Journal!*); and small-sized comicbooks, found in the Rye Lane Woolworths. These had titles like *Famous Funnies*, cost just twopence for 68 pages of tiny little pictures, and were even more marvellous by 1939 when incredible characters like "Superman" and "Batman" first came leaping off the pages.

With World War II these Yankee comics, as we called them, vanished, but what a thrill when somebody called Gerald G. Swan began to put out British comic books on the American style! I bought No.1 of *New Funnies* in January 1940, and with it I began consciously and consistently to collect. Once a week I cycled to Peckham, ostensibly to visit my Grandma but really to buy the latest Swan comic. By now I was drawing and printing my own comics, *The Junior* and *The Spotter*, and selling them for a penny a time at school. Meanwhile the paper shortage had inspired other minor publishers to follow Swan into the comic racket, and all sorts of little twopenny one-shots were turning up in Woolworths. I bought them, saved them, and now, following an unsuccessful attempt to research them in the British Library, discover that I have the world's only complete collection of these comic curiosities.

For many years comics were my life. I had always wanted to draw comics and before I left school I was freelancing "Pansy Potter" and other established strips to *The Beano*. Whilst serving in the RAF, I spent my Duty Clerk weekends drawing superhero comic-books for some of those minor publishers, and after demob I drew "Our Ernie", "Steadfast McStaunch" and others for *The Knockout*. But my real interest in comics, as a collector and a historian, did not develop until I somehow segued into showbiz, writing comedy on radio, then devising and compiling shows for television. Perhaps it was no longer cartooning for a living that made me more interested in the artwork of others. At any rate, I began to collect again, not from personal nostalgia, but from a sense of history, ever digging backwards to root out the origins of comics and strip cartooning. It has been, nay is, a fascinating hobby, for always there is something more to find out (I'm sure that by the time this book is published, I will have found at least one comic, character, or artist who has been undeservedly overlooked).

Comics have now taken me far beyond my bedside chair and my mum's coal cupboard, beyond the shelves of the British Library, beyond indeed the borders of Britain. I have carried the story of British comics to conventions in Spain, Italy and New York, and wherever I go I manage to find some comics, old or new, to add to my knowledge and my collection. Every comic in this book comes from my collection, and if your own favourite is missing, perhaps it's because I haven't got it. Send it to me at once!

Denis Gifford
Sydenham 1984

COMIC MAGAZINES:
From Punch to Puck

The first comic magazine was entitled, aptly enough, *The Comick Magazine*. It was published by Mr Harrison of 18 Paternoster Row, London, on, again aptly enough, 1 April 1796. Mr Harrison described it as, "The Compleat Library of Mirth, Humour, Wit, Gaiety and Entertainment." Although it was wholly text, it came "enriched with William Hogarth's Celebrated Humorous, Comical and Moral Prints", one per monthly issue. Hogarth's prints formed the series "Industry and Idleness". When these were put together in their narrative sequence, they could be described as an early form of comic strip. Hogarth's contemporary, caricaturist Thomas Rowlandson, provided plates for *The Caricature Magazine*, the next to come

along, in 1808. The following year *The Poetical Magazine* (1 May 1809) introduced the first continuing cartoon hero, "Dr Syntax". He was drawn by Rowlandson to illustrate "The Schoolmaster's Tour", a serial by William Combe. This was reprinted in book form in 1812 as *The Tour of Dr Syntax in Search of the Picturesque*. It had 31 coloured plates and was priced at one guinea. "Syntax" became the first cartoon cult figure, inspiring such merchandising spin-offs as Syntax hats, coats and wigs!

The French funny-paper *Figaro* prompted *Figaro in London*, a four-page weekly, which began on 10 December 1831. Robert Seymour drew the cover cartoons, which occasionally spread to inside pages as

well. This first British funny weekly ran for eight years and inspired so many imitators (*Figaro in Liverpool*; *Figaro in Sheffield*) that it was a genuine case of *Figaro* here, *Figaro* there! The longest-lived comic magazine of them all is, of course, *Punch*, born 17 July 1841 and still going strong. But *Punch* itself was a spin-off, having been preceded by *Punch in London* (14 January 1832), a weekly which celebrated its 17th and final issue with no fewer than 17 cartoons! *Punch* bore the subtitle, "The London Charavari", which was a nod to its actual inspiration, the French comic paper, *Le Charavari*, edited and published by Charles Philipon from 1 December 1832. *Punch* introduced the word "cartoon" into the language on 1 July 1843 when the editor announced the coming publication of "several exquisite designs to be called *Punch's Cartoons*". The first appeared two weeks later, drawn by John Leech. Leech also drew "The

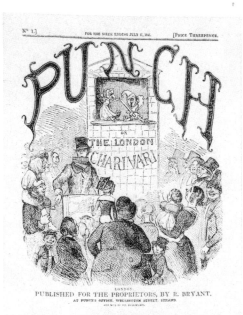

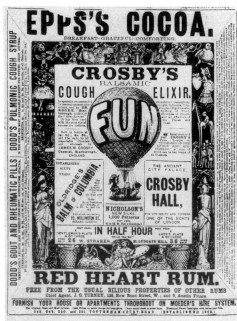

Pleasures of Housekeeping", a slap-stick strip about a suburban gent called Mr Briggs. This was published on 28 April 1849; ten years later a collection of Mr Briggs strips appeared in book form as *Pictures of Life and Character*. As late as 1905, Mr Briggs was still being reprinted in six-penny paperbacks.

Best of the many imitators of *Punch* was *Judy*. Subtitled "The London Serio-Comic Journal", *Judy* started on 1 May 1867 and, three months later, introduced the character destined to become the greatest comic strip hero of his day, "Ally Sloper". Of the many other comic weeklies, mention must be made of *Fun* (21 September 1861), which regularly featured a full-page strip by J. F. Sullivan, and *The Man in the Moon*, which from No. 4 (April 1847) ran a monthly serial strip, "Mr Candle's Rapid Career Upon the Town", by H. G. Hine and Albert Smith. Other serial strips followed after Mr Candle was extinguished. In Germany, cartoon magazines began with the weekly *Fliegende Blätter* (*Flying Leaves*) in 1845. Their first regular strip character was called "Der Staatshamorrhoidarius". But their great discovery was Wilhelm Büsch, who began contributing strips in 1859. Büsch's first attempt at a pantomime, or purely visual, strip appeared in No. 783 (1860), "The Mouse, or Sleep Disturbed". Five years later, Büsch created two little terrors whose influence on the world's comics was enormous, "Max und Moritz". Curiously, it was from Germany that the great American comic magazines sprang. Joseph Keppler, a Viennese cartoonist, moved to New York and started *Puck* in September 1876 as a German language weekly. An English language version followed in March 1877, and when colour printing was introduced a year later, the magazine settled down to 40 years of fun. Frederick Opper, who became one of the great fathers of American strip cartooning, joined *Puck* in 1880. *Judge*, the second great cartoon weekly (soon to become first in popularity), was born on 29 October 1881. More future comic artists had their beginnings here: "Zim" Zimmerman, R. F. ("Buster Brown") Outcault and George ("Krazy Kat") Herriman. *Life* was the third great magazine. It started on 4 January 1883 and introduced cartoons by Rudolph Dirks and F. M. Howarth, who would later give the comic world "The Kat-

zenjammer Kids" and "Lulu and Leander". *Judge* became a monthly and faded away; *Life* became the famous photographic news weekly; *Puck* became the title of William Randolph Hearst's Sunday comic section, retaining its original motto: "What fools we mortals be".

Figaro in London *No.17* © *31 March 1832 William Strange. Drawn by Robert Seymour*
Punch *No.1* © *17 July 1841 R. Bryant (facsimile edition). Drawn by Ebenezer Landells*
Judy *No.1* © *1 May 1867 Judy Office (facsimile edition). Drawn by Holman*

Comic News *No.24* © *11 June 1864 Smith & Co. Drawn by 'J. G.'*
Fun © *9 January 1878 Fun Office*
Fliegende Blätter *No.2196* © *1887 Braun & Schneider.*

Illustrated Bits *No.1* © *17 January 1885 William Lucas. Drawn by Matt Morgan*
Pictures From Punch *No.1* © *25 January 1904 Bradbury Agnew. Drawn by John Tenniel*
Puck's Library *No.43* © *February 1891 Keppler & Schwarzmann. Drawn by Frederick Opper*
Judge's Library *No.35* © *February 1892 Judge. Drawn by Hamilton*

CARICATURE MAGAZINES: Inventing the Comic

C. J. Grant signed himself AAE. The CJ stood for Charles Jamison, and the AAE for Author, Artist and Editor. Following on in neat if minute letters came his credits: "Author of Maclean and Aiken's *Sporting Ideas*, the (original) *Caricaturist*, a Monthly Show-Up, Comic Songs, Tregear's *Flights of Humour*, Frontispieces to the *Penny Magazine* etc. *Comic Almanac*, *Emigration*, and upward of 400 of the most Popular Caricatures of the Day." All this penned at the bottom of his fortnightly sheet of cartoons entitled *Every Body's Album and Caricature Magazine*; and still there was room for publication data: "London. Published by J. Kendrick, 54 Leicester Square, corner of Sidney's Court, and where may be had a great Variety of Cheap Books, Caricatures, Album Scraps, etc. etc." A few issues later and Grant had to drop his credit line to make room for distribution details: "Sold by T. Dewhurst, Manchester; T. Drake, Birmingham; R. Thorley, Bath; Wisehart, Dublin; Ross and Nightingale, Liverpool; etc. etc. etc." *Every Body's Album* was clearly a success and spreading post-haste through civilized England and Ireland. The printer also got a credit: Dean & Munday of 40 Threadneedle Street. They were lithographers, and the fairly new technique of lithography allowed a lighter, looser line than the heavy-handed woodcuts of traditional magazine printing. An earlier abbreviated credit-line of Grant's, used on his series of strip cartoon frontispieces, was "Invent.Del.& Lith.", meaning Inventor, Delineator and Lithographer.

Every Body's Album was a single sheet, tabloid-size, printed on one side like the *Images d'Epinal*, but there the resemblance ceased. Grant's *Album* was a scrapbook of cartooned comment on current political and social issues, and definitely not meant for children. First published on 1 January 1834, each bi-weekly edition looked different, according to Grant's chosen topics. Often a strip appeared among the single cartoons: one called "My Brother" ran for two weeks (issues 36 and 37). Another filled the entire sheet with six large panels, retailing the slapstick misadventures of four tradesmen and their dogs on a day's shoot. No.10 carried a large single panel of furious massed activity (No.10: "The Tailors' War"), forecasting the "Yellow Kid" cartoons of the 1890's. Some of Grant's strips illustrated hand-lettered captions, others carried the story in speech balloons. Virtually everything typical of the modern comic was "inv. del. & lith."-ed by C. J. Grant, even colour: *Every Body's Album* came in two versions, sixpence plain, one shilling coloured.

Yet, a decade before Grant issued his *Album*, William Heath in Scotland had begun to draw the *Glasgow Looking Glass*. John Watson published this from 11 June 1825, issuing it from his Lithographic Press, 169 George Street, Glasgow. This was not a single sheet, but a folded tabloid of four pages, all drawn and lettered by hand, and holding the record of being the first caricature magazine in Europe, perhaps the world. It sold at one shilling for "common impressions", 1s 6d for "best", with covers costing 1s 6d, or 4s for "superior" ones, 5s for "best", and 6s for "beautifully coloured". The artist also advertised for contributions thus: "Hints taken, Ideas illustrated, and Fancies illuminated". Heath introduced a serial strip in No.4, "The History of a Coat", and drew the first front-page strip on No.6. This was the issue that changed title to *Northern Looking Glass* (18 August 1825), achieving big-city distribution down south via the famous print publisher, R. Ackermann of 101 The Strand.

William Heath moved across to Ackermann's rival in caricature prints, Thomas McLean of 26 Haymarket. Here he started a new and very well produced series entitled *McLean's Monthly Sheet of Caricatures or The Looking Glass*. No.1 was dated 1 January 1830, and was so handsome it cost 3s plain, 6s coloured. The magazine was garnered into volumes as *The Caricature Annual*. From No.8 a new cartoonist took over, Robert Seymour, and the printer was credited as C. Motte of 70 St Martin's Lane. These were the satirical sheets for the rich, those who collected the prints of William Hogarth and Thomas Rowlandson. But in the rough and ready, slapdash, and sometimes slapstick, cartoons and strips of Charlie Grant we find the roots of the common man's comics, the great-grandfather of Ally Sloper and Andy Capp.

Every Body's Album and Caricature Magazine *No.34* © *1 April 1835 J. Kendrick. Drawn by C. J. Grant*

McLean's Monthly Sheet of Caricatures or The Looking Glass *No.14* © *1 February 1831 Thomas McLean. Drawn by Robert Seymour*

McLean's Monthly Sheet of Caricatures N° 14.

Vol: 2.ᵈ

February 1ˢᵗ 1831.

OR THE LOOKING GLASS,

PUBLISHED ON THE FIRST OF EVERY MONTH.

Price 3ˢ Plain

6. Col.ᵈ

TURKISH POLICY.

STATE OF THE IRON TRADE.

LAW.

MADAME V'S LEG IN THE HAND OF A CONNOISSEUR.

BEAUTIES OF OPEN VOTING AS SHOWN IN THE ELECTION OF CITY CHAMBERLAIN.

AWFULL VISION WHICH APPEARS TO EARL G—Y AFTER EVERY PUBLIC MEETING.

Printed by C. Motte 23 Leicester Sqᵉ

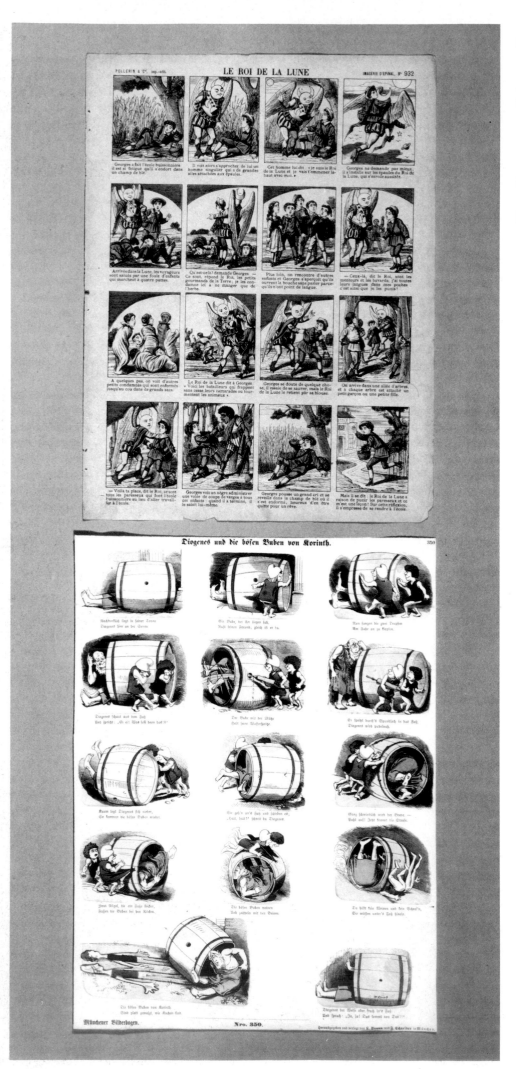

COMIC SHEETS: The Humoristic Co of Kansas City Mo

Comic sheets came from Europe in their thousands, single-sided picture pages sold singly and cheaply, linked numerically, and designed purely for the entertainment (and instruction) of children. With their uniform tabloid size, and their uniform panels of pictures, 16 to a page, and their bright colours (originally hand-painted, later printed), these are the true ancestors of the modern comic. The narrative is printed beneath each picture, sometimes in verse, setting a tradition which would hold good for European comics until recent times. The pioneer publisher of these prints was Jean-Charles Pellerin, who set up shop at 42 Quai de Dogneville in Epinal (Vosges) in 1796. Pellerin's *Imagerie d'Epinal* were founded on an earlier tradition of *Imagerie Populaire*, pictorial printed sheets which have been traced as far back as 1657. But Pellerin concentrated on strips to catch the interest of children (and their parents, who were the ones with the spare centimes). By the 1850s (Pellerin died in 1836) almost every variety of comic strip had been predicted by one or other of the Epinal images. Two naughty boys play all kinds of pranks in "Les Gamins"; funny animals dressed as humans appear in "L'Esprit des Bêtes" ("Spirit of the Beasts"), which was also an early serial, being continued in two parts; literary classics are condensed into picture stories, as with "Robinson Suisse" (*The Swiss Family Robinson*); science fiction makes a start in "Le Roi de la Lune" ("The King of the Moon").

But perhaps the most remarkable discovery is that it was one of these French comic sheets that became the first comic ever sold in America. The Pellerin company translated into English a special edition of 60 selected and suitable sheets for export across the Atlantic. Each bears the additional legend, "Printed expressly for the Humoristic Publishing Co, Kansas City, Mo." No.1 was entitled "Impossible Adventures" and illustrated the fantastical braggings of an old gent in true *Baron Münchhausen* style. Unfortunately the series was not dated, and research reveals confusion among the experts. Jean-Marie Dumont in *La Vie et l'Oeuvre de Jean-Charles Pellerin* claims that the 60 special sheets were "exported by the hundreds of thousands in 1894–1895". Bettina Hurlimann in her *Three Centuries of Children's Books in Europe* dates the American edition at 1856. My own enquiry of the Kansas City Public Library reveals that the only reference to the Humoristic Publishing Co was printed in the 1888 city directory. For the record, the company was located at 38 Hall Building, Walnut and Ninth Street (north-west corner).

Meanwhile, in Munich, the *Münchener Bilderbogen* (picture sheets) had begun in 1849. Published by Braun and Schneider, these followed the French pattern to some extent, but their artists preferred the less formalized approach. They abandoned the neatly-ruled, equal-sized frames for borderless pictures loosely arranged on the page. One thing remained common: the typeset captions. The *Bilderbogen's* greatest discovery was Wilhelm Büsch, a Hanoverian cartoonist, born 1832, who had begun to contribute caricatures to the cartoon weekly, *Fliegende Blätter*, at the age of 27. Two years later he began drawing *Bilderbogen*. From time to time two naughty little boys would play the mischievous leads. In 1865 they crystallized for all time as "Max und Moritz"; and comics and kids were united for eternity.

Le Roi de la Lune: Imagerie d'Epinal *No.932* © *Pellerin (France)* Diogenes: Münchener Bilderbogen *No.350* © *Braun and Schneider (Germany). Drawn by Wilhelm Büsch*

Impossible Adventures: *No.1* © *Pellerin/Humoristic Publishing Co*

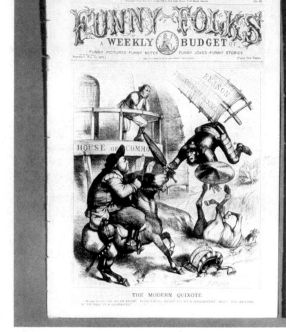

FUNNY FOLKS: The First Comic

"*Funny Folks*! 'Tis just a budget,
Full of pictures, jokes and fun,
Pleasantly and not unkindly
Showing what is said and done.
Funny Folks, it seems to tickle,
Funny Folks presents to view
As a camera that all things
To its Funny focus drew."

Looking back from 110 years away, that first versified editorial to the first issue of the first comic is just about the funniest thing in it, thanks to one of the world's worst puns. But in its day (which was Saturday 12 December 1874 to be precise) *Funny Folks* must certainly have lived up to its bold bannerline: "A Weekly Budget of Funny Pictures, Funny Notes, Funny Jokes, Funny Stories". To add a touch of class, so essential to the Victorians, it added by W. Shakespeare: "Our true intent is all for your delight."

For almost a century British comics followed the format pioneered by *Funny Folks*: eight tabloid pages (double the area of its *Punch*-like predecessors), a 50–50 ratio of text and pictures, and, for many years, the low price of one penny. The proportion of cartoons to strips would change gradually until strips came to dominate, and the somewhat satirical topical tone (*Funny Folks* later changed its slogan to "The Comic Companion to the Newspaper") would descend to social slapstick as the target audience shifted from middle-class to working-class to schoolchildren. "Rupert", writing an introduction to the No.1 (which was given away free as part of *The Weekly Budget Christmas Triple Number* for 1874) described the policy of the new publication: "In *Funny Folks* we have plenty that is

amusing; nothing that is ill-natured. A penny invested in a copy will serve a good evening's amusement; pictures to puzzle at; jokes to laugh over; cartoons to ponder; tales to stimulate interest; and suggestions, notably those of Mrs Grundy, to think about and remember. It is not a paper for the elders only. They will read it and enjoy; but the children will also grow merry with it, and even baby will laugh and crow over the picture pages. A home comic is a novelty, and one for which there is surely an opening."

Indeed there was, and *Funny Folks* appeared every week for 20 years, retiring on 28 April 1894 at number 1614, defeated by the halfpenny comics of its cutprice rivals. Contributors to the first issue were John Proctor, whose cover cartoons were caricatured political comments, G. Montbard with his "Comic Fancy Page", and Wilhelm Büsch's strip, "The Tale of a Tooth", reprinted from the German. One of the funny stories was "The Horrible Disclosures of S. Probe, Private Detective", a clear ancestor of "Dudley Dunn the Dud Detective" who would appear in *Radio Fun* 70 years later. Although *Funny Folks* featured more than one strip a week, the idea of a regular recurring character, which would become so important to comics, eluded them (although, to be fair, a cartoonist called Shirl ran a few adventures of "Tympkins" during 1875, and Julius Stafford Baker, whose uncle, John Stafford, had taken over the front page cartoon, drew a weekly panel featuring an Irish labourer called "Hooligan", 1891).

Funny Folks was a project of the pioneering popular publisher, James

Henderson, and grew out of his original *Lancashire, Yorkshire, and Northern Weekly Budget of News, Politics, Tales* etc. This began on 5 January 1861 and developed into *The Weekly Budget* ("To Inform, to Instruct, to Amuse") in 1874. *The Funny Folks Budget*, originally conceived as a pull-out supplement to the 1874 Christmas Number, was immediately recognised for its potential as a publication in its own right. Nine years later Henderson issued No.1 of a companion paper. This second comic he christened *Scraps* (29 August 1883), an apt choice, for it was compiled, scrapbook fashion, from items subtitled "Literary and Pictorial, Curious and Amusing". *Scraps* would last even more years than *Funny Folks*, turning into a coloured comic, *The Merry-Thought*, in 1910. Henderson's third comic, *Snap-Shots* ("Humorous Pictures and Amusing Reading") followed the format, but was rather different. It consisted entirely of American cartoons and strips selected from *Puck*, *Judge*, *Life* and *Harper's Weekly*. Thus from 1890 British readers were able to chuckle at the drawings of Fred Opper, F. M. Howarth, Hy Mayer, "Zim" and the others who would become pioneer comic men in the States.

Funny Folks No.23 © 15 May 1875 Henderson. Drawn by John Proctor
Scraps No.215 © 1 October 1887 Henderson. Drawn by "S"
Snap-Shots No.234 © 26 January 1895 Henderson. Drawn by Fred Opper
Funny Folks Christmas Number © 24 December 1887 James Henderson. Drawn by John Stafford

FUNNY ~ FOLKS

1887

CHRISTMAS NUMBER.

TWENTY PAGES.   PRICE TWOPENCE.

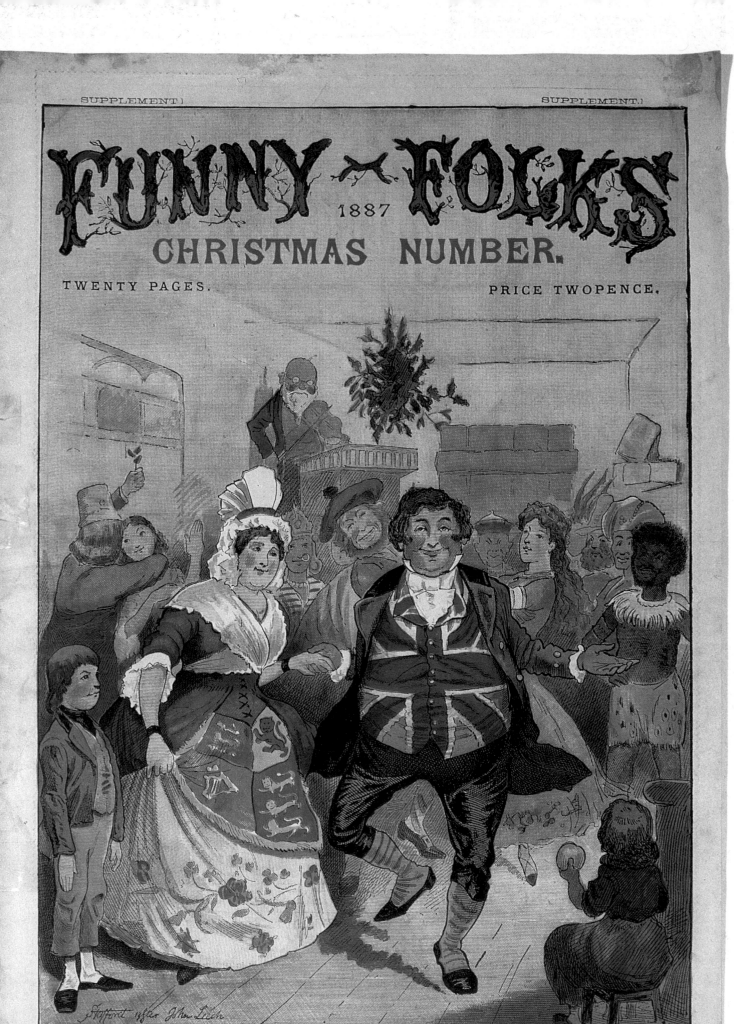

MR. JOHN BULLIWIG'S BALL.

ALLY SLOPER:
First Comic Hero and FOM

The first edition of *Ally Sloper's Half-Holiday* was published on Friday 3 May 1884, dated for the Saturday (which by recent Victorian edict had become a half-day off work for millions). Subtitled "Being a Selection, Side-Splitting, Sentimental and Serious, for the Benefit of Old Boys, Young Boys, Odd Boys Generally, and Even Girls", it had no editorial introduction from the FOM (Friend of Man) himself. The comic didn't need one: Ally Sloper was already the best-known comic character in Britain, and his own weekly paper was simply the latest in a long series of spin-offs dating back all of 17 years.

The historic date was 14 August 1867 when A. Sloper and I. Moses, soon to attain fame under their full names of Alexander Sloper (Ally for short) and Isaac Moses (Ikey Mo), opened for business in *Judy*. This weekly magazine was, of course, an imitation of *Punch*, and Ally was hardly an original, either. Bald of dome, bulbous of nose, the batter-hatted Mr Sloper was a dead (but lively) ringer for Mr Dickens' Mr Micawber. But where that penniless person was con-

tent to wait for something to turn up, Ally went right out and did the upturning for himself. His premier effort at raising the ready was called "Some of the Mysteries of Loan and Discount". The mystery of how two tattered bankrupts expected to profit by lending money to lesser unfortunates was soon solved. Ally and Ikey sold their Loan Application Forms at twopence a time! Their first adventure ended with Ally getting the boot, but he made good in an unexpected way. He became the world's first regular comic strip hero, coming back to the pages of *Judy* week after week with ever new, yet ever doomed, enterprises. He opened a theatre, but forgot to pay the gas bill! He started a Matrimonial Agency, but the only client was his own wife! He invented instantaneous photography, but it was so fast it didn't give the sitter time to sit! Sloper was soon a national institution. When an American newspaper sent H. M. Stanley to find the lost Dr Livingstone, *Judy* promptly sent Sloper. He found the source of the Nile instead, and typically fell in! Being Ally, he immediately opened the first African divorce court, and was nearly trampled to death in the rush by a local King's massed wives! The first publication totally devoted to the old bean was *Ally Sloper's Comic Kalendar*, a 24-page annual which began in December 1875. In June 1880 it was joined by a midsummer event, *Ally Sloper's Summer Number*. Paperback reprints of rejigged *Judy* strips began to appear from November 1873, with the publication of the 220-page *Ally Sloper: A Moral Lesson* (confusingly the inside title reads "Some Playful Episodes in the Career of Ally Sloper"), the world's first comic-book.

Ally Sloper was aptly named: in Victorian slang it meant one who sloped up the alley, especially when the rent collector was due. Ally himself sloped off when his creator, Charles Henry Ross, sold him for a lump sum to Gilbert Dalziell, a famous engraver-turned-publisher. It was Dalziell who started the *Half-Holiday*, the first comic to be linked to a regular character. The awkward, slightly amateurish style of Ross (who used his wife, Marie Duval, as inker), was banished to reprints on the inside, and in came the careful, cross-hatched penmanship of W. G. Baxter. Baxter made over Sloper into the outlandish cartoon character best known today. Baxter's tenure was short, thanks, 'tis said, to the booze,

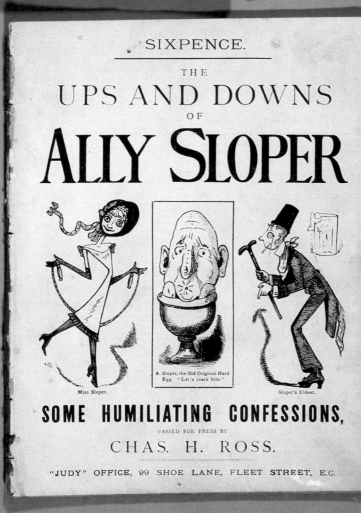

but W. F. Thomas came along to substitute, right through to the Twenties. Although Sloper's own comic collapsed on 14 April 1923, ending a record lifespan of 56 years, the old FOM refused to give up the ghost. He has been revived on several occasions, latterly by myself in a 1976 effort to give Britain a new, adult-oriented comic magazine. We failed after four

numbers, but Ally continues to rise again. One of his many Victorian spin-offs, a brass door-porter, was the model for annual Ally Sloper Awards for veteran comic artists.

Ally Sloper's Half-Holiday *No.1* © *3 May 1884 W. J. Sinkin.* Ally Sloper A Moral Lesson © *1873 Judy. Drawn by Marie Duval*

Ally Sloper's Summer Number *1887* © *Judy. Drawn by Charles H. Ross* Ally Sloper's Comic Kalendar *1888* © *Judy. Drawn by Charles H. Ross* The Ups and Downs of Ally Sloper © *1882 Judy. Drawn by Charles Ross* Ally Sloper *No.1* © *1976 Alan Class/Creative Comics. Drawn by Denis Gifford, W. G. Baxter*

COMIC CUTS: "One Hundred Laughs for One Halfpenny!"

Comic Cuts, the world's first comic, started on 17 May 1890. Only it was not the world's first comic, as we have already seen. That false honour has been claimed for it many times over the years, by its editors and publishers and others, including, for a time, its founder, Alfred Harmsworth. When Mr Harmsworth became Lord Northcliffe, the great British press baron, the fact that his fortune was founded on a cheap comic was hidden under the luxurious carpet. But once he had been proud of his comics, as the dark-blue bound volumes, embossed and bearing his personal bookplate (and now in my collection) testify. His editorial address in Number One admits *Comic Cuts* is nothing new: he greets his "excellent friends, *Scraps* and *Sloper*"! Nor was the format new: eight pages alternating text and cartoons. Even the cartoons and strips were not new, being reprinted from back numbers of Henderson's comics. Finally, the title was not new, being in long use as printers' jargon for

humorous woodcuts or blocks. What was new about *Comic Cuts* was its price, one halfpenny, half the cost of any other comic weekly: an un-comic cut to the trade. Many newsagents refused to stock it, but public clamour soon broke down their resistance.

Wrote Harmsworth: "Remember the following facts about *Comic Cuts*. It is as large as any penny paper of the kind published; this you can prove by measurement. It employs the best artists, is printed on good paper, is published every Thursday, will give big prizes, is the first halfpenny illustrated paper ever issued, and has plenty of money behind it. How is it possible for anyone to provide an illustrated paper, containing nearly 50 pictures, over 18,000 words, and many valuable prizes, for a halfpenny? Well, it is possible to do it, but that is all." The wholesale theft of artwork from five-year old copies of *Scraps* helped, but Henderson's sharp eyes soon spotted the swipes and Henderson's former editorial assistant found him-

self faced with a copyright action. Mending his ways, Harmsworth hurriedly inserted an advertisement in his third issue:

Wanted! Original Sketches for Comic Cuts.
Handsome Pay Offered. Professional Artists Only Need Apply.

First pro to apply was Roland Hill, swift enough to make the cover of No.4 with "Those Cheap Excursions". Oliver Veal arrived in No.10, for a while drawing silhouette strips, before developing a looser style that would give him a long career in comics. He proved a great influence on the young David Low, inspiring the boy who would grow to be Fleet Street's greatest newspaper cartoonist.

Harmsworth's ha'porth may not have been the first comic, but its success certainly started the comic boom. In his "What the Editor Says" in No.3, Harmsworth drops the hint that imitators are on the way: "Well, gentlemen, I have got a good start, and you will have to put in several thousands of

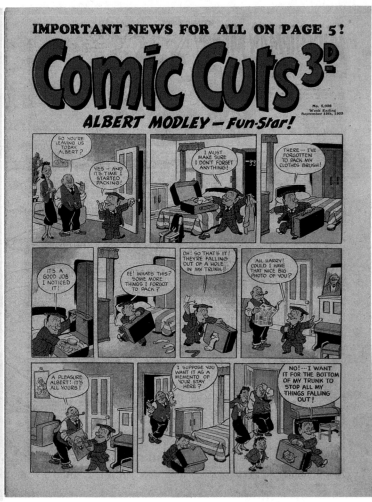

pounds, much hard work, and a few other attributes of success before you get ahead of the first halfpenny illustrated." First out was *Funny Cuts* (2 July 1890), published by Trapps, Holmes & Co and edited by Gordon Phillip Hood, billed as "the Funniest Man on Earth" and a "very Samson or Sandow of Humour". Hood was also handy with the scissors, filling his eight pages with all the American cartoons Henderson and Harmsworth had missed! *Funny Cuts* became the first comic to run a full front-page strip every week, beginning with No.16 (25 October 1890), although artist Alfred Gray did not develop a regular hero.

By the time the end came, *Funny Cuts* had clocked up a 30-year run: it was bought up by Harmsworth's Amalgamated Press, and incorporated with his long-running *Funny Wonder* (began 30 July 1892).

Harmsworth's second comic weekly was destined to last as long as *Comic Cuts. Illustrated Chips* was launched on 26 July 1890, relaunched after a false start, and a year later turned permanently pink. The first successful strip series in *Comic Cuts* was a burlesque on Sherlock Holmes, "Chubb-

lock Homes" (1893) drawn by Jack B. Yeats. "Comic Cuts Colony" (1894) was Frank Wilkinson's depiction of doings in darkest Africa, and Frank Holland contributed a pair of rogues called "Chokee Bill and Area Sneaker" (1897). Strips began to take over after the century turned: Tom Wilkinson's "Lucky Lucas and Happy Harry" (1904), Arthur White's "Commodore Pott" (1905), and Percy Cocking's extraordinary "Mulberry Flats" (1906). By the Great War of 1914, *Comic Cuts* and its companions had regularized to four pages of serials in text and four pages of strips, the centre two forming a spread packed with carefully scrap-booked series. By the Thirties, with the war-time price of a penny-halfpenny reduced to a penny, and printed on coloured paper, *Comic Cuts* was at its best. It ran strips by all the Golden Age cartoonists: Roy Wilson, Albert "Charlie" Pease, John L. Jukes, Cyril "Taffy" Price, Arthur Martin, G. W. "Billy" Wakefield and Frank Minnitt, with a back-page adventure serial drawn by John "Jock" McCail. The Forties were the war years, with pages reduced by the paper shortage and a second colour, orange, added to compensate. From 1952 the

pages were enlarged again, increased from eight to 12, and the quota of adventure strips increased to introduce the newly burgeoning talents of Ron Embleton ("The Forgotten City"), and James Holdaway, drawing Cal McCord, the *Riders of the Range* radio cowboy.

Comic Cuts and *Chips* ran in editorial partnership for more than 60 years, dying together of "old-fashioned" sickness on 12 September 1953. Their founder, Lord Northcliffe, in his mad grave these many years, did not witness the ignoble end, *Chips* going into *Film Fun* and *Cuts* into *Knockout*, but may have been comforted by the advance knowledge that those two comics were destined to suffer similar fates.

TOM BROWNE'S SCHOOL: "The World Famous Tramps"

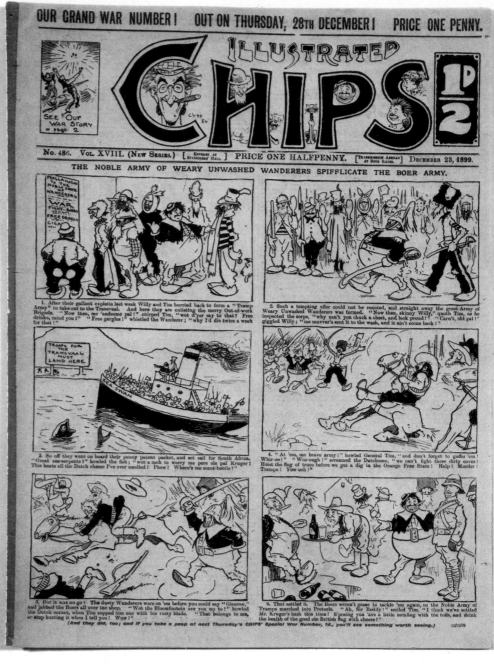

The history of British comics really began on 16 May 1896, on the front page of *Illustrated Chips* No.298, Alfred Harmsworth's companion paper to *Comic Cuts*. The six-picture strip was entitled "Innocents on the River" and it showed how two tramps, a thin one called Weary Waddles and a fat one called Tired Timmy, hitched a ribby horse to a rowing-boat for a tow and got spilled in the drink for their pains. "Great pip!" they cried in the caption beneath; so, apparently, did editor Cornelius "Corny" Chips, alias Mr G. H. Cantle. Sensing something eternal in these casually-created characters Cantle called for more, and the artist, Thomas Browne of Nottingham, cheerfully obliged. With "Weary Willie and Tired Tim" (as his heroes were shortly rechristened) he had created the first great comic heroes; more, he had created British comic style. For 50 years artists would imitate and emulate, but never equal, Tom Browne.

Tom was born in 1870 of humble parentage, educated briefly at St Mary's National School, and put out to carry hat-boxes for a milliner at the age of 12. Handy with a pencil, Tom was apprenticed to a local lithographer at one shilling a week, a salary which rose by 18 pence a year until he left in 1891. To eke out his existence young Tom moonlighted, freelancing cartoons for the London comics. His first-ever strip was printed in Henderson's *Scraps* when he was 18. The eight-panel strip was called "He Knew How To Do It", a prophetic title. Henderson paid Tom 30 shillings, over six months' wages knocked off in a night! As soon as his apprenticeship was done, Tom moved down to London and tackled the ha'penny comics in earnest.

Tom's favourite cartoonist was Phil May, the brilliant artist who simplified sketching to its bare essentials, stripping away all the overloaded cross-hatching so beloved of the Victorian period *Punch*. May's clean line, capturing character in a few skilful strokes, was the last word in modernity, and Tom was the first to apply Phil's pared-down style to the comics. Crisp linework coupled with carefully-spotted solid blacks was perfect for the comic weeklies, especially Harmsworth's ha'porths with their cut-price printing, low-quality newsprint paper, ill-etched blocks and cheap, near grey ink.

All Tom's early contributions were one-off sequences, but gradually the idea of series characters crept in. His first was "Squashington Flats" in *Comic Cuts* (1895), followed by the double-act that made his name and fame, "Weary Willie and Tired Tim". Based on his favourite fictional heroes, Don Quixote and Sancho Panza, Willie and Tim would remain on the front page of *Chips* for the best part of 60 years, only departing in the final edition (12 September 1953) to plush retirement in the mansion of Murgatroyd Mump, Millionaire! Browne had retired to his own mansion in the sky 43 years earlier, a mere 39, but his "World Famous Tramps" had carried on, drawn very much in Tom's traditional style by Percy Cocking. Percy drew their adventures for over 40 years, yet never once signed his name. Not because he was modest; the publishers would not let him!

Willie and Tim shot the circulation of *Chips* up to 600,000 copies a week. Tom was soon in demand to create similar strips for other comics. He drew "Airy Alf and Bouncing Billy", a pair of cyclists (Tom was a keen "wheeler") for *The Big Budget* (1897), "Lanky Larry and Bloated Bill" for *Comic Home Journal* (1897), and a nice burlesque of his original heroes, "Don Quixote de Tintogs" for *Comic Cuts* (1898). For six months Tom drew five front pages of six panels each, every week. It earned him £150 a week, still a record wage in British comics. But it tired him out, and by 1900 Tom left comics to do other things. Paintings, postcards, posters; he even went to the States for a spell as cartoonist on the *Chicago Daily Tribune* (1906). He helped found the London Sketch Club, he was made an RI and he was buried with full honours, but his true living legacy may be seen in any copy of almost any British comic.

Illustrated Chips No.486
© 23 December 1899 Harmsworth.
Drawn by Tom Browne
Illustrated Chips No.2500
© 6 August 1938 Amalgamated
Press. Drawn by Percy Cocking

CHIPS 1D EVERY WEDNESDAY

CHIPS, CHIPS—HOORAY! 2500TH NUMBER TODAY!

ILLUSTRATED CHIPS 1D EVERY WEDNESDAY

[No. 2,500.] WEARY WILLIE AND TIRED TIM, THE WORLD-FAMOUS TRAMPS. [AUGUST 6, 1938.]

1. The tired Weary and the weary Tired were gracefully decorating the doorstep of their diggings at Cockle Bay when two hearty "Woofs!" smote their ears. "By my bunions, it's Hecky," said Willie.

2. "Tickle my tootsies!" cried Tim. "It's a letter for us he's got, too! Whoop-ee! Hand it over, hound! Maybe it's glad tidings!" Saying which, Tim tore the missive from Hec's mouth.

3. And together the happy tramps perused it. "Well," crowed Willie. "Treasure for us at Cockle Bay, hey?"

4. "Twenty-five hundred pounds' worth, too!" parped the plump 'un. "Come, dear heart! Let us go forth and dig for this wealth!" So, borrowing pick and shovel, Willie and Tim went gaily forth.

5. "When we find this great treasure," guffed Tim, "I will stand you a jar of the best, Willie, my love!" "Best what?" inquired Willie. "Washing soap!" smirked Tim. "I—zowie! What's that bloke digging up over there, hey?" he howled.

6. Lancelot, the longshoreman, was indeed putting in some good spadework, and when Willie and Tim heard him say he only wanted ten more to make two thousand five hundred, they got worried. "Pal," hissed Willie, "he's after our treasure!"

7. "He can have it—when we've done with it!" yapped Tim, as he and Willie tunnelled 'neath the groyne. And never had they been known to toil so hard. But at last Tim bobbed out of the beach beside Lancelot's sack of doings and grabbed it.

8. "Come, treasure—come to Tim, who loves you so!" crooned Tim, as he pulled the sack through the tunnel and legged it for the cliffs. "We're rich at last!" wiffled Willie.

9. With singing hearts and faces smeared with gladness Willie and Tim emptied out the sack. And then what? It was cockles they'd won—hundreds of them! Oh, poor Tim!

10. Poor Willie! How we could sob for them! Then up leapt Longshoreman Lancelot. "Ye pair of cockle-poaching lubbers!" he roared. "Take the sack as well."

11. And so he left the pair very much wrapped up in themselves. It so happened, though, that old Corny Chips came cruising along and he recognised those dancing feet.

12. "By the pink of perfection!" roared our Ed. "It's Willie and Tim, and somebody's given 'em the sack, and now the silly fellows are going to have a drop too much! But I'll save them!" he nobly cried, as he stepped on the gas at the moment Willie and Tim went and stepped clean over the edge of the cliff. Down they came with a rush—

13. To plonk on to the awning of the launch. Saved! Not half! "Welcome to our jolly old two thousand five hundredth birthday party, dear lads!" yodelled Corny. "And so say all of us!" chanted the other cheery CHIPS fun-chaps. And then Willie and Tim discovered that they'd only got half the letter Corny had sent them, and that the bit about the treasure was just all bosh.

SUNDAY FUNNIES:
"Polychromatic Effulgence!"

In America, comics and colour have been inseparable from the start. They were born in the Sunday newspapers, out of the sometimes violent circulation wars between the 19th century press barons. Unlike their British cousins, American Sunday papers became sectionalized a century ago, dividing into parts that could be handed around the family. In Chicago, the *Inter Ocean* pioneered colour printing from 18 September 1892, and a detachable children's supplement, *The Youth's Department*, in 1893. Colour and cartoons went well together, and in the Spring of 1894 the section, now named *The Inter Ocean Jr*, introduced a full front-page cartoon called "The Ting-Lings". Each week Charles Saalburg pitched his pint-size Chinakids into a different situation ("The Ting-Lings Go A-fishing" on 22 May 1894). By 15 May 1897 the whole gang of 20 arrived in England and visited Queen Victoria to help her celebrate her Diamond Jubilee. *Home Chat* printed the cartoons and editress Aunt Molly remarked, "We are paying a tremendous price for these pictures because they are drawn by a very clever artist."

The *Sunday World Comic Weekly* started in the *New York World* on 21 May 1893. At first it was full of cartoons, no strip sequence appearing until 4 February 1894: "The Unfortunate Fate of a Well-Intentioned Dog", a combined operation by Walt McDougall and Mark Fenderson. On 5 May 1895 there was published an historic first, "At the Circus in Hogan's Alley". Like the Ting-Lings and their predecessors "The Brownies" (Palmer Cox 1879), the slum kids of Hogan's Alley cut their weekly capers in one large cartoon, and although one of their number, the readily recognizable bald Oriental in a hand-lettered nightgown, has gone down in history as the first comic strip hero, "The Yellow Kid" was seldom seen in panelled format.

The concept of a regularly recurring character in his own comic strip did not jell until 26 May 1895, when Frank Ladendorf drew the first adventure of "Uncle Reuben". Although Uncle ran for six years, as did Ladendorf's second strip, "Cholly", it was some time before the supplements began to concentrate on comic strips. The catalyst was William Randolph Hearst, the already legendary proprietor of the *New York Journal*. On 18 October 1896 he launched his *American Humorist*, his answer to Joseph Pulitzer's prize *Sunday World*. "Eight full pages of color that make the kaleidoscope pale with envy!" screamed his editorial advertising. "Eight pages of polychromatic effulgence that makes the rainbow look like a lead pipe!" And the star of Hearst's supplement was "The Yellow Kid",

lured over from the *World* with Richard Outcault, his artist, to star in a new series of big panels entitled (cautiously because of copyright), "McFadden's Row of Flats". By the time Gordon Bennett's *New York Herald* launched their *Funny Side*

comic supplement strips were standard fare: Carl "Bunny" Schultz's "Foxy Grandpa" (7 January 1900). Of the many early comic heroes of the American funnies, only two remain, still obstinately German: Hans and Fritz "The Katzenjammer Kids".

Comic Supplements *1900–1934*

COMIC KIDS: Max and Moritz meet Hans and Fritz

Max and Moritz, a pair of prankish brats, made their devilish debut by unreeling a fishing line down the chimney, hooking some cooking chickens, and tucking in at a safe distance while their innocent dog takes the blame and a beating. It was in 1865 and just another sheet of cartoons with rhyming captions turned out by Wilhelm Büsch for just another issue of the *Münchener Bilderbogen*. But the echoes of that premier prank were destined to resound down the century with cries of "Owitch!", "Vot giffs?", and "Dod-rot der dod-gasted dumkopfs!" Büsch, realising he was on to a good formula, drew some more adventures of the bad boys, winding up with a suitable punishment: they are ground into crumbs and eaten by ducks! The strips were gathered into a book, which was duly issued in an English edition in 1873: *Max and Moritz, a Story in Seven Tricks*. Four years later Rudolph Dirks was born in Heinde, the son of a German woodcarver who shortly brought his family to the United States, settling in Chicago in 1884.

Young Rudolph tried his hand at carpentry – and almost cut it off! Frightened off sharp tools forever, he decided to emulate his elder brother Gus and become a cartoonist. At the age of 17, young Rudolph was selling joke drawings to *Life* and *Judge*; at the age of 20 he joined the art staff of the *New York Journal*. Rudolph Block, who edited the comic supplement, asked Dirks to develop a regular comic strip to counter their rival's "Yellow Kid" cartoons. Dirks remembered the Büsch bilderbooks he had grown up with and produced a half-

page episode. It appeared on 12 December 1897 and he called it "The Katzenjammer Kids". Just to be different, Dirks featured three brothers, but by the next Sunday had reduced them to two, Hans and Fritz. At first Dirks tried to keep his strips wordless pantomimes in the manner of his mentor, but finding this too restricting, and the printers not being too keen to typeset librettos under each panel, Dirks developed the idea of speech balloons. Extra fun was added when he made his Germanic characters speak in broken English (dialect comedy, particularly German and Dutch, was a vaudeville staple of the time). Gradually Dirks developed his permanent cast: Hans and Fritz "der liddle anchels", der Mama, der Captain and der School Inspector, he of the tall hat and taller beard.

Dirks soon exceeded his starting salary of $25 a week, but in 1912 decided to move over to the *New York World*, who were offering him much more money. William Randolph Hearst promptly sued, and a legal battle of epic proportions ensued. The final decision, and one that made copyright history, was that Hearst had the right to continue the strip under the original title, drawn by another artist, while Dirks had the right to continue to draw his creations for anyone he chose, but under a different title. So "The Katzenjammer Kids" became the only comic characters with dod-gasted doppelgangers! The new Dirks strip began in 1914, without a name. In 1915 it became "Hans and Fritz", but when the States went to war with Germany, Dirks changed it for all time to "The Captain and the

Kids". Over on the Journal, "The Katzenjammer Kids" had been carrying on (alarmingly as usual) under the new guiding hand of Harold Knerr. This Pennsylvanian cartoonist of German descent had already run a slight rip-off of the Katzies called "The Flenheimer Kids", complete with a one-legged Captain. He was to draw the daily and weekly doings of the Katzies for 36 years. Dirks himself retired from the drawing-board in 1958, leaving his son John to take over the oldest pair of kids in the comics.

Max und Moritz © 1865 Braun & Schneider. Drawn by Wilhelm Büsch

Okay Comics No.1: The Captain and the Kids © *July 1940 United Features*
The Captain and the Kids 50th Anniversary © *1948 United Features*

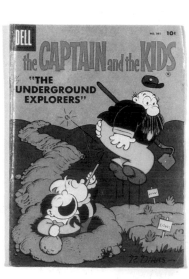

The Captain and the Kids *No.1 (OS 881* © *February 1958 United Features/Dell. Drawn by Rudolph Dirks*
Bravo! *No.44* © *28 October 1948 Defosse (Brussels). Drawn by Rudolph Dirks*

The Katzenjammer Kids *No.3* © *Winter 1947 David McKay/King Features. Drawn by Joe Musial*
Katzenjammer Kids *No.17* © *Summer 1951 Standard Comics/King Features*

Katzenjammer Kids *No.25* © *October 1953 Harvey Comics/King Features*
Pim Pam Poum *No.31* © *15 August 1969 Editions Lug (France)*

From Ball's Pond to Bash Street!

Comics and kids were made for each other. Obvious in retrospect, it was less so in those faraway beginnings, despite James Henderson's prediction that baby will crow over the cartoons in *Funny Folks*. There was little point in a publisher designing a comic to sell to children when children had no money to spend on them. Even the traditional Saturday penny would not go far if half of it was spent on Harmsworth's half-price *Comic Cuts*. But the essentially visual nature of the comic, especially once strip cartoons began to take precedence, was fascinating to the younger members of the family, and editors often slipped in a simple strip headed "Something for the Children": Tom Browne's "Billy Buster the Steam Engine" in *Comic Cuts* (14 March 1896) was described as "a tale of a toy engine to be read aloud to the youngsters while they look at the pictures".

The first child characters to appear regularly in a comic were "The Ball's Pond Banditti", a gang of urchins every bit as delinquent as the more usual tramps and burglars. They proved too much even for Ally Sloper, who introduced them in his front page *Half-Holiday* cartoon on 29 April 1893. Wrote daughter Tootsie in her caption, "Poor Pa was naturally curious to make the acquaintance of these gentlemen, so he invited them all to a winkle tea in the back garden of Mildew Court". The battle royal, with Sloper fending off the masked lads with his battered old brolly, was vividly depicted by W. F. Thomas, but the actual artistic creator of the Banditti was G. Gordon Fraser. They raged all over the front page of *Larks* (No.1, 1 May 1893), a wild bunch, mostly shop-boys: Gorger Pain the doctor's boy, Piggy Waffles the grocer's lad, Lurcher Geeson the butcher's boy, Sweppy Titmarsh from the rag shop, and Bocco the bloodhound, led by Ticko Scuppins of the Ball's Pond Road Clothing Stores. Their very names link a kinship to "Lord Snooty and his Pals", Dudley Watkins' gang from *Beano* No.1 (30 July 1938). "Son of a Duke but always pally – With the Beezer Kids of Ash Can Alley": Hairpin Huggins, Skinny Lizzie, Scrapper Smith, Snitchy and Snatchy, Happy

Hutton, Sweet Rosie, and Gertie the Goat. Even closer links could be claimed for "The Bash Street Kids", Leo Baxendale's schoolful of scruffy misfits (Smiffy, Sidney, Danny, Spotty, Fatty, Wilfred, 'Erbert, Plug and Toots) who have been bashing about in *The Beano* since 13 February 1954.

Much naughtier than their workshy fathers, "Weary Willie and Tired Tim", the World Famous Tramps of *Illustrated Chips*, were "Little Willy and Tiny Tim", their sons. Also drawn by Tom Browne, these fat-and-thin kids got up to much mischief on the front page of *The Wonder* from 9 July 1898. "Chips off the old block, ain't they?" punned parent Tim. Early echoes of "Max und Moritz" might be detected in "Those Terrible Twins", drawn by Frank Holland for *The Halfpenny Comic* (5 March 1898). Originally tucked away inside, they moved to the large front-page strip after four weeks, totally ousting Tom Browne's "Mr Stanley Deadstone and Co" for good and all, proving that even the master could fail to click sometimes. Although "Max and Moritz" were well known in Britain via comic-paper reprints (they turned up in *Comic Cuts* as "Tootle and Bootle"), it was not until Rudolph Dirks hit his American success with "The Katzenjammer Kids" that British rip-offs began. "Those Twinkleton Twins" (complete with Mamma) started in *The Big Budget* on 3 February 1900, but were quite overshadowed by "The Bunsey Boys". Yclept Georgy and Ferdy, this pair of lookalikes and prankalikes filled the front page of *The Jester* from 1902. Copying its style from the American strip, it helped regularize the use of speech balloons in British comics. Something else the strip stole was a character from another American strip, combining two into one. This was "Happy Ike", modelled so closely on "Happy Hooligan" that he even wore a tin-can for a hat!

A much more home-grown schoolboy hero was "Billy Bunter", British to the corpulent core. Formerly the fat villain of a series of stories about Greyfriars School, created by Frank Richards (Charles Hamilton) for *The Magnet*, a story-paper, on 15 February

1908, Billy became a comic strip hero from No.1 of *The Knockout Comic* on 4 March 1939. As drawn by Frank Minnitt, "the Owl of the Remove" was so popular that he eventually moved to the full-colour front page and took over the title: *Billy Bunter's Knockout* (10 June 1961). Unfortunately, Minnitt did not live to see the triumph of "the Fattest Schoolboy on Earth". The same sadness was in store for David Law, who first drew "Dennis the Menace" in *The Beano* on 17 March 1951. "The World's Wildest Boy" as he was billed became the most popular character in the comic, graduating to the front page on 14 September 1974, complete with a scribble of black fur and sharp teeth called Gnasher. But by this time David Law was dead. Dennis and Gnasher, however, show every sign of comic immortality.

COLOURED COMICS:
"Bright Wings of Colour and Fancy!"

Alfred Harmsworth, wonderkid of the Victorian popular publishing world, dropped his first hint of excitements in store in No.329 of *Comic Cuts*, dated 29 August 1896. "I am preparing a special number which is to be unlike any number before produced, and unlike any paper ever before published in this country. This may seem to boast and brag, but I am confident that when it goes out to the trade it will be an eye-opener, and few people will believe it was printed in England. The printing trade will jump to the conclusion that it was printed in Paris. It will not be so. It will be the product of English labour, and may cause the biggest rush ever known in the history of the halfpenny paper trade." A sentence later he added, somewhat contradictorily, "It will be the most marvellous pennyworth ever offered to the British

public, and perhaps may mark an epoch in illustrated journalism."

Harmsworth was about to publish Britain's first attempt at a coloured comic, and had already discovered that colour printing was going to cost him twice as much as his usual black ink. His readers therefore needed a little priming to be convinced that the addition of colour was going to be worth a 100 per cent price increase from a halfpenny to a penny. The much-heralded, somewhat delayed, "Special Art Number of the World Famed Halfpenny Comic Paper" at last emerged on 12 September 1896, dated simply September because of printing problems, which included the absence of publisher and printer indicia. Of the 12 pages, the front, back and spread were in four colours, four pages were in blue, and two in green.

It was oversize, and although it was boosted editorially – "This coloured number we expect will break the record of the world" – even Harmsworth later admitted its failure. On 28 November he wrote to his readers, "*Comic Cuts* made a strenuous effort to advance our lost reputation and produced a bizarre but pre-eminently startling number." He was trailing his second go at a coloured comic, next week's Christmas Number (5 December). "More successful, less gaudy, yet strikingly effective" wrote Harmsworth, referring to one reader who thought the title should be changed to *Chromatic Cuts*, and commenting that "The one great excitement about colour printing is its uncertainty!" On the full-colour front, a laughing Colonial remarked, "Dis am coloured and no mistake!"

28

The Harmsworth comics continued to flirt with special coloured numbers: *Funny Wonder Xmas Number* (19 December 1896), *Jester Coronation Number* (31 May 1902), but it was left to his very minor rivals, Messrs Trapps and Holmes, to publish Britain's first regular weekly coloured comic. They called it, with obvious pride, *The Coloured Comic*, and, incredibly, were able to charge only the usual halfpenny. "The Editor's Colour Box" in No.1 (21 May 1898) thought the proprietors must have "been to the Klondike and struck oil", and predicted that the first issue, dated 21 May 1898, would one day be worth at least ten times the price! The only trouble with *The Coloured Comic* was that it used Trapps and Holmes' regular cartoonists, a decidedly second-rate crowd. The cover stars were the usual double-act of footpads, this time called "Frog-Faced Ferdinand and Watty Wool Whiskers". After 72 weeks, the oil from the Klondike dried up. Trapps and Holmes justified their

continuity of title by printing *The Coloured Comic* in blue ink.

Puck, headlined as "The Greatest Novelty of 1904", arrived on 30 July. G. H. Cantle, the editor, waxed lyrical. "He has come to stay, to gladden your eye with his bright wings of colour and fancy. He is the first of his kind, the great main squeeze, the only one on the bunch, and he's come permanently to talk rot to you till you're as happy as a dog with two tails." He also added, in block caps, that *Puck* No.1 was "the first number of the first coloured comic paper." And Cantle's boss, Alfred Harmsworth, characteristically did nothing to correct him. *Puck* had not, of course, "come permanently": the comic was combined with the brighter *Sunbeam* on 11 May 1940 after 1,867 editions. The wonder is that it lasted six months, for a study of the first volume shows that the comic changes its mind and appearance with almost every issue. Some have strips on the front, some a large single cartoon, others a fashion sketch.

Clearly the comic was not finding a market. Adults, for whom it was intended, did not like the bright colours. But children did. In No.11 *Puck* began a section for children called *Puck Junior*. Ten weeks later the juvenile interest had spread through the entire comic, and once "Billy Smiff's Pirates" by Julius Baker got plundering and "Johnny Jones and the Casey Court Boys" by H. O'Neill took over the front page, the children's comic had been born.

Comic Cuts Christmas Number
No.395 © *4 December 1897 Harmsworth Brothers*

Funny Wonder Xmas Number
No.203 © *19 December 1896 Harmsworth Brothers*

The Coloured Comic *No.38* © *4 February 1899 Trapps Holmes*

Puck *No.1* © *30 July 1904 Amalgamated Press. Drawn by Fred Bennett*

THE FIRST AMERICAN COMIC-BOOKS

American comic-books were born on 23 November 1902 when the following exciting news was printed atop the comic supplement of the *New York Journal* and other William Randolph Hearst newspapers across the States:

Announcement !
The popular characters of the comic supplement have been published in book form. Your newsdealer can get them for you. They are the best comic-books that have ever been published. For sale everywhere 50 cents each.

There followed a list of the titles, five in all, one for each of the most popular Hearst characters: "Happy Hooligan", Fred Opper's tramp in the tin-can hat; "The Katzenjammer Kids", Rudolph Dirks' pranky brats; "The Tigers", the original anthropomorphic animals by Jimmy Swinnerton; "Alphonse and Gaston", the over-polite Frenchies, also by Opper; and, "On and Off Mount Ararat", more animals by Swinnerton, this time inhabiting Noah's Ark.

This flood of five, nicely timed for the Christmas rush, contained nothing new but the specially designed covers. The contents were all reprints from the Sunday sections of the previous year or so, somewhat indiscriminately arranged. This lack of care in editorial assembly was to become only too typical of the reprint comics, and the bane of all serious students of stripology. Although Hearst's nationwide marketing of his comic-books is a clear milestone, as always with any commercial success there are pioneers pointing the way.

The first US comic-book featured reprint adventures of the character many American historians regard as the first comic hero of them all. The Yellow Kid, who had been appearing in the *New York Sunday World* since 1895, moved to Hearst's *Sunday Journal* in 1896, and was issued as a 5-cent comic-book in 1897. The same year an "autobiography" of the bald boy was written by E. W. Townsend and published by the Dillingham Company as *The Yellow Kid in McFadden's Flats*. The Kid's adventures were seldom drawn in comic-strip format,

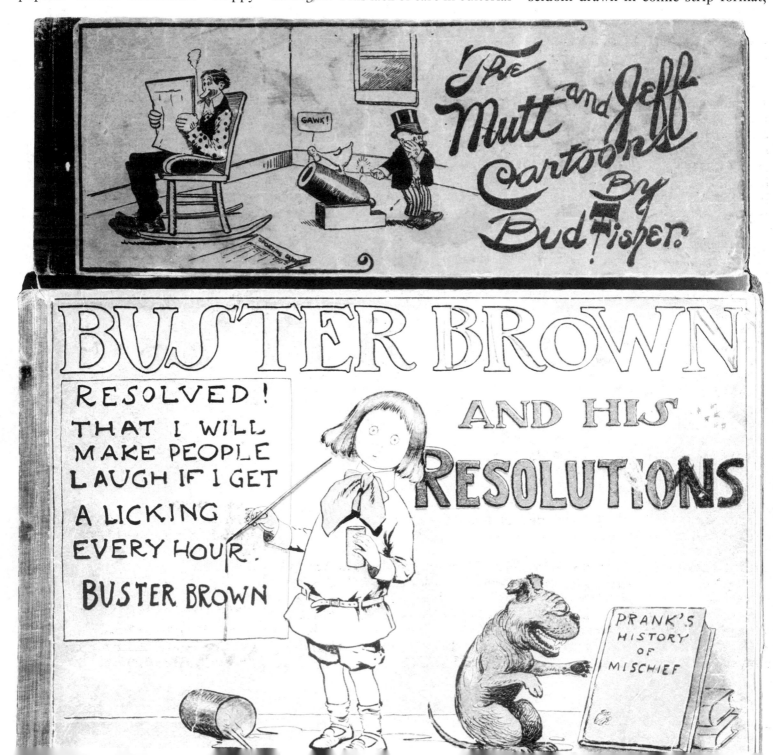

artist R. F. Outcault apparently preferring to fill his space with one, large crowded scene. However, when Outcault tired of the slum antics of the Hogan's Alley kids, he left the Hearst stable and returned to the *New York Herald* to create the most popular boy hero of his time, Buster Brown. This radical switch to middle class fun and games made Outcault's fortune: Buster went on the stage and into films, and even today is the trademark of a popular American shoe. In the first of a long series of reprint comic-books, *Buster Brown and his Resolutions* (1903), Outcault wrote: "Buster is not a bad or naughty boy, as the thousands of parents of Buster know. These pictures of his pranks are simply records of the usual everyday happenings in any healthy household."

"Bunny" was the pen name of Carl Schultze, whose two strips started on the same Sunday in the *New York Herald*, 7 January 1900, and both were collected into reprint comic-books by the end of the year. Bunny's "Herald Vaudeville," which introduced a different "act" every week, came out as *Vaudeville and Other Things*, a one-shot, while *The Adventures of Foxy Grandpa* was the first of many annual editions. Foxy was a wily old boy who always managed to turn the tables on his naughty nephews, which seems to have delighted young readers as much as their parents.

These comic-books of the early years are almost all of similar size: great oblongs covered in cardboard. The strips they contained were all reprinted without reduction in size. As they had come from the great broadsheet newspaper supplements, they could only be fitted on to the smaller comic-book pages by being split into halves, the top being made into one page and the bottom into another. The pages were all printed on one side of the paper only, so a book of 30 pages would actually contain only 15 complete strips. Because of their unwieldly size they easily became damaged and it is virtually impossible to find a perfect copy today, 80 years after their publication; but these big books do turn up, for they had a wide distribution. In England they were published by W. R. Chambers of London and Edinburgh. Even more awkward in size, however, were the reprint books of daily newspaper strips. *The Mutt and Jeff Cartoons*, the first collection of Bud Fisher's famous funny men, is a card-covered collec-

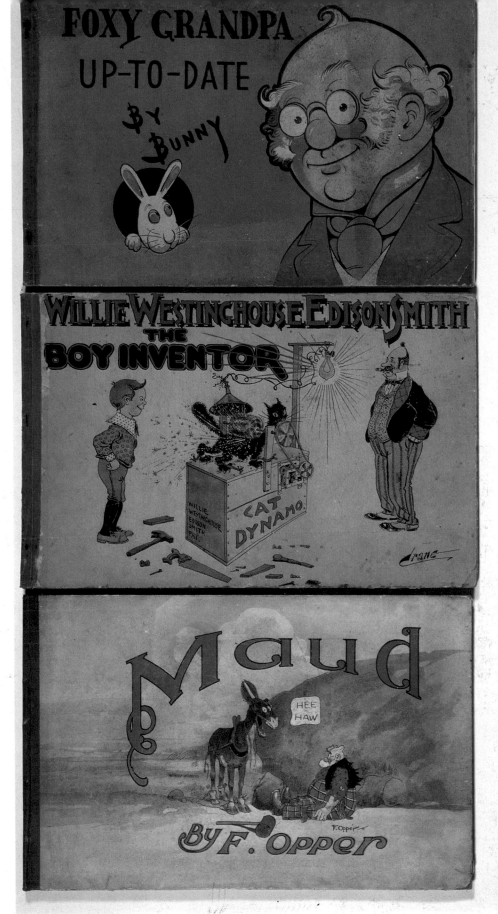

tion of 1908 strips, one to a page, $5\frac{1}{2}$ inches high by $15\frac{1}{2}$ inches wide!

The Mutt and Jeff Cartoons *No.1* © 1910 Ball Publishing Co/H. C. Fisher. *Drawn by Bud Fisher*
Buster Brown and his Resolutions *No.1* © 1903 Frederick A. Stokes Co/New York Herald. *Drawn by Richard Felton Outcault*

Foxy Grandpa Up-to-Date © *1904 Frederick A. Stokes Co/American Journal Examiner. Drawn by Carl Edward Schultze*

Willie Westinghouse Edison Smith © *1906 Frederick A. Stokes Co/New York Herald. Drawn by Frank Crane*

Maud © *1906 Frederick A. Stokes Co/American Journal Examiner. Drawn by Frederick Opper*

"A Million Laughs in a Carload!"

William Randolph Hearst, after his first great comic-book push of 1902, quit the field entirely. Perhaps finding the children's book market beyond his range as a newspaper publisher, he passed the reprint rights of his comic strip characters over to the Frederick A. Stokes Company. From 1904, Stokes was the premier reprint company, winding up in 1916 with the final "Bunny" book, *Foxy Grandpa's Merry Book*. By that time, Stokes had been completely outclassed by Cupples and Leon, New York publishers with a special bent for cheap children's books.

The first Cupples and Leon comic-book was published in 1906: *Buster Brown, His Dog Tige, and Their Jolly Times*. At the same moment, Stokes issued *My Resolutions by Buster Brown*. The following year it all became clear when Cupples and Leon published *Buster Brown's Frolics* and Stokes issued *Outcault's Buster Brown and Company*. Cupples and Leon's reprint books were not by the original artist, R. F. Outcault! The Buster Brown character and strip had become the subject of the first lawsuit concerning a comic. Outcault had left W. R. Hearst and his "Yellow Kid" cartoon in 1902. He returned to the *New York Herald* and created Buster Brown, who made his debut in that paper on 4 May. As we have seen, Frederick Stokes began his reprint books of Buster in 1904.

By 1905 the bad boy of the funny pages was so popular that Hearst signed Outcault to an exclusive contract. Buster Brown transferred to Hearst's *New York American* comic supplement on 14 January 1906. There was a copyright contest in the courts, and an historic decision was made. Outcault's old employer was given the right to the character with its name, while Outcault was given the right to continue his character for whomever he pleased, in this case his current employer, Hearst. But he was not allowed to entitle his strip "Buster Brown". So he gave his page a different descriptive title every week, and nobody really noticed the difference! Stokes, having a tie-up with Hearst, automatically acquired reprint rights to the Outcault version, while the *Herald* passed over their reprint rights to Cupples and Leon. This company added to their output with reprints of other successful Sunday strips; *The Monkeyshines of Marseleen* by Norman Jennett, and the fabulous fantasies of *Little Nemo in Slumberland* by Winsor McCay, were both issued in 1909. But their real success came with the reprinting of daily strips.

The daily newspaper strip, an obvious outgrowth of the full-page Sunday strips, did not begin to appear until 1904. First came "A. Piker Clerk" by Clare Briggs, followed a year later by A. D. Condo's "The Out-

bursts of Everett True". The latter was the first daily strip to be reprinted in comic-book form, by Saalfield in 1907. Cupples and Leon, whose main line in juvenile books was the cheaper end of the market, soon saw that the black-and-white daily strips would be a lot easier, and more importantly, cheaper, to reprint than the four-colour, large format Sunday pages. From 1914, they took over the Mutt and Jeff series from Ball and began a new run with *Mutt and Jeff Book 1*. Instead of the impractical oblongs of the Ball books, Cupples and Leon split the strips in halves, pasting them up so as to form a handy-sized square book, measuring about $9\frac{1}{2}$ inches around. Bound into a card cover, with a new coloured cartoon, the 48-page result sold for 25 cents. In 1918 Cupples and Leon added *The Gumps* to their lineup, then *Bringing Up Father*, and in 1920, *Keeping Up With The Joneses*. The series, called "Famous Comics in Book Form", was advertised as offering "A Million Laughs in a Carload!". A series in smaller format was introduced in 1926 with Harold Gray's *Little Orphan Annie*. This was the first fruit of a tie-in with Colonel Joseph Patterson's *Chicago Tribune* Syndicate. More strips from that famous stable followed: Frank Willard's *Moon Mullins* (1927), *Smitty* by Walter Berndt (1928) and *Harold Teen* by Carl Ed (1929). Unsold copies of earlier comics were rebound into triple-sized volumes and issued as the "Big Book" series, beginning with *Bringing Up Father Big Book* in 1926, price 75 cents. Cupples and Leon issued nine new titles in 1933, none in 1934. Ten cent comic-books, born with *Famous Funnies*, had taken over. Cupples and Leon's "World of Laughs for Young and Old" was suddenly out of date. What kid of the Thirties would spend 50 cents on a cardboard-covered reprint in black and white when, for a fifth of that sum he could buy 68 pages of comic strips "all in color for a dime"! The *Chicago Tribune New York News* Syndicate moved their stable of strips across to the Dell Publishing Company's *Popular Comics* (No.1 February 1936) and "Little Orphan Annie", "Harold Teen", "Smitty", "Moon Mullins" and other former Cupples and Leon favourites were joined by "Dick Tracy", "Terry and the Pirates", "Gasoline Alley and the rest in a monthly package labelled "America's Favorite Funnies".

Bringing Up Father *No.3* © *1919 International Feature Service/ Cupples and Leon. Drawn by George McManus*
Moon Mullins *No.7* © *1933 Chicago Tribune/Cupples and Leon. Drawn by Frank Willard*

Popeye *No.1* © *1935 King Features/David McKay Company. Drawn by Elzie Crisler Segar*

Little Orphan Annie *No.1* © *1926 Chicago Tribune/Cupples and Leon. Drawn by Harold Gray*

Smitty *No.1* © *1928 Chicago Tribune/Cupples and Leon. Drawn by Walter Berndt*
Harold Teen *No.1* © *1931 Chicago Tribune/Cupples and Leon. Drawn by Carl Ed*
Popular Comics *No.7* © *August 1936 Dell Publishing Co*

BRITISH STRIPS: A Laugh a Day, A Book a Year

The British invented the newspaper strip but, like many British inventions, it was allowed to languish until taken up with enthusiasm elsewhere. The first newspaper strip appeared on 23 February 1850 in *The Penny Illustrated News*. It was called "The Sentimental and Dramatic Adventures of Mr Green". Unfortunately, it was unsigned. The adventures were serialized over three issues of the paper, thus establishing "Mr Green" as the first hero of a continuity strip.

It was not until Alfred Harmsworth launched his *Daily Illustrated Mirror* in 1904 that strips began to appear with any regularity in British newspapers. Harmsworth had created the boom in comics with *Comic Cuts* in 1890, so perhaps it was no wonder. The first daily strip was a six-frame comment on a topic in the news, drawn by a former clerk and amateur artist, W. K. Haselden. Along the way Haselden developed the true comic strip by creating several original characters whose escapades he would recount in daily episodes. One such serial was "Mr Simkins On His Holidays", all 16 episodes of which were reprinted in the first collection of Haselden's strips, *Daily Mirror Reflections* of 1908. This chunky paperback was the first real newspaper strip comic-book in Britain. It became an annual publication and by the time the last issue appeared in 1935 it had run through 28 editions. A separate collection was published of Haselden's popular wartime strip, which used cartoon characters of Kaiser Wilhelm and the Crown Prince of Germany in "The Adventures of Big and Little Willie".

By the Twenties, every popular

Dot and Carrie *No.1* © *1923 The Star. Drawn by James Francis Horrabin*
The Japhet Book *No.1* © *1924 Daily News. Drawn by James Francis Horrabin*
Daily Mail Nipper Annual *No.1* © *1934 Associated Newspapers. Drawn by Brian White*

newspaper ran its popular comic strip, and many of them were reprinted in occasional or annual strip books. J. F. Horrabin was a stylist who drew two strips a day, one for the office commuters who read the evening paper, *The Star*, the other for the children whose parents bought *The Daily News*. "Dot and Carrie", heroines of the former, were typists for the irascible Mr Spillikin. They clocked in on 20 November 1922 and were retired on the death of their artist, on 2 March 1962: a forty-year career with no pension! The first of three books of their daily doings was published in 1923. Horrabin's other characters were animated wooden toys. They were known variously as "The Adventures of the Noah Family", "The Noahs", "The Arkubs" (when they ran a children's club called by the same name) and "Japhet and Happy" (when Happy the Bear grew more popular than his master). These were collected into books, beginning with *The Japhet Book* in 1924 and, after a long lapse, continuing with *The Japhet Holiday Book* from 1936. The most popular British newspaper strip of all, and the first to be syndicated to the States, was "Pop". J. Millar Watt's rotund wisecracker enjoyed the longest series of reprints of any British strip. The first *Pop Annual* was published in 1925 and the last in 1949. An additional book, *Pop At His Best*, came later and contained reprinted strips drawn by "Gog" (Gordon Hogg), the cartoonist who took over on Watt's retirement. "The Nipper", best of the several purely visual strips of the Thirties, was also reprinted in an oblong annual issued by its parent paper, the *Daily Mail*. This series began in 1934 and later editions included an unusual 16-page section in full colour.

Popular among children as these annual collections were, there was never any crossover between the newspaper strips and the weekly comics. The closest was the twice a year "Gloops Comic", a collection of *Sheffield Telegraph* daily strips, which ran from 1928 to 1940. This was slap bang in the kiddies' corner, costing only twopence for a large 32-page format.

The Christmas Book of Gloops
No.1 © *1930 Sheffield Telegraph.*
Drawn by 'Cousin Ken'
Captain Reilly-Ffoull © *1946*
Daily Mirror. Drawn by Bernard Graddon

Jane Strips in the Mirror

From the Twenties home-grown British strips began to take their place alongside American syndicated imports like "Mutt and Jeff" and "Bringing Up Father". By the Forties only "Blondie" and "Popeye" were left. Soon the *Daily Mirror* dropped Popeye in favour of a British strip, and the American syndicates lost a market which they have never regained.

British newspaper strips are virtually synonymous with the *Daily Mirror*. Even in the darkest days of World War II, when paper shortage reduced the size of the *Mirror* to a mere eight pages, a full page-and-a-half was given over to strips: two pages if you count the cartoons by Donald Zec, and Jack Greenall's "Useless Eustace". If this proportion was maintained in today's 40-page paper, there would be an eight-page comic section every day!

The *Mirror's* love affair with strips began in 1904 with a daily feature by Haselden. In the same year, the *Mirror* ran a few trial children's strips but by failing to persevere with them they lost a niche in history. One strip marked the first appearance of "Tiger Tim", about whom more later! The first real *Mirror* strip was "Pip, Squeak and Wilfred" (respectively a dog, a penguin and a rabbit), which began on 12 May 1919, disappeared in the war and returned in 1947 for another long run.

Strips really began in the *Mirror* with the arrival of "Jane" on 5 December 1932, although Jane's own "stripping" did not really begin until the war! She began life in a gag-a-day sequence entitled "Jane's Journal, the Diary of a Bright Young Thing", as recorded by Norman Pett. Her pioneering work in a two-piece bathing suit around 1937 showed the shape of things to come. By 1940, Jane was seen as no other strip queen in history had been seen – in her undies, in her bath and, finally, in the "altogether". The American Army newspaper *Round-Up* marked this moment with a banner headline: *Jane Gives All!*

Mirror executive Basil D. Nicholson is credited with the development of the paper's strip stable. Inspired by the tabloid *New York Daily News* strips, he introduced a sequence of strips, each British in character but each modelled on a successful American strip. First came "The Ruggles" (11 March 1935), a family saga with father John a chinless echo of Andy of "The Gumps". Next was "Belinda Blue-Eyes" (30 September 1935), a curly-top orphan with a wandering but wealthy "daddy": clearly modelled on "Little Orphan Annie". "Buck Ryan", a tough detective, signed on (22 March 1937), inspired by, but luckily not looking like, "Dick Tracy". "Beelzebub Jones" (28 December 1937) was a wiry little sheriff who talked funny: was "Popeye" far from the creator's mind? "Just Jake" (4 June 1938) tried to make a "Li'l Abner" out of English country bumpkins. It became quite a cult when artist Bernard Graddon switched the strip's focus from hayseed hero Jake to cigar-chomping villain, Captain A. R. P. Reilly-Ffoull, FFI and Bar. "Garth" (24 July 1943) was the *Mirror's* answer to "Superman", a musclebound hunk of a hero who came drifting in from the sea. "Garth", still wrestling with crime and goddesses, became the longest running newspaper serial in Britain.

Mirror strips, geared to the adult eye, never crossed over to comics. They remained to be gathered into occasional books, as far as Britain was concerned. It was not until an enterprising Australian publisher put the strips together in American-style comic-books that British newspaper strips appeared in children's comics. But what Australian parents thought of their youngsters studying Jane and her strip teases seems to have gone unrecorded!

COMIC SUPPLEMENTS:
Teddy Tail v
the Gugnuncs

The American idea of giving away a weekly comic supplement inside a newspaper was first tried in Britain in the Twenties. "Uncle Oojah", an out-size elephant, had started his adventures in the children's corner of the *Daily Sketch* on 18 February 1919. Originally a single panel by Thomas Maybank illustrating a serial story by Flo Lancaster, the pyjama-clad pachyderm progressed to strip format in the first British comic supplement. In his honour it was named *The Oojah Sketch*, and No.1 was dated 8 October 1921. The *Daily Mirror*, not to be outdone by its tabloid rival in the picture paper stakes, put together their own similar section, and the following Saturday presented No.1 of *Pip and Squeak* (15 October). This, of course, starred the *Mirror*'s own children's strip heroes, "Pip, Squeak and Wilfred", the dog, penguin and bunny rabbit that had been running in the daily edition since 12 May 1919. These three characters, supported by such eccentrics as Auntie ("Oosh!"), a ragged old bird, Wtzkoffski the Russki anarchist, and his pup Popski, endeared themselves to millions of children through the charming stories of "Uncle Dick" (Bertram Lamb) and the lively illustrations of Austin Payne, a comic paper veteran. Once the "World Famous Pets" started their Gugnunc Club, the WLOG (which stood for the Wilfredian League of Gugnuncs), their success was assured. Thousands upon thousands of children enrolled, holding rallies at the Albert Hall and yelling their secret password, "Ick ick pah boo!" (The Gugnuncs were named after Wilfred the bunny's only words: "Gug", because he was a baby, and "Nunc" for uncle.)

There was a great revival of comic supplements in the Thirties: they became weapons in the newspaper circulation wars. First in the field was the *Daily Mail* with a carefully planned comic of eight pages, based on their own regular children's strip character, "Teddy Tail". Teddy, first of all the

many British newspaper strips for children (if we exclude Tiger Tim's single appearance in 1904), had begun on 5 April 1915, a bright light in a dark war. Charles Folkard, a popular illustrator of juvenile books, was

Teddy's creator, and it was Harry Folkard, the artist's son, who drew the Teddy Tail comic. No.1 was published inside the *Daily Mail* dated 8 April 1933. On the same day, the *Mail*'s great rival, the *Daily Express*,

Teddy Tail comic in the *Mail* was due entirely to that newspaper's success in luring Herbert Foxwell away from Tiger Tim, and having him remodel Teddy in the highly popular *Rainbow* manner. Soon their sister paper, the *Sunday Dispatch*, launched its own two-colour comic, *Jolly Jack's Weekly* (20 August 1933). Again Foxwell refashioned Harry Folkard's "All Aboard the Fun Ship" in his beloved *Rainbow* way. Soon provincial newspapers were following the nationals in introducing their own comic sections, many of them handled by the enterprising Adams and Fidler Agency. This Fleet Street purveyor of puzzles quickly ballooned into a comic strip studio, hiring such youthful talents as Basil Reynolds (later to do supreme colour work for *Mickey Mouse Weekly*), and Reg Perrott (soon to develop into England's finest adventure strip artist), with young veterans like H. Stanley White (to become the first British science-fiction strip artist). One of these local supplements, that of the *Bristol Evening World*, was such a hit with the kids that it was made a twice-weekly, then thricc-weekly, and finally the world's first daily comic!

The longest run of any British comic supplement began on 8 March 1936 when the Scottish *Sunday Post* issued its first *Fun Section*: it continues to this day. All the other comics had died by the Second World War, but the new Sunday newspaper, *The Mail on Sunday*, started a full colour American-style supplement on 17 October 1982. More indigenous, and therefore more interesting, is *The Newspaper Comic* with its robot mascot "Scoops". Like the provincial supplements of the mid-Thirties, this one was produced in Portsmouth for the local *News*, beginning 10 September 1982. It was the brainchild of comics-collector Ron Holland, a T-shirt manufacturer: he lost his T-shirt on the project.

rushed out its own comic supplement. It beat the *Mail* in one sense – it was printed in two colours instead of on yellow paper – but was only issued with their Scottish edition. The London edition followed a few weeks later, but although a breezy, fun-filled comic, it failed to catch on and was soon dropped, perhaps because the *Express* did not pin it to their own popular children's strip, "Rupert".

The continued success of the

THE FUNNIES: "Watch Us Step!"

The first American comic to go on sale at the newsstands every week was not a comic-book. It was a comic very much on the British pattern, although its title was very much on the American: *The Funnies*. The word "funnies" had been coined early on, an affectionate abbreviation of "the funny papers", or "funny pages", as the Sunday comic supplements had come to be called. *The Funnies* was the first comic to be published by the Dell Publishing Company, a name that was a commercial contraction of the founder's, George T. Delacorte Jr, and a name that would be associated with some of the highest quality comic-books ever issued (motto: "Dell Comics Are Good Comics"). Dell's *Funnies* format followed the popular tabloid size of the comic section of the *New York Sunday News*, much more manageable as a newsstand item than the broadsheet format. This was why *The Funnies* failed: it was easily mistaken for a regular Sunday supplement, and children saw no good reason to part with 10 cents for something they got free every week! Even when Dell cut the price in half to 5 cents (from No.25; the page-count went down from 24 to 16), there weren't enough takers to continue the comic beyond No.36. But failure was in the future; when No.1 of *The Funnies* went on sale early in 1929 (the comic was undated, but the title had been registered with the US Post Office on 27 December 1928), the Editor had a jaunty jazz-age message for his readers: "Watch Us Step!"

Steppin' out on page one was "Frosty Ayre", stowing away with his pal Goofy on the first leg of a Polar expedition. The artwork, owing a lot to Moon Mullins crossed with Harold Teen was signed "Arch", a pen-name concealing Joe Archibald, a sports reporter and juvenile fiction-writer who would wind up as editor of the N. L. Pines comic chain. Another cartoonist who was to cut out a career in comics, present more than once in this first *Funnies*, was Gordon Rogers. His pages featured "Rock Age Roy", a comic caveman, "Campus Clowns", a college caper, and "Deadwood Gulch", a wild western which he signed "Charles McGraw". In later years he would sign "Boody" to his satirical superhero, "Sparky Watts". Among the other full-page strips were "Buck Buford", a baseball hero, "Corporal Tim", a World War serial, and "Bug Movies", funny insects by Stookie Allen. Only eight pages were in full colour, the centre 16 being black and white, mainly illustrated stories and features in the English style.

Changes began with No.4: the front page was given over to one large cartoon, which would become standard once the comic-book format was established. This first cover cartoon was signed VEP, a pen-name which concealed Victoria Pazmino, the first lady artist in comics. In No.9 she introduced her strip "Clancy the Cop", which was later issued as a oneshot reprint comic-book. From No.5 *The Funnies* became a monthly, a significant point in comic history: it had proved that a weekly comic in the European manner would not work in America. The Editor returned with prizes for young contributors. He reported on the response to his previous request for comments thus: "About all we got was a lot of bunk about *The Funnies* being so unutterably superlative that (if we believed it) we'd apply for Mussolini's job and then try to run the world!" One letter was quoted, from Chester N. Miller of Jackson Heights, who reckoned "My Big Brudder" by Tack Knight the best funny page he had ever seen. "I wish I could see it every day", he said, then went on to suggest that "a different type of heading on your front page would be better." Replied the Editor, "Smart boy, Chester!" and promptly changed the title design, sending young Miller his choice of fountain pen, microscope, Boy Scout knife, pencil-that-writes-six-different-colours, or a book on How to Fly.

The Funnies had stepped out only to fall; but it had been a first step for comic-kind. For the record, the editor was Harry Steeger and the comic art editor, the first so accredited, Abril Lamarque. In October 1936 *The Funnies* would return, this time to succeed in the new comic-book format. From No.65 (July 1942) it would change to *New Funnies* and carry strips starring the Walter Lantz animated cartoon characters, finally winding up with No.288 (March 1962) as *TV Funnies*.

The Funnies *No.1 © January 1929 Dell Publishing. Drawn by Joe Archibald*

The Funnies *No.4 © January 1937 Dell Publishing*
New Funnies *No.109 © March 1946 Dell Publishing*
TV Funnies *No.261 (No.1) © November 1958 Dell Publishing*

14 COMICS 14

THE FUNNIES

Flying – Sports – Adventure

No. One　　　　　　　　　　　　10 Cents

Copyright 1929, Film Humor, Inc.

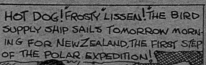

FAMOUS FUNNIES ON PARADE

The American comic-book, destined to dominate the world, was born in humble circumstances. The first appeared in the midst of the Depression and could only be given away. Today a mint copy of that first edition is valued at $700. Max Charles Gaines, a salesman with the Eastern Color Printing Co of New York, worked out the idea of a scaled-down reprint of the broadsheet Sunday funnies, stapled into a specially drawn cover and printed on better class paper. He talked Proctor and Gamble into giving the book away as a promotional premium. This pioneering production consisted of 32 pages of reprints in a collage cover, illustrating the familiar characters within. Gaines christened it *Funnies On Parade*. The strips featured were "Nipper" by Clare Dwiggins, "Reg'lar Fellers" by Gene Byrnes, "Mutt and Jeff" by Bud Fisher, "Keeping Up With the Joneses" by Pop Momand, "Hairbreadth Harry" by F. O. Alexander, "The Bungle Family" by H. J. Tuthill, "Joe Palooka" by Ham Fisher, "S'Matter Pop" and "Honeybunch's Hubby" by C. M. Payne, and "Somebody's Stenog" by A. E. Hayward. There were also eight two-colour pages of "Magic by Blackstone the Magician", and various puzzles. The book, published in the summer of 1933, was successful enough for Gaines to interest the Wheatena Corporation in a similar giveaway. On 1 October 1933 this advertisement appeared in the *Chicago Sunday Tribune* comic supplement for *Famous Funnies: A Carnival of Comics*.

Free! Famous Funnies! *A book of popular comics. Boys and Girls — here's a book you'll all like. 32 pages including Mutt and Jeff, Hairbreadth Harry, Joe Palooka, Reg'lar Fellers and a lot more. It's full of puzzles, jokes, magic tricks — all sorts of things. You can get a copy of this book free. Just fill out the coupon and mail it to us with the top cut from a package of Wheatena. If you haven't a Wheatena package in your home, ask your mother to get you one from her grocer the first thing tomorrow morning!*

In addition to the strips listed in the advertisement, *Famous Funnies* included "Dixie Dugan" by McEvoy and Striebel, "Nipper", "Keeping Up With the Joneses", "Somebody's Stenog", "The Bungle Family", "The Nebbs" by Hess and Carlson, "S'Matter Pop", "Connie" by Frank Godwin, and puzzle items. It was similar to the pioneering *Funnies On Parade*, but had one big difference. *Famous Funnies* had the first specially-drawn comic-book cover, showing the characters from the strips having fun at a fairground.

The third comic-book, this time called *Century of Comics*, was a bigger effort: 100 pages of strips, again reprinted from recent Sunday sections. It included the usual Mutt and Jeff, Joe Palooka and Co. This time Gaines' book was used as a premium by Milk-O-Malt, Wanamaker's Stores and Kinney's Shoes, as well as Wheatena. Obviously, Gaines was on to a good thing. Eastern Color backed his idea to the tune of a 35,000-copy print-run when he suggested publishing a comic-book for sale at 10 cents. *Famous Funnies (Series 1)*, with twice the page count of the giveaways (64 plus covers), went into the chain stores in early 1934. It was the usual gathering of reprint strips, half of them reprinted for the second time: Gaines used material from his first two giveaway comic-books. It sold out swiftly enough for Eastern Color to publish *Famous Funnies* on a regular schedule through the shops and newsstands, just like any other publication. And so, at last, with *Famous Funnies* No.1, dated July 1934, the genuine American comic-book was born. The only original thing about *Famous Funnies* No.1 was the cover. It was a front-to-back spread with a crude cartoon by Jon Mayes, showing some of the well-known comic characters playing golf. Inside was the usual parade of reprints, although several strips new to the format were introduced, including "Toonerville Folks" by Fontaine Fox, "Tailspin Tommy" by Hal Forrest, "Donald Dare the Demon Reporter" by A. W. Brewerton and "Ben Webster" by Edwin Alger. The only new material, cover apart, was that curse of the comic-book, the two-page text story. This, apparently a legal requirement of the US Post Office, became a fixed feature of every comic-book to come. For the record, this historic first was "Dick Whittington" by Jane Corby.

Famous Funnies No.2 introduced something which was to upset purists through the years. The vast reduction of the newspaper strips from broadsheet to 7 × 9 inches meant a similar vast reduction in the size of the lettering. Gaines solved this problem in his No.2. He had all the speech balloons relettered in a larger, more readable size. This was undoubtedly easier on your eyes, but ruinous to artwork. The new balloons, crudely uniform in style and pasted haphazardly over the panels, often intruding into margins and overlapping other panels, spoilt the original quality of the strips.

One by one, other popular newspaper strip heroes arrived in the pages of *Famous Funnies*. "Buck Rogers in the 25th Century" by Dick Calkins rocketed into No.3, closely followed by "Dan Dunn Special Operative" by Norman Marsh, and a scattering of original strips including "Seaweed Sam the Rhyming Rover". Subtitled "The Nation's Comic Monthly", No.19 was something of a special edition. It introduced no fewer than ten new strips. This issue also saw a breezy editorial page, "Let's Get Into a Huddle", which advised readers that "Next month we start another corking, good story, that of 'Apple Mary'. She is a grand person and her life is filled with adventure and thrills." The feature was signed by "The Famous Funnies Family".

As the years went by, and original comic-books came on to the market, *Famous Funnies* was forced to fight back. It reduced the number of frames on a page from a packed 15 to six, and began to add characters of its own editorial creation. "Fearless Flint the Flint Man", which reflected the super-hero trend, arrived in No.89. Frank Frazetta began to provide original Buck Rogers covers from No.210. The end of the story came in July 1955. With issue No.218 the first American comic-book gave up its rather slender ghost. M. C. Gaines, its famous father, had long since moved elsewhere – as shall be seen.

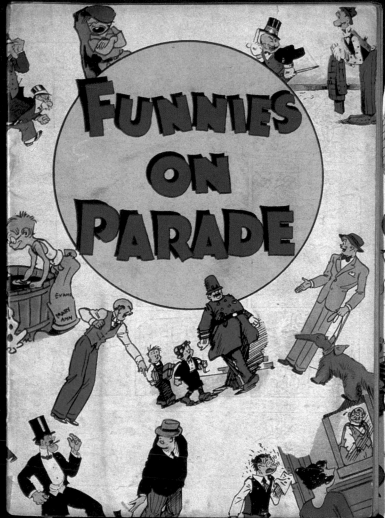

FUNNIES ON PARADE

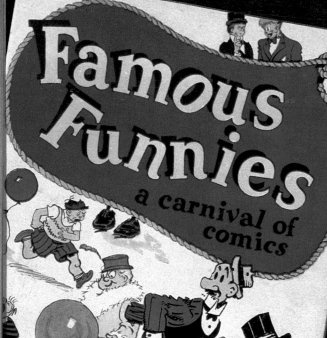

Famous Funnies
a carnival of comics

FAMOUS FUNNIES

100 COMICS AND GAMES—PUZZLES—MAGIC

10 CENTS

No. 1

Toonerville Folks · Mutt & Jeff · Hairbreadth Harry · S'matter
Dixie Duggan · The Bungle Family · Connie · Ben Webster ·
Pam · The Nebbs · Highlights of History · Amaze-a-Minute ·

FAMOUS FUNNIES

No. 100

HAPPY BIRTHDAY!

100TH ANNIVERSARY

"AMERICA'S FAVORITE FUNNIES!"

Popular Comics, which arrived once a month from February 1936, modelled itself closely on the *Famous Funnies* format, right down to the regular catchline. *Famous* called itself "The Nation's Comic Monthly", so *Popular* coined the phrase "America's Favorite Funnies". And just like the early *Famous*, *Popular's* covers were crudely-drawn likenesses of their syndicated reprints. The immediate success of his new comic-book prompted Dell Publishing's president, George T. Delacorte Jr., to launch a companion. As promotion he instituted a competition with $25 as the prize for the best name for the new comic-book. On 10 September 1936 the first issue of the new magazine hit America's newsstands. The winning title was *The Funnies*, the same title that had graced Dell's tabloid comic flop of 1929!

Lead strip in *The Funnies* was "Dan Dunn Secret Operative 48" by Norman Marsh, backed up by "Tailspin Tommy" by Hal Forrest and "Captain Easy Soldier of Fortune" by Roy Crane. Easy came from N. E. A. Service, as did most of the strips in *The Funnies*: Edgar Martin's "Boots", V. T. Hamlin's "Alley Oop", and Clyde Lewis's "Herky". Also around were our old friends "Mutt and Jeff", plus a few completely new strips. These included "Spargus 'n' Chubby" and "Happy Mulligan", both unsigned, plus some more adventures of Sheldon Mayer's boy cartoonist, Scribbly. Like many other early comic-books, *The Funnies* gradually increased its proportion of original strips, whittling away at the syndicated reprints until, with No.65 (June 1942), it changed into an animated cartoon comic and changed its title to *New Funnies*.

King Comics No.1 was dated April 1936 and, as its title suggests, was compiled entirely from the strip stable of King Features Syndicate. David McKay was the publisher, and his slogan was "Laughs and Thrills". This described, if baldly, the lineup of "Flash Gordon", "Brick Bradford", "Mandrake the Magician", "Radio Patrol", "King of the Royal Moun-

ted", "Ted Towers, Animal Master" and "Popeye". But the ratio suggests a better slogan would have been "Thrills and Laughs". King's covers, usually showing "Popeye", "Henry" and other characters at play, were drawn by Joe Musial, a King Features artroom staffer, and were always on the side of laughs. King's major rival in the newspaper strip syndicate field was United Features. Getting wind of King's activities, they launched No.1 of their own comic-book, *Tip Top Comics*, in the same month. This fabulous compilation boasted "Over 100 Funnies" for 10 cents, and introduced reduced Sunday strips of Hal Foster's "Tarzan", Al Capp's "Li'l Abner" (with its supporting feature "Washable Jones"), Harry O'Neill's double feature "Bronco Bill" and "Bumps", "The Captain and the Kids", currently drawn by Bernard Dibble in addition to his "Danny Dingle" and wacky "Dub Dabs" series, H. E. Homan's "Billy Make-Believe" and J. Carver Pusey's baffling "Benny".

But the favourite feature for many young readers was "The *Tip Top* Cartoonists' Club" – "Think of the fun of seeing your drawing and name in print to show all your friends!" *Tip Top* was clearly a profitable publication for, within a few issues, the editor was offering lucky young cartoonists not only the thrill of print but a dollar bill prize too! And history was made in *Tip Top* No.22 (February 1938). One of the four winners was young Morton Walker of Kansas City, Mo., the self-same Mort Walker who today draws the world-famous soldier strip, "Beetle Bailey"!

Dell added a third comic-book to their schedule in March 1937 with No.1 of *The Comics*. Although Crane's "Wash Tubbs" and Charles Coll's "Myra North Special Nurse" were starred, the rest of the magazine was entirely original material. A crudely drawn crowd, "Tom Beatty", "G-Man Jim", "Arizona Kid", "Prairie Bill", and even the film star "Tom Mix", all seemed to have been drawn

by the same hasty hand. This material was packaged by Stephen Slesinger Inc, an outfit that worked with Dell comics for many years.

David McKay came back quickly with his second comic-book, *Ace Comics*, No.1 April 1937. This was edited by a character called "Ace Hi", evidently a close relation of *King Comics*' "Jo King". They shared the same address – 604 South Washington Square, Philadelphia – although Jo called it his King's Castle! They also shared the same slanguage: "Squivels!" Ace would ejaculate while Jo cried, "Gollykawollybirds!"

Ace Comics used the rest of the King Features characters. A second string lineup led off with Chic Young's "Blondie", Allen Dean's "Tex Thorne", Ruth Carroll's "The Pussycat Princess", and Billy De Beck's "Barney Google", not yet sharing his logo with "thet shif'less skonk Snuffy Smith". Joe Musial was again to handle the covers, proving that he was funnier at drawing "The Katzenjammer Kids" than his own inside strip, "Teddy and Sitting Bull". *Ace* would be followed later by *Magic Comics* (No.1 August 1939), which would fill itself with unused daily strips featuring King Features characters.

And so the parade of comic-books continued to march through the Thirties. *Feature Funnies* (October 1937), *Comics On Parade* (April 1938), *Super Comics* (May 1938) and *Crackajack Funnies* (June 1938). But gradually the all-original comic-books were taking over the market. The super heroes were just around the corner.

Peter Rabbit: Large Feature Comic
No.1 © 1941 New York Tribune/
Dell Publishing Co. Drawn by
Harrison Cady

The Comics *No.1 © March 1937*
Dell Publishing Co
Crackajack Funnies *No.1 © June*
1938 Dell Publishing Co
Tip Top Comics *No.1 © April 1936*
United Feature Syndicate. Drawn by
Mo Leff

Super Comics *No.1 © May 1938*
Dell Publishing Co
Comics On Parade *No.1 © April*
1938 United Feature Syndicate

JUNGLE JINKS WITH TIGER TIM

On Tuesday 11 April 1904 C. Langton Townley Esq, cartoon editor for Alfred Harmsworth Publications, wrote a letter to Mr J. Stafford Baker, comic artist, requesting a new strip for the recently refurbished *Daily Illustrated Mirror*. "Mr Harmsworth's idea is to emulate the success of 'Jungle Jinks' in *Home Chat*", he wrote, explaining that the strip, which first appeared in *The Playbox*, a four-page pull-out supplement in that magazine for women on 29 October 1898, "is without doubt the most successful children's series ever published in this country. The circulation increased over 50,000 after it started, and it is now so much a part of the paper that it could not be

stopped without risking a big slump. The secret of its popularity is the serial (i.e. comic strip) story form in which it is served up and the domestic touches which appeal to both parents and children alike."

In this first ever attempt to analyse the popularity of a children's strip which was the first ever published in Britain, Townley continues: "I rather think that dressing up the animals in clothes adds to the humour and enables the artist to indicate better the age of the characters. It also adds to the reality of the thing, and makes the children believe that Jungle Town really exists. All the animals in the school have character: Jumbo the big boy, for instance, is very good-natured and always ready for a lark; Jacko the monkey is full of mischief and always getting into hot water; Dr Lion the headmaster is stern in school but a good old scout at heart; Mrs Lion is a motherly old soul; the twin Boars play the part of villains in the story. They are unpopular greedy pigs and tale-bearers. For the sake of a moral, their ill-nature usually recoils upon themselves. The great thing is to provide something funny that is absolutely free from vulgarity and will please the mothers almost as much as the children. There is a distinct line between broad comic paper humour and the nursery atmosphere which is the backbone of Jungle Jinks." In this historic document, preserved by the artist's grandson, we see the beginnings of the "nursery school" of British comics, which would grow directly out of Jungle Jinks, via *The Playbox*, and come to full flower with *The Rainbow*.

Following Townley's further instructions to draw a school entitled "Mrs Hippo's Kinder-Garten" ("a nice old girl in spectacles with a birch beside her") with "new animals and birds as far as possible, such as Tommy Tiger, ostrich, giraffe, parrot, bear and artful Willy Fox", Baker turned in the three-panel job and it duly appeared in the *Daily Mirror* on 16 April 1904, the first proper comic strip in a British newspaper. The characters' names were a little different: Freddy Fox, Peter Pelican, Willy Giraffe, Billy Bruin, and Tiger Tim.

The cute little cub in the stripey suit is now 80 years old and still up to his tricks, the oldest strip cartoon hero in the country: he currently cuts up in *Jack and Jill*.

The *Mirror* children's corner did not catch on as Harmsworth hoped, but Townley's faith was undimmed. Charged with producing a new children's supplement for a Rolls Royce among magazines, *The World and His Wife*, he contracted Baker to produce more kindergarten comicalities, this time in full colour. No.1 of the new magazine, complete with a 16-page extra *The Monthly Playbox*, was dated November 1904. Tiger Tim and his pals, in hand-painted pictures, celebrated Guy Fawkes' Day on the front and played soldiers across the centre spread. Tim soon emerges as the major mischief-maker, starring in the first of all children's Christmas annuals as well as *The Playbox*, and graduating to the front page of the first comic really designed for children, *The Rainbow* (No.1 14 February 1914).

William Fisher, editor of the new project, commissioned Baker on 11 December 1913: "It is for a new thing, and your pictures will be reproduced in full colour similar to the front page of *Puck*. Will you kindly remember this and not work the sketches up too much, otherwise the colour effect does not get a chance. I should be pleased to pay you three guineas (£3.3.0) a set." Not a lot for six pictures, but Baker was a quick worker and was also providing "Casey Court" for *Chips*, in a very different style. Eventually his style, which was very much closer to comic than cuddly, got him the push from *The Rainbow*, and the poor man spent the rest of his very long life seeing his creations drawn by the jollier hand of Herbert Foxwell. The full circle of fate awaited, however: the last artist to draw Tiger Tim for the last years of *The Rainbow* (it wound up in 1956) was Julius Stafford Baker's son, Julius Stafford Baker II. Comic art came as a contrast to his previous job, official war artist to the RAF!

The Monthly Playbox *No.1* © *November 1904 Harmsworth Publications. Drawn by Julius Stafford Baker*
Tiger Tim's Tales *No.1* © *1 June 1919 Amalgamated Press*

The Rainbow *No.1* © *14 February 1914 Amalgamated Press. Drawn by Julius Stafford Baker*

No. 1. A SPLENDID TOY MODEL GIVEN FREE WITH THIS NUMBER. 1ᵈ

THE RAINBOW 1ᴰ

No. 1. Vol. 1.   PRICE ONE PENNY.   February 14, 1914.

THE JOLLY ADVENTURES OF THE BRUIN BOYS.—THEIR SNOW-MAN HAS A WARM TIME.

1. There was a great surprise awaiting the boys at Mrs. Bruin's Boarding-School when they awoke the other morning. "Look!" cried Tiger Tim excitedly. "It has been snowing in the night! Isn't it grand!" "I wish we could go out," grumbled Willie Ostrich. "It will all have melted away by the time we've finished our lessons."

2. "I know!" exclaimed Tim. "Let's dress and go up on the roof before Mrs. Bruin gets up! We can have some fine fun up there." The other boys thought it a jolly fine idea, too, and in less than half a minute they were climbing through the roof door. "Come along, boys!" piped Joey, the parrot. "Who'll take me on for a snowball fight?"

3. But Tiger Tim had a better idea than that. "Let's make a snow-man," he said. "He'll look fine sitting up here on the chimney!" So they all set to work, and this is the beauty they made. "Now, that's what I call a real work of art!" cried Jumbo, as Tim put on the finishing touch. "Well done, sir! You ought to get a medal for that!" "Bravo, Tim!" chimed in Joey. "That's the coolest piece of work I've seen for a long time!"

4. But while all this was going on Mrs. Bruin was busy down in the kitchen below, preparing breakfast for her pupils, and as soon as the fire began to burn up, down the chimney came a great heap of snow—plomp!—which put the fire out. "Goodness me!" she exclaimed, with a start. "I've never known it to snow such large flakes as this before! What ever can be the cause of it all?"

5. And she promptly went up on to the roof to find out. Meanwhile, the naughty boys were wondering what had become of their snow-man. "He needn't have left us in such a hurry," cried Georgie Giraffe, who was looking down the chimney for him. "He has done the disappearing trick, if you ask me!" "I wish I could do the same," groaned Jumbo, who just then spotted their teacher. "Oh dear! We're in for it now, I can see!"

6. And Jumbo had guessed quite right, for Mrs. Bruin pretty quickly had them downstairs again, and they had to put up with a cold breakfast. "Isn't she cool to us this morning!" remarked Jacko. "Yes, and so is everything else," agreed Fido. "Cold tea, eh! Burr-r-h!" Anyway, Mrs. Bruin made up for it by giving them all a good dinner, because they promised to be good in future. Do you think they will be? We shall see next week!

NURSERY COMICS:
Hy-phen-a-ted Fun for Ev-er-y One!

"My Dear Chicks," wrote Unc-le Dan in his let-ter in num-ber one of *The Chicks' Own* (25 Sep-tem-ber 1920), "And now you have a pa-per of your ver-y own!" Unc-le Dan did not forget to add the all important message, "You must ask your Dad-dy to buy you *The Chicks' Own* ev-er-y Tues-day!" The Amalgamated (insert your own hyphens) Press had discovered a high-ly viable section of the comic market as yet untapped, the children not yet old enough to read! They had no money either, of course, but this did not deter Alfred Harmsworth's old boys. They devised a comic that parents would buy in order to help their youngsters to read, using big pictures, big print, and, most importantly, the hy-phen-a-ted syll-a-bles which formed the traditional reading system of the

period. Children's delight in attractive anthropomorphic animals, proved since the Nineties with "Jungle Jinks" in *Home Chat*, was well catered for, and Arthur White, who had created Dr Lion and his jungle pupils so long ago, now drew "Dicky Duck" on the front page. Later he replaced this strip with a more suitable title character for the comic, "Ru-pert the Chick". In-side the 12 pages were "Pussy Cat Tales" by L. Church, "Tales of the Jolly Jumbos" by H. P. Jenner, and "Tales of Robert Rabbit" by the ex-cellent Walter Holt. Many of these tales would wag right to the last issue on 9 March 1957. A companion comic was duly produced on 22 October 1927, *Tiny Tots*. On the front page were "Tiny and Tot" drawn by Fred-er-ick Cromp-ton – yes, hyphens were still in fashion, although they had disappeared by 24 January 1959, when *Tiny Tots* disappeared too. Full-colour photogravure failed to save them in a changing children's world, and both comics were incorporated with *Playhour*, one of the new breed of nursery comics which had started on 16 October 1954.

In America, comic-book publishers aim at the kids with hot dimes to spend; in consequence parental buys are fairly infrequent. Strips to amuse the very young tend to be confined to newspaper supplements. The monthly magazine, *St Nicholas*, was the breed-ing ground for "The Brownies", Palmer Cox's jam-packed pictures of the adventurous elves. The influence of this series was enormous, from Jimmy Swinnerton's "On and Off Mount Ararat" through to Julius Baker's "Casey Court", especially after Cox's cartoons were issued in book form in 1887. *The Brownies* were updated by Walt Kelly and appeared as Dell comic-books from 1948. "The Teeny Weenies" was a newspaper series much influenced by the Brow-nies, but artist William Donahey added an attractive touch: each week there was a different Teeny Weeny to cut out. The cartoons ran in the *Chicago Tribune* from May 1914, and made it into comic-books in 1950. Another crowd of inch-high charac-ters was Walt Scott's *The Little People*,

which Dell introduced in 1953. *Rag-gedy Ann and Andy*, rag-dolls who came to life, are an American chil-dren's classic, created as illustrated story-books by strip cartoonist Johnny Gruelle. They also had a run in Dell comic-books, but, sadly, not until some years after Gruelle's death in 1938.

Walt Kelly's advance as an artist may be seen at a glance. Compare the cover he drew for No.1 of *Dell's Fairy Tale Parade*, published in 1942, and the one he drew for *Mother Goose and Nursery Rhyme Comics* in 1944. Within two years this ex-animator from the Disney Studio had become one of the most delightful stylists ever to draw young people's comics. *Tiny Tots Comics* followed, and somewhere in the Okefenokee Swamps a possum called Pogo lay a-dozin'. A comic genius of a related yet different kind to Kelly was George Carlson, a wild and wayward talent whose drawings were funny, whose words were funny, and whose stories, design, layout, every-thing, were funny. Carlson did the covers and best strips for *Jingle Jangle Comics*, from 1942 a companion to *Famous Funnies*. No.1 leads off with the first "Jingle Jangle Tale", an epic entitled "The Calico Fisherman and the Left-Handed Clay Pipe", and Carlson backed this with the opening adventure of "The Pie-Face Prince of Pretzleburg", whose name was Dimwitri, or Casper Algernon Nicodemus for short, only son of King Hokum of the steam-heated suspen-ders. Carson was the Dr Seuss of the comic-book, with a touch of Bill Hol-man's "foo"!

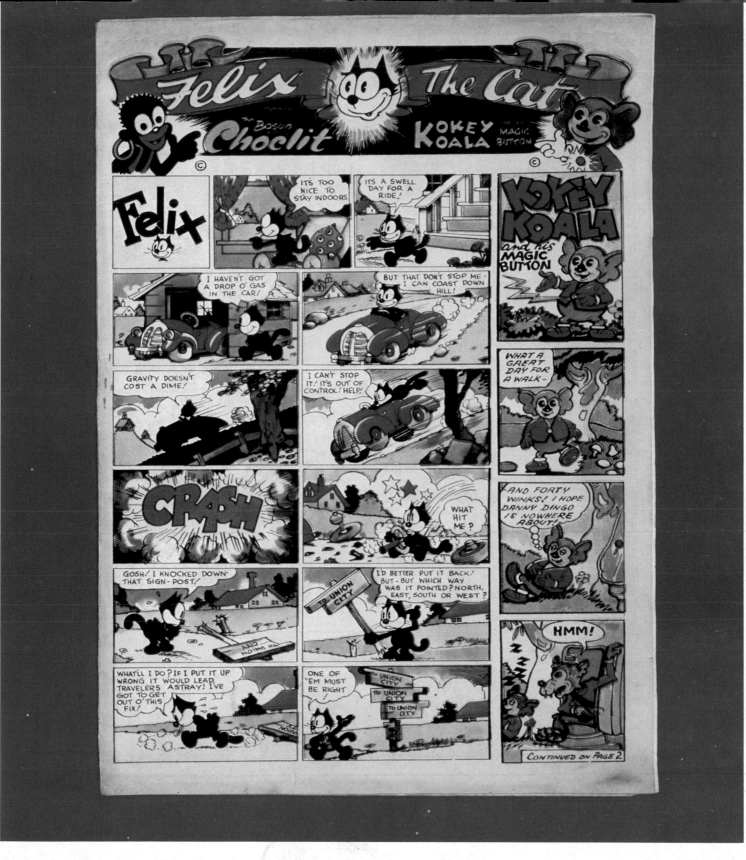

CONTINUED ON PAGE 2

Government that it would be okay to reprint American Felix strips, despite wartime restrictions, as they were "family". So the 32-page Australian *Felix* magazine came into being. With only a set of proofs to work from, some redrawing plus new colour covers were necessary, and this was duly supplied by the expert hand of John Leahy. The British *Felix Funnies* (1949) reworked the Australian material into popular British format.

Felix's latest life-renewal came when comic artist Joe Oriolo not only took over the strip, but set up a new animation production company: "Felix and his Friends" came to television! This gave new life to the comic-book series, and even revived *The Felix Annual* in England (1961). This was an all-original strip book drawn by John Mortimer, who was shortly to give up comic art to become one of the top television comedy writers in the country. New adventures of the oldest cartoon cat in the business continue to be drawn and published throughout Europe, and if that doesn't add up to nine lives, how about Felix's foray into the stereoscopic comics of the Fifties?

Felix *No.8* © *1945 Elmsdale Publications (Australia).*
Felix de Kat *No.2* © *1980 Opera Mundi/King Features*
Felix *No.10* © *January 1966 Bastei Verlag/King Features*
Felix the Cat 3D Comic Book *No.1* © *1953 Toby Press/King Features. Drawn by Otto Messmer*
Felix the Cat (Felix Funnies) *No.1* © *May 1949 S. G. Bruce/King Features. Drawn by Otto Messmer*

MICKEY MOUSE: "Fun for the Whole Family!"

"Dear Folks!" wrote Mickey Mouse on 8 February 1936 from an address in Covent Garden, London. "Here it is at last – no, not the elephant's tail, but the Very First Issue of my Very Own Weekly Paper! And it's what the fire-irons called the kitchen range: isn't it ... just *grate*!" And that certainly was the verdict of the hundreds of thousands of British children who paid out their twopences for No.1 of *Mickey Mouse Weekly*, for in return they were handed a package of laughs and thrills the like of which had never been seen before. There were twelve tabloid pages, four of them in bright, shining full-colour photogravure. The back page was made up of five American daily strips, coloured in to tell the story of "Clarabelle's Court-ship". These, and the centre page series, "Silly Symphony – the Robber Kitten" and "Mickey Mouse", were the main American reprints, taken from newspaper strips syndicated by King Features and drawn by a former animator at the Disney Studio, Floyd Gottfredson. The rest, although Dis-neyfied, was British, expertly edited by the American Disney exploiteer, William B. Levy.

The covers were painted by Wilfred Haughton, a wise choice, for he had been the first man in England to draw Mickey Mouse under licence for com-mercial purposes, and since 1932 had been drawing the entire 128-page issues of *Mickey Mouse Annual*. Haughton was later forced to leave the comic because he refused to update his style of drawing Mickey and his pals in line with the Disney Studio develop-ments. "Shuffled Symphonies", a serial incorporating all the Disney car-toon characters, was written and drawn by "A. Merrimaker", a pen-name for the flowering talent of Basil Reynolds. Basil, from a long line of artists, quickly developed into the best of the British Disney-style cartoonists, contributing delightful covers to the *Weekly* and its several later reincarna-tions. He also drew "Skit, Skat and the

Captain", a funny full-page which made a small ripple in comics history by being reprinted in Dell's *Popular Comics*. Another first was Hugh Stanley White's exciting science-fiction serial, "Ian on Mu, or Pioneers on the Mystery Planet". Quaint today, both in style and science ("We are going at terrific speed, due to your marvellous petrol mixture, Uncle", remarks Ian as the propellered spaceship zooms towards Mu), it was brand new in 1936 and fulfilled the comic's motto, "Fun for the Whole Family".

That slogan was, in fact, borrowed by Bill Levy from *Mickey Mouse Magazine*, the American monthly launched in the Summer of 1935 by Kay Kamen, the main merchandiser of Disneyana. Kamen did so well out of Mickey that he was able to launch his own KK Publications and continue

in quality comic-books for many years. *Mickey Mouse Magazine* was a high-class monthly, mixing strips and stories in equal proportions. Copies came over to the London office and probably inspired Levy to publish the 64-page *Mickey Mouse Holiday Special* in December 1936.

But even the 1935 *Mickey Mouse Magazine* was not the first, for in November 1933 Hal Horne edited No.1 of *Mickey Mouse Magazine* on behalf of a chain of dairies. Most of the gags had a milky flavour: "Top of the morning to you, Mickey!" "Top of the bottle to you, Pluto!" And even before that, back in January, there was another *Mickey Mouse Magazine* sponsored by stores and given away at local cinemas. Travelling forward again, the transition from magazine to comic-book was quite slow, and it was

not until June 1940 that the page-size was reduced to standard format. Then, in October, the title changed to *Walt Disney's Comics and Stories*. Mickey's name was no longer the pulling power, and, as the cover showed, the dominant force was Donald Duck.

Mickey Mouse Magazine *No.1*
© *November 1933 Walt Disney Enterprises*
Mickey Mouse Magazine *No.12*
© *September 1936 Kay Kamen/Walt Disney Enterprises*
Mickey Mouse Holiday Special *No.1*
© *December 1936 Willbank/Walt Disney-Mickey Mouse. Drawn by Wilfred Haughton*
Mickey Mouse Weekly *No.1*
© *8 February 1936 Willbank/Walt Disney-Mickey Mouse. Drawn by Wilfred Haughton*

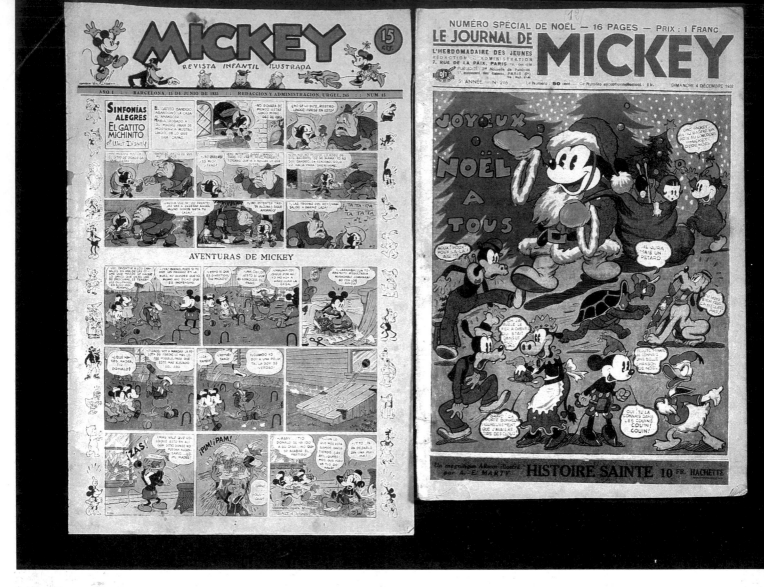

The World of Mickey Mouse

Walt Disney World may be a modern concept, but the world was Mickey's, and therefore Walt's, half a century ago. Legend has it that Disney, inspired by a cheeky rodent that nibbled crumbs at his drawing-board, created his immortal mouse (originally christened Mortimer, renamed by Walt's wife) on the Hollywood-bound express after losing his original cartoon character, "Oswald the Lucky Rabbit", to his distributor, Charles Mintz. Other sources prefer to credit Disney's long-term assistant, the brilliant animator Ub Iwerks, and point to veteran Paul Terry's constant use of cartoon mice in his *Aesop's Fables* series through the Twenties. Certainly Mickey Mouse bears a family resemblance to Oswald, the circular ears replacing the long floppies of the rabbit, and equally Oswald might be likened to a lop-eared Felix the Cat. Further backtracking might link Felix with Pat Sullivan's even earlier piccaninny, "Sammie Johnsin", who in turn grew out of Billy Marriner's comic-strip kiddies (Sullivan had been

Marriner's assistant). Be all that as it may, what Mickey had that the others had not, back in 1928, was a voice! *Steamboat Willie*, with Mickey jazzing up a river-trip, was premièred on 19 September at New York's Colony Theatre and, helped 100 per cent by its synchronized soundtrack, was an outstanding hit. As the print travelled around the world's suitably wired cinemas, Mickey Mouse was raised to international stardom and everybody forgot poor old Felix, who was tossed aside just like so many of his silent screen-star counterparts.

The logical step was to take Mickey into comic strips, and on 13 January 1930 the long-running series began, credited to Ub Iwerks. Soon one of Disney's less important animators took over, and Floyd Gottfredson was given a free hand to develop the strip. It became an exciting, suspenseful mixture of adventure and cartoon humour that ran for many years before other pens let it lapse into gag-a-day dullness. Sunday comic pages, which were shared between Mickey and

adaptations of current *Silly Symphony* cartoons, were added from 17 January 1932. And on the last day of December in that year the world's first Mickey Mouse comic was published.

Topolino was the name the Italians gave to Mickey Mouse, and *Topolino* was the name of that first comic, published at a price of 20 centimos by Casa Editrice Nerbini of Florence. Edited by Collodi Nipoti, the eight-page comic starred a rather ill-drawn Mickey signed Buriko. There was no mention anywhere of Walt Disney, save in a short article on how animated cartoons are made. When No.2 had no Mickey, but a strange-looking chicken on the front page, readers may have suspected something was amiss. But within a few weeks all was well; Nerbini came to an arrangement with the Disney organization, and in return for a share of the 20 centimos were granted the right to run translations of the American strips. So from a spot of Italian piracy grew a world-wide network of foreign-language Disney comics.

On 9 March 1935 No.1 of *Mickey* was published in Barcelona, Spain, with the American Sunday page forming the entire front cover. Other King Features strips filled the colour pages: Nicholas Afonsky's "Little Annie Rooney", C. D. Russell's "Pete the Tramp", and Walt Hoban's "Needlenose Noonan" translated as "El Guardia Petronio". Spanish contributions were confined to the black-and-white pages. The French comic, *Le Journal de Mickey*, started on 21 October 1934. Again the American Sundays filled the front page, except on such special occasions as Christmas when Wilfred Haughton's British *Mickey Mouse Weekly*

covers were traced off (for letterpress reproduction) and used. All the other strips came from King Features, with "Tim Tyler's Luck" translated as "Richard le Téméraire", "Don Winslow of the Navy" as "Bernard Tempête", and "The Katzenjammer Kids" as "Pim Pam Poum". Even a German-language edition managed to escape Hitler's censors by being published in Zurich. *Micky Maus Zeitung* (January 1937) ran Disney dailies plus Donald Duck rechristened "Schnatterich". "Tim Tyler's Luck" was also serialized as "Tim und Tom". Today there is probably no country without its Walt Disney comic: in Holland Donald Duck's

weekly is the national best-seller, while Britain, once such a stronghold, is down to a monthly reprint.

Mickey *No.15* © *15 June 1935 Ventosa (Barcelona)/Walt Disney. Drawn by Floyd Gottfredson* Le Journal de Mickey *No.216* © *4 December 1938 Dablanc (Paris)/Walt Disney. Drawn by Wilfred Haughton* Topolino *No.1 (facsimile)* © *31 December 1932 Nerbini (Florence)* Mickey Maus Zeitung *No.14* © *July 1937 Bollman (Zurich)/Walt Disney* Miki *No.295* © *15 July 1972 (Beograd)/Walt Disney* Miky *No.85* © *September 1974 (Greece)/Walt Disney*

The Rivals of Mickey Mouse

Here's a rabbit called Bugs Bunny,
Who spends his time acting funny,
He's always playing pranks and jokes
On all the other cartoon folks.

Where Walt Disney led, could Leon Schlesinger be far behind? Or Walter Lantz, Paul Terry, and all the other producers of animated cartoon films? The only major name missing in the rush to get their cartoon characters into comic-books was Max Fleischer: his hero, Popeye the Sailor, was already there, having come into cartoon films from the comic strips in the first place.

First in the field to follow *Walt Dis-*

ney's *Comics and Stories* (No.1 October 1940) was Leon Schlesinger's *Looney Tunes and Merrie Melodies Comics*, a long-winded title embracing that producer's twin series of cartoon films made for Warner Brothers. Dell's comic-book was topped and curly-tailed by the star of the series, Porky Pig, bursting through his familiar drum on the cover, and bidding us farewell with his cheery "That's all, folks!" on the back page. But starring in the lead strip was that fast-rising, buck-toothed bunny called Bugs, popping out of his hole to startle that fearless wabbit-hunter, Elmer Fudd, with his call-sign, "What's up, Doc?" The strip was adapted directly from *A Wild Hare*, the 1940 Merrie Melody directed by Fred "Tex" Avery, which is reckoned by historians of the genre to be the definitive origin of Bugs Bunny. However, Bugs' designer, Ben Hardaway, might point to *Hare-um Scare-um*, which he directed in 1939.

The premier issue of *Looney Tunes and Merrie Melodies* forms quite a collectors' item for cartoon buffs in that, unusually, it runs no fewer than five strip adaptations of recent Warner cartoons. Porky Pig, who first strutted his stuttering stuff by courtesy of funny voice man Mel Blanc in the 1935 cartoon *I Haven't Got a Hat*, stars here in *Porky's Hired Hand*, a Dick Bickenbach animation of 1940. Chuck Jones has an entry in *Tom Thumb in Trouble*, also from 1940, while two more stem from Tex Avery, the 1938 burlesque of Pilgrim Father days, *Johnny Smith and Poker Hontas*, which featured Egghead, forerunner of Fudd, and the 1939 burlesque of Robert L. Ripley's "Believe It Or Not" feature, *Believe It Or Else*. Among the supporting programme was an original series built around "Sniffles", the cutesy little mouse who had made his debut in Chuck Jones' *Naughty But Mice* (1939). Dell did so well with their new cartoon title that in July 1942 they transmogrified *The Funnies* into *New Funnies*, packing it with characters from the Walter Lantz productions made for Universal. Several of them – Andy Panda, Oswald the Rabbit, Woody Woodpecker – soon spun off into comic-books of their own, a privilege never granted to Li'l Eightball, the bald black boy.

Terry-Toons, produced by veteran

Paul Terry, never looked as good on the screen as they did in the comic-book as designed by Marvel. Credits were given just like the movies, with publisher Martin Goodman listing himself as Executive Producer, and editor Stan Lee as Director. The cartoonists were listed under Production Assistants (Vincent Fago, Ernest Hart, Gary Kay) and Chief Animators (G. D. Klein, Jim Mooney, Mike Sekowsky and Ed Winiarski), with Mel Barry as Technical Advisor, and Bill King as Associate Director. This historic moment (No.1 was dated October 1942) represents the origin of Marvel Comics' famous credit-listings for writers, pencillers, inkers, colourists and letterers. The early heroes of *Terry-Toons Comics* were "Gandy Goose and Sourpuss", "Oscar Pig", "Dinky Duck" and "Andy Wolf and Bertie Mouse", but the comic really took off once "Mighty Mouse" arrived in No.38 (November 1945). This halfpint-sized parody of Superman (he was beaten to the title of Supermouse by the comic-book hero) proved enormously popular with children and from 1946 clouted the cats in his own title. When the Terry comics moved to other publishers, several of his staff animators supplemented their wages by drawing strips, including Connie Rasinski and Art Bartsch.

Columbia Pictures' cartoon stars, "The Fox and the Crow", moved into comic-books in 1945, taking the lead in DC's *Real Screen Comics*. MGM's cat and mouse comedians, "Tom and Jerry", had been in *Our Gang Comics* from the word go, but as supporting players. Their rapidly rising popularity among young movie fans soon moved them to front-cover stardom, and they finally ousted Our Gang in July 1949 when the comic-book changed its title to *Tom and Jerry Comics* (No.60). Paramount cartoons, made by their subsidiary Famous Studios, came to comics a title at a time: *Little Audrey* in 1948, *Casper the Friendly Ghost* in 1949, *Baby Huey* in 1956. The rest got together in *Paramount Animated Comics* from 1953: "Herman and Katnip", their answer to Tom and Jerry, and "Buzzy the Crow". The UPA (United Productions of America) cartoons whose styling changed the face of animation, also combined in a comic-book: *Gerald McBoing-Boing and Mr Magoo* (Dell 1952). After a few issues the near-sighted Magoo took top billing.

Looney Tunes and Merrie Melodies
Comics *No.1* © *1941 Dell/Leon
Schlesinger*
Terry-Toons Comics *No.43* © *April
1946 Timely Comics/Paul Ferry*
Paramount Animated Comics *No.2
(Comics Hits 62)* © *April 1953
Harvey/Paramount*
Andy Panda *No.1 (OS 25)* © *1943
Dell/Walter Lantz*

Woody Woodpecker's Back to
School *No.1* © *October 1952 Dell/
Walter Lantz*
Oswald the Rabbit *OS 43* © *April
1947 Dell/Walter Lantz. Drawn by
Dan Gormley*
Porky Pig *OS 191* © *June 1948 Dell/
Warner Brothers*
Tweety and Sylvester *No.1* © *June
1963 Gold Key/Warner Brothers*

Bugs Bunny's Christmas Funnies
No.1 © *November 1950 Dell/Warner
Brothers*
Tom & Jerry Comics *No.67*
© *February 1950 Dell/MGM*
Gerald McBoing Boing and Mr
Magoo *No.2* © *November 1953 Dell/
Columbia*
Real Screen Comics *No.29* © *April
1950 National Comics/Columbia*

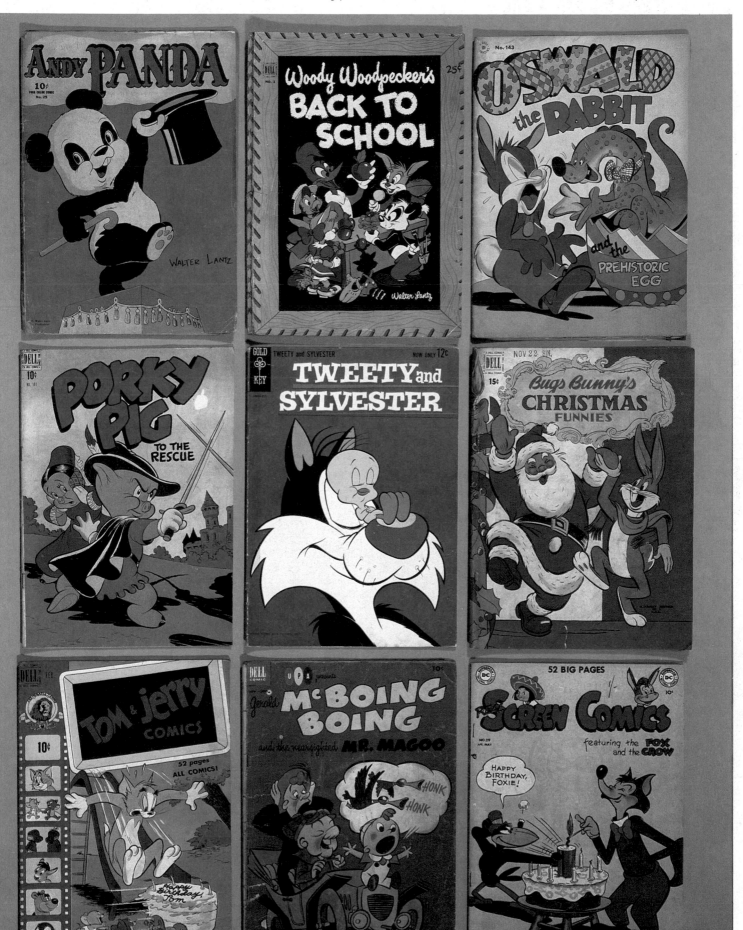

FUNNY ANIMALS:
Krazy about Pogo

"Krazy Kat", the first true Klassic Komic animal, was fathered by George Herriman, mothered by Offisa Pupp, and christened by a brick bunged by Ignatz Mouse ('Owitch! The liddle dollink!') back in 1910. Moving out of the basement of a daily strip called "The Family Upstairs", and into a Sunday colour page in 1916, Krazy Kat starred in as surreal a series of wacky happenings as ever dreamed in anyone's philosophy. When the amazing Herriman ascended to a higher plane in 1944, King Features let Krazy go with him, a signal act of homage. Or so the story goes. In fact, the great man and animal had hardly slumbered some seven years before King gave the okay to Dell to run a series of *Krazy Kat* comic-books. Not reprints of the glorious years (as had been run in *Ace Comics*, back in '37), but brand new, not very well drawn, not very inspired, not very funny stuff.

The Dutch are more sensible: they republish the vintage strips as *Krazy Kat Komix* (1976). Pogo, on the other hand, is the funny animal that made the opposite trip, from comic-books to newspaper strips. A rare event, but Pogo is a rare possum. He began in a small way, very small, as a ratty-looking background player in a series

entitled "Bumbazine and Albert the Alligator". This was but one of several strips in Dell's *Animal Comics* (1942), an attractive collation of animal adventure ("Rover" by Dan Noonan), animal cartoons ("Jigger" by John Stanley), animal veterans ("Uncle Wiggily" by Howard Garis), and animal photos. Bumbazine, an Okeefenokee piccaninny, was soon shunted away, leaving the swamp to Ol' Albert, Pogo, and such other critters as the wise Dr Howland Owl, the singing turtle Churchy La Femme, prickly ol' Porkypine, Deacon Mushrat, Beauregard the retired bloodhound, and P. T. Bridgeport the fancy-talking bear, plus full supporting cast of li'l tads and woodchucks.

When Dell closed the comic-book in the Christmas of '47, Pogo (and co) moved into his own comic-book. More, he moved to the *New York Star* as a daily strip. Having successfully closed that newspaper in '49, Pogo joined the Post-Hall Syndicate and became a nationwide favourite especially with his Sunday page. Although not aspiring to Krazy Kat pyrotechnicalities of design, the fun and philosophy were the finest since that feline's departure. Pogo also, like Krazy, left his cartoon world when his

creator did: Walt Kelly died in 1973. Between them they gave the world a legacy of laughter and a motto to live by: "We have met the enemy and he is us."

It was in 1942 that the comic-books discovered funny animals and animators. Many of them (and Walt Kelly was one) added to their movie-making income by freelancing strips to the comic-books, a particular boon to those who had worked at the Max Fleischer Studio: it closed after the box-office failure of *Mr Bug Goes to Town*. *Goofy Comics* No.1 (June 1943) is virtually an all-Fleischer animator issue, with strips by Carl Wessler, Otto Feuer, Gordon Sheehan, Jim Davis and Bill Hudson. *Real Funnies* No.1 (January 1943) is another, with Milton Stein and Al Pross. *Funny Funnies* No.1 (April 1943) has Rube Grossman and Sidney Pillet, and *Barnyard Comics* No.1 (June 1944) Thurston Harper and John Gentilella. *Funny Animals* No.1 (December 1942) had Captain Marvel! This Fawcett comic made sure of winning a big readership by having their top superhero introduce one of the first of the funny animal superheroes, "Hoppy the Marvel Bunny". The funny animal phase hit its peak in 1945 when *Leading Comics*, a DC title, dropped "Crimson Avenger", "Green Arrow" and the rest and replaced them with "Nero Fox, the Jive Jumpin' Emperor of Ancient Rome" and "Spylot Bones" the dog detective.

Pogo Possum *No.1* © *October 1949 Dell. Drawn by Walt Kelly*
Funny Animals *No.1* © *December 1942 Fawcett Publications. Drawn by Chad Grothkopf*
Krazy Kat Comics *No.5* © *August 1952 Dell Publishing*

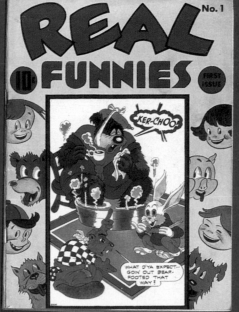

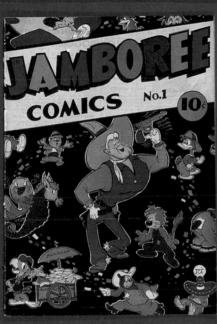

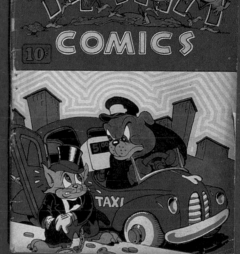

Goofy Comics *No.1* © *June 1943*
Nedor/Pines. Drawn by Joe Oriolo
Real Funnies *No.1* © *January 1943*
Nedor/Pines. Drawn by Milton Stein
Funny Funnies *No.1* © *April 1943*
Nedor/Pines. Drawn by Larry Riley

Jamboree Comics *No.1* © *February*
1946 Round. Drawn by Jason
Funny Films *No.1* © *September*
1949 American Comics Group. Drawn
by Dan Gordon
Ha Ha Comics *No.8* © *May 1944*
Creston

Krazy Komics *No.2* © *September*
1942 Marvel Comics
Frisky Fables *No.2* © *Fall 1945*
Novelty Press. Drawn by Al Fago
All Surprise Comics *No.1* © *Fall*
1943 Marvel Comics

COMICS AND THE CINEMA:
Charlie Chaplin's Comic Capers

Charles Spencer Chaplin, one of "Fred Karno's Speechless Comedians", switched to the Keystone Comedy Company to try his hand (and flat feet) at the booming new medium of silent cinema. His first film, *Making a Living*, was released on 2 February 1914; exactly one year later his 36th film, *His New Job*, was released. It was his first for Essanay, and his salary had shot up from $175 a week to $1,250 plus a cash bonus of $10,000. In twelve months the little tramp with the twitchy moustache, the flat-footed shuffle and the whangee cane had become the world's King of Comedy. Six months later, Charlie was starring in his own comic strip, filling the front page of *The Funny Wonder*, where he was modestly billed as "The Scream of the Earth!" And Charlie was to remain on the front page for many years, long after the credit line "The Famous Essanay Comedian" had been exchanged for the more topical "The Great Dictator of Mirth". Displaced to an inside page during World War II, the Chaplin strip finally closed on 13 May 1944. For most of Charlie's 30-year comic career, right from the first full page of 7 August 1915, he had been drawn by Bertie Brown. Brown was as natural a comedian with pen and ink as Charlie was with his body. As a boy he had won a scholarship to the Slade School of Art, but family poverty had prevented him from taking it up. Instead he learned from comics, and especially from his idol, Tom Browne. Browne was not only the creator of Weary Willie and Tired Tim, he was the originator of the British comic style. Bertie recalled visiting the sick cartoonist at his home in Blackheath. Bertie showed the dying Tom his own cartoons and was encouraged to submit them to the comics. Soon Bertie was on the art staff of *Illustrated Chips*,

remaining with the same publisher for 50 years (1908 to 1958). Bertie was always good at caricature and, inspired by one of his frequent visits to the local cinema, made a few quick sketches of Charlie Chaplin and showed them to his editor. The idea found instant approval, coinciding as it did with the Chaplin boom which Essanay publicists were boosting. Soon Charlie was being introduced to *Funny Wonder* readers with these well-chosen words: "He is the pick of the fun market and will keep you bright and jolly!"

Meanwhile, in America, a surprisingly similar series of events occurred. "By Arrangement with the Essanay Company" publisher James Keeley started a Chaplin strip in his newspaper, the *Chicago Record-Herald and Inter-Ocean*. Called "Charlie Chaplin's Comic Capers", it was far cruder than the British strip, reducing Charlie to the status of a standardized cartoon character with gags more verbal than visual. However, the strip is of enormous importance in the history of the art because on 12 March 1916 it introduced a new cartoonist, Elzie Crisler Segar. But it would have taken a genius greater even than Chaplin's to have foreseen that this tyro cartoonist's hackwork would one day lead to the evolution of the mighty Popeye! Two early comic-books came from these Chaplin strips. In England, the Bertie Brown strips were reprinted as *The Charlie Chaplin Fun Book*, which, as it was published in late 1915, was the world's first book about the comedian. In the States, the American strip was collected into a run of four comic-books, commencing with *Charlie Chaplin's Comic Capers* (1917).

The French name for Charlie was Charlot, and it was not long before Thomen, a brilliant if slapdash cartoonist, was drawing "Les Aventures

The Charlie Chaplin Fun Book © 1915 Amalgamated Press. Cover drawn by Seymour
Les Aventures Acrobatiques de Charlot © Société Parisienne d'Edition. Drawn by Thomen
Charlie Chaplin No.1 © 1973 Top Sellers/Bubbles Inc. Drawn by Torre Grosa

Charlie Chaplin's Comic Capers No.1 © 1917 J. Keeley/M.A. Donohue
Funny Wonder No.72 © 7 August 1915 Amalgamated Press. Drawn by Albert T. Brown

Acrobatiques de Charlot" for the weekly comic *Cri-Cri*. Thomen's strips ran in serial form, and unlike the British and American strips, were close to the Chaplin concept of silent comedy. Charlot never spoke. Nor, for that matter, did any of the other characters in the serials, the story being told in printed continuity underneath the pictures. Thomen's strips were regularly gathered into albums, the first being *Charlot Fait des Farces*. It is also worth mentioning that only in the comics has Chaplin ever appeared in colour. And only in the 1973 series of *Charlie Chaplin* comic-books can he be seen in colour on every page. This comic was an international venture, published in London by Top Sellers, drawn in Spain by Torre Grosa, and printed in Sweden. Charlie, who considered himself a citizen of the world, would have liked that!

"All the Fun of the Films!"

"Startling news!" shrieked the headline. "An absolutely New and Original Comic paper entitled *Film Fun*! Nothing else like it on the market! All the Real Film Favourites in Flickers of Funniosity!" Thus spake the diamond studded gent we would soon come to know as Eddie the Happy Editor. Actually his name was Fred Cordwell, and when the Amalgamated Press asked their staff editors to come up with concepts for new comics in the postwar peace of 1919, it was Cordwell's which won the race. His *Film Fun* was destined to run from 17 January 1920 to 8 September 1962, a total of 2,225 weekly editions. The quotation comes from the illustrated leaflet tucked inside all the other AP comics, promoting the new venture.

"It is the Most Wonderful Comic for Boys and Girls", ran the blurb, proceeding to list the all-star attractions like some fabulous film programme. Page one led off with "The Adventures of Winkle the Pathé Mirth Wizard". This was really Harold Lloyd, renamed for British release for reasons lost in the dim distance. Then came "The Lively Adventures of Lawrence Semon, the Popular Vitagraph Comedian", "The Playful Pranks of Baby Marie Osborne, the Famous Pathé Star", "Mack Swain the One and Only Ambrose of the W & F Film Service", "The Screamingly Funny Adventures of Earle Montgomery and Joseph Rock of Vitagraph Fame", "Ben Turpin and Charlie Conklin, Heroes of the Paramount Mack Sennett Comedies", "Slim Summerville's Side-Splitters" and "James Aubrey the Vitagraph Fun Spark". In addition to these strip cartoons there was a serial story, "Fatty Arbuckle's Schooldays", written, it was claimed, by the Famous-Lasky Film Service Star himself. All this, together with a "Free Plate of Fatty Arbuckle", for twopence!

More important, perhaps, than the obvious value *Film Fun* has as a cartoon record of bygone cinema stars, is the style of the comic. In an attempt to capture the look of silent movies, the artwork was boldly black-and-white, and the action visual, modelled on the slapstick sight gags of the comedians of the period. British comics had always been very visual, of course, but with *Film Fun* there came a definite improvement in the construction of slapstick sequences which could be understood at a glance. Many of the gags were lifted directly from the films: the Twenties were the Golden Age of silent film comedy, and two-reelers could be seen in every cinema programme. To draw his new comic,

Cordwell used the artists who had been working on his *Merry and Bright*, a comic which often featured Music Hall stars. Tom Radford drew Harold Lloyd and Montgomery and Rock, Harry Parlett drew Lawrence Semon and Slim Summerville, and George William Wakefield drew Baby Marie, Mack Swain and Ben Turpin and illustrated Fatty's Schooldays. Billy Wakefield was to be the cartoonist who would set the style of *Film Fun's* art work with his own drawings. He did this by becoming its master artist and originating many of its famous series over the years: Jackie Coogan (1921), Wesley Barry (1924), Grock (1929), Laurel and Hardy (1930), Joe E. Brown (1933), Wheeler and Woolsey (1934), Max Miller (1938), George Formby (1938) and Lupino Lane (1939). In addition, he designed the caricatures that served as models for other artists to follow when drawing strips.

The success of *Film Fun* led to Cordwell creating a companion paper, and on 24 April 1920 there appeared No.1 of *Kinema Comic*. This time "The Funniosities of Fatty Arbuckle" appeared in strips drawn, of course, by Billy Wakefield. He also contributed "The Screen Screams of Ford Sterling", whilst other pens drew "The

Larks of Louise Fazenda", "The Priceless Pranks of Polly Moran" and "Mabel Normand in a Reel Comedy". The predominance of film comediennes, virtually ignored by *Film Fun*, suggests either *Kinema Comic* was looking for a female audience, or they were scraping the barrel a bit. Despite having to make do with decidedly second string stars, *Kinema Comic* managed a 12-year run before combining with its stablemate.

Most remarkable of the several cinema comics was *Film Picture Stories*, another Fred Cordwell enterprise, but one which crashed after only 30 issues. This time the concept was to adapt films directly as strips; dramatic films, not comedies. This was something completely new in comics, and No.1, published 28 July 1934, was, in consequence, the first all-adventure strip comic published in Britain. The four films given strip treatment were "Police Car" by Billy Wakefield, (proving, not very successfully, that he could turn his hand to adventure strips), "Ace of Aces" and "Dick Turpin" by J. H. Valda, and "Fighting Code" by Joseph Walker. The artists, joined in No.3 by Harry Lane, were all experienced in illustrating boys' stories in the many Amalgamated Press weeklies, but unaccustomed to

the continuity required by strip work. From No.12 the film strips were reduced to two an issue, then only one, as adventure strips featuring cowboy stars Ken Maynard, Tim McCoy and Buck Jones were introduced. Then readers of No.30 were advised to buy *Film Fun* next week. *Film Picture Stories* was no more.

Of all the many cinema stars cartooned in the comics, none can be rarer than the great goddess Garbo. Did Greta or MGM ever know that, back in the Thirties, she was starring in a strip on the front of the Italian comic, *Bombolo*?

Film Fun *No.1* © *17 January 1920 Amalgamated Press. "Winkle". Drawn by Tom Radford*

Kinema Comic *No.1* © *24 April 1920 Amalgamated Press. "Fatty Arbuckle". Drawn by Billy Wakefield*

Film Picture Stories *No.16* © *10 November 1934 Amalgamated Press. "The Eagle and the Hawk". Drawn by Joseph Walker*

Bombolo *No.37* © *28 February 1936 Mazorati (Milan)*

Film Fun with
Laurel and Hardy

When Stan Laurel met Oliver Hardy in Hollywood in 1926, there was laughter in Paradise. Not only in Paradise, but in every other cinema and movie theatre that carried Hal Roach releases. Their comedy was in the classic mould of vaudeville double acts, and comic strip double acts, too. Like Weary Willie and Tired Tim, they were fat and thin, and fond of the slapstick, and hence the very stuff of which comic strip heroes are made. So it was no surprise to readers of *Film Fun*, the British comic that had been starring screen comedians since 1920, that Eddie the Happy Editor should announce that Laurel and Hardy would arrive in the centre spread of their favourite comic in No.564 dated 8 November 1930.

"I promise you that you'll have a real good laugh when you see them," chuckled Eddie, hoping that his readers might overlook the fact that Stan and Ollie had already made their comic strip debut in a rival, but now defunct, weekly, *The Realm of Fun and Fiction* No.46, published 28 December 1929! In that paper the cartoonist had been Reg Carter, a former picture postcard artist who, amazingly enough, had also drawn the comic strip adventures of Babe Hardy (as Ollie had previously been billed when a solo star) in *Kinema Comic* in 1920. But the editor of *Film Fun* handed the new L. and H. strip over to Billy Wakefield, a brilliant cartoonist whose clean black-and-white work was ideally suited to a comic based on black-and-white movies.

Wakefield was top man at *Film Fun*, the man who, armed with a pad and pencil, was sent to see every new film comedian with the task of turning him into a cartoon character for the comic. He started off every new strip, setting the pattern which would eventually be imitated by lesser artists. He was working on the first Abbott and Costello strip when he died in 1942. His son, Terry, succeeded him on Laurel and Hardy.

The Laurel and Hardy strip, subtitled "The Comical Capers of the Screen's Cutest Couple", was so popular that it moved to the front page of *Film Fun* from 10 March 1934, and stayed there until 15 November 1957, a run of 27 years in all, longer than their real-life partnership on the screen!

The popularity of Stan and Ollie

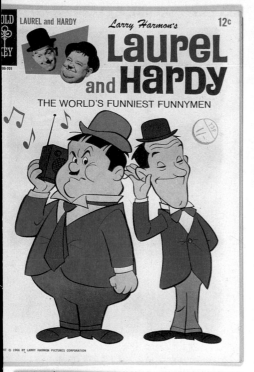

beyond the English-speaking world was huge, and so the *Film Fun* strip was syndicated abroad. In Italy it appeared in both *Bombolo* (1934) and a film oriented comic, *Cine Comico* (1934). A local publisher produced a rival strip called "Stan e Oli", and put them on the front page of yet another comic, *Mastro Remo* (1934). Here the boys had the advantage of appearing in full colour, although the Italian artist, Missigoi, was not in the Wakefield class. Neither was Mat, the French cartoonist who drew Laurel and Hardy, also in colour, for the comic *Cri-Cri* (1934). After the war an Italian publisher, Mario Conte, introduced the first all-Laurel and Hardy comic-book, *Criche e Croc* (1946). The artwork by Dap was crude but lively.

In the Sixties Larry Harmon, a television puppeteer, turned Laurel and Hardy into an animated cartoon series. This gave the comedians a new lease of life, and their small-screen popularity soon led to a new flow of comic-books. The most successful series was not published in America, as might have been expected, but in Europe. This was *Laurel and Hardy* (No.1 March 1969), a full-colour comic-book published by Top Sellers in England and in foreign language versions by Williams. It was scripted in London, drawn in Spain and printed in Poland. Although long gone from English shops, it continues in Spain as *Gordo y Flaco*. Whoever said "Laurel and Hardy will live forever" seems to have been right!

Film Fun *No.904* © *15 May 1937 Amalgamated Press. Drawn by George W. Wakefield*
Cri-Cri *No.850* © *10 January 1935 Société Parisienne d'Edition. Drawn by "Mat"*

Laurel and Hardy *No.1* © *1966 KK Publications/Larry Harmon Pictures Corporation*

Criche e Croc *No.17* © *30 November 1946, Editrice Edital. Drawn by "Dap"*
Album el Gordo y el Flaco *No.2* © *1980 Nueva Frontiera/Larry Harmon Pictures Corporation*
Laurel and Hardy *No.1* © *August 1972 National Periodicals/Larry Harmon Pictures Corporation*

THE YOUNG ADVENTURERS

On the 15 May 1920 the adventure began. It was described as "The Picture Story of a Brave Boy who was All Alone in the World", and was called, after its young hero, "Rob the Rover". Floating mysteriously in from the sea, Rob was washed up in the pages of *Puck*, the high-class twopenny comic, to become the world's first adventure strip hero. For 20 years, in a weekly page of a dozen pictures, Rob roved the globe seeking his true identity in the company of Dan, the grizzled old fisherman who had found the boy on the beach. Who Rob really was will never now be known; *Puck* was suddenly suspended because of the wartime paper shortage and our hero was cut down in mid-rove. Rob was created by Walter Booth, who had spent the previous ten years drawing comic characters like "Professor Potash", and this sudden change of direction into adventure was both surprising and permanent. From now on Booth would draw such picture serials as "Orphans of the Sea" (1930), "Captain Moonlight" (1936) and "The Pirate's Secret" (1939). But Rob would remain his classic, with stories set under the sea, in lost cities, and aboard Professor Seymour's amazing submarplane, "The Flying Fish". Rob journeyed even further than his creator knew; he was syndicated throughout Europe, turning up in full colour in Denmark and as a member of the Young Fascisti in a redrawn uniform in Mussolini's Italy!

Boy heroes and their adventures were usually confined to the inside or back pages of British comics, but in 1934 "Jerry, Jenny and Joe" began their cheery serial on the front page of *Tip Top*, followed by "Nutty Bolt and Tom Random, Cycling Round the World on a Tandem", who took over page one of *Jingles* in 1937. Then *Crackers* followed suit, moving its back-page serial stars ("The Adventures of Bob and Betty Britten") to the front and full-colour. All these and more followed a common story-line, sending their boy/girl or boy/boy teams wandering through a world of wild animals, savage cannibals, mysterious orientals and lost cities. No-

body seemed to mind, neither the heroes, nor their readers.

Five years after Rob, the American newspaper strips published their first boy hero, "Phil Hardy", drawn by George Storm. "This is the story of Phil Hardy's climb to fame and fortune" announced scriptwriter Edwin Alger (J. J. Jerome), and soon 15-year-old Phil was doing his best to support his widowed mother by being shanghaied for Cape Town. Alger went on to write another adventure strip, "Bound to Win", while Storm both wrote and drew a new boy hero, "Bobby Thatcher" (1927). To make certain Alger had no grounds for a suit, Storm made Bobby a 14-year-old orphan, otherwise life was much the same for boy heroes – gangsters, flying, sailing, riding the range. See also "Frankie Doodle", Ben Batsford's boy hero of the Thirties, and the young orphan star of "Tim Tyler's Luck". This got a lot more exciting once artist Lyman Young shipped Tim and his chum Spud Slavins off to Africa to join the Ivory Patrol.

"Dickie Dare" began 1933, the first solo effort of a rising new talent called Milton Caniff. A year later and his genius had been recognized by Captain Patterson of the Tribune-News Syndicate; "Terry and the Pirates" was born. At first it looked like a remake, with Terry Lee replacing Dickie Dare as the titular boy hero, and Pat Ryan replacing Dan Flynn as his grown-up, two-fisted companion. But Caniff's setting for his serial, the exotic, authentic Orient, was breathtakingly illustrated (especially in the Sunday colour pages), and equally breathtakingly peopled with a cast of characters more real, more rounded out, than any the comics had ever known. Under Caniff's brilliant hand as both writer and artist, the strip matured into the finest adventure saga of them all. It broke completely away from the "funny style" that still dominated most American and European adventure strips, as with Hergé's exciting, but equally amusing, boy reporter "Tintin".

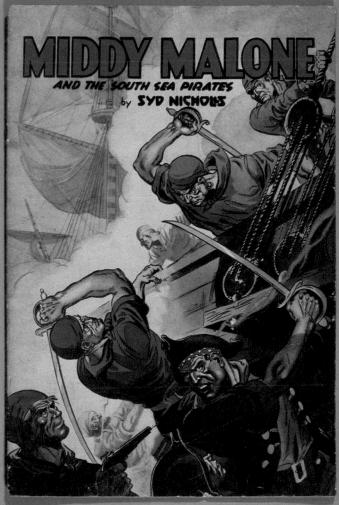

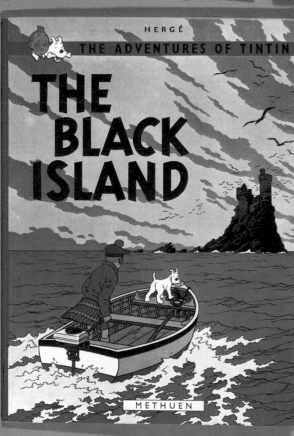

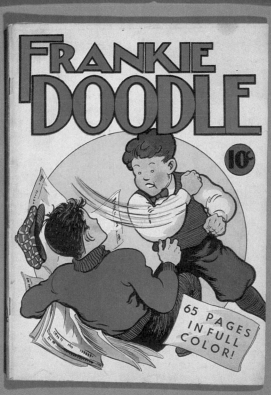

La Revista de Tim Tyler *No.19* ©
1936 Hispano American (Spain).
Drawn by Lyman Young
Il Giornale di Cino e Franco *No.14*
© *10 November 1935 Lorenzini*
(Italy). Drawn by Lyman Young
Tip Top *No.243* © *10 December*
1938 Amalgamated Press. Drawn by
W. D. Davies

Crackers *No.527* © *25 March 1939*
Amalgamated Press. Drawn by
Alexander Akerbladh
Terry and the Pirates *No.2 (FC 44)*
© *1944 Dell/Chicago Tribune. Drawn*
by Milton Caniff
Middy Malone *No.2* © *1942*
Nicholls (Australia). Drawn by Syd
Nicholls

Adventures of Tintin *No.1: Black*
Island © *1966 Methuen/Casterman.*
Drawn by Hergé
Frankie Doodle *No.1 (SS 7)*
© *1939 United Features. Drawn by*
Ben Batsford

NEW FUN: "Mystery, Thrills and Cuckoo Birds!"

"Hello everybody! Fun speaking – stand by all stations! I'm bringing you this first issue of *Fun* magazine – to be followed by more and more – carrying with every issue a new cargo of mystery and thrills ... and the rest of the cock-eyed crew of cuckoo birds." So spake "Fun the Fantastic", a black-bearded gnome purporting to be the Editor of *New Fun*, the next American attempt at an original comic, six years on from the failure of *The Funnies*. Like that 1929 effort, *New Fun* was a tabloid, justifying its slogan of "The Big Comic Magazine". Unlike *The Funnies*, *New Fun* No.1 was entirely black-and-white save for its full-colour cover, the western strip "Jack Woods" by C. Brigham. Even when colour did arrive with the third issue, it was confined to 16 of the 32 pages. But colour or not, at 10 cents *New Fun* was an exciting buy and its design plus quality paper covers made it stand out from the free supplements that had killed earlier experiments.

New Fun was the brain child of Major Malcolm Wheeler-Nicholson, a pulp magazine writer who set up National Allied Publications in late 1934. His original idea had been to syndicate weekly strips to those newspapers using tabloid supplements. Unable to get enough contracts he had saved the project by assembling his material (which included a number of text features on radio, movies and sports, destined for a magazine section) into a new form of magazine. *New Fun* No.1, dated February 1935, promised to become a weekly (the Major realised his serial strips, designed for a weekly supplement, would scarcely sustain interest with four weeks' wait between instalments), but this was not to be. Neither would the outsize format be maintained, nor the monthly schedule, nor indeed the title. No.7 carried the new logo *More Fun*, was reduced in size to an odd 9¾ by 11½ inches and was belatedly dated January 1936. Two issues later (dated March-April) the size was reduced even further, the page count increased to 64, and lo: *More Fun Comics* was now a proper comic-book. It would remain so for the rest of its long life, finishing in November 1947 at No.127, at that time the longest-lived title in the DC Comics group.

The original editor of *New Fun* was not, of course, "Fantastic Fun", but Lloyd V. Jacquet. He was assisted by art editor Dick Loederer, an Austrian artist who drew "Bubby and Beevil" and "Caveman Capers". The strips were a good mix as promised. For "Mystery and Thrills" there were "Sandra of the Secret Service", "Barry O'Neill" by Lawrence Lariar (later the notable magazine cartoonist who would edit many an anthology of cartoons), Sir Walter Scott's "Ivanhoe" illustrated by Charles Flanders in a style many miles from his yet-to-come "King of the Royal Mounted", "Don Drake on the Planet Saro", a science-fiction trip by balloon(!) drawn by Clemens Gretter, who also drew "2023 Super Police", in which the hero Rex piloted an aero-sub called the Hi-lo. A close ripoff of a sporty radio serial, "Jack Andrews, All-American Boy", was drawn by Lyman Anderson, soon to do the daily "Inspector Wade" strip. Among the "Cock-eyed Crew of Cuckoo Birds" were "Judge Perkins" by "Bert", Jack Warren's funny cowboy "Loco Luke – Nope, He Didn't Get His Man", and a sports strip, "Scrub Hardy", by Joe Archibald, who will be recalled from similar stuff in *The Funnies*. There was also a scratchy strip of "Oswald the Rabbit" which could not have pleased Walter Lantz at Universal Pictures.

The odd-sized issue that inaugurated the *More Fun* series from No.7 ushered in several staff changes. Jacquet had departed, but would shortly return to the comic-book field as owner of Funnies Inc, a studio that would produce complete comic-books for several different publishers. Editorial offices had moved from West 45th Street to Fourth Avenue, and William Cook was in charge with Vincent Sullivan as assistant. Sullivan, who contributed several strips, notably the serialized "Spike Spalding", would graduate to his own publishing house, Magazine Enterprises (1947). Whitney Ellsworth also arrived with "Little Linda", the new cover strip. He, too, would stay with comic-books, becoming Editorial Director at DC

and producer for the original *Superman* television series. No.7 also featured a full page cartoon entitled "Down by the Old Mill Stream". It featured a bunch of brownies called "The Little Folk Over the Hill" and was drawn by Walt Kelly, a young hopeful about to join the Walt Disney Studios as an animator. But of all the bright new talents beginning to feel their way into the brand new world of the comic-books, none would have more lasting effect on the field than the two friends who, as writer and artist, had teamed up in No.6 of *New Fun* to present two new serials. One, "Doctor Occult the Ghost Detective", was signed Leger and Reuths, a partial anagram, as the editor didn't want the same names to appear on more than one strip. So the other serial, "Henri Duval", a swordplay story set in old France, was the first strip to carry the legendary byline, Jerome Siegel and Joe Shuster.

More Fun Comics No.9, the first comic-book format issue, has an interesting editorial called "Hello Again!". The Editors (now changed to Sullivan and Ellsworth) wrote, "Yessir, we've had our face lifted. So many people wrote in asking for *More Fun* in a smaller, handier size that we had to go into a huddle and admit that they were right, as the customer always is." They continued, "Everything between these covers is brand new, never before published. All the pictures, type and lettering are clear and legible, no eye-strain reading about the adventures of the heroes that flash across the pages." A nice swipe at their rival *Famous Funnies*! The issue

introduces a well-drawn hero in "Bob Merritt, Gentleman Adventurer and Inventor" by Leo O'Mealia and a cartoon submitted by a 14-year old reader. Kenneth Bald of Mount Vernon won a dollar and went on to draw "Captain Marvel", "Bulletman", and the newspaper strip of "Dr Kildare".

New Fun *No.1* © *February 1935 National Allied. Drawn by Brigham*
More Fun *No.7* © *January 1936 More Fun Magazine. Drawn by Whitney Ellsworth*

More Fun Comics *No.9* © *March 1936 More Fun Inc. Drawn by Vincent Sullivan*
More Fun Comics *No.127 (final issue)* © *November 1947 National Comics. Drawn by Howard Post*

NEW COMICS:
"Picturized Stories Chock Full of Thrills!"

"Salute! Hello!" cried the three editors of *New Comics* No.1 in December 1935 (Malcolm Wheeler-Nicholson, William H. Cook and Vincent A. Sullivan). "Here we are with the first number of the International Picture Story Magazine. Here's something you have always wanted, 80 pages packed and jammed with new comic features, written and drawn especially for *New Comics*, never printed before anywhere." They went on for a page describing their "magazine of picturized stories, chock full of laughter and thrills, comic characters of every hue, knights and Vikings of ancient days, adventuring heroes, detectives, aviator daredevils of today and (wait for it – significant phrase coming up!) hero supermen of the days to come!" Had the tyro team of Jerry Siegel and Joe Shuster been around with their first draft for "Superman"? Perhaps, but there is no sign of any kind of science-fiction strip in the eighty "packed and jammed" pages, and when Siegel and Shuster make their debut in No.2 with the first episode of "Federal Men", it is undercover cop Steve Carson who swiftly rises to be *New Comics*' top hero. No.3 actually offers an original drawing of Steve by Joe to every reader who writes in! Where are these collectors' items today? Tucked away, perhaps, with the membership certificates for the

Junior Federal Men Club which was launched with the next issue. By No.9 "Federal Men" had turned into a science-fiction serial subtitled "The Invisible Empire", with Steve in a glass-domed, submersible island battling a colossal robot. For the laughter that laced the thrills, there was "J. Worthington Blimp Esq." by the young Sheldon Mayer, and "Gulliver's Travels" illustrated by the young Walter C. Kelly, shortly to shorten to Walt. *New Comics* started the new year of 1937 by slipping the small word *Adventure* into its title, a significant switch. Within that issue (No.12) a scientist shows Steve Carson a Federal Man of the future in action: his name was Jor-L. Soon the *New* shrank, and by No.32 (November 1938) had disappeared completely: *Adventure Comics* was born at last, and would become the longest running comic-book in American history.

The Comics Magazine No.1 arrived in May 1936, and from No.2 took the title of its editorial, *Funny Pages*: "The Funny Pages presented in this magazine are all original and every one of them new!" Perhaps so, but some of them had a familiar face: Sheldon Mayer's "J. Worthington Blimp", William Allison's "Captain Bill of the Rangers", even Siegel and Shuster's "Dr Mystic the Occult Detective". Clearly the new breed of comic-book

artists felt they could sell their strips to anyone with the necessary five dollars a page. Kelly, already shortened to Walt, is also here with "Cannonball Jones" ("the scourge of the jungle – muscles of steel and a head of iron!"), No.2, with the new title and a nice cover by Sheldon Mayer, was unusual in that the editorial referred to "the pick of the country's funniest and cleverest freelance artists." Siegel and Shuster were here again, this time with a version of their other *New Comics* hero, "Bart Regan, Federal Agent". But the most important and innovative feature of any to this date was the seven-page adventure, "The Golden Idol" by Tom Cooper. This was introduced by a full-page announcement: "This story is told entirely in pictures and records a new departure in narrative form. The publishers of this magazine are happy to be the first to offer this style of story-telling to its readers, and ask all of you to write your opinion frankly. Do you want more stories told in this fashion?"

Evidently the answer was in the affirmative, for in November 1936 the publishers, the Comics Magazine Company, launched the first 100 per cent all-adventure strip comic-book ever, No.1 of *Funny Picture Stories*. "The Real McCoy!" shouted their full-page advertisement. "At last – Thrilling Stories in Pictures! Detective, Adventure, Mystery, Western, Action, and in Vivid Colors! It's a Natural!" The star hero was the masked crimebuster "The Clock", who had been introduced in No.6 of *Funny Pages* in a two-page teaser, "The Clock Strikes". "Who is the Clock and what is his purpose?" asked his creator, George Brenner. To find out you simply forked out your thin dime for No.1 of *Funny Picture Stories*, where "Alias the Clock" took the cover and the first seven pages. The Clock would continue to strike through the years, with Brenner billing him as "the oldest comic-book character" when he transferred to *Crack Comics* No.1 in May 1940. Heavily influenced by the fiction pulp magazines in design, *Funny Picture Stories* presented eight further completes, including "Red Dolan the Young News Hawk" by Joe Campbell, "The Floating City", a science-fiction strip by Arthur Pinajian starring Dick Kent, Soldier of Fortune, and "The Case of the Broken Skull" featuring Bert Christman's story-teller, The Spinner. It was in No.4 dated February 1937 that "The Brothers Three" (They Dared the Scourge of the Desert) was headlined with the byline

William Eisner, a name that was destined to ring down the comic-book years.

Star Comics, "A Rapid View of Fun that's New", arrived in February 1937, published by Harry "A" Chesler, who edited in asociation with George Nagle. (When I asked the veteran Harry why his "A" was always printed in quotation marks, he said it was because it stood for "Anything"!). *Star* in harness with *Star Ranger* was somewhat oversize for the first six issues; thereafter pressure from his distributors forced Chesler to conform to the new standardized comic-book size. A pity, for the added inches gave the comic-books added stature: their excellence of design and high standard of artwork already made them stand out against their several rivals. Harry Chesler was the first publisher to organize an art studio, or "shop" as they came to be called in the trade. He advertised for new cartoonists, and the first to apply, samples under his arm, was young Fred Schwab, a zany stylist much influenced by E. C. Segar's "Popeye". If Schwab's "Riggin' Bill, that Lyin' Sailor Man" was wildly new, then Dick Ryan's "Bug-Ville"

was vintage, to put it kindly. If Clemens Gretter's "Dan Hastings" was tomorrow, then Winsor McCay Junior's "Impy" was yesterday. But Chesler's mix of nostalgia plus novelty, so carefully packaged under Charles Biro's tight art supervision, worked, and his twin comic-books, never excelled in his own long publishing career, remain the finest of the pre-superhero era.

By DASHIELL HAMMETT

DETECTIVE COMICS: "Swelegant!"

"Swelegant!" was the word for *Detective Comics*, according to the advertisement for No.1 which filled the back page of *More Fun Comics* for March 1937. "A brand-new comic magazine filled with brand-new features by your favorite artists! Action-packed stories in color!" *Detective Comics*, which would give its initials to America's major comics publishing house, DC, has now become the longest continually running title in the field. One record it cannot claim, but always does, is that it was the first comic-book to devote itself to a single theme. Four months earlier than its own No.1 came the first edition of *Detective Picture Stories*, dated December 1936 and excitingly trailered in the previous month's issue of *Funny Pages*: "Now you see it! You see the killer backed against the wall – You see the low gun muzzle rammed against his throat – You see the police pack actually run the murder-mad man into his hole – You see it all because the whole detective story is told in pictures."

The Comics Magazine Co modelled their third publication on the popular detective pulps of the period complete with contents page listing stories and artists. Headlined on the cover was "The Phantom Killer", billed as a "New Clock Mystery" by George E. Brenner. "The Clock", a masked detective, was a carry-over from *Funny Picture Stories*, but in fact he failed to appear in this particular strip, a curious editorial error. Lead story in the comic was "The Diamond Dick", well-drawn by William Allison, but

Joe Buresch's "Roadhouse Racket" was crude in the extreme. Among the nine items was one funny, "Murder in the Blue Room", in which John Patterson introduced his burlesque "Spurlock and Watkins". Headlined on No.4 (March 1937) was "Muss 'Em Up", billed as "a Cartoon Thriller by Bill Eisner". This seven-page strip in black-and-white is a key work in the comic career of the influential artist who was to create his own masked detective "The Spirit". In the crudely drawn, jaggedly laid out, hard-hitting adventure of tough cop Hammer Donovan can be seen the shape of things to come, only three short years away. Perhaps a little harder to predict was a future for the cartoonist who provided "The Case of the Missing Heir" in No.5 (April 1937), although the profusion of shadowy night scenes could have been a clue. It was drawn by Bob Kane. Only two years later Kane would create "Batman". *Detective Picture Stories* lasted only seven issues, but its influence was enormous. Centaur Publications took it over and changed the title to *Keen Detective Funnies* from No.8 (July 1938), adding regular heroes of their own such as "Dean Denton, Scientific Adventurer" by Harry Campbell, but retaining Brenner's "Clock". New discoveries continued to be made: in No.13 a six-pager called "Little Dynamite" was signed Jack Cole, who was later to combine his cartoony style with drama to produce the wholly original "Plastic Man".

Detective Comics, published by

Malcolm Wheeler-Nicholson and edited in partnership with Vincent Sullivan and Whitney Ellsworth, was generally better drawn than its rival. The lead strip was by Creig Flessel, a pulp illustrator whose economical brushwork suggested a wealth of detail. "Speed Saunders" was his hero. Sven Elven, a Scandinavian artist with a very different, fine penline style, drew "Cosmo the Phantom of Disguise", an elegant pipe-sucker. Jerry Siegel and Joe Shuster supplied two series between them, "Spy", a serial starring Bart Regan, and "Slam Bradley" with his sawn-off assistant Shorty, described by the authors as "two unorthodox madcaps". Slam's wham-bam way of detecting seems to be a stepping-stone to "Superman".

Detectives in newspaper strips began with "Dick Tracy" on 4 October 1931. The artist was Chester Gould, and Dick's debut was in the *Chicago Sunday Tribune*, an appropriate place, recalling the Hollywood gangster movies set in that city. Dick, in the course of his still-continuing career, has done battle with the most grotesque gallery of crooks ever depicted: Larceny Lu, Boris Arson, Stooge Viller, Whip Chute, the featureless "Blank", the midget "Brow", the wrinkled "Pruneface", the vibrating "Shaky", the level-headed "Flattop". Dick Tracy comics appeared early, as Cupples and Leon books from 1933, as *Feature Books* from 1937, and he was No.1 in Dell's *Four Colour Comics* series in 1939. His own proper comic-book began in January 1948.

Alex Raymond, not yet ready to take off with "Flash Gordon", was hired to illustrate King Features' answer to Tracy, "Secret Agent X-9". The strip started on 22 January 1934, scripted by the top thriller writer of the day, Dashiell Hammett of *The Thin Man*. Artist and writer would be changed many times during X-9's career, but the first comic-book edition, published by McKay, preserves the originals. Curiously, Raymond would later abandon outer space and return to the detective genre with "Rip Kirby", from 4 March 1946. The adventures of this be-spectacled private eye and his lady, Honey Dorian, were only a daily strip, never a Sunday page. In consequence the only full-colour version that ever appeared was the McKay comic-book.

Detective Picture Stories No.1 © December 1936 Comics Magazine Co. Drawn by William Allison

Detective Comics No.4 © June 1937 Detective Comics. Drawn by Creig Flessel
Secret Agent X9 No.1 © 1934 David McKay/King Features

Dick Tracy Monthly No.1 © January 1948 Dell Publishing
Kerry Drake Detective No.1 © 1944 Life's Romances. Drawn by Alfred Andriola
Rip Kirby Feature Book No.51 © 1948 David McKay/King. Drawn by Alex Raymond

Charlie Chan No.1 © June 1948 Crestwood. Drawn by Simon and Kirby
Ellery Queen No.2 © July 1949 Superior Comics
Mike Shayne Private Eye No.1 © November 1961 Dell Publishing
Perry Mason Feature Book No.49 © David McKay. Drawn by Vernon Greene
The Saint Detective Cases No,7 © 1949 Avon Periodicals
Edgar Wallace Comic No.4 © Herald (Australia)

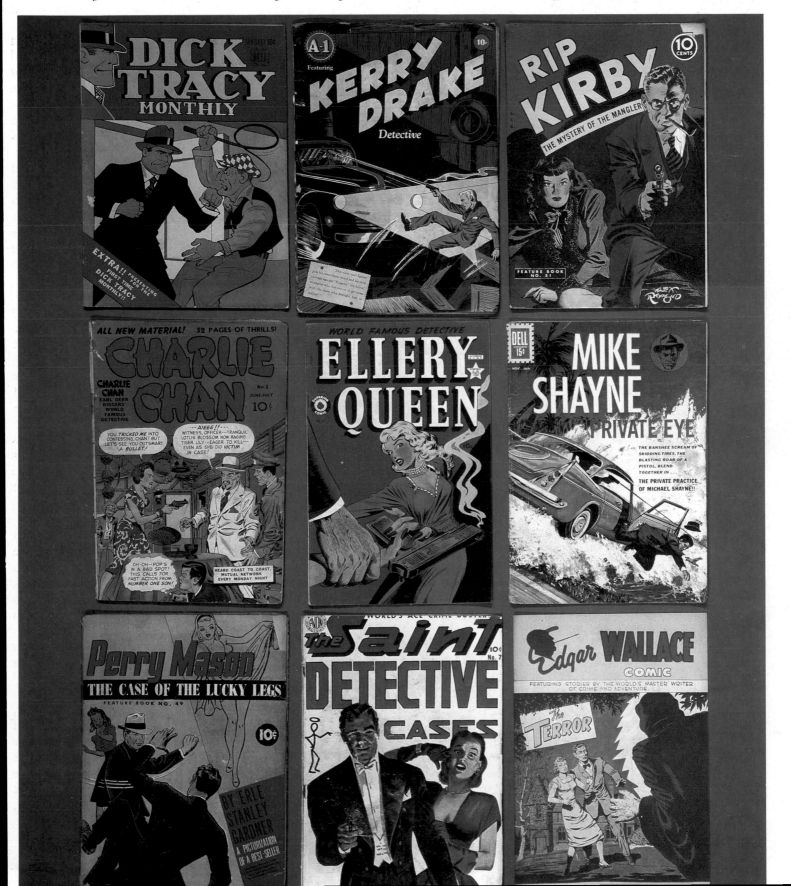

SHERLOCK HOLMES and the Baker Street Highly Irregulars

Sherlock Holmes, the world's first consulting detective, set up for business in the January of 1881, at 221B Baker Street, London. He shared quarters with Dr John H. Watson, who subsequently became the detective's chronicler, publishing his first case, "A Study in Scarlet", in *Beeton's Christmas Annual* for 1887. Four years later the first of a long series of short stories, "A Scandal in Bohemia", was published in *The Strand Magazine* for July 1891, and with it Sherlock Holmes' name was swiftly established as a household word. Sir Arthur Conan Doyle, his creator, established in Holmes the prototype private detective, a figure whose deductive methods still influence the world's fiction. Holmes was turned into a stage play in 1899, and many films, beginning with *Sherlock Holmes Baffled* in 1903. But before all these there was a comic strip.

Sherlock Holmes was not yet seven years old when Jack B. Yeats cartooned him for *Comic Cuts*. "The Adventures of Chubblock Homes" first appeared on 16 June 1894, one of the first regular characters in British comics. Jack B. (John Butler) Yeats was the brother of the great Irish poet W. B., and in later years became famous as an impressionist painter. Admirers and biographers, however, choose to ignore Yeats' many and important contributions to the comics. "Jack Bee's" version of Holmes trans-ferred to *The Funny Wonder* in August 1894, turned into a serial in December (the first week-by-week continuity in comics), and was so popular that it made the front page from 10 April 1897. Holmes was helped, not by a Watson parody, but by Shirk the Dog Detective, a swipe at a serial story in *Illustrated Chips* called "Dirk the Dog Detective". The first comic strip Sherlock in America was also a burlesque, "Sherlocko the Monk". Gus Mager had introduced the cartoon into his varied "Monks" feature, then from 9 December 1910 as a regular daily strip in the *New York Journal*. The gag failed to please Conan Doyle, who threatened to sue. Mager quickly switched his title to "Hawkshaw the Detective" from 23 February 1913, and everybody was happy. Except, perhaps, the shade of Tom Taylor, who had created Hawkshaw for his play, *The Ticket-of-Leave Man*, back in 1863. Sherlock Holmes did not appear again in a British comic until 1955, when *Super Detective Library* No.65 presented a pair of the classic short stories in pocket-sized format.

Classics Illustrated No.33 (January 1947) was entitled *Adventures of Sherlock Holmes*, but contained "The Hound of the Baskervilles". A striking cover by H. C. Kiefer disguised the crudely drawn contents by Louis Zansky. He had already done his worst with "The Sign of the Four", one of *Three Famous Mysteries* issued as No.21 (July 1944). The first attempt at a comic-book series was tried by Charlton Comics with their No.1 of *Sherlock Holmes*, published October 1955. Transplanted to New York the great detective cuts a quaintly Victorian figure in company with snap-brimmed Sergeant Flaherty. In his second case Holmes has a moustachioed assistant who looks familiar, if his name isn't: "Elementary, my dear Frothingham!" The series expired at No.2. Dell Comics issued two *New Adventures of Sherlock Holmes* in 1961, nicely drawn cases perhaps because authorized by the Estate of Conan Doyle. Equally authorized, or at least credited with being "adapted from the writings of Sir Arthur Conan Doyle by Mr Dennis J. O'Neil and Mr E. R. Cruz Esquires", was the DC edition of *Sherlock Holmes* (October 1975). It contained two from the canon, "The Final Problem" and "The Empty House", but once again a failure must be recorded: there was no No.2.

Super Detective Library: Sherlock Holmes *No.65* © *1955 Amalgamated Press*
The Funny Wonder *No.219* © *10 April 1897 Harmsworth. Drawn by Jack B. Yeats*

Classics Illustrated *No.33* © *January 1947 Gilberton. Drawn by H. Kiefer* Sherlock Holmes *No.1* © *Charlton Comics October 1955* New Adventures of Sherlock Holmes *No.2* © *January 1961 Dell Publishing* Sherlock Holmes *No.1* © *October 1975 National Periodicals. Drawn by E. R. Cruz*

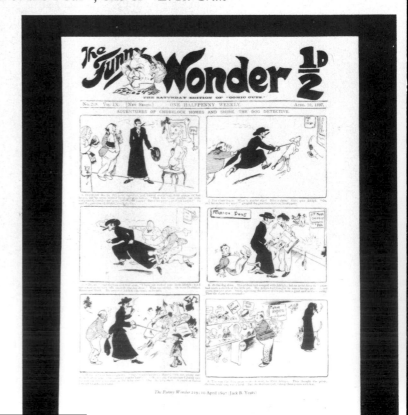

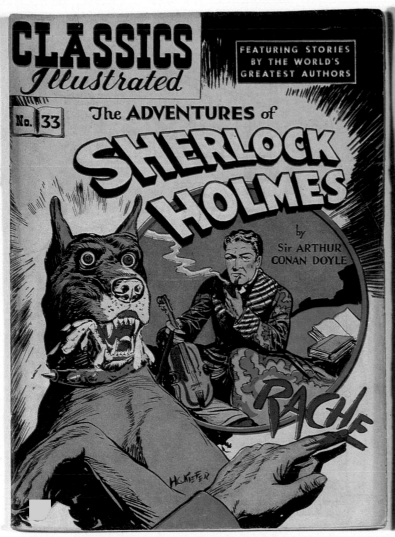

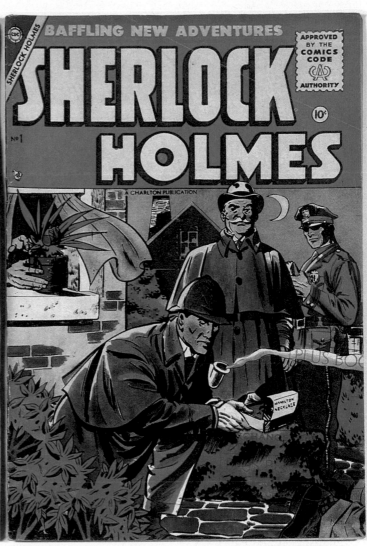

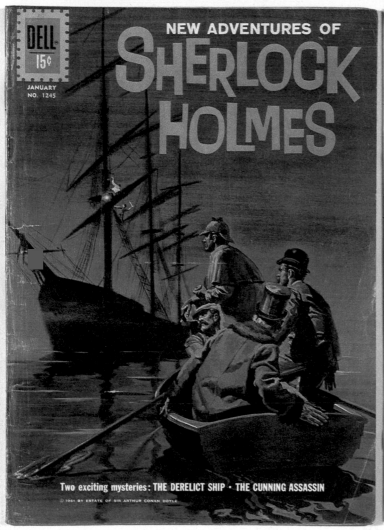

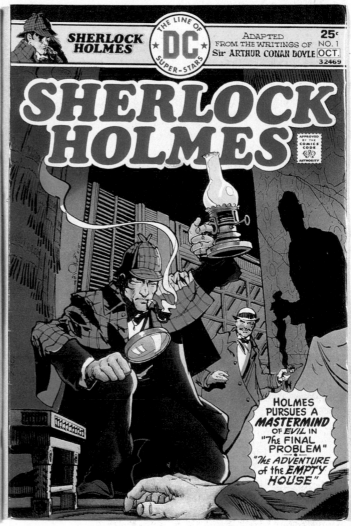

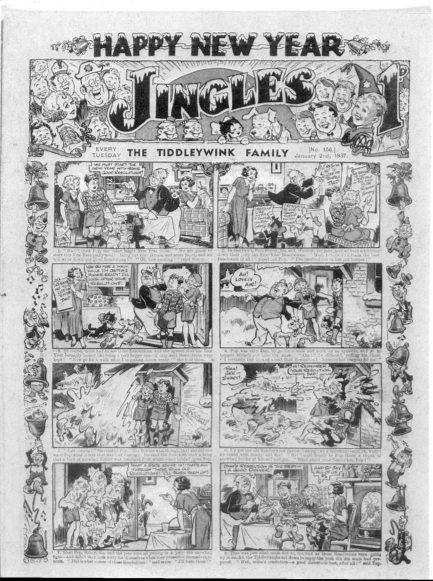

HAPPY FAMILIES: or Bringing Up Blondie

"The family that laughs together, stays together" might have been the motto of the American comic strips. From the Teens with Jiggs and Maggie to the Eighties with the Bumsteads, family life has always been right at the top of syndicated strip polls. This is less true of the comic-books, for, although they have reprinted their quota of popular family strips, they are bought by a sector of the market demonstrably less interested in the doings of "poor old pa" than in the capers of caped crusaders. In Britain, families have figured even less in comics than in the States. In the rare instances where families have featured on the front pages, the accent is heavily on the offspring, with dear old dad as the object of most of the slapstick. Typical victim is portly Pop, bespectacled head of Roy Wilson's "Tiddleywink Family" from *Jingles* (13 January 1934), who gets mud, paint or custard in the eye much to the mirth of Sonny, Sis and the pets, not to mention Mum. "Poor old Dad!" was the usual payoff line.

First family of the American funnies was the jumped-up Irish lot of "Bringing Up Father" (1913). Labourer Jiggs and Maggie, his missus, won the Irish Sweepstake and spent the rest of their very long life (they outlived their creator, George McManus, by many years) trying to crash society. Maggie's ambitions for their languorously lovely daughter, Nora, were ever thwarted by Jiggs' craving for corned beef and cabbage with his cronies down at Dinty Moore's. McManus's meticulous strips were syndicated world-wide, making the rolling-pin an internationally recognized symbol of family life. "The Gumps" (1917) was the first family strip proper, a soap opera that serialised the doings of what Captain Joseph Patterson of the *Chicago Tribune*, who devised it, called a typical American middle-class family ("Gump" was Patterson's word for idiot!). Andy, the chinless wonder, was wed to Min, queen of the purse-strings, and they had a child, Chester, and a rich uncle, Bim. The strip was an immediate success, despite some of the crudest cartooning ever seen, and made Sidney Smith the highest-paid cartoonist in the world. He died in a car crash having just signed a new contract, but the artwork didn't improve. His successor, Gus Edson, was forced to imitate Smith's atrocious style. "Moon Mullins" (1923) began as a low-life sporty strip but resolved into one of the more intriguing sitcoms. Moonshine Mullins, layabout gambler, and his kid brother Kayo, roomed with rotund Uncle Willie, Mamie the cook (Willie's estranged wife), Emmy Schmaltz the landlady, and the apple of her eye, the retired Lord Plushbottom; as unlikely a menage as ever managed.

"Gasoline Alley" (1918) made history; it was the first strip to reflect real life – its characters grew older, day by day. Frank King began his saga of small-town America with bachelor Walt Wallet finding a baby on his doorstep. The boy was duly called Skeezix, and he began to grow. Walt married, fathered Corky in 1928, adopted a little girl Judy in 1935; meanwhile Skeezix went to school, went to war, and married his long-standing girlfriend, Nina Clock, in 1944, and fathered baby Chipper. The only one ever to die was cartoonist King, whose assistants continue the family tradition to this day.

"The Nebbs" (1927), introduced by scriptwriter Sol Hess as "just a little family like thousands of other families", had one advantage over the rest. They were drawn by Wallace Carlson, one of the pioneers of animated cartoon films. But even Carlson's qualities paled beside the stylishness of Chic Young as he developed his "Blondie" (1930) from a fluff-headed flapper strip to the most consistently amusing family outing of them all. Once Blondie Boopadoop settled down and married Dagwood Bumstead on 13 February 1933, the strip followed the Gasoline Alley formula: everybody grew a little older, day by day. Alexander was born on 15 April 1934, and was immediately dubbed "Baby Dumpling". His baby sister Cookie arrived on 25 April 1941, and Daisy the dog had quinpuplets. The strip has long been the top of King Features' syndication list; evidently Chic Young's tight formula of home, kids, dogs, neighbours (Herb Woodley), mailman (Mr Beasley), boss (J. C. Dithers) touches a global nerve.

Crackers No.403 © 7 November 1936 *Amalgamated Press. Drawn by Reg Parlett*
Jingles No.156 © 2 January 1937 Amalgamated Press. Drawn by Roy Wilson

Blondie Comics No.1 © Spring 1947 David McKay/King Features. Drawn by Chic Young
The Nebbs No.1 © 1945 Croydon. Drawn by Wallace Carlson
Dotty Dripple No.1 © 1946 Magazine Enterprises. Drawn by Buford Tune
Hi and Lois No.1 (OS 683) © March 1956 Dell/King Features. Drawn by Mort Walker and Dik Browne
The Gumps No.4 © September 1947 Bridgeport Herald. Drawn by Gus Edson
Gasoline Alley No.1 © September 1950 Star Publications. Drawn by Frank King
Moon Mullins No.1 © December 1947 Michel. Drawn by Dan Gordon
Jiggs and Maggie No.12 © October 1949 Standard Comics/King Features. Drawn by Frank Fletcher

COMIC KIDS: Dennis and the Other Menaces

The comic-book kids were, for a while, the same crowd as the comic strip kids: either straight reprints, or newly-drawn adventures, of the boys and girls from the Sunday funnies. Among the earliest to depart from the caricatured outrages of the Katzenjammer Kids were the gang known as "Reg'lar Fellers" (1918). Jimmie Dugan, the brothers Puddin'head and Pinhead Duffy, overweight Zoolie with the oversize hair-ribbon plus Bullseye the pup, made up a typical bunch of suburban kids, written and drawn with an affectionate pen by Gene Byrnes. He was the first to use weighted lettering for emphasis. "Just Kids" (1923) by Ad Carter, a scratchily sketched series starring Mush Stebbins and pals, never won a solo comic-book, but "Skippy" (1925) did. In fact, *Skippy's Own Book of Comics* (1934) was one of the first ever, being a premium for Phillips toothpaste. Skippy Skinner was the creation of Percy L. Crosby, who drew with the same hasty short-hand as Ad Carter, but with a brush. But his depiction of boyhood street life was far truer, and captured a youthful lifestyle now long gone. Another strip true to boyhood days was "Cap Stubbs and Tippie" (1921), the tale of a dog, a boy and his Grandma Bailey. This delightfully drawn series was by one of the few lady cartoonists, Edwina Dumm.

The first of the modern comic kids was "Henry", who was born in the pages of that slick magazine for grown-ups, the *Saturday Evening Post*, in 1932. Henry, a curious, dumb, bald-headed cypher, was created by Carl Anderson, who was 67 years old at the time, quite a long way from boyhood. Anderson had been drawing for the Sunday funnies since the century turned, but it was not until he thought of Henry that he struck gold. Although only one single panel a week to start with, "Henry" was an immediate hit and came to Britain as a series of coloured cigarette cards that soon filled several albums. By 1934 Henry was a proper newspaper strip, continuing the pantomime style in always excellent visual gags. When Henry was turned into a comic-book by Dell, however, he suddenly found the power of speech!

The direct opposite of Henry, but only in the matter of sex, is "Little Lulu": otherwise she might have been mistaken for Henry in drag! Lulu was created by a cartoonist who signed herself Marge. She was Marjorie Henderson Buell (and not Carl Anderson in drag!), and she had been commissioned by the *Saturday Evening Post* to create a replacement for Henry, whom they had lost to King Features. Lulu, like Henry, was deadpan and dumb, until, like Henry, Dell decided to star her in a comic-book. Not only did she begin to speak, but her new artist John Stanley devised for her a delightfully contrived series of adventures involving her parents, Mr and Mrs Moppet, her boyfriend Tubby Tompkins, and a small nuisance named Alvin. Other young girls who starred in their own comic-books include "Nancy", the little niece of "Fritzi Ritz", who grew so popular with newspaper readers that she took over her glamorous aunt's strip entirely from 1940, thanks to Ernie Bushmiller's brilliant way with gags; and "Little Iodine", a brat who emerged from Jimmy Hatlo's "They'll Do It Every Time" feature in 1943.

The star of the most successful comic strip of all time (annual income from licensed spin-offs etc. has been estimated at $50,000,000!) is "Good Ol' Charlie Brown", but much to the continued irritation of creator Charles Schulz, the strip is called "Peanuts" and not, as he named it, "Li'l Folks". United Features, his syndicate, changed it back in 1950, but at least they didn't interfere with Charlie B., his hag-rider Lucy Van Pelt, Linus (he of the security blanket), Schroeder the Beethoven boy, big-hearted Peppermint Patty, scruffy Pigpen, black Franklin, or Charlie's strip-stealing beagle, the one and only Snoopy, who achieved immortality on behalf of the comic-strip world when the Apollo 10's Lunar Excursion Module was named after him. "Dennis the Menace", a tousle-headed four-year-old, was born in the USA on Monday 12 March 1951, of cartoonist Hank Ketcham. By the most curious comic coincidence of them all, it was the same day that the British *Beano*, dated 17 March 1951, went on sale featuring the first appearance of another "Dennis the Menace". That said, the two kids have little in else in common, for while David Law's menace is the equivalent of Hans and Fritz rolled into one, Hank's half-pint hero is a very human, joyful little boy. Among the many, many kids created for comic-books, the most successful have been Harvey Comics' two, *Little Dot* (1953) and *Richie Rich* (1960), the Poor Little Rich Boy.

A COMIC FOR ALL SEASONS

Christmas Numbers and Summer Holiday Numbers had been regular treats for British comic readers since the earliest of times, and in pre-First World War years double-sized editions had been the holiday order of the day for all the Amalgamated Press comics, and most other publishers. But the idea of a special comic, one published purely for holiday sales, was a completely original thought. It occurred to those in command at the venerable publishing house of C. Arthur Pearson, the great pioneer of popular magazines. Pearson's had been unlucky in comics, for although their policy was to match whatever weekly their rivals at Amalgamated Press produced, their only attempt at a regular comic, *Merry Moments*, launched 12 April 1919, had floundered after 194 weeks. The concept of a single issue comic (a "one-shot" as it later came to be called), was completely new. Pearson followed the standard format of the AP twopenny comics exactly: full colour on the front page, red and black on the centre spread and back, and in between a selection of stories, strips and features. To supervise the design of his comic, and draw the front page, Pearson hired Walter Bell. Bell was an excellent comic man, a cartoonist who had learned his trade as assistant to the veteran W. F. Thomas, the man who had drawn Ally Sloper from the Eighties to the Twenties, and whose last comic work would be to come out of retirement to draw new Sloper cartoons for my revival of the comic in 1976. Walter's main line in the Thirties was the nursery style: he had been drawing "Peter and Peggy in Jungle Land" for Tiny Tots since 1927. The publication of Pearson's first *Seaside Comic* on 27 June 1930 caused a small sensation at Fleetway House, Farringdon Street, where the AP had their headquarters. Walter always remembered a sneered greeting from a top comic editor there, "How's Bell's Weekly?", a harkback to the long-gone *Bell's Weekly News* of the Victorian era.

Seaside Comic, unnumbered as all Pearson's holiday comics would be, was dated Summer 1930, and although no copy seems to exist, an advertisement for it shows Bell's jolly front page strip, "Milly and Billy and their Jungle Friends" (shades of "Peter and Peggy in Jungle Land") having "Jolly Good Fun at Winkle-On-Sea". Although some copies of *Seaside Comic* were sold in the usual newsagents' shops, the main sales were concentrated at seaside resorts, a pattern followed to this day by the many hundreds of Holiday Specials that have followed in Pearson's pioneering wake.

The next year's issue of *Seaside Comic* was accompanied by a companion, *The Holiday Comic* (27 June 1931). This also featured Bell's "Milly and Billy", and his back page funny animals, at "Doctor Hee-Haw's School". A third title was added to the growing Pearson stable on 8 December 1931, the first edition of *The Christmas Comic*: "Milly and Billy and the Jungle Boys Make the Christmas Puddings and Cause a Big Stir!" In March 1932 there arrived another seasonable special, *The Spring Comic*, with Milly and Billy going fishing and the Jungle Boys Making a Grand Splash! In June came the first *Summer Comic*, the first to be designed by a new artist, A. W. Browne. Bell, busy at the AP, drew no more for the expanding Pearson specials. The last two new titles were added on 2 June 1939, *Sunny Sands* and *The Monster Comic*. The latter was Pearson's first to follow Thomson's successful *Dandy* format, a 28-pager in smaller size. It saw just one more edition, a Christmas number published 17 November 1939 in harness with the traditional tabloid *Christmas Holiday Comic*. They were the last two holiday specials from Pearson's, and were blacked out for ever by that first winter of war.

The Monster *No.2* © *December 1939 C. Arthur Pearson. Drawn by Larkman*

Christmas Comic *No.5* © *December 1935 C. Arthur Pearson. Drawn by Ray Bailey*
The Spring Comic *No.1* © *March 1932 C. Arthur Pearson. Drawn by Walter Bell*
Summer Comic *No.4* © *June 1938 C. Arthur Pearson. Drawn by Norman Ward*
The Seaside Comic *No.6* © *June 1935 C. Arthur Pearson. Drawn by Ray Bailey*

80

PACKED WITH FUN FOR YOUR XMAS HOLIDAY

FOR BOYS AND GIRLS
CHRISTMAS COMIC 2D

THE BEST COMIC YOU CAN BUY!

FOR BOYS AND GIRLS
THE SPRING COMIC 2D

FULL OF STORIES AND COMIC FUN FOR YOU!

FOR BOYS AND GIRLS
SUMMER COMIC 2D

6 Stories—Picture-Adventures—Big Play Page!

THE FOR BOYS AND GIRLS
SEASIDE COMIC 2D

HURRAH FOR A PICNIC BY THE SEA!

Puzzles, Tricks, Catches, Jokes and Lots More Funny Pictures Inside.

CHRISTMAS IN FAMOUS FUNNYLAND

The first comic-book Christmas was celebrated in 1935, dated December, on sale November! The month ahead saledate would prove a curse to the comic-books, eventually creeping forward as many as three months ahead of the date as printed on the cover. This made it difficult to market Santa Claus and snowballs, unless the comic-books were dated January or February: not a very good idea. So after the early years Christmas Numbers of regular titles tended to disappear, to be replaced by one-shots and annuals specially produced for seasonal sales.

The first "Christmas in Famous Funnyland", a party cover by "Vep", was celebrated by *Famous Funnies* No.17. The "Let's Get Into a Huddle" page wished all readers a Merry Christmas, especially Johnny Conway of Cambridge, Massachusetts, who fell off the roof of his home and was photographed by his local paper enjoying *Famous Funnies* in hospital! This page apart there was little Christmassy about the contents, as the reprint strips continued their timeless serialized adventures. This was another problem, of course, although the Christmas *Tip Top Comics* of 1936 managed to find a holly-bordered "Ella Cinders" strip to add a little seasonable seasoning. *Feature Funnies'* first Christmas issue (1937) had less luck, but made up for it by offering a year's subscription for a dollar, the normal price of ten, as a Christmas present. *Popular Comics* (1938) livened up an otherwise average issue with an unusual Christmas competition: what presents would you give to Tailspin Tommy and the Toonerville Folks? More might have been expected from the all-original comic-books, but once you got past Dick Ryan's rather Victorian cover of the Christmas *Funny Picture Stories* (1937), the only other Christmassy feature was Dick Ryan's rather Victorian centre spread.

The first one-shot Christmas Special was also America's biggest comic-book ever: although standard page size, *Xmas Comics* No.1, published December 1941, contained 324 pages. Boosted as the "Giant Xmas Gift for Every Boy and Girl", Fawcett

Publications sold this for 50 cents. How did they do it at the price? Simple: *Xmas Comics* was made up entirely of reprints of earlier Fawcett comic-books (*Whiz Comics* No.21, *Bulletman* No.2, and three others). At least it sported a new, Christmassy cover. From No.3 *Xmas Comics* concentrated

on reprinting *Funny Animals*, reducing the price to a more popular 25 cents, but also reducing the pagecount to 132.

The first specially-drawn Christmas comic-book was *Santa Claus Funnies*, published annually by Dell from 1942. The first issue, and the succeeding five, were illustrated by Walt Kelly, the brilliant cartoonist who was already developing his "Pogo Possum" in Dell's *Animal Comics*. From 1945 Kelly added another annual treat to his workload, *Christmas with Mother Goose*. There would be

five of these before his Pogo news-paper strip claimed his fulltime attention. Kelly's Christmas comics, funny, charming, and delightful, remain among the finest ever American comic-books for the young. *Walt Disney's Christmas Parade* was another annual special from Dell, beginning 1949. The lead story, "Letter to Santa", starred Donald Duck and his nephews, Huey, Dewey and Louie, in a 24-page adventure with their Uncle Scrooge. Scrooge McDuck, "the richest (and meanest) tycoon in the universe", had been created for a Donald Duck oneshot entitled *Christmas on Bear Mountain*, published by Dell in 1947. Uncle Scrooge was an instant favourite with young readers, and the creator, cartoonist Carl Barks, began to feature him in his monthly Donald Duck strip for *Walt Disney's Comics and Stories*. Soon Uncle Scrooge and his magnificent meanness, coupled with his astronomic wealth, became a cult figure among comic-book fans. He was awarded his own comic in 1952, which continued after Barks' retirement in 1965. Uncle Scrooge, created for comic-books, became unique when he crossed over into animation to star in the Mickey Mouse film adapted from Charles Dickens' *Christmas Carol*.

Famous Funnies *No.17* © *December 1935 Eastern Color Printing. Drawn by Victoria Pazmino*
Tip Top Comics *No.8* © *December 1936 United Features*
Feature Funnies *No.3* © *December 1937 Comic Favorites. Drawn by Lank Leonard*
The Funnies *No.16* © *January 1938 Dell Publishing*
Popular Comics *No.35* © *December 1938 Dell Publishing*
Funny Picture Stories *No.4 Vol.2* © *December 1937 Ultem Publications. Drawn by Dick Ryan*

Xmas Comics *No.7* © *1947 Fawcett. Drawn by Chad Grothkopf*
Gift Comics *No.4* © *1949 Fawcett Publications*
Adventures of Tom-Tom *No.3* © *1947 Magazine Enterprises*
Walt Disney's Christmas Parade *No.1* © *November 1949 Dell/Walt Disney Productions*
Santa Claus Funnies *No.8* © *November 1949 Dell Publishing*
Christmas with Mother Goose *No.4* © *November 1948 Dell Publishing (Canada). Drawn by Walt Kelly*

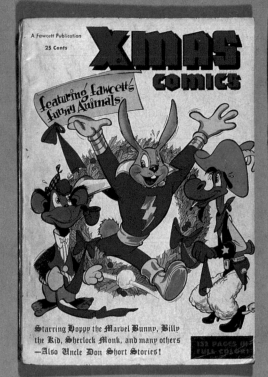

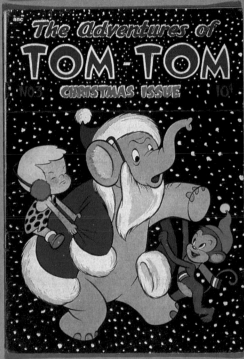

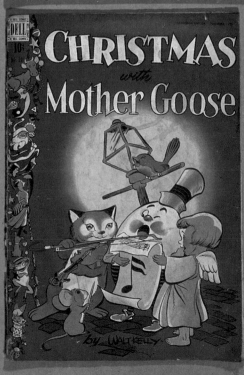

COMIC CELEBRATIONS:
from Baron Sloper to King Ally the First

Comics and royalty have always been the best of chums, at least so the comics would have us believe. From the earliest days, Ally Sloper could be found in the van of every grand occasion, and sometimes in the royal carriage itself. Small wonder, then, that when Queen Victoria celebrated her Golden Jubilee the special edition of *Ally Sloper's Half-Holiday* (18 June 1887) gave away not only "Ally Sloper's Jubilee March" by Louis Mallett, but a great centre-spread engraving by W. F. Thomas, showing the FOM (Friend of Man) himself being created Baron Sloper of Mildew Court by Her Majesty, who performed the ceremony not with the sword of state, but with Poor Papa's beloved, battered brolly! By way of further celebration, the Eminent also gave away 20 Silver Keyless Sloper Watches, 10,000 Gilt Jubilee Medals (with ribbon attached), and 10,00 Red Leather Sloper Jubilee Purses, with Gilt Inscription, four different pockets, and carefully packed in a box. Never would such comic-paper generosity occur again. *Scraps* Jubilee Edition was content with Oliver Veal's silhouette strip, "Podger's Jubilee Cricket Match". Sloper celebrated the coronation of Edward VII with a 16-page special (28 June 1902), which included a cartoon of the Coronation of Ally the First as King of the Comics.

The Silver Jubilee of King George V and Queen Mary in May 1935 was the cause of the biggest celebration British comics had ever put on. Half-way through the Golden Age, every comic, penny and twopenny, dressed itself up in a specially-designed front page and hung bunting from its headings. Arthur A. Wagg, editor of *The Joker*, signed himself Flag Wagg for the occasion and claimed to be "all of a flutter", while cross-talk comedians Bright and Gay opened their Jolly Jubilee Jubilations with "D'you know the diff' between a bent sixpence and the decorations in the High Street?" "One's a battered tanner and the t'other's a tattered banner!"

Two years later came the coronation of King George VI and Queen

Elizabeth, and the comic celebration was even jollier than the Jubilee. Roy Wilson, at the height of his powers, drew several special covers, some of them in colour like the Coronation *Puck* (15 May 1937).

The next great national celebration was VE (Victory in Europe) Day, with

VJ (Victory over Japan) Day three months later. Of the many comics which celebrated with special fronts, the most colourful was *Mickey Mouse* (2 June 1945). There were a few comics which celebrated the Festival of Britain in 1951, but the big event was the Coronation of Queen

Elizabeth I in 1953. Even the Scottish comics of D. C. Thomson joined in, with "Desperate Dan" of the *Dandy* getting a tow from Cactusville, via the "Queen Elizabeth", and stopping Big Ben by sitting on the hands! The Queen's Silver Jubilee came in for comic celebration 25 years later, and in 1981 the Royal Wedding of the Prince and Princess of Wales was a cue for Britain's comics to turn red, white and blue.

American comics seem to have produced few celebratory editions, although both New York World's Fairs, in 1939 and 1964, had special comicbooks. The first, *New York World's Fair Comics*, was a 96-page 25 cent souvenir featuring all DC's heroes, from Superman and Slam Bradley, to "Zatara the Magician" and Fred Schwab's "Butch the Pup". The second was a 68-page, 25 cent special starring all the Hanna-Barbera cartoon characters. The United States Bicentennial of 1976 was celebrated by two outsize comics from the rival publishers, DC and Marvel: *Superman Salutes the Bicentennial* cost a dollar, while *Captain America's Bicentennial Battles* cost 75 cents. Both made unusual and exciting souvenirs.

Scraps Jubilee Number © *25 June 1887 James Henderson. Drawn by W. J. Urquhart*
Ally Sloper's Half-Holiday Coronation Number © *28 June 1902 Dalziel. Drawn by W. F. Thomas*
Joker Jubilee Number © *11 May 1935 Amalgamated Press. Drawn by John L. Jukes*
Puck Coronation Number © *15 May 1937 Amalgamated Press. Drawn by Roy Wilson*

Mickey Mouse Victory Number © *2 June 1945 Willbank/Walt Disney Productions. Drawn by Victor Ibbison*
Dandy Coronation Number © *6 June 1953 DC Thomson. Drawn by James Crichton*
Buster Jubilee Number © *11 June 1977 IPC Magazines. Drawn by Robert Lee*
Whoopee Royal Wedding Number © *1 August 1981 IPC Magazines. Drawn by Nick Baker*
New York World's Fair Comics No.1 © *1939 Detective Comics. Drawn by Vincent Sullivan (facsimile)*
The Flintstones at the New York World's Fair © *1964 Hanna-Barbera*

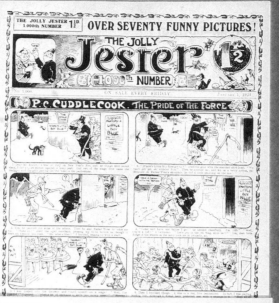

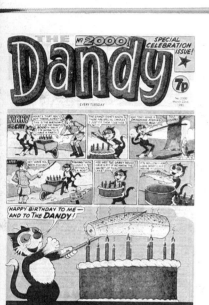

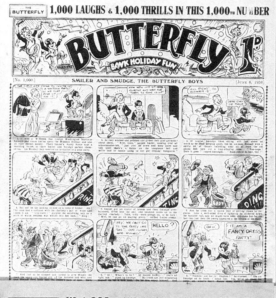

"Painting the Old Town Pink!"

"Thirty years ago 2-day
Chips woz born and kame 2 stay.
Kame 2 fill this dull old erf
Wiv joy and jollity and merf.
So let us awl be B gay and arty,
And hav a good old berfday party.
Doant waist your kash on useless lumber,
But bye this splendid Berfday Number,
Larf and chear wiv awl yor mite,
And paint the old town pink 2-nite!"

And with that misspelled ode, a misspent youth called Philpott Bottles, who billed himself as "The World Famuss Ossif Boy", celebrated the 30th birthday of *Illustrated Chips* on 24 July 1920. "Paint the old town pink" was an in-joke: *Chips* had been printed on pink paper since its early years as a ha'penny comic. The editor, Cornelius Chips, in toasting his good health in ginger pop, wondered if he would still be writing his cheery chats in another 30 years. He would, and more, for it was not until 12 September 1953 that *Chips* would be forcibly retired by an unsentimental publisher just three issues short of its 3,000th edition. The first comic to pass that incredible total was *Chips'* companion, *Comic Cuts*. That red letter day (or red and black letter day: it was a two-colour comic) was 1 August 1953, but Clarence C. Cutts, the old-time editor, no longer wrote his weekly chats. Instead a "Now and Then" feature showed readers how times had changed: "When *Comic Cuts* was first published, men with red flags walked in front of cars, horse buses were used, and the penny farthing bicycle was still seen." There were also long-winded type-set captions under every picture, another anachronism that had long since disappeared. But *Comic Cuts'* record-breaking run was fated not to continue: just six weeks later an uncomic cut ended its 63-year career.

Comics have celebrated themselves since they began, annually with their own birthdays, and in between with such meaningful numbers as 50, 100,

200, 500, and any and every multiple thereof. The longest-lived title of the current crop of British comics is *Dandy*, which celebrated its 2,000th edition on 22 March 1980. It would have happened much earlier, had *Dandy* not been reduced to fortnightly publication during the war.

The first American comic-book to reach the magic number 100 was *Famous Funnies* in November 1942, while the first to hit No.500 was *Action Comics* in October 1979. American comic-books also have a happy habit of celebrating the birthdays of their characters. Thus we have No.144 of *Popeye* celebrating the spinach-eating sailor's 50th anniversary in March 1979, and No.526 of *Detective Comics* celebrating Batman's 500th appearance in May 1983.

No comics celebrate themselves so splendidly as do those of Europe, bringing forth multi-coloured specials bulging with nostalgia for old readers and fascinating history for the youngsters. *TBO*, the long-running Spanish comic which gave its name to strip

cartoons (they call them "tebeos"), has appeared every week since 17 March 1917. In 1983 they published a superb *Numero Extraordinario* reprinting 30 classic covers from number one to date. The Belgian comic *Journal de Spirou* started on 21 April 1938, and the hero was the title character, a bell-boy at the Hotel Moustic. He is still hopping bells, but the style of his creator, Robert Velter, has changed somewhat since "Jije" (Joseph Gullain) took over after the war. To celebrate its 40th birthday, *Spirou* gave away a superbly reproduced fac-simile of its No.1. The comic is known in its Dutch edition as *Robbedoes*.

Beano *No.1,000* © *16 September 1961 DC Thomson. Drawn by Dudley D. Watkins*
Dandy *No.2,000* © *22 March 1980 DC Thomson. Drawn by Charles Grigg*
Hotspur *No.1,000* © *16 December 1978 DC Thomson*
The Jolly Jester *No.1,000* © *1 January 1921 Amalgamated*

Press. *Drawn by Percy Cocking*
Butterfly *No.1,000* © *6 June 1936 Amalgamated Press. Drawn by Bertie Brown*
Funny Wonder *No.1,000* © *27 May 1933 Amalgamated Press. Drawn by Reg Parlett*

Captain Marvel Adventures *No.100* © *September 1949 Fawcett Publications. Drawn by C. C. Beck*
Batman *No.100* © *June 1956 National Comics*
Wonder Woman *No.300* © *February 1983 DC Comics*
Detective Comics *No.500* © *March 1981 DC Comics*
Donald Duck 25th Anniversary © *1977 Oberon/Walt Disney Productions (Holland)*
TBO *1917–1983* © *1983 Ediciones TBO (Spain). Drawn by "Tha"*
Robbedoes *No.1682* © *9 July 1970 Dupuis (Holland)*
Spirou *No.2097* © *22 June 1978 Dupuis (Belgium). Drawn by F. Walthery*

THE COMICS GO WEST!

"We're a-callin' yuh!" was editor Ken Fitch's headline to his Personal Chat with the young readers of *Star Ranger*, the first comic-book devoted 100 per cent to the American West, published by Harry A. Chesler in February 1937. Editor Fitch's first Roundup feature opened with "Hi, Rangers!" and continued "Jest tie yore broncs to th' hitchin' posts out thar an' push yore

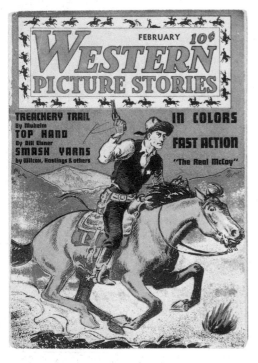

stetsons back off yore foreheads!" City kids did their best with their scooters and beanies as they picked their way through the patois. *Star Ranger*, Fitch explained, was "a book like yuh ain't never seen afore! Mostly in pitchers what artists draw an' color. The dust is a-goin' t' fly an' bullets is a-goin' t' zing through th' air." There followed 68 pages packed with that sort of stuff, guaranteed to give the vapours to any teacher of English, especially in England! The proclaimed "Pictorial Stories of the Golden West" included "Death's Head Range" ("Why you dirty double-crossing half-breed!"), "The Ghost Riders" ("We'll show them buzzards what tough is!"), "Valley of Living Death" ("Dog of a dog, it will be the wolves for you!"), "Empty Sixguns" ("Draw and be danged, yuh white-livered coyote!") and "The Joker" ("I'm pluggin' you in the guts!").

Although the wild frontier stuff was salted with hilariously drawn comic fillers by the young Fred Schwab, the lingo was a mite bodacious, "Say, whut in tarnation is a piece of rubbur(*sic*) tire(*sic*) doin' in my hash?" "Like you said Jess, the auto is replacin' the horse everywhere!" (*Plop*!) But kids didn't

complain; the artwork and design, tightly supervised by bossman Chesler ridin' tight rein over his posse of tenderfeet cartoonists, was top notch. Apart from the blossoming talent of Fred Schwab, there was drawing by Creig Flessel, Fred Guardineer, W. M. Allison, Rafael Astarita, Jim Chambers, and later Charles Biro, Will Eisner and Jack Cole. *Star Ranger*, originally in a handsome oversize, dropped to regular format from No.7 and changed title to *Cowboy Comics*, with No.13 (July 1938) reverting to *Star Ranger Funnies* from No.15 (October).

Riding in harness, datewise, was *Western Picture Stories*, No.1 of which hit the trail also in February 1937. This was put out by the Comics Magazine Company in the wake of their pioneering *Detective Picture Stories* and followed their popular pulp-magazine format, billing strips and artists on the cover and a contents page. More action-packed, less colourful than *Star Ranger*, the comic's language was just as tough to take, Victor Dowling's "Windy Parks" ("I'll send some clean fresh air a-whistlin' through that pizenous, low-down, ornery carcase o' yourn!"), Arthur Pinajian's "Guns of Revenge" ("Blast yore hide, I'll git yuh fer thet!"), and Will Eisner's "Top Hand" ("Stop thet stompin' yuh onry critter!"). The

third cowboy comic, *Western Action Thrillers*, a Dell 100-page one-shot (appropriate term) of April 1937 introduced strips of Buffalo Bill.

"Young Buffalo Bill" was the original title/hero of Harry O'Neill's newspaper strip: it started in 1930 and became the more familiar "Bronco Bill" in 1935. O'Neill's boy cowboy was reprinted in *Comics On Parade*, and featured as the cover star in the fifth British edition. The next western strip to spread from the Sunday supplements to his own comic-book was *Little Joe* (1933 the strip; 1942 the comic). The static but picturesque quality of this conversational comic had a lot to do with artist Ed Leffingwell being assistant to Harold Gray, the "Little Orphan Annie" man. The first *King of the Royal Mounted* comic-book was also the first of the famous *Feature Book* series, large format comic-books reprinting daily strips in monochrome. It contained 52 pages of the 1936 strip, purportedly written by western novelist Zane Grey and undoubtedly drawn by Allen Dean. Then in 1938 "the restless urge of a wandering cowboy brings Red Ryder down the slopes of the Shokanoes into Devil's Hole in the broken country of the Southwest", and into the newspapers, and thence into *Crackajack Funnies* No.9, and finally into his own *Red Ryder Comics* (1940), which became *Red Ryder Ranch Magazine* from October 1955. One of the most popular, authentic and best-drawn westerns ever, Fred Harman's rangy hero met his cute sidekick bang in strip one: "My papa name Chief Beaver; me Little Beaver!" Red was well drawn from the off; not so that other long-lasting western hero, the masked man of the plains. *The Lone Ranger* No.1 (1938) was a crudely cartooned affair published as a premium for Lone Ranger Dripless Ice Cream Cones. The art was a feeble imitation of the feeble newspaper strip by Ed Kressy, which had begun in September 1938. Kressy was soon replaced by the more macho Charles Flanders, and when the professional comic-book got going, abandoning reprints for new art by Tom Gill, it was so successful that companion comic-books spun off which were devoted to LR's redskin sidekick, Tonto, and LR's faithful steed, Silver. LR's origin, told so frequently that it was a wonder how he kept it secret, revealed that he was really John Reid, Texas Ranger, sole survivor of a massacre by the Butch

Cavendish Gang. His battle-cry "Hiyo Silver, away-y-y!" was first heard in the radio serial by Fran Striker, broadcast regularly from 30 January 1933. (His signature tune was "The William Tell Overture".)

Western Picture Stories *No.1* © *February 1937 Comics Magazine Co. Drawn by W. M. Allison*
King of the Royal Mounted (Feature Book *No.1*) © *May 1937 David McKay. Drawn by Allen Dean*
Star Ranger *No.3* © *May 1937 Chesler Publications. Drawn by Fred Schwab*

The Lone Ranger Comics *No.1* © *1938 Lone Ranger Inc*
Little Joe (Four Colour Comic *No.1*) © *1942 Dell/Chicago Tribune. Drawn by Ed Leffingwell*
Crackajack Funnies *No.9* © *March 1939 Whitman Publishing. Drawn by Fred Harman*
Red Ryder Ranch Magazine *No.145* (*No.1*) © *October 1955 Dell/Red Ryder Inc*
Comics On Parade (*British Edition*) *No.5* © *L. Miller/United Features. Drawn by Harry O'Neill*
Casey Ruggles Comic (*British Edition*) *No. 1* © *1951 Donald F. Peters. Drawn by Warren Tufts*

89

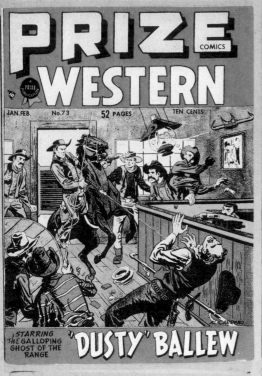

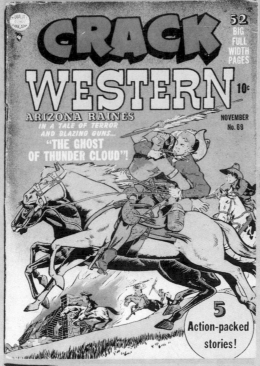

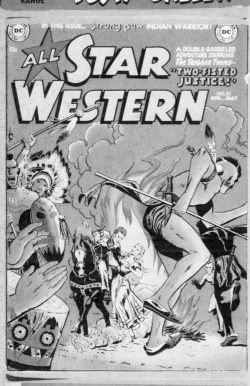

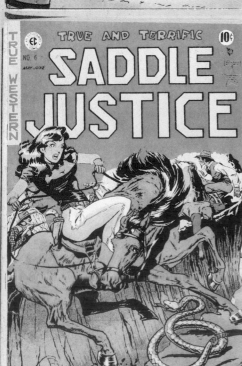

QUICK ON THE DRAWING-BOARD

American comic-book publishers were ever instinctive; fast to react to the slightest whiff of a trend. The moment it was obvious that westerns were "in", with Saturday Matinee heroes riding high at the box-office, there was a stampede to stock the news-stands with comic-book cowboys. All the old-time pulp magazine heroes and dime novel desperadoes were dusted down and togged up with tailor-made comic-books. Street & Smith Publications, an old-time outfit that had issued many dime novel series in the 19th century, published *Buffalo Bill Picture Stories* in 1949, reworking the old fictional adventures of real-life hero Colonel William F. Cody, "the greatest scout, soldier and hunter of the old West". *Pawnee Bill*, billed as "the white man craftier than the wiliest Indian", starred in his own comic-book from 1950, supported by such notorious notables as Bat Masterson and Wyatt Earp. The latter legendary frontier marshal was so popular (and so out of copyright) that he had two comic-books devoted to his exploits, issued by rival publishers Atlas and Charlton. *Daniel Boone* ("Pioneer, Hunter and Indian Fighter") also had two, although one was spelled Dan'l, just in case legal eagles came a-gunnin'. *Davy Crockett* outdid both his rivals as well he should, by notching up three. Dell's was safely based on the tremendously popular TV series by Walt Disney, which made a star of Fess Parker and a hit of his theme song. Avon and Charlton issued their own, safe in the knowledge that Davy was a national heritage.

The western boom found the major publishers quick on the trigger, too. Like lightning, several of their slightly-slipping superhero series were switched to the western trend. *Prize Comics* was the first: from April 1948 it became *Prize Comics Western*, starring "Dusty Ballew the Galloping Ghost of the Range" complete with comedy sidekick, Gumption Jones. The artist, Al Carreno, was an old hand at westerns, having drawn the syndicated strip "Ted Strong" from 1935 to 1938. In June 1948 the prestigious Parents Magazine Company converted its loss-leader *Calling All Boys* to *Tex Granger Adventure Magazine* ("I'm Tex Granger, Sheriff of Jacknife. Put up your gun, Billy the Kid!"). But the fighting Frontier Sheriff lasted just seven issues: Parents Magazine morality was not wanted by the western fans. DC Comics pulled a fast one in November 1948, switching their long-running *All-American Comics* to *All-American Western*. Top of a well-drawn team was "Johnny Thunder", who rode a white horse called Black Lightning. But as the art was by Alexander Toth, nobody objected. DC found the experiment a success and in April 1951 turned *All Star Comics* into *All Star Western*. This starred an unusual double act, "The Trigger Twins": Sheriff Walt Trigger and his identical brother, Wayne, the peaceful merchant. Meanwhile *Crack Comics* had become *Crack Western* from November 1949, co-starring "Arizona Raines and his small companion, Spurs". But probably the most curious title-change was the one which must have fazed lovers of teenage shenanigans. From Spring 1948 *The Happy Houlihans* became *Saddle Justice*, a "True and Terrific" western from E. C. Sex rode the comic-book range with "The Grinning Gun Girl".

Tex Granger Adventure Magazine *No.23* © *July 1949 Parents Inc*
Buffalo Bill Picture Stories *No.2* © *August 1949 Street & Smith. Drawn by Douglas Wildey*
The Cisco Kid *No.35* © *April 1957 Dell Publishing*
Daniel Boone *No.1163 (No.1)* © *May 1961 Dell Publishing*
Davy Crockett *No.1* © *1951 Avon Periodicals. Drawn by Gene Fawcette*
Wyatt Earp *No.29* © *June 1960 Marvel Comics. Drawn by Dick Ayers*
Pawnee Bill *No.1* © *February 1951 Story Comics*

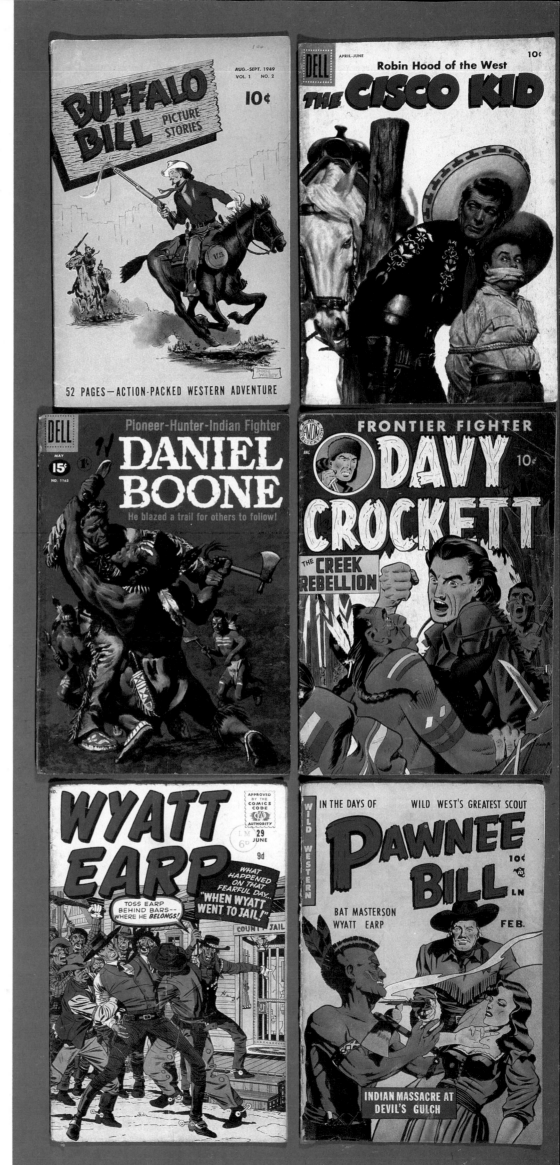

TOM MIX AND THE RIDERS OF THE SILVER SCREEN

Comic-books were to the *Saturday Evening Post* what B-westerns were to *Stagecoach*. Small wonder then that the cowboy heroes so beloved of the Saturday Matinee posse should ride their way into the comics. Tom Mix, "six feet two, bronzed, and lithe as a panther, slid out of the saddle, tied his horse, and went into the Long Horn Bar" – and into *Popular Comics* No.4 dated May 1936: the first film-star cowboy in the comic-books. Come September 1940 and he was also the first to have his own comic-book, writing the editorial in *Tom Mix Comics* No.1: "I'm mighty proud of this comic magazine the folks at the ranch have printed. Just like our radio program, it is full of clean, wholesome entertainment and promotes honesty, fair play, and good sportsmanship so necessary among youth in the world today." Tom had another message in his comic: "Ever tried fried Ralston for Sunday breakfast? It sure tastes keen!" Yes, the comic was produced by the sponsors of the Tom Mix radio serial ("The Ralston Straight Shooters are on the air from Coast to Coast – Blue Network – Monday thru Friday – 5.45 pm!"), and could only be obtained through the mail in exchange for the blue seal from the pouring spout of a package of Ralston. A month later Tom Mix was dead, killed in a car crash; but his radio serial lived

on, and his comic-book lived even longer until 1953.

Gene Autry, formerly a feeble impersonator of the original yodelling brakeman, Jimmy Rodgers, shot to stardom in a series of Republic musical westerns. He failed to make the grade in the Sunday supplements with a strip based on his movie serial, *The Phantom Empire*, but hit paydirt with his own comic-book, which ran from 1941 to 1959. Another long run was achieved by the next western star to ride through the comics. "Hopalong Cassidy", in the persona of William Boyd, was tried out as a supporting hero in *Master Comics* (November 1942) and within a year was top-hand in his own title. *Hopalong Cassidy* notched up 135 issues between 1943 and 1959, surviving a jump from Fawcett to DC Comics in 1954. Hoppy actually beat Gene in the numbers stakes: his publishers brought out a companion comic called *Bill Boyd Western*, carefully billing him as "Famous Star of the Hopalong Cassidy Movies". This added another 23 to Boyd's total. Roy Rogers, "King of the Cowboys", was tried out by Dell Publications in 1944. After 13 one-shots, *Roy Rogers Comics* started at No.1 in January 1948 and wound up 14 years later at No.145.

The boom years for the B-western, comic-book style, began in late 1948.

Fawcett, more than happy with Hoppy, added *Monte Hale* to their posse and turned the failing superhero title *Wow Comics* into *Real Western Hero* at No.70. Like some super-B movie, the cast list for this comic read Hopalong Cassidy, Tom Mix, Monte Hale and, true to form, that all-purpose comedy sidekick, Gabby Hayes. The following year Fawcett designed comic-books for *Rocky Lane* and *Lash LaRue*, and in 1950, *Rod Cameron*, *Ken Maynard*, *Tex Ritter* and *Bob Steele*. Vincent Sullivan's quality house, Magazine Enterprises, signed up *Tim Holt* and *The Durango Kid*, a Columbia series which starred Charles Starrett as Steve Brand, cowpoke, and his alter ego, the black-masked righter of wrongs. By 1950 Dell, in addition to Gene and Roy, was running *Johnny Mack Brown*, and soon introduced *Rex Allen, Buck Jones* and *Wild Bill Elliott*. DC Comics signed up *Jimmy Wakeley*, and in the winter of '49 Toby Press announced with pride "The Greatest Cowboy Star of Them All" in *John Wayne Adventure Comics*. Fox Features, never ready with folding money for right buying, brought up the rear with a couple of movie cowboys who, if not already dead, were nigh to dying, *Hoot Gibson* and *Will Rogers*. Charlton did little better when they tried to boost their *Cowboy Western Comics* with Sunset Carson, not forgetting his horse, Cactus Junior. Sunset starred in penniless westerns for Yucca Pictures and his handle just about spelled the twilight of the Hollywood cowboy.

But while the sun still shone out of their saddles, the cowboy comics rode high. There were titles devoted to their heroes' horses: Gene's *Champion* (1950), Roy's *Trigger* (1951) and even Rocky Lane's *Black Jack* (1957) all had comic-books. So did their sidekicks: *Gabby Hayes* (1948), *Smiley Burnette* (1950) and *Andy Devine* (1950). Even the gals were not forgotten, with *Reno Browne*, "Hollywood's Greatest Cowgal" (1950) riding for Marvel, and *Dale Evans*, "Queen of the Westerns" (1953) at DC. There was even a completely phoney film cowboy, the non-existent *Bob Colt* (1950). Fawcett had a male model pose for the obligatory photo cover and cheekily billed him as "The Sensational New Western Star".

Tom Mix Comics No.1 © *September 1940 Ralston Cereal. Drawn by Fred Meagher*

Roy Rogers and Trigger *No.1*
© *April 1967/1957 Gold Key/KK*
Buck Jones *No.2 (No.1)* © *April
1951 Dell Publishing*
Gene Autry and Champion *No.1
(British Edition)* © *1956 World
Distributors/Dell*
Hopalong Cassidy Comic *No.50 (No.*

1) (British Edition) © *1946 Miller/
Fawcett*
John Wayne Adventure Comics *No.1*
© *1949 Toby Press*
Ken Maynard Western *No1*
© *September 1950 Fawcett
Publications*
Lash La Rue Western *No1* © *1949
Fawcett Publications*

Tex Ritter Western *No.1* © *October
1950 Fawcett Publications*
Tim McCoy *No.16 (No.1)* ©
*October 1948 Charlton Comics.
Drawn by Lee Sherman*
Cowboy Western Comics *No.28*
© *June 1950 Charlton Comics*

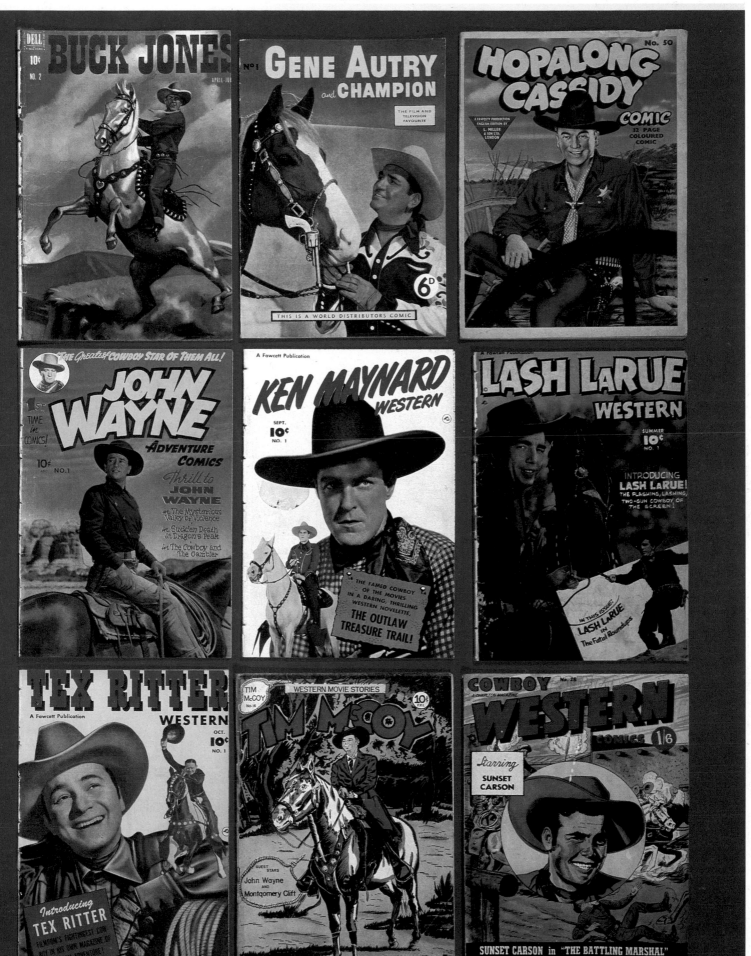

COMICS ON THE WARPATH

The son of a Potawatomi Chief, having seen his fourteenth winter, set forth from his father's camp to win his place in the Council of Braves. Captured by Sioux raiders, he survived torture to become the last of his tribe. Seeing his dead father about to be scalped by the Sioux leader the boy charged blindly. A shot rang out, the Sioux fell dead, and a lifetime partnership began. The white boy who fired the shot became the Lone Ranger, the man the Indian called "Kemo Sabay – trusty scout"; the Indian boy was *Tonto*. Together they rode the dangerous trails of the old west, over the radio waves and into the newspaper strips and comic-books, until the time came when the Indian rode alone – into his own comic-book in 1951. Tonto was not the first Indian sidekick to branch off in this way. Three years earlier Red Ryder's brave buddy *Little Beaver* did his own thing with many an Injun whoop of "Awah!", "Waugh!", "Hola!", "Aii-ee!" and "You betchum, Red Ryder!" Tonto, being a fully-fledged brave, was less prone to comic-book-style Injun lingo tending to lapse only when leaping into the saddle: "Get-um up, Scout!"

Straight Arrow, another rider of the radio range, cantered into comics in 1950 by courtesy of the National Biscuit Company. Straight Arrow's speech patterns were less the traditional talk-um, more the microphoney: "Stand ready, great palomino! This is your master who speaks. This is ... Straight Arrow!" This clarity of speech was not an honourable attempt to restore dignity to the first Americans. It was because Straight Arrow was really white man Steve Adams, owner of the Broken

Tonto *No.6* (*British Edition*)
© *1953 World Distributors/Lone Ranger Inc*
Little Beaver *No.817* (*No.11*) © *Dell Publishing/Red Ryder Enterprises*
Straight Arrow *No.2* © *April 1950 Magazine Enterprises/National Biscuits. Drawn by Fred Meagher*
Young Eagle *No.1* © *December 1950 Fawcett Publications*
Long Bow *No.1* © *1951 Fiction House*
Big Chief Wahoo *No.7* © *Famous*

Bow cattle spread, who donned Comanche disguise to fight the cause of justice on Fury the Golden Palomino, crying "Kanee-wah!" as he did so. Other more genuine Indian heroes were *Young Eagle*, whose exploits were assisted by Clawfoot, his trained Golden Eagle, and *Long Bow* the Blackfoot boy, who appeared in *Indians* (1950) before graduating to his own title the following year.

Indians had a great round-up of red brothers in support of young Long Bow: "Petalasharo of the Pawnees", "Starlight, Wildcat Daughter of the Hurons", and "Manzar the White Indian", who turned out to be Dan Carter in disguise, despite his warcry of "Hoka-Hai!" This pioneering comic-book was too strong for some white-eyes. Gerald P. Algerton of Washington DC wrote to the Editor's Pow-Wow: "There ought to be a law against such a magazine, and if people are uncivilized enough to read it, something ought to be done about them, too." What Mr Algerton thought of *Indian Braves* ("Trail of the Plundering Pariahs"), *Indian Warriors* ("The Mohawk Massacre") and *Fighting Indians of the Wild West* with its all-star line-up of Geronimo, Crazy Horse and Chief Victorio, is unrecorded, but hopefully he saw the joke in *Big Chief Wahoo*. This newspaper strip, originally designed to star "The Great Gusto", a W. C. Fields lookalike, soon focussed its attention and title on Gusto's assistant medicine man. In time Wahoo and his tribe, papoose Tommy Hawk ("Oskeewawa! Heap fun!") and squaw Minnie-Ha-Cha, raised enough laughs in *Famous Funnies* to warrant their own comic-book from 1942. Elmer Woggons' strip is probably the only case of the redskin successfully driving out the white man.

Funnies/Publishers Syndicate. Drawn by Stephen Douglas
Indians *No.2* © *1950 Fiction House*
Indian Braves *No.4* © *September 1951 Ace Magazines*
Indian Warriors *No.8 (No.2)* © *Star Publications. Drawn by L. B. Cole*
Fighting Indians of the Wild West *No.2* © *November 1942 Avon Periodicals. Drawn by Everett Raymond Kinstler*
Chief Crazy Horse *No.1* © *1950 Avon Periodicals. Drawn by Gene Fawcette*
Geronimo *No.1* © *1950 Avon Periodicals. Drawn by Gene Fawcette*

95

THE WESTERN WORLD

Westerns not only went West: they went North, East and South. The popularity of the cowboy is universal, and although the popularity of western comics waxes and wanes in the land of their birth, this is not so in Europe, or indeed in Australasia. The French have loved western fiction since the days of J. Fenimore Cooper and his *Last of the Mohicans*, while many Aussies still live on horseback in the outback much as the old westerners did on the prairies. Down under is probably the last place on earth where a yodeller can top the hit parade. Two of the outback cowboys achieved comic-books of their own. The first, *Tex Morton's Wild West Comics* (1948), starred the hillbilly singer with his "mates", Jacky, Shorty and Slim, in strips drawn by Dan Russell. There was also a Tex Morton Club, with a lapel badge, a Handsome Certificate, an autographed photo and a Letter of Welcome from Tex Himself – all for 1s 6d! *The Adventures of Smoky Dawson* (1960) had no club, but you could hear him on the radio every Thursday by courtesy of Kelloggs Corn Flakes. But the most famous, some might say notorious, Australian Western was *Action Comic* (1946), a title which soon took second place to its hero, "The Lone Avenger". This masked man of the old west notched up Australia's longest run for a monthly comic-book, 13 years. But it turned out an unlucky number for cartoonist Len Lawson: he was accused of rape, tried and sentenced to death (later commuted to 14 years' imprisonment).

In France the first comic weekly to be named after a Western hero was *Zorro* (1946). Artist Oulié drew him complete with famous "Z" trademark and whip, but made no direct acknowledgement to Justin McCarthy, the novelist who created the character in his much-filmed classic, *The Curse of Capistrano*. Zorro starred on the front page only, the rest of the comic being given over to such non-western heroes as "Luc Bradfer", the French translation of "Brick Bradford". *O.K. Texas* (1949) was a title which showed the rise in popularity of the Western: it had begun life as simply *O.K.* in 1946.

Now "Nick Boston au Far-West" rode the front page, while "Rodeo Kid" and the film, "Massacre at Furnace Creek", brought up the rear.

The Italians were producing original Western comics of their own long before Leone began filming his famous "Spaghetti Westerns". *Pecos Bill* (1949), subtitled "The Legendary Hero of Texas", wore his blond hair with a black streak and tossed his lasso with all the deadly accuracy of Zorro's whip. His noble steed, called Turbine in the original Italian, was translated as Tempest in the British edition. Another Italian cowboy to see a British edition was *Il Piccolo Sceriffo, The Little Sheriff* (1950). He suffered a little in translation, appearing as Kit Hodgkin in the strip and Kid Hodgkin on the cover. Cowboys had been riding the rear pages of British penny comics for many years, usually drawn by George Heath, but the first all-cowboy comic was *Ace-High Western Comics* (1945), an eight-page twopenny so crudely drawn that International Publications should have asked for their £12. 10s back! (I had improved, but not much, when I drew the next all-western comic, *The Sheriff* (1948): as the strips were adapted from movies, I could copy the stills!)

The western boom of the Fifties brought a stampede of titles from Miller & Son, mostly via the King-Ganteaume Productions studio: *Kid Dynamite, Rocky Mountain King, Buffalo Bill Cody, Pancho Villa*. The best western came from Die Cast Metal Toys, who published *Lone Star Magazine* (1953) to promote their products. Each strip linked to a toy weapon: "Captain Dirk Cutlass" to a pirate pistol, "Space Ace" to a spacegun, and the main character, "Steve Larrabee the Lone Star Rider" to "a life-size Cowboy Night Rider Gun in gleaming silver or blue, with horsehead grips in realistically carved bone finish. Handsomely scroll-engraved it fires a roll of 100 caps. At your Toy Shop Now!" Steve Larrabee was a "real cowboy", and like his Aussie comic-book pardners, toured the variety halls with his horse and his yodel.

HOW THE WEST WAS FUN!

"Land o' Goshen, Loco!" whooped Texas Slim to his faithful cayuse, a critter his scruffy sidekick preferred to call "Thet ***!!! four-laigged piece o' skonk meat!" The scrawny redhead and his bewhiskered buddy were the co-stars of "Texas Slim and Dirty Dalton", a comic strip combination launched by Ferd Johnson in the *Chicago Tribune* Sunday section on

30 August 1925. They were the first of the cartoon cowboys who have cantered through the comics ever since, riding off into a sudden sunset in 1928 only to come back with a bang in 1940. This time a longer run took them to 1958, when their artist, who had been running them as a sideline to his main work, assisting Frank Willard on "Moon Mullins", took over the latter strip completely on its creator's death.

Cowboys, popular in Britain from the films, were burlesqued in *The Monster Comic* with "Tom Mixture" (1926) and Bertie Brown's "Prairie Pranks" in *Larks* (1927), but these were only filler strips. The same can be said for "Desperate Dan" in *The Dandy* (1937), but this stubbly tough-guy soon burst from his half-page confines to become a full-page star with a half-century of weekly strips on the horizon. Dan was created by the brilliant Dudley D. Watkins in the image of *The Dandy's* editor, Albert Barnes. According to his official biography, Dan was born in Tombstone. "His Paw was a quarry-man at the granite quarries. When Dan was six months old his Paw used to bring

home useless chunks of granite too hard for making tombstones, for his baby to chew. That helped his teeth come through the gums!" And, presumably, gave the lad the taste for cow-pie with the horns in, his favourite supper! Dan operates out of Cactusville, a town which mixes western America with Northern Scotland (*The Dandy* is published in Dundee). Among the shacks and shanties may be spied street-corner lamp-posts, trams and even gasometers! Although Dan is the undoubted star of *Dandy*, he has never starred on the cover. However, when *Dandy Comic Library* was published in 1983, No.1 was devoted to a 64-page strip of Desperate Dan.

When "Lucky Luke" came riding out of the sunset, he was singing "I'm a poor lonesome cowboy and a long way from home." The rest of the time he spoke French! Lucky Luke began in a small way as a page in the French comic weekly, *Spirou*, on 12 June 1947; today he stars in his own albums and comic-books in English, Italian, German and almost any other language you can name. Yet always (and this is part of the hero's unique charm) his lonesome signature song appears in English. Luke, an affectionate burlesque deeply rooted in well-researched western lore (Luke has encountered

Jesse James, Judge Roy Bean, the Daltons, and a battleaxe called Jane Calamity), was created by cartoonist Maurice de Bevère, who signed himself "Morris". He was shortly joined by scriptwriter René Goscinny, whose brilliance would later steer the team into another bygone world, that of the Ancient Romans and "Asterix the Gaul".

Burlesque westerns were just part of Benito Jacovitti's wacky oeuvre. Italy's most original and prolific talent in the funnybook line, Jac's first strip, "Pippo and the English", appeared in the weekly *Vittorioso* from 1940 to 1967. Among his many other strips were parodies of such well-travelled American heroes as "Mandrake the Magician" and "Tarzan", so it was inevitable that the artist should discover the joys of the old West. His first excursion was "Cocco Bill" for *Il Giorno* (1957), duly followed in 1968 by his burlesque of Zorro, "Zorry Kid". Originally a page in the weekly *Corriere dei Piccoli*, this salami-nosed, masked avenger also has his own monthly comic in France.

Meanwhile, back at the ranch in the land where the West begins, Billy the Kid rode into yet another comic-book. As it was *Funny Animals*, the outlaw was a goat (Billy the *Kid*, get it?). And, just to be different, his sidekick, Oscar, was an ostrich! No wonder the West was wild.

Dandy Comic Library *No.1* © *April 1983 D. C. Thomson. Drawn by Charles Grigg*
Lucky Luke *No.8* © *October 1974 Dargaud. Drawn by Maurice de Bevère*
Chicos *No.512* © *21 November 1948 Gil (Spain). Drawn by Moro*

Texas Slim and Dirty Dalton *A.1. No.4 (No.1)* © *1944 Compix/Chicago Tribune. Drawn by Ferd Johnson*
Billy the Kid *No.1* © *Winter 1945 Fawcett Publications. Drawn by William Brady*
Cowboys 'n' Injuns *No.4* © *1947 Compix*
Shorty Shiner *No.2* © *August 1956 Dandy Magazines. Drawn by Charles Biro*
Mick and Muff *No.1* © *1971 Aredit (France). Drawn by George Boxade*
Zorry Kid Super *No.1* © *Société Française de Presse Illustrée. Drawn by Benito Jacovitti*

TARZAN OF THE COMICS

"Something absolutely new!" proclaimed the Editor of *Tit-Bits*. "A serial story in pictures. *Tarzan of the Apes* – your home picture-play! Edgar Rice Burroughs' world-famous novel to be presented in a weekly series of Vivid Pictures!" The date was 20 October 1928, and the extraordinary thing about this first British publication of the Tarzan strip was that it was three months ahead of the American première. The cartoon adaptation was the idea of an advertising agent, Joseph H. Neebe, who had bought the rights of Burroughs' popular novel (first publication, *All-Story Magazine* October 1912) and hired another advertising man, artist Harold R. Foster, to draw the pictures. Although *Tit-Bits* took it up in England, Neebe had less luck in the States, and it was not until the Metropolitan Syndicate took it on that the strip was published in American newspapers, beginning 7 January 1929. The second strip sequence, adopted from *The Return of Tarzan*, was drawn by Rex Maxon, Foster having returned to advertising art.

As the popularity of the strips built up, Maxon was asked to tackle a Sunday colour-page. This started on 15 March 1931, but soon proved too much for Maxon, and Foster was called back into service. He started from 27 September and there was an immediate improvement. Instead of a series of static pictures illustrating the narrative, Tarzan leaped into the kind of action moviegoers enjoyed in the Johnny Weissmuller jungle-operas. By the time Foster tired of drawing another man's creation, and left the strip to create his own, brilliant epic of medieval adventure, "Prince Valiant", he had evolved the Tarzan page into the finest adventure strip yet seen. But more wonders were yet to come, for beginning on 9 May 1937 Burne Hogarth arrived to draw a series of such superlatively designed Tarzan pages that even Foster was left in the shade.

The Tarzan legend is well-known: how the infant son of the shipwrecked Lord and Lady Greystoke was raised in the African jungle by apes and grew to become a physical wonder. Burroughs wrote a total of 24 books about him; there have been radio serials and more than 40 films since the original epic starring a silent Elmo Lincoln was made in 1918. And, of course, there have been many comic-books. Grossett and Dunlap issued the first in 1929, a reprint of the original daily strips entitled *The Illustrated Tarzan Book*. The same strips were reprinted a decade later as Dell's *Black and White Comic* No.5 (1939), but meanwhile Tarzan in the Hal Foster version was running in *Tip Top Comics* (1936), with Rex Maxon dailies coloured up for its companion, *Comics On Parade* (1938).

The first all-original Tarzan comic-book was published in 1947, *Tarzan and the Devil Ogre*, a one-shot in Dell's *Four Color Comics* series, No.134. *Tarzan and the Fires of Tohr* followed as No.161, and the books were so successful that Dell initiated a regular monthly series from January 1948. The artist, Jesse Marsh, used a thick brush and a bold, blocked-in style a long way from the detailed penmanship of Burne Hogarth, but it worked well for the comic-books. *Tarzan* ran with Dell until 1972, when with issue No.207 the title passed to DC Comics and the artwork to Joe Kubert. Burroughs' other great science-fiction hero, "John Carter of Mars", joined as the back-up feature. DC lost interest at No.288, so Marvel Comics signed up the Ape Man for a new series, *Tarzan Lord of the Jungle*, beginning June 1977. Meanwhile there was a slightly piratical *Jungle Tales of Tarzan* published by Charlton Comics in 1964, and a sub-series from Gold Key, *Korak Son of Tarzan*, illustrated by Russ Manning from January 1964. This latter title was also taken over by DC from May 1972, and like the parent title was given another ERB hero as back-up, "Carson of Venus". There have been numerous Tarzan comics published around the world, including a big British tabloid *Tarzan the Grand Adventure Comic* (15 September 1951), that was a translation of the French version, and a *Tarzan Adventures* from 8 April 1953 that was the first editorial assignment for the young fantasy novelist-to-be, Michael Moorcock.

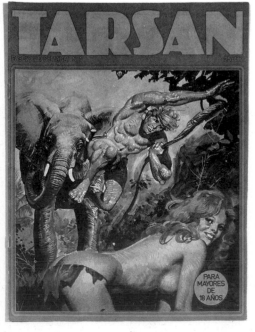

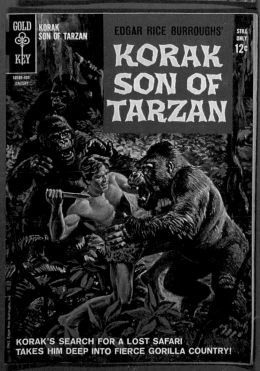

JUNGLE KINGS AND JUNGLE QUEENS

Edgar Rice Burroughs sired more than a new kind of hero when he dreamed up *Tarzan of the Apes*. He spawned a whole new generation of heroes, and soon the comic-books were full of far-away jungle places teeming with strange-sounding names. There were Kaänga and Ka-Zar, Jo-Jo and Zago, Lo-Zar and Zangar, Wambi and Jann. And for every King of the Jungle there was a White Queen: Sheena and Shanna, Rulah and Zegra, Nyoka, Camilla and Jungle Lil. First in the field was Fiction House who had once published a pulp magazine called *Jungle Stories*. Under the editorship of Larabie Cunningham and with Gene Fawcette as art director, *Jungle Comics* was born in January 1940. "Kaänga, Jungle Lord" was the cover star and leading man, sharing his living-space with a leopard-skinned lady whom he usually referred to as "Mate Ann". This "Mighty Monarch of the Congo" mended the regularly-broken peace with the aid of Marmo the elephant and a war-cry of "Mayomba!" Frank Ridell's dialogue was Hollywood Congo: "Wait! Don't go alone, Kaänga!" ... "No matter, it is a chance a Jungle Lord must always take!"

Fox Features got the jungle bug in 1947. First came *Jo-Jo, Congo King*, not to be confused with his later compatriot, *Jungle Jo*; the former's shorts were spotted and brown, the latter's striped and blue. Otherwise it was hard to tell, for, like Kaänga and the Fiction House crowd, they spoke a similar junglese. "Your evil eyes alone are vulnerable, crazed monster!" cried Jo to a creature from Forbidden Valley, "My blade will sink deeply into them!" (The monster answers "Grrunnt!"). Then there was *Zago, Jungle Prince* (black trunks), more than a match for white man's fire-stick. "Waa! The smell of death is in my nostrils! Someone in the jungle plots against my life!" Marvel Comics joined in in 1954 with *Jungle Tales*, starring "Jann of the Jungle", and *Jungle Action* with "Tharn". "Ka-Zar, Lord of the Hidden Jungle", assisted by Zabu the Sabertooth, was a Marvel hero from their pre-war pulp-magazine years.

Edgar Rice Burroughs can also take a slice of credit for originating Queens as well as Kings of the Jungle. His 1932 novel, *Jungle Girl*, was used by Republic Pictures as the basis for their serial, *Perils of Nyoka*. Fawcett Publications took the comic-book rights and issued *Jungle Girl* No.1 in 1942. From the second issue the comic was retitled *Nyoka the Jungle Girl*, and completely new adventures began. But Tarzan himself was more likely the inspiration for the first comic-book Queen of the Jungle. "Sheena" began her adventures as a full-page serial in No.46 of *Wags* (14 January 1938), the tabloid comic produced by Sam Iger and Will Eisner for export to the British Empire. The artwork, which rapidly improved, was by Mort Meskin, and the script was credited to a W. Morgan Thomas, a pen-name for Iger. Sheena made her American debut in No.1 of *Jumbo Comics* (September 1938), which Iger packaged for Fiction House out of the pages produced for *Wags*. Bob Reynolds and Professor Van Dyke are captured by the White

Queen's tribe. "Maguali tua no't!" says Sheena in "a remnant of an almost forgotten language". Sighs Bob, "She's beautiful . . . beautiful!" Once *Jumbo Comics* shrank down to the popular comic-book format (No.9, August 1939), Sheena appeared in full colour and immediately became the comic's leading lady. Three years later she was given her own title, by which time she had learned to speak regulation jungloid: "This dagger for you, black-hearted villain!", she cries, saving Bob once again with the aid of Chim the Chimp. Sheena was such a hit that Fiction House soon introduced an even lovelier, even tougher jungle queen, "Tiger Girl", into their previously he-manned *Fight Comics*. Fox Features, having successfully imitated the Fiction House Jungle Kings, now did the same with the Queens: *Zoot Comics* converted to *Rulah, Jungle Goddess* with No.17 (August 1948), and *Tegra, Jungle Empress* (August 1948) inexplicably switched to *Zegra, Jungle Empress* from No.2. As the excellent Matt Baker, one of America's few Negro cartoonists, drew them both, he made Zegra a blonde and Rulah a brunette: only the jungle remained unchanged.

Jungle Comics *No.32* © *August 1942 Fiction House. Drawn by Zolne Rowich*
Zago *No.4* © *March 1949 Fox Features. Drawn by Matt Baker*
Jungle Jo *No.2* © *July 1950 Fox Features*
Jo-Jo Comics *No.23* © *January 1949 Fox Features. Drawn by Matt Baker*
Ka-Zar *No.1* © *January 1974 Marvel Comics. Drawn by Mike Royer*
Yarmak Jungle King *No.24* © *Herald Gravure (Australia). Drawn by Stanley Pitt*

Jungle Girl *No.1* © *1942 Fawcett Publications*
Sheena Comics *No.1* © *Spring 1942 Fiction House. Drawn by Zolne Rowich*
Zegra *No.4* © *February 1949 Fox Features. Drawn by Matt Baker*
Rulah *No.23* © *February 1949 Fox Features. Drawn by Matt Baker*
Shanna the She-Devil *No.1* © *December 1972 Marvel Comics. Drawn by George Tuska*
Fight Comics *No.73* © *March 1951 Fiction House. Drawn by Bob Lubbers*

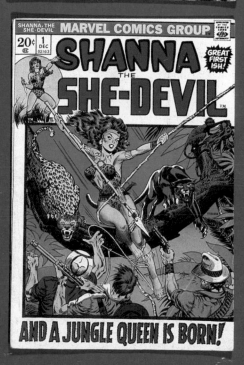

THE COMICS FLY HIGH!

As the air-minded Twenties zoomed into the high-flying Thirties, so the comic strips reflected America's excited interest in aviation. The sky was the new frontier, and pioneering pilot of the Sunday sections was "Tailspin Tommy" (1928) created as a 50-50 partnership by newspaperman Glenn Chaffin and cartoonist Hal Forrest. Thomas Tomkins, "Tailspin" to his pals, hooknosed sidekick Skeets and blonde Betty Lou Barnes, formed the entire aircrew of Three Point Airlines, and as such encountered more than their fair share of mad inventors and despotic deities, such as the High Ullah of the Lost Inca City of Puerto Bahongo. Small wonder Skeets was given to crying, "Well, I'm a ring-tailed monkey!" Forrest's linework was rather thin for aircraft and action, but he had a way of flipping a flowing skirt above a shapely knee that must have affected many a lad reading his reprints in *Popular Comics*. Readers of *Famous Funnies* had no such problems with "Skyroads", a more masculine air affair which was so serious that each day's strip ended with "Wingtips" ("There are four forces continually acting on a plane while in the air, lift and thrust which are positive, and drag and gravity which are negative."). Skyroads Unlimited was Ace Ames and Buster Evans in a biplane, and the strip, which started in 1929, was also a partnership, Lester Maitland and Dick Calkins. The latter, however, soon withdrew his nib for an even higher flier into the wide blue yonder.

"Scorchy Smith" (1930) was created by John Terry, ex-animator brother of Paul Terry, but by the time the strip arrived in *Famous Funnies* it was being drawn by Noel Sickles. The dauntless aviator would have many limners in his long lifetime, but none so good or so influential as this Sickles: his assistant was the young Milton Caniff. Unfortunately the reduced, five-strips-to-a-page format of *Famous Funnies* did little justice to Sickles' style, and the additional colour tints obscured his chiaroscuro. Zack Mosley's cartoony artwork on "Smilin' Jack" (1933) was absolutely ideal for the comic-book medium, however, and jolly Jack's action-packed aerobatics lent an air to *Popular Comics*. Last of the prewar pilots to fly from the

papers to the comic-books was the freckle-faced hero of "Barney Baxter in the Air". Drawn in an eccentrically overwrought style by Frank Miller, Barney flew the blue with his grizzled sidekick Gopher Gus, who talked like a refugee from a Gene Autry B-movie ("Oxygen? Shucks-a-shootin'! I done left it in Chicago!"). His strip, according to *King Comics*, was "Approved by the Junior Bird Men of America".

The comic-books, meanwhile, were quietly developing airmen of their own. *Crackajack Funnies* introduced "Captain Frank Hawks, Air Ace", a debut for Alden McWilliams, who was later to draw the daily science fiction serial, "Twin Earths". Much more identifiable to young readers was "Hop Harrigan", Jon Elby's ill-treated farm-boy who learned to fly by immediate instinct in No.1 of *All-American Comics* (April 1939) and was promptly awarded that essential item in every flier's equipment, the funny sidekick. In Hop's case it was "Ikky Tinker, world's best aviation mechanic" and possibly the first red-headed Jew in the comic-books.

The first all-air-oriented comic-book flew onto the newsstands in September 1940. This was No.1 of *Wings Comics*, a spin-off from Fiction

House's story pulp. Excellently drawn and coloured, as were all this publisher's comics, *Wings* went out on a limb glorifying a war in which the USA was officially neutral. As the Editor wrote on the comic's first birthday: "They Called *Wings* 'warmonger' and 'alarmist' because, long before Pearl Harbor, it chose to dramatize and glorify the Yank aces, those dauntless, unconquerable chips off the old block who had rushed to join the RAF in high battle". *Wings* glorified the Yank gals too, who were also aces with their thigh-slashed skirts that flew higher than a kite. Stand-out among an otherwise all-male cast that included Skull Squad, Clipper Kirk and Suicide Smith was Jane Martin, War Nurse; her role model was the movies' "Mean, Moody and Magnificent" Jane Russell. Rival pulp publishers did well with their "Airboy", star of *Air Fighters Comics* (1941), who took over the title, too, from No.23. Airboy (teenager Davy Nelson) had two secret weapons: Birdie the Batplane, an "ornithopter" invented by a monk, and Valkyrie, a different sort of bird. She was supposed to be one of Hitler's secret weapons (she commanded the Airmaiden Squadron of the Third Reich), but with her sky-diving neckline of a kind never before seen in comics, she opened her own second front! In her first appearance (*Air Fighters* No.14)

she strips Airboy to his goggles, whips him, then kisses the secrets of the bird-plane out of him, and changes sides. Airboy forgets his scars and that he called her a "female knockwurst", sealing the deal with a climactic kiss: "G-gosh! We should do this more often!" Well, once a month in *Air Fighters Comics* anyway.

Sex was one problem that seldom bothered Biggles, the British airman whose career began in *Popular Flying* magazine. This 1932 short story by the magazine's editor, Flying Officer W. E. Johns, proved so popular that over 70 Biggles books appeared during the ensuing 35 years. Biggles (Captain James Bigglesworth RAF) had the longest career a flier ever knew, beginning with service in the Royal Flying Corps in the Great War of 1914–18, continuing through the Battle of Britain in 1940, and concluding as a postwar Air Detective with Interpol. Small wonder he also made it into comic-books; the curiosity is that it was the Australians who drew and published it! Also from Down Under came "Air Hawk and the Flying Doctors", one of the best-drawn flying strips ever. John Dixon started Jim Hawk's adventures with the Royal Flying Doctor Service as a Sunday strip serial in 1949; the comic-book came along in 1962.

Best-Seller Comics: Tailspin Tommy *No.1* © *1946 Service*
Barney Baxter in the Air *No.6* © *Invincible Press* (*Australia*)
Bruce Gentry Airways Investigator *No.12* © *February 1951 Real Adventure Comics* (*Australia*)
Smilin' Jack © *1947 Popped Wheat/ Sig Feuchtwanger/Famous Artists*
Air Hawk and the Flying Doctors *No.1* © *1962 Horwitz Publications* (*Australia*). *Drawn by John Dixon*
The Adventures of Biggles *No.1* © *Strato Publications* (*British Edition*). *Drawn by Albert Devine*

True Aviation Comics Digest *No.1* © *1942 Parents Institute*
Flyin' Jenny *No.1* © *1946 Pentagon*
Sky Blazers *No.1* © *September 1940 Hawley Publications/Phillips Lord. Drawn by Tom Hickey*
Sky Sheriff *No.1* © *Summer 1948 DS. Drawn by Edmond Good*
Air Fighters Comics *No.14* © *November 1943 Hillman Periodicals. Drawn by Fred Kida*
Wings Comics *No.91* © *March 1948 Fiction House. Drawn by Bob Lubbers*

SING A COMIC SONG!

Barney Google apart, songs about comic heroes seldom make it into the international Top Tens. They don't travel well; their success depends totally on their hearers' familiarity with the funnies. Barney Google was the exception that proved the rule. You didn't have to know Billy De Beck's cartoon to sing and dance along with "Barney Google and his Goo Goo Googly Eyes". It was just the silly, jazzy type of number the Roaring Twenties adored, and the writers were Billy Rose, he of the "Diamond Horseshoe", and Con Conrad.

The *Chicago Tribune*, always very promotion conscious, inspired a series

of songs based on their comic strip characters, and gave them away with the newspaper during 1929. "Moon Mullins", from Frank Willard's derby-hatted stogie-smoker, was written by Grace Ingram and George Hill:

"Oh! Moon Mullins is a very funny guy,
At Moon Mullins you will laugh until you cry;
Tho' he don't amount to much,
It seems he always gets in Dutch,
Oh! Moon Mullins is a very funny guy."

Walter Berndt's strip about kids, "Smitty", prompted this song from Harry Harris and Larry Shay:

"If a kid throws a stone thro' your window
And you're looking for someone to blame,
Blame it on to Smitty, blame it on to Smitty,
That devilish boy."

"I'm Popeye the Sailor Man" had more going for it than E. C. Segar's comic strip, and spinach. Max and Dave Fleischer had acquired the rights for their animated cartoon films, and Paramount staff composer Sammy Lerner wrote the song as the signature tune. It was sung by the original voice of Popeye, Billy Costello, who quickly incorporated it into his stage and radio act and thence on to records. Soon every dance band crooner was straining to copy Costello's gravelly tones:

"If anyone dasses to risk me fisk,
It's wham an' it's bam, under-stan',
So keep good behaviour, it's sure one life saver,
Sez Popeye the Sailor Man."

In England songs about the comics were more genteel; but then, so were the comics:

"Toys are busy as bees,
The pets are making holiday,
Let them do as they please
And they'll spend a jolly day.
Just imagine if we could see
The Party of Tiger Tim."

This "characteristic novelty" was written by Percy Edgar and Reginald Morgan "by kind permission of Tiger Tim's paper, *The Rainbow*". The first British newspaper strip to be immortalized in music was "Pip, Squeak and Wilfred". This remarkably popular *Daily Mirror* series began in 1919 and within two years the creators, Austin Payne (art) and Bertram Lamb (author, alias "Uncle Dick"), worked with composer Olive Turner on an album of eight piano pieces for children. Directly inspired by incidents in the strip, they included "Uncle Gus from Paris", "Marmaduke the Buck Rabbit of Sydenham" and "Popski the Bolshevik Dog".

George E. Studdy's "Bonzo" was another post-World War I phenomenon, but this time the cartoons were intended for adults. Bonzo emerged from a weekly series of half-tone painted cartoons which appeared in *The Sketch*, a classy magazine. Soon Bonzo was everywhere, on postcards, ashtrays and souvenirs of all kinds. Eventually he would star in a comic strip, too; but first came the popular foxtrot, "Where's Bonzo?", by Wyn Ewart and Mark Strong:

"How's Bonzo? How's Bonzo?
Is he OK?
How's Bonzo? How's Bonzo?
Oh tell us, pray.
Though his big baby eyes are soft as silk,
Who put the pepper in the tom cat's milk?
Not Bonzo, not Bonzo, not him I vow,
He'd never get mixed up in any row,
If he's snoozing or he's scrapping,
You can never catch him napping,
Bonzo, how are you?
Tray-bonzo, bow-wow!"

But the honour of the first comic character to have a song written about him belongs to our old "Friend of Man, Ally Sloper". It was published in December 1886 and given away as a seasonable supplement to *Ally Sloper's Christmas Holidays*:

"Then a Merry Christmas to Sloper
All under the mistletoe,
And freedom from ills and from Doctors' bills
May that Marvel ever know.
Then here's good cheer and a Happy New Year
To Sloper and Iky Mo!"

And, every year from then on, a new Sloper song was commissioned and presented with the annual Christmas edition. Titles included, "The Tootsie Gavotte", "Tootsie's Serpentine Dance", featuring the dainty Miss Sloper, and "The Rumfoozlers Chorus", celebrating the favourite Sloperian tipple.

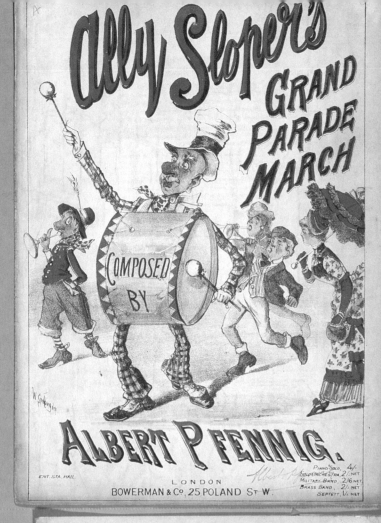

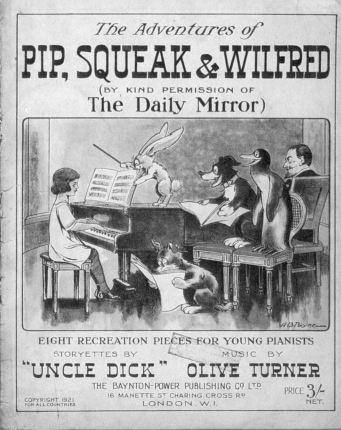

Moon Mullins © 1929 Will Rossiter.
Drawn by Frank Willard
Smitty © 1928 Harris and Shay/
Famous Artists Syndicate. Drawn by
Walter Berndt
Tiger Tim's Party © 1941 Victory
Music. Drawn by Julius Stafford
Baker Jr

Ally Sloper's Grand Parade March
© Bowerman and Co. Drawn by W.
Spalding
How's Bonzo © 1924 Cecil Lennox.
Drawn by George Ernest Studdy
Adventures of Pip, Squeak &
Wilfred © 1921 Baynton-Power Co.
Drawn by Austin Payne

I'm Popeye the Sailor Man
© Famous Music Corporation/King
Features

107

A GOLDEN AGE OF HAPPY DAYS

The Thirties were the Golden Age of British comics. With more than 40 years of evolution behind them, the weekly children's comics had developed their own unique style of humorous and adventure strip illustration, patterns which traced back to the early masters, Tom Browne for the funnies, and the story-paper illustrators for the serials. The comics now fell into two distinct types, the "penny blacks" (as they were known in the trade, although most were by now printed on coloured paper), and twopenny coloureds. They appealed to two classes; the penny comics were the ones children bought with their pocket money and were by the Thirties essentially knockabout slapsticks designed for working-class or council-school kids; while the twopennies were bought by parents and were therefore less slapstick, more polished, appealing to the middle class and tending to reflect a better-mannered way of life. In both penny and twopenny areas, editorial standards were high and strict, and artists were constrained by having to emulate those who had gone before, or those who were at the top of the tree. It was the comic characters who were considered important, not the men who drew them; many characters lived on for 20, 30 or more years, while their cartoonists came and went anonymously, forbidden to sign their work.

Of the few top artists who were permitted to sign some of their strips, Wilson (he was not allowed to add the Roy) was the undoubted king. He had learned his art in the Twenties, assisting Don Newhouse, an established comic artist in the Tom Browne school. To fool his London editors, Newhouse did all the lettering, mystifying the Amalgamated Press with the improved quality of his output. A clever editor, Len Stroud of *Butterfly*, finally penetrated the mystery and lured the modest Wilson away from his master. Immediately the assistant blossomed into AP's finest front-page artist, ousting the former favourite, Bertie Brown. Wilson soon became the essential stylist all others had to copy and designed the fronts for all new titles: "The Tiddlewink Family", *Jingles* (1934), "Jack Sprat and Tubby Tadpole", *Jolly* (1935), "Lieutenant Daring and Jolly Roger", *Golden* (1937), "George the Jolly Gee Gee", *Radio Fun* (1938) and his masterpiece, *Happy Days* (1938).

"Hallo, Happy Hearts! I am Uncle Happy the proud Editor of your new paper. How are you all?" Uncle Happy was really John L. Bott, and he had a right to be proud, for *Happy Days* was the crown of AP achievement. Inspired by the success of *Mickey Mouse Weekly* by their rival publisher, Odhams Press, the AP spent a small fortune devising their own first comic to be printed in full-colour photogravure. Naturally Roy Wilson was given the cover, and he used the whole area to the full, composing a front page that was designed differently every week. "At Chimpo's Circus" was also the AP's first attempt at funny animals presented at a higher age level than Tiger Tim and his nursery chums, depicting the usual jungle combination in the kind of slapstick action previously preserved for the penny black heroes like Weary Willie and Tired Tim. Young Fred Robinson, a progressive cartoonist under the animated cartoon influence, was given the back page to develop as a unified pictorial whole, depicting Merry Mick and Jolly Molly's serialized adventures in "Crazy Castle". The centre spread introduced two serials using colour techniques to the full, "Wonder Island" and "Sons of the Sword". This epic of the crusades was drawn by another newish talent, Reg Perrott, who had been drawing amazing historical serials for *Mickey Mouse Weekly*. Unhappily for *Happy Days*, its mixture of age-appeal was too confusing to reach a steady circulation, and after a drab few weeks when it was reduced to economical letterpress colour, it suffered the embarrassment of absorption into the hyphenated *Chicks' Own*.

The end of *Happy Days* marked the end of an era. It happened on 5 August 1939; one month later Britain was at war. Paper shortage killed many of the old titles, reduced others in size and shape. The happy days were gone for good. But as the Thirties died, a new force in comics had dawned, far away from the traditions of Alfred Harmsworth's Amalgamated Press. In Dundee, Scotland, the publishers of a successful string of story-papers for boys began experimenting with comics. *The Dandy* (4 December 1937)

and *The Beano* (30 July 1938) and *The Magic* (22 July 1939), drawn in a deliberately different style closer to the American school of captionless strips, were seen by traditionalists as crude, by children as wonderful. They were the first twopenny comics kids bought for themselves. D. C. Thom-son had chanced on a secret the AP and its successors would never learn, the art of making comics that children really wanted to read – and buy.

Golden *No.1* © 23 October 1937 *Amalgamated. Drawn by Roy Wilson* The Dandy Comic *No.1* (*facsimile*)

© *4 December 1937 D. C. Thomson. Drawn by James Crichton* The Beano Comic *No.1* © *30 July 1938 D. C. Thomson. Drawn by Reg Carter*

Happy Days *No.1* © *8 October 1938 Amalgamated. Drawn by Roy Wilson*

THE YANKS ARE COMING!

The American comic invasion was spearheaded by William Randolph Hearst as early as 1910. Buying the antique and declining *Weekly Budget* (whence had sprung that prototype British comic, *Funny Folks*, in 1874) from antique and declining James Henderson, Hearst converted it to the first British Sunday newspaper to be sectionalized in the American style. Unable to find a British printer to cope with four-colour broadsheet printing, Hearst had his comic supplement specially printed in the States and shipped across. The first four-page comic section was wrapped around the

News and Magazine Sections to make a 20-page "Popular Family Story and News Paper". It went on sale on 16 October 1910, price one penny ("if posted with coloured sheet, three ha'pence"). Although some of Hearst's syndicated strips had seen British publication in such comics as *The Big Budget* in 1902, this was for millions the first sight of "The Katzenjammer Kids", "Happy Hooligan", "Buster Brown", "Their Only Child", and later, "Little Nemo", as they were intended to be seen: in newspaper size and full colour.

In the mid-Thirties Joshua B.

Powers of New York formed Editors' Press Service, a syndicate for syndicates. His idea was to specialize in overseas distribution only, selling reprint rights of American comic strips to English-speaking countries. His main customer was the British Empire. Thwarted by the problem of cheap four-colour printing, Powers came up with the concept of printing and publishing an Export Only comic. Like Hearst's *Weekly Budget* comic, it would be printed in the USA, then shipped overseas for distribution in Great Britain, Australia and New Zealand. Instead of the *Weekly Budget* broadsheet size, Powers settled for the handier tabloid format. Not only was it handier to pack, it was virtually the standard shape and size of the British

weekly comic and thus would cause no display and distribution problems. Needing a title for his comic, Powers came up with "*Wags*" which, apparently, he felt was a typically English word to describe its essentially humorous contents: "Smitty" on the front page, and "Smokey Stover", "Moon Mullins", "Mutt and Jeff", "Mickey Finn", and "Winnie Winkle" on the inside. There were adventure strips, too: "Tarzan", "Terry and the Pirates", "Tailspin Tommy", and the rather rare "Ted Strong" by Al Carreno. No.1, 16 pages for twopence, went on sale in Australasia on 8 September 1936. It was an instant success, and was followed on 1 January 1937 by the first issue of the British Edition. This was even more of a success than the Australian Edition, having no fewer than 32 pages for twopence, an unprecedented bargain.

Then, with *Wags* No.17 (23 April 1937), came startling changes that would have a great effect on the development of the American comic-book; changes that, at the time and for many years in the future, were unknown to American historians and afficionados. Powers' agent in London, T. V. Boardman, decided to publish his own comic. Breaking with Editors' Press, he took with him the British rights to a number of the syndicated strips. Needing to fill his blank pages, Powers got in touch with Universal Phoenix Features, a two-man set-up run by Sam Iger and Will Eisner, a couple of cartoonists who had met during the brief run of *Wow!* (1936). Rounding up some of their former freelancers, Eisner and Iger set to fill the required eight pages a week. Working as "Willis B. Rensie", Eisner started the long-to-run "Hawks of the Seas", a piratical picture serial, later (as "Dennis Colbrook") drawing "Spencer Steel", and later still drawing "Scrappy", from the Charles Mintz Columbia cartoons. Eisner's old schoolmate, Bob Kane, came up with "Peter Pupp", a brilliant mixture of funny animals and sci-fi adventure, with a fabulous one-eyed villain. Dick Briefer restarted his *Wow* serial based on "The Hunchback of Notre Dame", and Don De Conn drew "The Adventures of Tom Sherrill". Later in the year George Brenner came along with new exploits of his masked detective in "The Clock Strikes", and on 14 January 1938 Mort Meskin drew the first ever adventure of the fabulous "Sheena, Queen of the Jungle". Two

new serials started in No.64 (20 May), Vernon Henkel's "Gallant Knight", and "The Count of Monte Cristo", which was attributed to a Jack Curtiss. He would become better known as Jack Kirby, one of the most innovative artists ever to work in comics.

The final British Edition of *Wags* was No.88, dated 4 November 1938, but apparently the Australasian Edition continued to 1940. In Britain *Wags* had competition from *Okay Comics Weekly*. This was published by T. V. Boardman, and, although presenting only 16 pages for twopence, its selection of US syndicated strips ("Joe Palooka", "Alley Oop", "Don Winslow of the Navy", "Toonerville Folks") still meant it needed to be printed in the States. Soon Boardman found a British printer, Greycaines, who could produce the requisite colours, but at a price which meant that alternate pages would have to be

in black and white. He cleverly capitalized on this economy by introducing several text stories and features for the uncoloured pages, which had the added attraction of bringing *Okay Comics* into line with traditional British comic format. Another skilful editorial touch was to publish new stories built around "Larry the Lamb", S. G. Hulme Beaman's highly popular hero of the *Toytown* radio plays. In addition Boardman commissioned Harry Parlett to draw a "Larry the Lamb" strip, and even instituted a Larry the Lamb Club. But the mix of British and American content failed to jell, and *Okay* had to fold.

Wags No.24 © 11 June 1937 Joshua B. Powers. Drawn by George Scarbo

Okay Comics Weekly No.1 © 16 October 1937 T. V. Boardman. Drawn by Will Eisner

COMICS OF "THE WHATCHUMACALLIT KIND"

"Hello Boys and Girls!" wrote Joseph Hardie, editor/publisher of Centaur Comics. "You've been asking for something new and your Uncle Joe, who's been staying up nights thinking of ideas to amuse all his nieces and nephews, now hands you *Little Giant Comics*, a whatchumacallit kind of magazine. It's a little book, yet it's a big magazine, all in one. It has giggles and gags, puzzles and tricks, funnies and stories, 128 pages of them – more than any other magazine!" *Little Giant Comics* No.1 came out in July 1938, an odd oblong of a booklet measuring $6\frac{3}{4}$ by $4\frac{3}{4}$ inches, full of black and white reprints from back numbers of other Centaur comic-books. It was followed by *Little Giant Detective Funnies* and *Little Giant Movie Funnies*, again both reprints, but the latter using the delightful newspaper strip, "Minute Movies", in which Ed Wheelan burlesqued the silent screen. His serial "Alaska" starred Dick Dare as Gilbert Gay, "dissipated son of a very wealthy multi-millionaire", Ralph McSneer as his dissolute Uncle Desmond, and Miss Hazel Dearie as "Bessie the Blonde, a frail little flower of the Curly Wolf Dance Hall". In the top right-hand corner of the comic was an

animated cartoon "riffler" by Martin Filchock. Dell also tried an oblong format comic-book in 1938, *Nickel Comics*, which as its title suggests sold at the low price of 5 cents. This was a unique comic for America, most of the strips being British, culled from back numbers of *Mickey Mouse Weekly*. There was Basil Reynolds' "Skit, Skat and the Captain", Reg Carter's "Bob the Bugler", Harry Parlett's "Wally the Wooly Cowboy", renamed "Wyoming Willie", and the same cartoonist's "Little Lulu" renamed "Miss Adventure" to avoid a copyright clash with Marge's *Saturday Evening Post* heroine. Curiously, Otto Messmer's "Bobby Dazzler", which was retitled "Bobby and Chip" for its English publication in *Mickey Mouse*, was reprinted in *Nickel Comics* under its English title to the probable bafflement of Mr Messmer.

Small-format comic-books of a squarer shape were introduced in the Forties by Alfred Harvey. *Pocket Comics* No.1 (August 1941) measured around 5 by 7 inches and boasted 100 full-colour pages for 10 cents: "The Biggest Comics Value in the World!" Unusually the star of the lead strip was a villain, "Satan-Mad Dictator of the

Underworld", while Al Avison's superhero, "The Red Blazer" ("Swooping and zooming, propelled by fiery Pyro Rays!") took second place. Other heroes included "The Zebra", "The Phantom Sphinx", "British Agent 99" (bylined William Churchill!), and the only one who would be heard from again, Hollywood's Mystery Girl "The Black Cat". A companion comic-book was called *Spitfire*, but the promised *Pocket Comics Library* which was to include such titles as *Patriotic Comics*, *Historic Comics* and *Digest Comics*, seems not to have materialized. (Curiously, when the concept of pocket comics was revived successfully in the Sixties, they were termed by the trade "Digest Comics".) Nationwide Comics, a Chicago outfit, launched a string of 5-cent pockets in 1950, and although they covered the main genres popular at the time (superhero, western, animal and teenage) again the small format failed.

There were other experiments in size and shape before comic-books settled down to their familiar format. Whitman issued two outsize one-shots that reprinted tabloid Sunday strips of Burke's "Lily of the Alley" and Meb's

"Buttons and Fatty", and also *Mammoth Comics* (1937), an 84-page reprint of 20 different newspaper strips, from "Dick Tracy" to "Terry and the Pirates". A curiosity was Dell's *Famous Feature Stories* (1938) which ran Dick, Terry and even "Smokey Stover" in fiction format, illustrated with panels from their strips. Dell was also responsible for *100 Pages of Comics* (1937), in which all the strips tied in with their *Big Little Books*. *Gags* (1937) was odd in that it used comic-book format to reprint the Sunday supplement cartoon page, "Life's Like That", by Lichty (George Lichtenstein). *Jumbo Comics* (September 1938) was the big one that made it – although it had to shrink down from tabloid to comic-book format to do it. It was launched in September 1938, a huge dimesworth of "Bigger and Better Funnies", the first comic from the eminent pulp-magazine publisher, Fiction House. The strips were all new to young Americans, but would have been old hat to the British. Bob Kane's "Peter Pupp", Will Eisner's "Hawks of the Seas", Jack Kirby's "The Count of Monte Cristo", Mort Meskin's "Sheena, Queen of the Jungle": all and more were reprints from the many issues of *Wags*! Sam Iger and Will Eisner, the original packagers, had bought back the printing plates from Joshua B. Powers, and sold them afresh to Fiction House. As "Jerry" Iger told me (his nickname comes from a comic character called "Jerry on the Job"), "When Thurman T. Scott said 'What do we do about colour?' I said 'Easy – just print on coloured paper!'" The early issues of *Jumbo Comics* are on alternate pages of orange and green. From No.10 (October 1939), *Jumbo* was reduced to regular comic-book format and printed in full colour, and became the Fiction House flagship, running to April 1953 and 167 editions. Obviously, in America at least, the comic-book had come to stay.

Jumbo Comics *No.1* © *September 1938 Fiction House. Drawn by Will Eisner*

Pocket Comics *No.1* © *August 1941 Harvey Publications. Drawn by Al Avison*
Yankee Comics *No.7* © *1943 William Wise/Harry Chesler*
Nickel Comics *No.1* © *1938 Dell Publishing. Drawn by Harry Parlett*
Little Giant Movie Funnies *No.2*

© *October 1983 Centaur. Drawn by Ed Wheelan*
Little Giant Comics *No.1* © *July 1983 Centaur. Drawn by Martin Filchock*
Mammoth Comics *No.1* © *1937 Whitman*
Famous Feature Stories *No.1* © *1938 Dell Publishing*

Gags *No.1* © *July 1937 United Features. Drawn by Lichty*
100 Pages of Comics *No.1* © *1937 Dell Publishing*
Tops Comics *No.1* (2001) © *1944 Consolidated Books*
Midget Comics *No.2* © *April 1950 St John*
Captain Atom *No.1* © *1950 Nationwide*

SUPERMAN: It's a Bird! It's a Plane! It's a Comic!

"The Man of Steel" … "The Man of Tomorrow" … "The World's Greatest Adventure-Strip Character" … his subtitle may change, but Superman goes on forever, fighting for Truth, Justice, Freedom, and the American Way of Comic-books. There have been many changes in his lifestyle (and drawing style) since the infant Kal-El was tucked into a baby-rocket by his scientist father, Jor-el, and shot to Earth from the exploding planet Krypton. Adopted by kindly old Jonathan and Mary Kent, who called him Clark, the boy grew into the mild-mannered reporter of the *Daily Star* (later *Planet*), who was secretly "able to leap one eighth of a mile, hurdle a 20-storey building, raise tremendous weights, run faster than an express train", and whose skin could be penetrated by "nothing less than a bursting shell". In other words, "Superman, Champion of the

Oppressed, the Physical Marvel who had sworn to devote his existence to helping those in need!" His origins have been told, retold and elaborated upon many times since that fateful day in June 1938 when No.1 of *Action Comics* hit the American newsstands: they have never been the same since. For, more than creating a myth that threatens to resound through the aeons via radio, television and the movies, Superman created the comic-book. Until he streaked over the horizon, comic-books were but a reflection of strips that had gone before, in newspapers and Sunday supplements. Superman was created for comic-books, comic-books were created for Superman. From this moment on, comic-books and super-heroes became virtually inseparable.

Perhaps, however, it is not quite true to say Superman was created for comic-books. Two college boys in

Ohio, Jerome Siegel the would-be writer and Joseph Shuster the tyro cartoonist, got together to write and draw their own home-made fantasy magazine. In No.3 of their monthly *Science Fiction: The Advance Guard of Future Civilization* dated January 1933, appeared "The Reign of the Superman", written by Jerry, illustrated by Joe. The concept of futuristic supermen intrigued them, and the following year Jerry scripted out the first Superman strips for Joe to draw. Their idea was to run it as a daily strip for newspapers, but every syndicate they tried rejected it as "too fantastic". Not so the comic-books.

Siegel and Shuster had been into comic-books from almost the beginning, turning out "Henri Duval, Famed Soldier of Fortune" for *New Fun* (October 1935), and changing their names to Leger and Reuths' for "Dr Occult the Ghost Detective" in

the next issue. This strip was important, not only for the fantasy element
dear to the creators' hearts, but for one
story which had Doc as a prototype
superhero, cloaked and flying through
the air. The second super-step was
taken in their serial, "Federal Men",
in *New Adventure Comics* (January
1937), which featured a Federal Agent
of the future called Jor-L! There was
a good deal of fistic action in their
"Slam Bradley" series for *Detective
Comics*, too, and when publisher
Harry Donenfield decided to launch a
new title in the wake of his successful
Detective, Jerry and Joe mailed in their
much-rejected Superman strips. The
package was opened by Sheldon
Mayer, the only staff art assistant.
Mayer, another young veteran of the
same comic-books (he drew the
delightful "Scribbly", the adventures
of a boy cartoonist), loved the oversize
heroics and persuaded the less impressed Max Gaines to buy it. For his
pains, Mayer was given the task of cut-
ting up the strips and pasting them
into comic-book proportions. Shuster
was commissioned to draw one new
picture, the cover, and, despite
Donenfield's objections that it was
ridiculous, *Action Comics* No.1 was
published, with its classic image of
Superman smashing up a car. "Flash!
Here's a New Magazine You Can't
Afford to Miss!" yelled the first advertisement – today it is the magazine you
can't afford to buy! A mint copy, ten
cents then, is listed at $14,000 in the
current *Comic Book Price Guide*.

With Superman (duly followed by
Superboy, Supergirl, and the rest) the
American comic-book was "Up, Up
and Away!"

Action Comics *No.1* © *June 1938
Detective Comics/Famous First
Edition facsimile* © *1974 National
Periodicals. Drawn by Joe Shuster*
Superman *No.1* © *Summer 1939
Detective Comics/Famous First
Edition facsimile* © *1978 DC Comics.
Drawn by Joe Shuster*

Superman *No.100* © *September 1955
National Comics*
Superman Annual *No.7* © *Summer
1963 National Periodicals*
Superman *No.207* © *July 1968
National Periodicals*
Action Comics *No.500* © *October
1979 DC Comics. Drawn by Ross
Andru and Dick Giordano*

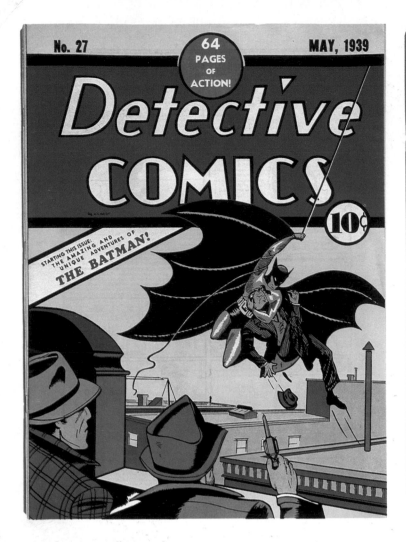

BATMAN AND THE BOY WONDER

"The Case of the Chemical Syndicate" was its title, and it appeared in No.27 of *Detective Comics*, dated May 1939. A black, vampiric silhouette posed behind the legend: "The Bat-Man, mysterious and adventurous figure, fighting for righteousness and apprehending the wrong-doer, in his lone battle against the evil forces of society. His identity remains unknown." But not to those kids who gulped, took another bite of their O-Henry bars, and dared to read on. For within a page or so Commissioner Gordon's young socialite friend, Bruce Wayne, is "lashing out with a terrific right" at one killer, grabbing a second "in a deadly headlock", and before a third can cry the traditional "What th'...?", socks a fourth into an acid tank. "A grim smile comes to his lips"; about all of the playboy readily identifiable, for the rest of him wears the black-and-blue mask, cloak and super-suit forever to strike terror into the heart of the underworld. Yes, wastrel Wayne is also "The Batman", created by Bob Kane in answer to

editor Vincent Sullivan's plea for a follow-up to Superman.

Kane, an ex-animator from Max Fleischer's studio, was brought up on Betty Boop cartoons, and more at home with the funny animal he had created for Jerry Iger's *Wags*, "Peter Pupp", than with heroics. Bob frankly admits his early Batman artwork showed his comedy leanings. Equally frankly, he admits he would have been happier had his career followed his personal preference for the funny side of art. But when Sullivan told him Siegel and Shuster were making $800 a week with Superman, Bob quickly changed his attitude!

In his New York batpartment, Bob told me how he created Batman "I took the Superman figure and traced over different costumes. I remembered a book I read when I was 12 years old. It showed Leonardo da Vinci's sketches of a flying machine, a man with skeleton bat-wings. His phrase was, 'And your bird shall have no other wings than that of a bat.' Douglas Fairbanks Senior was my ideal as a

kid. I got Batman's dual identity idea from his *Mark of Zorro.*" To help write the scripts, Bob brought in an old school chum called Bill Finger. Bob calls him "the Cecil B. De Mille of the comics – he always built his stories around some giant prop, the Statue of Liberty or an outsize sewing-machine!" Batman caught on, and Bob, taking a break at a resort, ran into a skinny college kid wearing a cartoonily decorated painter's jacket. Who drew the cartoons? "I did," said the kid, and Jerry Robinson (today a leading cartoonist) was promptly signed on as Bob's first assistant. Jerry assisted in the birth of Batman's own first assistant, Robin (named after Robin Hood) the Boy Wonder, and his most permanent opponent, The Joker. This character, the original super-villain, who "smiles a smile without mirth, a smile of death, the awesome ghastly grin of The Joker", made his devilish debut in No.1 of *Batman Comics*, a quarterly which began in Spring 1940. Batman, with us still through television series, cartoons, movies and, of course, comics, continues to hold second place to Superman.

Max Gaines, currently publishing *All-American Comics* (No.1 April 1939), having been instrumental in *Action Comics*' acquisition of Superman, introduced his own superhero in No.8 (November), "Gary Concord – Ultraman!" Two months later he put out No.1 of *Flash Comics* (January 1940), starring "The Flash – Fastest Man Alive". "Faster than the streak of the lightning in the sky . . . swifter than the speed of light itself . . . fleeter than the rapidity of thought . . ." and, as drawn by Harry Lampert, sillier-looking than any other superhero . . . except, perhaps, "Johnny Thunderbolt", who, with the elegant, winged "Hawkman", helped pad out the comic-book. Were three superheroes too many for one comic? Not if *All Star Comics* (No.1 Summer 1940) was anything to go by. For here, in one 68-page book, were assembled the Flash, Hawkman, Sandman, Spectre, Ultraman, Biff Bronson and Red, White and Blue! But No.3 was the real killer: in it was held the first meeting of the Justice Society of America, a whole clubroom of superheroes: "Gathered are the Mightiest Champions of Right and Justice in the World! The Roll Call: the Flash, the Hawkman, the Spectre, the Sandman, Doctor Fate, the Hour Man, the Green Lantern and the Atom!" The centre-spread was a panoramic advertisement for all the current comic-books issued under the DC (Detective Comics) emblem, and every one of them starred at least one superhero: *Flash Comics* with Flash and Hawkman; *All-American Comics* with The Green Lantern; *Adventure Comics* with Sandman; *More Fun Comics* with Spectre; *Action Comics* with Superman; *Detective Comics* with Batman. The superheroes had arrived!

Detective Comics No.27 © May 1939 Detective Comics/Famous First Edition facsimile © 1974 National Periodicals. Drawn by Bob Kane Batman No.1 © Spring 1940 Detective Comics/Famous First Edition facsimile © 1975 National Periodicals. Drawn by Bob Kane

Flash Comics No.1 © January 1940/Famous First Edition facsimile © 1975 National Periodicals All Star Comics No.3 © Winter 1940 All-American/Famous First Edition facsimile © 1975 National Periodicals

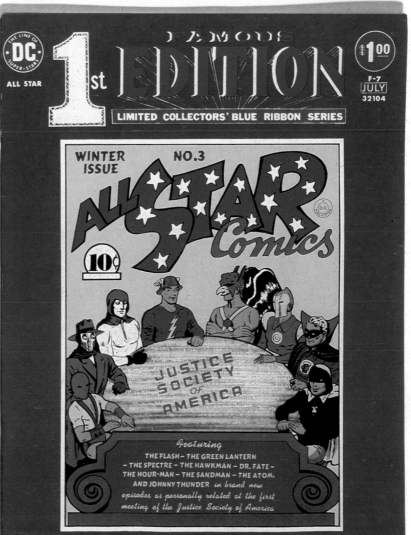

THE SUPERHEROES TAKE OVER

"Flash! Boys and Girls – Do you want one of the Masked Marvel's Red Masks?" Uncle Joe (Joseph Hardie, boss of Centaur comics) asked the question in the July 1939 issue of *Keen Detective Funnies*. He was offering the gimmick in return for opinions on "The Masked Marvel", the company's first superhero. Drawn by Ben Thompson, the super-sleuth donned a red mask as disguise, but it failed to hide his receding hairline. The first, but not the last, hero in comics to bear the name of Marvel, he led a trio of ex-G-men known only as ZR, ZY and ZL. They wore green masks; one was bald. The Masked Marvel flew an amphibious plane, made his HQ in a glass-topped mountain, and on occasion exercised inexplicable super-powers, like jumping up the stairs. Centaur's second superman was "The Fantom of the Fair". Inspired by the Phantom of the Opera, this totally

mysterious, black-clad, red-cloaked muscle-man swung around the New York World's Fair catching crooks, then dragged them screaming to his underground torture-chamber. Fantom made his debut by crashing through a glass roof into *Amazing Mystery Funnies* in July 1939. Closer to Batman than Superman, the link is more than on the surface, for Fantom's creator, Paul Gustafson, like Batman's Bob Kane, had hitherto been known as a funny artist.

Centaur's next superhero was the aptly named but oddly conceived "Speed Centaur". Drawn by Malcolm Kildale, this mythical survivor of a far north holocaust became the four-legged friend of an aged publisher who trained him to be a Crusader Against Crime. Speed made his debut in August 1939 and one month later came Centaur's first all-superhero comic-book, *Amazing-Man Comics*. "Amazing-Man", known as Aman for short, was an orphan raised in Tibet by the Council of Seven, endowed with the benefits of Kindness, Tolerance and Bravery. In a series of tests to see if he is ready to set forth into the outside world, Aman wins a tug-o-war with an elephant, bites the head off an attacking cobra, and survives a knife thrown through his throat by the Lady Zina. Finally he has to answer "one thousand diversified questions involving the languages of all the civilized and uncivilized countries". Fortunately for slow readers, this test was taken as read. Arriving in the outside world at last, uniformed in a blue serge suit and tril-by, Aman uses his will-power to save the President's train from falling down a ravine. The artist was Bill Everett. In a packed 68-page programme, No.1 also presented "The Cat Man" by Tarpé Mills, "The Iron Skull" by Carl Burgos, John Kolb's "Minimidget the Miniature Man", and Martin Filchock's "Mighty Man". Centaur wound up 1939 by introducing Paul Gustafson's hooded Robinhood, "The Arrow", in *Funny Pages*.

"The Blue Beetle", who arrived in No.1 of *Mystery Men Comics* (August 1939), was destined for a long life, although he would first need to develop powers and costume a little more super than seen here. In his debut strip, Patrolman Dan Garret simply pops on goggles and a snappy blue suit

to solve a crime. Front-of-the-book hero was Walter Friehm's "The Green Mask", whose true identity "must remain a secret until society is purged of crime". We will never know. *Mystery Men* was a comic-book created by Will Eisner for Victor Fox of Fox Features, a curious combination of the best and the worst in comic-books. Eisner's touch is also very apparent in No.1 of *Speed Comics* (October 1939), which introduced "Shock Gibson the Human Dynamo". Drawn by Maurice Scott, scientist Charles Gibson is experimenting with electrical and chemical forces when a bolt of lightning strikes his mountain top laboratory. To the amazement of Dr Blitzer, Gibson survives, bends a piece of steel, and throws it aside. "The lightning plus something in those chemicals did it!" deduces the doctor. "You have the power to change the world! Now go!" Charles goes, changes his name and clothes, and in next to no time is thwarting Baron Von Kampf's mad plot to conquer America with a death ray and one-eyed green zombies.

The year 1939 ended on a big note with the smallest superhero of them all. "Doll Man" ("Darrell Dane, a young scientist, possesses vast powers which enable him to become the dynamic Doll Man"), another Will Eisner creation, first shrank to five-inch height in the December issue of *Feature Comics* (No.27); it was the start of a 12-year career.

Pep Comics *No.1* © *January 1940 MLJ Magazines (facsimile). Drawn by Irving Novick*
Mystery Men Comics *No.1* © *August 1939 Fox Features. Drawn by Lou Fine*
Speed Comics *No.1* © *October 1939 Brookwood*
Amazing Mystery Funnies © *July 1939 Centaur. Drawn by Paul Gustafson*
Amazing Man Comics *No.1* © *September 1939 Centaur. Drawn by William Everett*
Hyper Mystery Comics *No.1* © *May 1940 Hyper*
Super-Mystery Comics *No.1* © *July 1940 Ace Magazines*
Black Terror *No.1* © *1942 Nedor*
Cat-Man Comics *No.1* © *May 1941 Helnit. Drawn by Charles Quinlan*

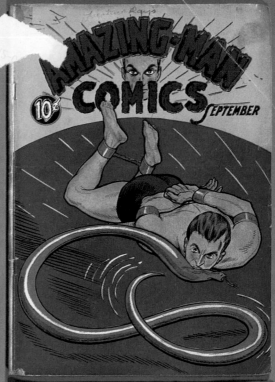

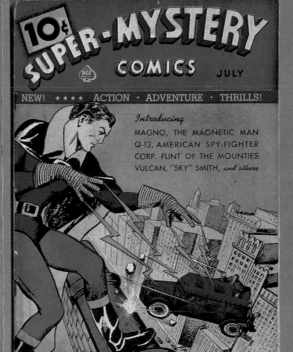

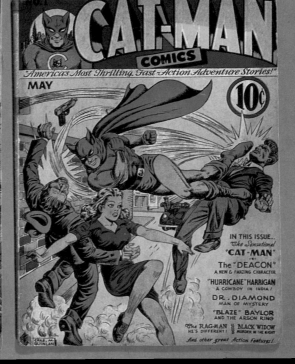

SUPERHEROES:
Into the Forties

The Marvel Age (as opposed to the Captain Marvel Age) of the superhero began in late 1939 when Martin Goodman published No.1 of *Marvel Comics*. Actually it began earlier in the year when Bill Everett drew the first adventure of "Sub-Mariner" for No.1 of *Motion Picture Funnies Weekly*, a promotional project that misfired. When Funnies Inc, a studio team formed by the first editor of *New Fun*, Lloyd Jacquet, talked pulp publisher Goodman into the comic-book business, Everett's Sub-Mariner was dusted off as lead feature. Everett, being the art editor of Funnies Inc, made sure of that! The underwater super-hero was in reality Prince Namor, "the much-feared and respected pheno-menon from the Antarctic Icelands", given to crying such fishy oaths as "Holy mackerel!" Also in that first of the Marvel comics was a hot number called "The Human Torch", created by a chap from Chesler's old studio, Carl Burgos, but in the strip itself created by Professor Horton. "I've been working on a synthetic man, an exact replica of a human being. In this airtight glass case lives my creation. I call him the Human Torch!" Acc-identally freed to roam the world and right wrongs, Torch cries, "I'm burn-ing alive! Why must everything I touch turn to flame?" Given his own comic-book, Torch was also given his personal Boy Wonder, Toro the teenage fire-eater. The Human Torch and Sub-Mariner quickly established themselves as Marvel Comics' top heroes, or possibly anti-heroes, for their fame rests on a fabulous series of battles fought out through their early comic-books. No.6 of *The Human Torch* is headlined "60 Thrilling Pages of the Human Torch fighting the Sub-Mariner in a Life and Death Struggle!" The first of this series was devised, scripted and drawn over one long weekend.

The first MLJ comic-book was the first of the new decade. The publishers, who were to discover teenagers and change their name to Archie Comics, began with super-heroes. *Pep Comics* No.1 (January) introduced "The Shield" (Joe Hig-gins, G-Man Extraordinary), whose bullet-proof, flame-proof uniform gave him "the speed of a bullet and the strength of Hercules. The four white stars on the field of blue signify to what he has devoted his life: Truth, Justice, Patriotism and Courage." Second fiddle was "The Comet": John Dickering discovers a gas 50 times lighter than hydrogen, injects it into his bloodstream, and in consequence makes great leaps and finds, when he crosses his eyes, beams from them make objects disintegrate! ("Puff! ... There goes my test-tube rack!") Funny? Well, the artist was Jack Cole, the brilliant cartoonist from Chesler's *Star Ranger*, who would in a year create the most perfect blend of fan-tastic adventure and comedy ever in a comic-book superhero, "Plastic Man" (*Police Comics* August 1941).

The second MLJ Magazine was *Zip Comics*, starring "Steel Sterling, the Man of Steel". John Sterling, to avenge his father's murder, covers his body with chemicals, dives into a tank of molten steel, and survives as "a man with the resistance, the magnetism and the strength of steel!" Next came "The Scarlet Avenger", who was not unlike DC's "Crimson Avenger", who was not unlike Harvey's "Green Hor-net". Followed by "Kalthar the Giant Man of the Jungle", who was not far different from Marvel's "Ka-Zar of the Jungle", who was not far different from "Tarzan the Ape Man". Then came "Zambini the Magician", who bore a faint resemblance to DC's "Zatara the Magician", who bore a faint resemblance to "Mandrake the Magician". Did anyone notice? Did anyone care? Certainly not the fast-growing breed of comic-book readers. Never had 10 cents bought so much fun! To read the front-page listings is almost enough: "The Sensational Cat-Man!" ... "Hurricane Harrigan!" ... "Dr Diamond, Man of Mystery!" ... "Blaze Baylor and the Arson Ring!" ... "The Rag-Man – He's Different!" ... "Black Widow!" ... "Strongman the Perfect Human!" ... "Sub-Zeroman!" ... "Sergeant Spook!" ... "Superhorse!" ... "Tornado Tom the Human Whirlwind!" ... "Volton the Human Generator!" ... "Hercules the Strongest Man in the World!" ... "Neon the Unknown!" ... "The Strange Twins!" ...

Zip Comics No.1 © February 1940 MLJ. Drawn by Charles Biro
Crash Comics No.1 © May 1940 Tem. Drawn by Scotty Walters
America's Best Comics No.1 © February 1942 Better Publications

The Human Torch No.1 © Fall 1940 Timely (facsimile)
Blue Bolt No.1 © June 1940 Novelty Press/Funnies Inc. Drawn by Joe Simon
Pep Comics No.1 © January 1940 MLJ. Drawn by Irving Novick
Hit Comics No.1 © July 1940 Comic Magazines. Drawn by Lou Fine
Doll Man Quarterly No.1 © Autumn 1941 Quality Comics (facsimile)
Plastic Man No.1 © 1943 Vital Publications (facsimile). Drawn by Jack Cole

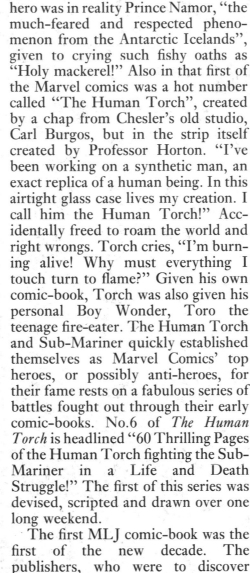

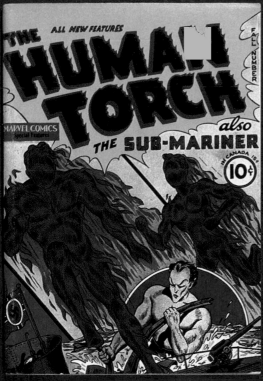

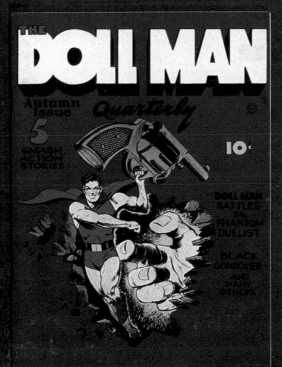

SHAZAM! The World's Mightiest Mortal

Whiz Comics proudly presents the World's Mightiest Man – Powerful Champion of Justice – Relentless Enemy of Evil – Captain Marvel!

"The World's Mightiest Mortal", as he was soon to be redubbed, had narrowly missed being called Captain Thunder. At the last minute, the pilot issue of *Whiz Comics* No.1 was cancelled, rejigged, and published as *Whiz Comics* No.2 (thus thoroughly foxing future comic-book collectors!). It was February 1940 and with it was born the future Fawcett Publications line of comic-books which would quickly grow to challenge, equal, but never quite top, the originals, DC.

William H. Fawcett had founded his magazine empire on the strength of a pocket-sized gagbook filled with "smokehouse stories", a World War One offshoot called *Captain Billy's Whizbang*. When editor Bill Parker was moved from movie mags to initiate the new comic-book, he contrived echoes of the company's origins: *Captain* Marvel – *Billy* Batson – *Whiz* Comics. The first issue was the usual parade of adventure heroes: "Ibis the Invincible" was an Egyptian magician (echoes of "Zatara"), "Golden Arrow" a western avenger (shades of "Lone Ranger"), "Spy Smasher" a cloaked airman, "Scoop Smith" a reporter, "Lance O'Casey" a sailor of fortune, and "Dan Dare" a private dick. All had counterparts in other comic-books, and so had their lead hero, "Captain Marvel" – or so

DC Comics, publishers of *Superman*, would soon claim in a court battle that would last for a decade. *Whiz*'s original cover, with Captain Marvel casually tossing a car to the left, certainly drew inspiration from *Action Comics'* cover with Superman about to chuck a car to the right. Otherwise, super-strength apart, "the Big Red Cheese", as he came to be called in affection, was quite a different concept. He was an orphan newsboy, Billy Batson, who magically turned into Captain Marvel whenever he shouted his magic word "Shazam!", whereas Superman was an alien from another planet who disguised himself as an adult Earthman. However, after much expensive legal wrangling, Fawcett threw in the towel and promised never to do it again. By that time, comic-books and super-heroes were on the decline anyway, – but in his mighty heyday, *Captain Marvel Adventures* sold in millions and was the first American comic-book published every other week.

C. C. Beck was the cartoonist who fashioned the Captain and whose simple, clean, and mildly humorous style made him so popular with younger fans. Quite a different style of drawing was used for "Captain Marvel Jr", the first spin-off series which started in *Whiz Comics* No.25 (December 1941). Mac Raboy favoured the illustrative techniques of Alex Raymond (and indeed would ultimately take over that artist's "Flash Gordon" strip), and his gracefully flying boy decorated some of the most striking covers in comic-

books. Junior was in reality crippled newsboy Freddy Freeman who attained super-powers by shouting the name of his hero, "Captain Marvel!"

Mary Marvel, next to arrive, was Billy's long-lost twin who found the original magic word, "Shazam", worked for her, too. However, the word's actual meaning had changed sex, too. For Billy it stood for the wisdom of Solomon, the strength of Hercules, the stamina of Atlas, the power of Zeus, the courage of Achilles, and the speed of Mercury. For Mary it meant the grace of Selena, the strength of Hippolyta, the skill of Ariadne, the fleetness of Zephyra, the beauty of Aurora, the wisdom of Minerva. Mary, drawn by Jack Binder, appeared both in *Wow Comics* and her own title. All three got together in *Marvel Family Comics* (December 1945), along with the fraudulent but lovable Uncle Marvel.

The final issue of *The Marvel Family*, No.89, dated January 1954, had the most prophetic cover in comics. The marvellous threesome appeared as black silhouettes, while an onlooker commented, "Holey Moley! What happened to the Marvel Family?" The lead story was entitled "And Then There Were None!" But Captain Marvel proved indeed to be the World's Mightiest Mortal: he survived even the United States Supreme Court! Out of copyright, MF Enterprises revived him (in name only) in April 1966. Then Marvel Comics did the same in May 1968. Finally DC, who legally owned the original character, brought him back in February 1973, drawn once again by good old C. C. Beck. Like the Marvel man said, "Holy Moley!"

CAPTAIN MARVEL JR. SINKS THE JAPS!

WONDER WOMEN AND SUPERGIRLS

Superman and the Supermen were not going to have comic-books all their own way for long, not if Max Gaines had any say in the matter. And as the man who had spotted the potential but missed the copyright in Superman, he was determined to be the first in the field with a superheroine, someone for the girls. After all, the macho masculinity of the supermen was basically appealing to boys; girls had dimes to spend too! He called in Dr William Moulton Marston, one of his Editorial Advisory Board. The doctor was billed as "Member of the American Psychological Association and Fellow of the American Association for the Advancement of Science". Under the pen-name of Charles Moulton he came up with a concept inspired by mythology and female psychology, and his first script appeared in *All Star Comics* No.8 (December 1941) illustrated by Harry Peter. Peter had a curving line that looked decidedly wrong for "Fearless Flint the Flint-Man" in *Famous Funnies*, but was definitely right for this lady. "At last, in a world torn by the hatreds and wars of men, appears a woman to whom the problems and feats of men are mere childsplay. With a hundred times the agility and strength of our best male athletes and strongest wrestlers, she appears as though from nowhere to avenge an injustice or right a wrong. As lovely as Aphrodite, as wise as Athena, with the speed of Mercury and the strength of Hercules, she is known only as *Wonder Woman!*"

And so Diana, daughter of Hippolyte, Queen of the Amazons on Paradise Island, became Wonder Woman, leaping across from *All Star* to become the leading lady of *Sensation Comics* No.1 (January 1942), pausing briefly to swap her star-spangled skirt for flappy culottes. Having saved and fallen for Captain Steve Trevor, a plane-crashed pilot, she returns him to Washington in her invisible airplane and poses as Diana Prince, bespectacled nurse, to conceal her super-qualities and "best the world's most villainous men at their

own game". Much dissected for her psychological undertones and sexological overtones, Wonder Woman is today seen as a fabulous forerunner of the feminist movement.

"Black Fury", shortly to change her name to "Miss Fury", was not only the first superheroine in the newspapers (her debut on 6 April 1941 predates Wonder Woman's by eight months) she was the first, and remains the only, to be actually drawn by a woman, Tarpé Mills. Her early one-off horror strip, "The Vampire" (*Amazing Mystery Funnies* February 1939), showed a taste for the macabre, as Sicilian girls are sucked dry of blood by an ex-college professor with filed teeth. Ms Mills followed through with her first continuing hero, "Daredevil Barry Flynn" (April), who is imprisoned by the dark and lovely Dacia, daughter of mad Dr Zaroff. His experiments in creating an amphibious race have resulted in Frogga, whom Dacia keeps at bay with her whip: "You fiendish-looking monstrosity. Get out of here or I'll give you another taste of the lash!" Whips, spiky heels, branding irons and the like were regular features of Miss Fury's arsenal in her fight against spies, interpolated between delightful studies of her "real self", wealthy socialite Marla Drake at her toilette.

"Black Cat", known as both "Hollywood's Glamorous Detective Star" and "The Darling of the Comics since 1941", also had an alter ego, Linda Turner, America's Sweetheart of the Screen. Originally drawn for the unsuccessful experiment *Pocket Comics* No.1 (August 1941) by Al

Gabriele, the red-headed heroine reached her attractive apogee during the six-year span by artist Lee Elias.

"Phantom Lady" was actually Sandra Knight, a senator's daughter. She started life in *Police Comics* No.1 (August 1941), but it is from her revival period for Fox Features, who gave her her own title from August 1947, that her true notoriety stems. Armed with not much more than her breasts, loosely covered by a backless halter, she knocked out the mere males of the underworld and gave comic-book critic Dr Frederic Wertham nightmares. Her latter day artist was Matt Baker, one of the few unsung Negro cartoonists to make a career out of comic work.

"Moon Girl and the Prince" were unusual in that they fought side by side as a man/woman team, or rather, woman/man. She was described as "a woman of sensational strength, superhuman speed, and surpassing loveliness," he as "one of the greatest athletes of all time, true son of Hercules." No man could match him; only Moon Girl, when she chose to use her Magic Moonstone! The comic, one of the Gaines EC group, changed title to *Moon Girl* from No.2. It became *Moon Girl Fights Crime* from No.7, then *A Moon, A Girl... Romance* from No.9. No.13 became *Weird Fantasy*. Not, it seems, a success.

The obvious opposite to Superman was Supergirl, and she (Kara from Krypton, Superman's cousin, alias Linda Lee from Midvale Orphanage) hurtled to earth and *Action Comics* in May 1959. Nobody but a copyright lawyer would confuse her with D. C.

THE SUPERHEROES ARE ABROAD!

Superman may have been quick to take off in the United States, but he was slow off the mark as far as the rest of the English-speaking world was concerned; partly due to bad timing – outside the USA the world went to war in 1939 – partly due to the strong and long-standing traditions of juvenile publishing. Staid, middle-aged editors found the superhero concept too fantastic to accept, although young readers lucky enough to be on the end of a lease-lend operation, and later near to one of Uncle Sam's GI PXs (Postal Exchanges), thought rather differently. Copies of *Action Comics* and *Superman*, dished out generously with the "gum, chum", quickly became gold-dust in the comic-swapping game.

In Australia, the import restrictions on American comic-books came into force in July 1940. Immediately local publishers began to issue native comic-books on the American pattern, but for economic reasons only the cover was in colour. The first was *Jimmy Rodney on Secret Service* (1940), drawn by Tony Rafty and published by New South Wales Bookstall. Many more followed, including *Dr Mensana* (1941), the first Australian superhero. Drawn by Tom Hubble, the doctor had developed two kinds of pill. One, the "S+", rapidly increased his muscles so that he became the "Samson of Science". The other, "M+", did the same, but only to his head! This gave him telepathic powers to probe men's minds. After an hour of either, the effect wore off and he shrank back to being a puny weakling. The idea was original, but as illustrated by Hubble, laughable, and set back the cause of the superhero until after the war, when reprints of the American originals became possible once more.

Captain Atom, "the Original Atoman", made his down-under debut in January 1948. Arthur Mather drew the full colour heroics of Dr Rador, who had only to utter the magic word "Exenor" to change places with his twin brother, Bikini, alias Atoman. This complicated concept did not seem to worry Australian boys, over 75,000 of whom dubbed up their shillings to join the Captain Atom Club and wear the Handsome, Gleaming, Plated Ring that by night

Glows with a Mysterious Blue Fire!

Captain Power (1949) although bang in the comic-book style (he and his brother Atommy flew with Buck Rogers-style Atojets, disappeared with Bela Lugosi-style Invisibility Belts, and saw through walls with Superman-style X-ray Goggles), was originally a newspaper strip. Stanley Pitt, Australia's answer to Alex Raymond, drew the Captain as a weekly half-page for the *Sunday Herald*, and they were gathered into oblong comic-books, a format so popular it was almost Australian standard. *Jet Fury* (1949) was drawn for this $10\frac{3}{4}$ by $7\frac{1}{2}$ inch format, originally as a back-up strip for a detective comic called *Michael Chance*. Jet was so popular, and so well drawn, that he took over the title. The artist was Jaroslav ("Larry") Horak, born in Manchuria of Russian and Czechoslovakian parents, a naturalized Australian who did his most famous work in England, the newspaper strip of "James Bond". Jet Fury was secretly Randolph "Randy" Gray, wealthy aircraft designer, who kept his amazing plane "The Comet" in a secret hangar above his penthouse. *Crimson Comet* (1948) was a creation of John Dixon, the "Air Hawk" artist and the best comic-book man Aussie ever produced. Ralph Rivers, a weak-looking fellow in his dark glasses, trenchcoat, and hunchback, is really something else: "Ralph peels off his outer garments and false hump, stretches his great wings, and

with a mighty swish, soars into the clear blue sky as ... The Crimson Comet!" His comic-book was oblong, but the hinges were at the top! *Catman*, also by Dixon, was originally the American superhero. When the reprints rights ran out, the comic was so popular that the publishers hired Dixon to continue the character.

Powerman (1975), the first African superhero, was produced in England but sold only in Nigeria. The adventures of this superhuman ("A bolt of lightning struck him when he was a child and gave him his special powers") represents the early comic work of Dave Gibbons, later to take on "Dan Dare" and "Dr Who".

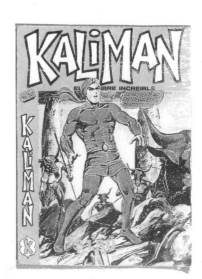

No. 32

THE ORIGINAL ATOMAN! - MYSTERY! - ADVENTURE!

CAPTAIN
ATOM

WORLD FAMOUS
COMIC

6d

An ATLAS Publication

The CRIMSON COMET

Nº4

COMIC

6d

BY JOHN DIXON

CAPTAIN POWER
COMIC

4D.

"LORD of the HURRICANES" and "TERROR from the EAST"

No. 23

CATMAN

15c

Jet FURY

6D COMIC

Michael CHANCE No 16

CANADA: Superheroes and the Gold Rush

Canada, like Australia, was a loyal outpost of the British Empire. Its sons were brought up on a strict diet of British comics, thanks to such export agencies as Gordon and Gotch. To make the business worthwhile, penny comics were doubled up, one inside the other, and issued with special Overseas Edition headings at five cents a time: *Comic Cuts and Chips*; *Funny Wonder and Jester*. Anglophile families preferred their offspring to read the mother language rather than the imported Americanisms of the new comic-books. Came September 1939 and the war, and in due course the War Exchange Conservation Act of 6 December 1940. The importation of American comic-books, considered a waste of precious dollars by the adults in charge, was banned. Enterprising entrepreneurs saw the sudden gap in the market caused by the vanished comic-books and quickly geared themselves to fill it. And so was born the short-lived but splendid era of the Canadian comic-book. *Triumph Adventure Comics* was the first, dated August 1941. It was produced by Hillborough Studios of Toronto under the supervision of a Welsh emigrant, Adrian Darley Dingle. For his comic-book Dingle created Canada's first superhero, or rather, superheroine. "Nirvana of the Northern Lights", a mythical beauty, was the daughter of King Koliak the Mighty. She used the magical powers of the Aurora Borealis to thwart the evil Ether People.

One month later came *Wow Comics* No.1, a title cheerfully swiped from the Fawcett comic-book which was now banned from Canada. *Wow* was published by Bell Features, the brothers Cyril and Gene who produced posters for the local Toronto streetcars. One of their staff artists, Edmund Legault, had ambitions to draw a newspaper strip, and it was his rejected samples that the Bell brothers cut up and used for their first comic, "Dart Daring, Daredevil Master Swordsman". As back-up, Legault quickly whipped up "Whiz Wallace", a Yankee Navy flier science-fictionally transported to the Invisible Planet. The second Bell book, *Active Comics* (this time the title was a side-swipe from DC's forbidden *Action*) arrived

in February 1942. Although Fred Kelly's "Active Jim", a sports hero, took the lead, he was backed up by "The Brain", Leo Bachle's masked and moustached muscle-man, and "Thunderfist", the Electric-Fisted Champion of Right who was really Randy King, Ace Reporter. Tedd Steele's drawings were as fast-moving as his brush, and he also supplied "Speed Savage" in *Triumph* and "Woody and the Wolf" in *Wow*. This sent up the whole genre, including himself, as heroic comic-book artist Woody Wilkins dons a tatty animal skin to fight crime as his own comic-book superhero, "The Wolf". Bell's *Dime Comics* (No.1 February 1942) starred Jerry Lazare's "Nitro" and the oddest superhero of the lot, a combination called "Major Domo and Jo-Jo" by Armand. Jo-Jo was a legless dwarf who rode on the back of the armless Domo, disguised together as a hunchbacked giant. *Joke Comics*, introduced as an all-funny comic in March 1942, soon found it needed a superhero to survive. Jerry Lazare filled the breech with "The Wing", a lovely lady in cloak and tights.

Bell did not have this profitable new field to themselves for long. The Anglo-American Publishing Co of Toronto soon began releasing their "Double-A" brand comics. AA had entered the business as repackagers of the forbidden fruit of Fawcett comics: they hired Canadian artists to redraw the American comics for black-and-white printing, apparently a loophole in the law. Now they began to produce original comics of their own, in a tight "house style" very different from the free and easy pages of Bell. A high standard of scripting was maintained through the use of Ted McCall, an experienced newspaper strip man ("Men of the Mounties", etc). McCall created an original superhero in *Freelance*, who wore a big L on his chest and worked with a piratical partner called Big John. Freelance was drawn by Ed Furness, whose style was virtually indistinguishable from the other AA artists. He may, or may not, have drawn "Commander Steel of the International Police Service" for *Grand Slam Comics*. This, like others in the AA line, was printed in full colour, a treat the other Canadian comics seldom knew.

The best Canadian comics came from Vancouver, where the Maple Leaf Co under editor Ted Ross and production director John St Ables produced as stylish a series as any ever issued. Maple Leaf began with *Better Comics* (1943), and they certainly were. Although following the now standard Canadian format of coloured cover and black-and-white interior, here was none of the hasty crudity so typical of the Bell books. St Ables rejected the usual poster effects of red, yellow and blue for unusual oranges and greens, laid with a variety of tints. His interior pages also used variegated dot tints for added effects, making a virtue of their economic monochrome. *Better* featured St Ables' own superhero, "Brok Windsor", and "Quest of the Solar Star" with spaceman Lon Martin, drawn by Bill Benz. The other Maple Leaf comics concentrated on comedy and adventure, save for *Rocket Comics*. This led off with the science-fiction saga of "Cosmo and his White Magic", an undersea science-fiction saga by Spike Brown.

Brilliant as the best of the Canadian comics were, and entertaining as they all were, they were unable to survive the postwar relaxation of restrictions which brought back the all-conquering Yankee supermen. An attempted Canadian comeback with Comely Comix' *Captain Canuck* (1975) has also failed, despite unusually good colour.

Freelance Comics *No.33* © *August 1946 Anglo-American Publishing. Drawn by Ed Furness*
Grand Slam Comics *No.54* © *August 1946 Anglo-American Publishing*
Better Comics *No.38* © *October 1946 Maple Leaf Publishing. Drawn by Jon St Ables*

Active Comics *No.28* © *1946 Bell Features. Drawn by Adrian Dingle*
Wow Comics *No.28* © *1946 Bell Features. Drawn by Adrian Dingle*
Triumph Comics *No.31* © *1946 Bell Features. Drawn by Adrian Dingle*
Joke Comics *No.18* © *1946 Bell Features. Drawn by Adrian Dingle*
Speed Savage Comics *No.1* © *October 1946 Associated Newspapers. Drawn by Tedd Steele*
Captain Canuck *No.1* © *July 1975 Comely Comix. Drawn by Richard Comely*

SUPERMAN OF THE WORLD

Superman took a little over a year to fly across the Atlantic to Britain. He landed on the front cover of *Triumph* No.772 on 5 August 1939, looking a little worse for the trip. Superman's sea-change was due to his anatomy being a little beyond the ken of his first British illustrator, John "Jock" McCail. Jock was an old hand at drawing heroes for both story papers and adventure strips: his "Duke, Dan and Darky" was currently running on the back page of *Comic Cuts*. But British comic heroes were realistic and not given to what was known as "Yankee exaggeration", and thus the Man of Steel's well-developed anatomy and simplified face-structure were conspicuously absent from his British debut. But inside *Triumph* all was well; genuine Superman strips filled the four middle pages, 48 panels of "the World's Most Wonderful Picture Serial", as the Editor described it. He called Superman "a Fighter for the Right", "a Rescuer of the Oppressed", and "a Foe to the Criminal", and had pasted up his pages from the Siegel and Shuster daily strip which had begun its run in American newspapers on 16 January 1939. (Curious to consider that Siegel and Shuster had created Superman as a newspaper strip, cut it up for No.1 of *Action Comics* after failing to sell it, then produced another daily strip for syndication, and had that cut up for a British comic!) Superman became so popular that another *Action Comics* hero, Fred Guardineer's "Zatara the Magician", was added to *Triumph*. But all too soon Britain was at war and *Triumph* closed. It was not until 1959 that Superman reappeared in a British weekly; his television series won him a place in *Radio Fun*. Ten years later Mick Anglo edited *Super DC*, a monthly comic pasting up Superman, Superboy, Batman, Jimmy Olsen and Lois Lane strips into acceptably British comic format. Another decade passed before Vanessa Morgan edited Superman, Batman and Wonder Woman comics into *The Superheroes Monthly* (1980). Once again a British artist was used for the cover, but 40 years on from Jock McCail, Alan Craddock was better able to cope (airbrush and all). In Australia, *Superman*, *Batman* and *Super Adventure Comic*, a title featuring both, were best-sellers in the standard post-war comic-book format. This meant coloured covers and black-and-white interiors, but for a while some issues sported full colour throughout. Also for a while there was an English edition (by Atlas) of the Australian edition (by K. G. Murray) of the American edition (by DC Comics). Australia also did curious things to their Fawcett reprints, turning *Captain Marvel* and company into oblong books, printing four pages to a spread.

The Marvel Comics superheroes began to infiltrate British comics in the Sixties. Odhams Press, who had lost the rights to *Mickey Mouse*, started a new comic called *Wham* in 1964. The original intention was to produce a super-*Beano*, and Odhams lured away that comic's top artist, Leo Baxendale, to design and create a new crew of characters. The comic was a great success, but after two years in crashed Marvel Comics' supergroup, The Fantastic Four. In 1967 came The Thing. *Smash*, a companion comic to *Wham* launched in 1966, started to run Batman, then added a trio of Marvels in The Incredible Hulk, Thor and Daredevil. The third Odhams title, *Pow*, started in 1967 with The Amazing Spider-Man, and then came *Fantastic* and *Terrific*, 100 per cent Marvel superheroes with not a British character in sight. On 7 October 1972 came No.1 of *The Mighty World of Marvel*, and in next to no time Marvel Comics UK had been organized and a whole new ball game came into play; a super-ball game.

Probably the oddest superhero editions to Western eyes are those published in the Middle East. There comics not only have their hinge on the right and their covers on the back, but even the panels are reversed to read from right to left: a paste-up job that puts that first ever Superman re-jig to shame!

New Triumph *No.772* © *5 August 1939 Amalgamated Press. Drawn by John McCail*
The Super Heroes Monthly *No.1* © *1980 Egmont/DC. Drawn by Alan Craddock*

Superman *No.1* © *January 1978 Maverick/DC (Japan)*
Superman © *1973 (Arabic Edition)*
Batman © *1973 (Arabic Edition)*
Roter Blitz (The Flash) © *1981 Ehapa Verlag/DC (Germany)*
Super Adventure Comic *No.54* © *K. G. Murray/DC (Australia)*
Daredevil *No.1* © *Horwitz/Marvel (Australia)*
Prins Namor en Rauwe Bonk (Sub-Mariner and The Hulk) © *1968 Hip Comics/Marvel (Holland)*
De Wrekers (The Avengers) © *1967 Hip Comics/Marvel (Holland)*
Fantastici Quattro (The Fantastic Four) *No.249* © *1980 Editoriale Corno/Marvel (Italy)*

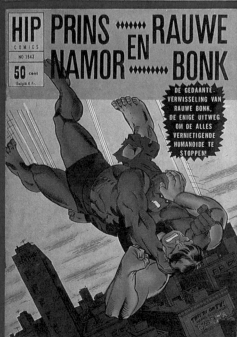

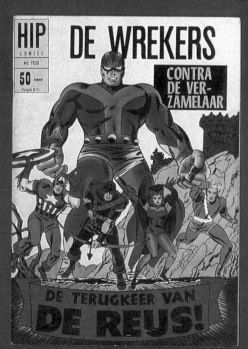

OF SUPERMICE AND SUPERMEN

"Announcing the Mouse of Might! I'm here to teach you wrong from right!" Fulfilling the terms of Rabbie Burns' auld maxim regarding the best-laid plan of mice and men, those of "Supermouse" ganged oft agley, ofter than Superman's, at any rate. Supermouse (the Big Cheese) made his comedy crime-busting debut in No.1 of *Coo-Coo Comics* (October 1942). Like his power-packed predecessor in the funny superhero stakes, Popeye, Soupie as he was intimately known, had a secret ingredient: not spinach, but something equally green and potent, supercheese! Soupie's adventures, drawn by a number of expert animators from Jack Bradbury to Milton Stein, were always a delight, and small wonder that with his battle cry of "Make way for the mouse of the day after tomorrow!" he graduated to his own comic-book in 1948. Hot on Soupie's paws came "Hoppy the Marvel Bunny". Unlike the rodent, the rabbit was an official burlesque of Captain Marvel, who actually

introduced the new superhero in No.1 of *Funny Animals* (December 1942). Hoppy, as drawn by Chad Grothkopf, was cuter and cuddlier, even after he had shouted his magic word, "Shazam!" and crash-boomed into a lop-eared likeness of his red-clad hero.

"Super Rabbit" was cut from tougher stuff, perhaps because he was fathered by Marvel Comics. Waffles, the much-abused shoe-shine bunny, rubbed his magic ring in *Comedy Comics* No.1 (1942), flashing into the red-cloaked, blue-clad Super Rabbit. Like Hoppy, he too won his own title; unlike Hoppy, his evil opponent was the bloodthirsty Dracula, hireling of Hitler, no less ("Heil me!"). Funniest of the funny animal supercrowd was "Superkatt", who made his debut in *Giggle Comics* No.9 (1944). As drawn by "Dang" (the comic-book pen-name of animator Dan Gordon from the Fleischer Studio), Superkatt, known as "Supe" for short (which he was), was as silly as his supercostume. In times of urgency, Supe snatched

Junior's bonnet and nappy when Petunia the coloured maid wasn't looking, and leaped to the rescue of Humphrey the Hound with his regular warcry: "Make way for the cat what is super!" Supe's superness was usually a matter of highly contrived coincidence. Other unlikely contenders in the funny animal field were "Super Duck the Cockeyed Wonder" (1944), and "Wiggles the Wonder Worm" in *Taffy Comics* (1945). Wiggles was not only unusual in that he turned into a superworm whenever he said "Omygosh!", but that his comic-book consisted of one long 48-page adventure. Late on the scene (1965) came the Walt Disney variant, *Super Goof*.

"Powerhouse Pepper", a hyped thumper in a striped jumper, was the first cranky Yankee to get tough with the rough stuff since Popeye the Sailor bailed a whaler. Powerhouse was born and drawn by the late, great Basil "Beanbrain" Wolverton, whose letterhead described him as "The Spaghetti and Meatballs Cartoonist". Basil, and hence his heroes, was fond of poetic prose. Thus an adventure in *Powerhouse Pepper* No.2 pits PP against Doug Slugmug, Ash Hashmash and Rush Slushcrush. This hip strip is entitled "A Fling in the Ring". Another highly individual cartoonist was Ed Wheelan, who had created the first strip to burlesque the cinema, "Minute Movies", back in 1921. Two of Ed's stars were revived for their own comic-book, *Fat and Slat*, but their vaudeville chitchat was a trifle whiskery for the kids of 1947. So Ed invented a new burlesque to suit the age, a strip satirising comic-books and their superheroes.

"Comics McCormick, the World's Number One Comic-book Fan" did fearless battle with several menaces, if only in his own imagination. The Sixties saw a couple of funny superguys arriving to burlesque the new crop, Odgen Whitney's *Herbie* (1964) – "Make way for the Fat Fury!" – and *Fat Man*, "The Human Flying Saucer" (1967). Amazingly this chubby chap was written and drawn by the men who had made Captain Marvel so great, Otto Binder and C. C. Beck. Finally, belatedly, but very successfully, a comical superhero from Britain: "Bananaman" (secretly the schoolboy Eric Wimp) started in *Nutty* in 1980 and three years later became the first-ever British comic character to transfer to television via animated cartoons.

Nutty *No.194* © *29 October 1983 D.C. Thomson. Drawn by John Geering*
Herbie *No.1* © *April 1964 American Comics Group. Drawn by Ogden Whitney*
Fat and Slat *No. 4* © *Spring 1948 EC Comics. Drawn by Ed Wheelan*
Powerhouse Pepper *No.2* © *April 1948 Marvel Comics. Drawn by Basil Wolverton*

Super Pumby *No.3* © *1964 Editorial Valencis (Spain). Drawn by J. Sanchis*
Giggle Comics *No.28* © *April 1946 Creston Publications. Drawn by Dan Gordon*
Cosmo Cat *No.1* © *July 1946 Fox Features. Drawn by Pat Chambers*
Hoppy the Marvel Bunny *No.4* © *August 1946 Fawcett Publications. Drawn by Chad Grothkopf*

Comic Capers *No.1* © *Fall 1944 Marvel Comics*
Atomic Bunny *No.16* © *May 1959 Charlton Comics*
Super Goof *No.1* © *July 1965 Walt Disney Productions/Gold Key*
Taffy Comics *No.2* © *1945 Orbit*
Supermouse *No.1* © *December 1948 Animated Cartoons*

SUPERHEROES AT WAR: Captain America v the Ratzis!

March 1941, and the United States were still nine months away from war. President Roosevelt, faced with the problem of seeking out Fifth Columnists in the Army, said "What would you suggest, gentlemen? A character out of the comic-books?" And that's exactly what he got. Professor Reinstein's serum turned weedy Steve Rogers into "the first of a corps of superagents whose mental and physical ability will make them a terror to spies and saboteurs!" In other words, *Captain America*! He was swiftly teamed with his own Boy Wonder, Bucky Barnes, and the pair formed "America's Greatest Fighting Machine". By No. 2 of their new comic-book they were giving Adolf and his Ratzis a taste of quick-fisted democracy. (They were content with merely socking him on the cover of No. 1). Cap, with his costume and shield inspired by the stars and stripes of Old Glory, was created by the top comic-book team of Joe Simon and Jack Kirby, Marvel comics' answer to Jerry Siegel and Joe Shuster. Unlike that DC team, both men wrote and drew, Simon working on *Blue Bolt* (1940), Kirby beginning earlier on *Wags* (1936). Like their first mutual creations Cap and Bucky, Joe and Jack would work magnificently as a team, creating new comic-book genres with their *Boy Commandos* and *Newsboy Legion*, and their later *Black Magic* and *Young Romance*. Kirby continues as a creative force in comic-books, occasionally shifting from Marvel to DC and back, but never changing his unique style.

Captain America was the first patriotic superhero. His club, the Sentinels of Liberty, invited young readers to "help rid the USA of the traitors who wish to destroy it." For one thin dime you received, "not a picture button toy, but a real high quality badge made of the same metal used in police and fireman badges!" Wow! Cap's major adversary was not Hitler himself, but a Nazi monster even Hitler feared, the Red Skull. Hitler, inhuman as he was, was still a human; nobody could be sure about the Red Skull! Cap's soaraway success soon spawned a host of comic-book super-patriots – "Captain Flag", "Captain Freedom", "Major Liberty", "The American Eagle", "Fighting Yank", "Yankee Eagle", and even "Miss Victory" and "Liberty Belle". Marvel Comics published a warning of legal action: "Imitators Beware! There is only one Captain America!" Meanwhile they milked their top hero, not only guesting him in other comic-books, but spinning off a sidekick comic starring both the boy wonders, Bucky plus Toro, the Human Torch's chum, as *The Young Allies* (1941).

Daredevil Battles Hitler (July 1941) was a one-shot that sold so well that it became a series. "Daredevil", a red/blue superhero with spikes on his belt, began his career in *Silver Streak Comics* No. 6 (September 1940), created by Don Rico and Jack Binder.

When Charles Biro came in as writer/editor, he introduced, not just one Boy Wonder, but a whole Monogram Movies-inspired gang called "The Little Wise Guys" (October 1942), who elbowed Daredevil out of the limelight. It seems a little early in the war for the climate to change – Captain America didn't begin to lose his grip until after VJ Day – but after such a debut as *Daredevil Battles Hitler*, perhaps there was no way to go but down. Following the title story came "The Claw Double Crosses Hitler" (The Claw was Daredevil's ugly answer to the Red Skull), "Daredevil and Lance Hale Fighting Hitler and his Jungle Hordes", "Daredevil with Dickie Dean, Boy Inventor, Smash Goebbels' Spy Net", "Daredevil and Cloud Curtis Wreck Goering's Sky Fighters", "Daredevil and the Pirate Prince versus Von Roeder, Nazi Sea Raider", and a pictorial postscript biography entitled "The Man of Hate: Adolf Hitler, Dictator of Germany". After all that, how could America not enter the War?

Captain America Special © *1942 Marvel Comics. Drawn by Sid Shores* USA Comics *No. 1 © August 1941 Marvel Comics (facsimile). Drawn by Jack Kirby* Daredevil Battles Hitler *No. 1 © July 1941 Your Guide (facsimile). Drawn by Charles Biro* Major Victory Comics *No. 1 © 1944 Glover/Harry Chesler* Wonder Comics *No. 1 © May 1944 Great. Drawn by Alex Schomburg* Young Allies *No. 1 © Summer 1941 Marvel Comics (facsimile). Drawn by Joe Simon and Jack Kirby* Sub-Mariner *No. 1 © Spring 1941 Marvel Comics (facsimile). Drawn by Bill Everett*

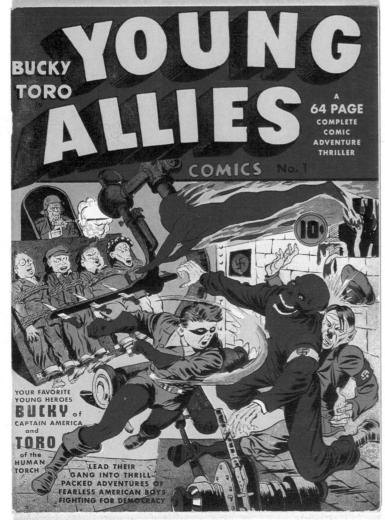

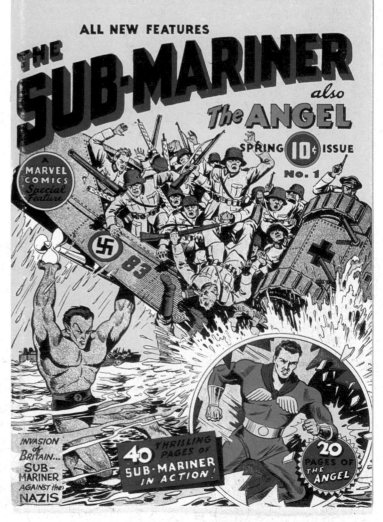

KIMOTA! The Great British Supermen

"Who is he? What is the Secret of his Amazing Strength? Every boy and girl will be speaking about the Mysterious Mr X! The thrilling adventures of this terrific superman appear in *The Dandy* in a fortnight!" The first announcement of the first British superhero appeared in *Dandy* No.271. And as promised, in No.272 dated 5 August 1944 there he was, Len Manners private enquiry agent, "tall and loosely built, but behind his glasses his eyes sparkled keen and bright". Spotting a ship in distress, Len whips off his specs and swiftly slips into black skin-tight trousers, white woollen jersey with a large red X on the chest, and black mask. (Len also slips on a black cloak according to the caption, but the artist apparently forgot to draw it!) Soon the sinking seamen are saved and Len is home again, grinning at the newspaper headlines, having stopped only to save a boy from falling logs. Although his later adventures were slightly more super and from episode two he found his cloak (but lost his X), "The Amazing Mr X" was dropped

after 14 strips. He had been defeated by the dread hand of British traditionalism. Superheroes just did not fit into the format of the British comic, and *Dandy* readers were obviously much happier when Mr X was replaced by the Dudley Watkins fantasy "Danny Longlegs – He's Ten Feet Tall and Up to the Ears in Trouble!"

But the new breed of British comic-book readers was growing up into a new breed of British comic-book artists, teenagers who were excited by the new American way of drawing and the new things that they could draw: holding back an express train with one hand, pulling an airplane in half, tearing up a tank. But such notions tried on traditional publications were rejected out of hand. So they turned to the new breed of British comic-book publisher, business opportunists who saw a "quick quid" in putting out one-shot comics on whatever paper they could con out of the wartime controllers. Knowing little of the ethics of juvenile publishing, operating without experienced editors, these

men were happy to slap together eight pages of artwork of almost any kind. Content and standards mattered little, just as long as the page size was right. Proof of this may be found in *Dynamic Comics* (1945) starring "Mr Muscle, Britain's Superman". Mike O'Leary drinks his father's "essence of strength" and saves the plans of the Stratford Bomber by juggling with a spy-laden taxi. This eight-page black-and-white crudity, published at twopence by International Publications, is a blot on British comic art — even if I was only 17 when I drew it! I can only plead that the many superhero comics drawn by Dennis M. Reader for Cartoon Art Productions of Glasgow ("Powerman", "Electrogirl", etc) were better, but only just.

The best of the British supermen was born on 3 February 1954, but well out of wedlock. A thoroughly illegitimate offspring of Captain Marvel, *Marvelman* made his debut in No.25 of his own title: the first 24 issues were called *Captain Marvel Adventures*, the 24th bearing the inserted subtitle of "The Marvelman". The publisher, Leonard Miller, half-hoped the readers wouldn't notice; he certainly hoped that the American DC Comics wouldn't notice. DC had just

triumphed in the US Courts of Justice, where their long-running lawsuit against Fawcett Publications had caused the latter to discontinue their entire comic line. This, of course, included *Captain Marvel Adventures*, Miller's British reprint best-seller. Mick Anglo, a quick-thinking cartoonist, converted Billy Batson the boy reporter of Station Whiz to Micky Moran the boy reporter of the *Daily Bugle*. Old Shazam the Mystic became Guntag Bargholt the recluse astro-scientist, and the magic word he gave the boy switched from "Shazam!" to "Kimota!" (atomic spelled backwards). Once it was uttered, the boy became, not Captain Marvel, but Marvelman, not "The World's Mightiest Mortal", but "The Mightiest Man in the Universe". Similar operations were performed on the Captain's close relations. Freddy Freeman, crippled newsboy, became Dicky Dauntless, messenger boy, who had only to shout his magic word to turn into Young Marvelman instead of Captain Marvel Jr. The operation on Mary Batson/Mary Marvel was trickier: she became crewcut Johnny Bates, alias Kid Marvelman! The comics continued to be Miller's best-sellers and ran for ten years, notching up the longest runs for British comic-books (370 issues). Even the death of Miller and the collapse of his little empire did not kill the Mightiest Family in the Universe. Nostalgic comics-publisher Dez Skinn recently revived them with great success in his adult-orientated *Warrior*, "Kimota" and all.

Super Duper Comics No.15 © 1949 Cartoon Art Productions. Drawn by Crewe Davies
Marvelman No.1 (Italian Edition) © December 1965 Edit Europa/Miller
Marvelman Family No.1 © October 1956 Miller
Captain Miracle No.1 © October 1960 Mick Anglo
Crash Comics No.1 © 1948 Rayburn/Martin and Reid. Drawn by John McCail
Streamline Comics No.1 © 1947 Cardal Publishing. Drawn by Denis Gifford
Masterman Comic No.1 © November 1952 Streamline/United Anglo-American. Drawn by King-Ganteaume
Electroman Comics No.1 © 1951 Scion Publications. Drawn by King-Ganteaume

THE MARVEL AGE OF COMICS: "Excelsior!"

"Excelsior!": James Henderson's triumphant cry announcing No.1 of the first *Funny Folks* in 1874, and Stan Lee's salute a century later – a crazy coincidence linking the man who created comics and the man who recreated them. For American comic-books were sinking in a rut of mediocrity under the Comics Code Authority, dragging the overly familiar old superheroes with them, when the Marvel Age of Comics dawned like an exploding nova, or more correctly a fiery "4" high in the sky. Superstars of the new wave were Dr Reed Richards, Ben Grimm, Susan and Johnny Storm, known (thanks to cosmic ray exposure) as Mr Fantastic, The Thing, The Invisible Girl and the Human Torch, a team called collectively *The Fantastic Four* (November 1961). But the real superstars, the fantastic two, were "Jolly" Jack Kirby, artist, and "Smilin'" Stan Lee: Kirby, a continuing innovator in comic-books since the Thirties, Lee a busy script-writer since the Forties.

Born Stanley Lieber, the talented teenager began working on his uncle Martin Goodman's comic-books, taking over as editor when Kirby and his partner Joe Simon left for DC Comics in 1942. Stan's sudden success in the sinking Sixties was due to two things: he devised a new line of super-men with human failings, creating a bond of sympathy which appealed to teenagers; and he developed a jokey, intimate relationship with his readers, writing a new kind of editorial that was not only in their own slangy lingo, it broke down the mystique of comic-book creation and made them feel part of "the Marvel Revolution". Soon "True Believers", as Stan called his subscribers, were enrolling in the Merry Marvel Marching Society, reading *Foom*, their "fanzine", and buying up every Marvel comic in sight. And there were plenty of new ones rolling fresh from the press.

The year 1962 saw No.1 of *The Incredible Hulk*, "half-man, half-monster, thundering out of the night to take his place among the most amazing characters of all time!" He was Dr Bruce Banner, bathed in gamma rays from the first G-Bomb, which turned him into a Boris Karloff lookalike. In September arrived *The Amazing Spider-Man*, Peter Parker, a "book-worm who wouldn't know a cha-cha from a waltz", who got bitten by a radioactive spider and turned into what "we in the comic-mag business refer to as a 'long-underwear character'!" (Stan Lee in his intro to Steve Ditko's picturization.) Exactly a year later came two new team-ups, *The Avengers* and *The X-Men*. The first combined "some of the Earth's Greatest Superheroes", Hulk, the Mighty Thor, Iron Man, Antman and the Wasp. The second was an all-new outfit run by the handicapped Professor Xavier: Slim Summers (the Cyclops), Bobby Drake (Iceman), Hank McCoy (The Beast), and Warren Worthington the Third (the Angel). They are swiftly joined by Jean Grey, the Marvel Girl.

"Can you guess why Daredevil is different from all other crime-fighters?" queried the cover of *Daredevil* No.1 (1964), a comic-book which appeared to bear the world's longest title, "Here Comes Daredevil the Man Without Fear!" The secret was that young Matt Murdock was blind, struck by a radioactive truck. Of the many other marvellous Marvels, two deserve singling out. *Doctor Strange*, Master of the Mystic Arts, took over the title of *Strange Tales* from No.169 (June 1968). A surgeon injured in a car crash, he is given the power of magic by the Ancient One of the Himalayas: "By the Hoary Hosts of Hoggoth!" he gasps. The second

star sailed in on a shining surfboard: "High o'er the roof of the world he soars, free and unfettered as the roaring wind itself! Behold the sky-born spanner of a trillion galaxies, the restless, streaking stranger from the farthest reach of space, this glistening, gleaming seeker of truth whom man shall call for ever more *The Silver Surfer!*" The Sentinel of the Spaceways shone forth solo in a giant 68-page, 25 cent special, a unique hero and, some say, Stan Lee's vision of Christ. Perhaps, for after his comic died in 1970, the Surfer had a second coming in 1982.

The Fantastic Four *No.2 © January 1962 Marvel. Drawn by Jack Kirby*
The Mighty World of Marvel *No.1 © 7 October 1972 © Marvel Comics (British edition)*
The Amazing Spider-Man *No.100 © September 1971 Marvel Comics. Drawn by Gil Kane*

The X-Men *No.1 © September 1963 Marvel Comics. Drawn by Jack Kirby*
The Avengers *No.1 © September 1963 Marvel. Drawn by Jack Kirby*
Daredevil *No.1 © April 1964 Marvel Comics. Drawn by Bill Everett*
Iron Man *No.1 © May 1968 Marvel Comics. Drawn by Gene Colan*
Sub-Mariner *No.1 © May 1968 Marvel Comics. Drawn by John Buscema*
Doctor Strange *No.1 (No.169) © June 1968 Marvel Comics. Drawn by Dan Adkins*
Nick Fury Agent of Shield *No.1 © June 1968 Marvel Comics. Drawn by James Steranko*
The Silver Surfer *No.1 © August 1968 Marvel Comics. Drawn by John Buscema*
What If *No.1 © February 1977 Marvel Comics. Drawn by Jim Craig*

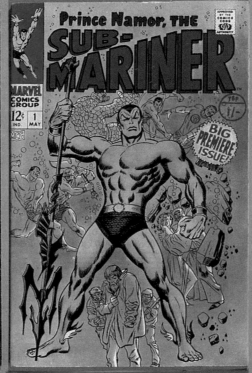

AMERICAN COMICS/ BRITISH EDITIONS: Price Ten Cents (Threepence)!

If the slogan of the American comic-book was "All in Color for a Dime", then the slogan of the British edition of the American comic-book should have been "Half in Colour for Fourpence" – but, of course, it wasn't. Full colour printing on every page had always been a problem in the UK. Full colour supplements had been produced in American newspapers since the 19th century, but they did not become a practicality in British papers until the *Mail On Sunday* introduced its 16-page colour comic in 1982. It was not that the technology for colour did not exist, it was simply that it was too expensive for an essentially low-cost product like a comic.

The declaration of war on 3 September 1939 put an immediate stop to the importation into the UK of American comic-books. T. V. Boardman, the London-based publisher who had pioneered the reprint tabloid comic, *Okay*, realized the potential in continuing the distribution of popular American comic-books. Consequently he made an arrangement with Everett Arnold of Quality Comics to republish two of his most successful titles, *Feature Comics* and *Smash Comics*, in British editions. Boardman found it impossible to produce the full 64-page comic-books at a price acceptable to Woolworth's, his main outlet, which still ran "Nothing Over Sixpence" chain-stores.

To get the price down to threepence Boardman split each comic in half, and divided the printing similarly, so that he had a 32-page comic, half in full colour, half in black and white. To use the remaining 32 pages of each comic, he created two new titles, and had new covers drawn for them. Thus he made four 32-page comic-books out of two 64-page books. In doing so, he caused a good deal of confusion to future collectors seeking original American editions of Boardman's *Mystery Comics* and *Super Funnies*, the titles he gave to half of *Smash Comics* and half of *Feature Comics*. After a couple of issues, increasing costs and the wartime paper shortage forced Boardman to reduce his comics to 16 pages plus covers, and raise their price to fourpence.

After the war Boardman continued his deal with Quality Comics and ran Anglicized editions of *Blackhawk* and *The Spirit*. This time they were even more reduced, becoming 12-page comics in two-colour photogravure. Denis McLoughlin, Boardman's one-man art staff, cut up and re-shaped the original comics to turn two 6-frame pages into one of 12-frames, and also drew the new cover designs. These followed the standard British format of introducing strips on the front page, a practice another ex-importer of comic-books turned publisher, Leonard Miller, had instituted earlier with his wartime reprints of the United Features comic, *Tip Top*. Miller had been the first to use the two-tone photogravure process in comics, a style of printing he later made very popular. *Tip Top Comics* was a 32-page reprint sold for fourpence, but it was soon reduced to 16. The Amalgamated Press, which had been publishing its own *Tip Top* as a weekly title since the Thirties, objected strongly to Miller's reprint and, after No.2, *Tip Top* was turned into United's other title, *Comic On Parade*, and the numbering continued.

Tip Top Comics No.1 © December 1940 L. Miller and Son/United Features. Drawn by Bernard Dibble
Blackhawk *No.11 (first issue) © 1949 T. V. Boardman/Quality Comics. Drawn by Denis McLoughlin*
The Spirit *No.12 (first issue) © 1949 T. V. Boardman/Quality Comics. Drawn by Denis McLoughlin/Will Eisner*

Feature Comics *No.29 (first issue) © 1940 T. V. Boardman/Quality*
Smash Comics *No.7 (first issue) © 1940 T. V. Boardman/Quality Comics*
Super Funnies *No.30 © 1940 T. V. Boardman/Quality Comics*
Mystery Comics *No.7 (first issue) © 1940 T. V. Boardman/Quality Comics*
Family Favourites *No.1 © 24 February 1954 Miller/Chicago Tribune*
King Comic *No.1 © 5 May 1954 Miller/King Features*

BRITISH COMIC-BOOKS: "The Laughs of a Nation!"

The first British comic-book was born of acumen out of neccessity. The conflict which began in September 1939 and soon grew into World War Two put a swift end to the profitable trade in American comic-books. Ever since back numbers of *Famous Funnies* were redated and shipped to the UK as ballast in the transatlantic freighters, American comic-books had been part of the British comic scene. Whilst they had no direct influence on native publications as far as format, style and content go, they had a tremendous influence on the children who read them. Unpopular with parents and teachers alike for their Yankee colloquialism (the main point of pre-war criticism; violence and the sexiness of comic-book heroines had yet to develop), American comic-books were popular only with the kids. Sold mainly in Woolworths and street markets, their handy size and thick, 68-page full-colour format was more than just a bargain for twopence a time; it was an excitingly different taste of the American way of life. Even the advertisements were thrillingly alien: if only we could send three cents to Detroit, Mich, for Johnson Smith's 576-page "catalog of novelties", so tantalisingly trailed in their jam-packed backpage ads! And what on earth did a Baby Ruth candybar taste like, packed with Dextrose and "NRG"?

With the war, all those "All in Color for a Dime" dreams vanished, except for those lucky few children who were evacuated to the USA instead of the blacked-out depths of the country. With the banning of "unneccessary" American imports, there came, too, a sudden gap in the income of those who handled the comics, the importers, wholesalers and salesmen. As ever, when crisis faces a nation at bay, there is one brave man to answer the call. This was "a tall, thin, kindly man, smartly dressed in dark pin-stripe suit, long overcoat, and wearing a black bowler hat. Indeed, he looked more like a successful City businessman than one trading as a stall-holder in a street market". The man was Gerald George Swan, recalled by W. O. G. Lofts, once one of his half-price comic

customers, now the respected authority on comics history. I sought out the retired Mr Swan shortly before he died in 1980; unhappily, old age had made him prouder of his hard-cover novels than his creation of the British comic-book. For it was Swan who, seeing the gap in the market caused by the vanished American comic-books, single-handedly and completely inexperienced in publishing, edited, prin-

ted and distributed *New Funnies* No.1 in January 1940.

The first British comic-book was closely modelled on the American format, the same page-count (64 plus covers), the same page-size (7¼ by 9¾ inches), and like *Famous Funnies* and the others, it even had a similar slogan: "The Laughs of a Nation". Major differences were that the cover was the only page in colour, and the price was tripled to sixpence. It was the price factor that proved the biggest problem. No British comic had ever cost more than twopence: sixpence was an entire week's pocket-money. Swan had quickly produced a companion title, *Topical Funnies*, at the same

size and price. Although *New Funnies* sold, *Topical Funnies* did not. Returned copies were halved and rebound as 32-page editions numbered 1A and 1B, and sent out again at threepence. This worked, and soon all the Swan comic-books settled down at 32 pages in a coloured cover for threepence. And here they remained, as far as price goes; paper shortage soon reduced the comics to 20, then 16 pages, but Swan, good market-man that he was, kept the value up by increasing picture count from eight to 12 panels a page.

Swan's comic-books were a curious mixture of pseudo-Yankee and British traditional. The early covers, schoolboys in caps posing riddles, were boring, but soon artist John Woods settled into action scenes featuring the inside characters. Only one of the early Swan artists was an old-timer from the weekly comics. This was Harry Banger who, although working in the classic Roy Wilson style, found the captionless pictorial format Swan offered a happy one, and produced many excellent four- and six-page continuities. Swan's other artists were a curious collection. Murdock Stimpson, who did some lively strips both funny ("Nibbo") and dramatic ("Flash Scarlet"), was a veteran from the so-called "saucy mags" of the Twenties. Douglas Lovern West was an untried amateur whose scratchy strips could be both topically humorous ("Winnie of the WATS") and thrilling ("The Seven Circles"). Another cartoonist who divided his Swan stuff both ways was William A. Ward, formerly an animator with the "Bonzo" films of the Twenties. He drew such pseudo-western capers as "Sheriff Fox" as well as a more serious version, "Hurricane Hurry". He also did the first horror strips in British comics. Another one who doubled up was Jock McCail, an out-of-work illustrator from the many boys' story papers which had collapsed with the war. He quickly mastered picture-story techniques and drew the Charlie Chan-style "Ah Wong the Wily Chinee", the macabre "Dene Vernon, Ghost Investigator", and the funny tough-guy, "Bring 'Em In Hank".

Swan's first two titles were followed by *War Comics* and *Thrill Comics* in April 1940, *Slick Fun* and *Fresh Fun* in May, and *Extra Fun* in August. In addition to the regular issues (the monthly schedule slipped after paper rationing came in) there were double-sized sixpenny Specials. After the war Swan changed the style of his comics from American to British, with Banger drawing traditional strips on the front pages. Once the paper quotas disappeared, Swan's comics lost their readers to the major publishers, and after a brief return to comic-book format with *Dynamic Thrills* and *Western War Comic* in 1951, the old pioneer's minor empire withered as quickly as it had bloomed.

COMICS AT WAR:
Basil and Bert in Nastyland!

The Second World War did not catch British comics totally unprepared. Like the grown-up world and its newspapers, comics had their own Munich Crisis late in 1938. Well, one comic did, the unique *Jester*, a penny pink'un which retailed the serialized misadventures of "Basil and Bert, Our Very Private Detectives" on the front page. This strip, begun years before in 1923 by Roy Wilson and Don Newhouse, had fallen into the happy hands of George Parlett in 1932. Third of the amazing Parlett family to make comics his life (following father Harry and brother Reg), George's distinctive style and way with words set him above the basically traditional line he followed. With Basil and Bert he came into his own, sending his fearless funsters into Taterland, where Dick Tater and his Stormtaters ruled with an iron heil. Once war broke out for real, Dick was revealed as none other than Ateful Adolf 'imself, boss of the Doublecross Party, ruling from the Ricebag with his three stooges, Dr Gobbles, General Snoring and Herr

Von Drippingtop. And in this way, with laughter and burlesque, British comics went to war. "Constable Cuddlecook" swapped his helmet for a tin titfer and pounded the blackout beat. "Big Hearted Martha", the *Comic Cuts* char, turned in her scrubber to sign on as "Our ARP-Nut". "The Cruise of the Crusoe Kids" clobbered Admiral Von Hamburger's pocket battleship "Ditchland" with an airborne sausage. In *Chips*, "Laurie and Trailer, Our Secret Service Lads" enlisted in the Coldcream Guards when their arch-enemies Crown Prince Oddsocksz and Serge Pantz suddenly swapped their Russki accents for der old Deutscher. Those highland rivals to the AP comics, *Dandy* and *Beano*, soon followed the trend, with strips of "Addy and Hermy the Nasty Nazis" and a fondly remembered swipe at the Eye-ties, "Musso the Wop – He's a Big a da Flop", both inspirations of Dundee artist Sam Fair.

The war brought about the first British comics to emulate the

American comic-books, published by Gerald G. Swan. Although a few serious war strips were introduced, such as William McCail's "Defenders of Great Britain" in *New Funnies*, Swan's strips, like those in the regular comics, were mostly for fun: Jock McCail's "Adolf the Awful" in *Topical Funnies*, and Harry Banger's excellent "Over There" in *War Comics* (which all too soon had to be switched to "Over Here", following Dunkirk). Also from 1940, the snowballing shortage of paper killed off many comics. No new regular title could be started so small publishers began to issue one-offs. Lacking editorial supervision or tradition, these little eight-pagers often included the kind of wartime adventure strip sadly lacking in the professional comics.

Jester No.1988 © *16 December 1939 Amalgamated Press. Drawn by George Parlett*
Funny Wonder No.1417 © *24 May 1941 Amalgamated Press. Drawn by Roy Wilson*

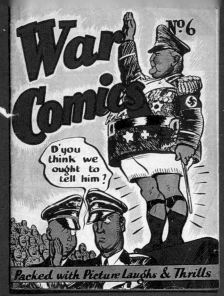

The Magic Comic No.21
© 9 December 1939 D. C. Thomson.
Drawn by Harry Banger
The Beano Comic No.213
© 28 August 1943 D. C. Thomson.
Drawn by Reg Carter
Knockout the Victory Comic No.245
© 13 November 1943. Drawn by
A. J. Kelly

War Comics No.6 © 1940 Gerald G.
Swan. Drawn by John Woods
Topical Funnies Special Autumn
Number © 1941 Gerald G. Swan.
Drawn by John Woods
Thrill Comics No.4 © 1940 Gerald
G. Swan. Drawn by John Woods
All Fun Vol.3 No.1 © 1943
A. Soloway. Drawn by Alan Fraser
Slick Fun No.22 © 1945 Gerald G.
Swan. Drawn by John "Jock" McCail

Reel Comics © 1944 Locker
Cyclone Illustrated Comic © 1945
*R. and L. Locker. Drawn by
R. Beaumont*
Four Aces © 1945 Newton
*Wickham. Drawn by Alfred
Farningham*
Grand Adventure Comic © 1945
*Martin and Reid. Drawn by
R. Beaumont*

Britischer Schwein v Heinie Hunkheads

The Second World War began, not on 3 September 1939, but on 6 October 1962 when "Captain Hurricane" heralded the first issue of *Valiant* with a "Thumbs up for Number One!" Or perhaps it was on 28 June 1958, when "Battler Britton", the aptly-named "Fighting Ace of Land, Sea and Air", took over the front page of the hitherto cowboy-crazed comic, *Sun*. Or a little earlier, in 1954 when "Johnnie Wingco" flew into *Knockout*. Always a patriotic little paper, this was the one which had subtitled itself *The Victory Comic* in the dark December of 1941. Thus in less than a decade from the signing of the peace, World War II was being fought all over again – in the comics. And causing, in time, almost as much comment and controversy as the non-fiction version, as newspapers and education authorities aired their opinions on whether or not so many strip-cartooned reruns harmed young readers, especially in a climate of a unified Europe. The readers themselves seemed not to worry, as comic weeklies escalated from the odd one or two war strips to entire 32-page war comics, and pocket-sized 64-page war "libraries".

When Wing Commander Robert Britton, RAF, "the amazing fighting-ace known to all as Battler Britton", swooped his Spitfire against the Messerschmidts on that first front page in the *Sun*, he cried "Tally-ho!" It was still a gentleman's war. When Captain Hercules Hurricane, "the toughest fighting man of World War II" stormed into action with the Royal Marine Commandos, four years later in *Valiant*, it was "Avast there, hunkhead!" War was slam-bang fun, especially when Hurricane went into one of his "raging furies". But the Mighty Marine did not have the comic all his own way. *Valiant*, like all other boys' comics of the period, had an assorted cast of heroes: "Hawk Hunter", a western, "Blade of the Frontier", a period tale of Empire-building, "Kid Gloves", a boxer and "Jack o' Justice", a highwayman. It was not until D. C. Thomson entered the lists on 28 September 1974 that the first all-war comic appeared in Britain. *Warlord* No.1 promised "Action, Drama, Thrills on Land, at Sea, in the Air"

(and on the side delivered an unusual Grand Free Gift, eight Golden Replica Medals complete with folder holder). Its 36 pictorial pages led off with "Union Jack Jackson", the only Britisher in the US Marines. Sole survivor of a Jap attack on his ship, Jackson slugs it out with bully O'Bannion to prove Limeys got guts. Lord Peter Flint, "the coward who was Britain's top secret agent", starred in the title strip, "Codename Warlord", a well-drawn serial of unusual length: nine pages. For variety, World War One was the setting for "Spider Wells", an ill-treated teenager who swapped his cruel stepfather for an easier life in the

Royal Flying Corps. There were also strip adaptations of two ex-story-paper heroes from Thomson's old "Big Five" range: Bomber Braddock, Sergeant Matt of that ilk and *The Rover*, who flew a converted Wellington fitted with an electrical ring for exploding Jerry mines, and "Young Wolf". Founded on the old *Wizard* stories, this pictured the boyhood of "The Wolf of Kabul", Bill Samson, who kept the peace along the Khyber Pass with his Pathan chum, Chung. In his turn, Chung kept the peace with the aid of Clicky-ba, his brass-bound cricket bat destined to crack many a rebel skull: "Lord,

Clicky-ba turned in my hand!"

Another kind of comic war flared up when the London-based IPC answered Dundee-based Thomson with No.1 of *Battle Picture Weekly*, "Blasting into Action" on 8 March 1975, complete with Free Combat Stickers. Leading this 32-page attack was "D-Day Dawson", the Sergeant with a bullet lodged next to his heart. Given a year to live, he becomes "the soldier with a date with death". *Battle's* answer to Peter Flint was "Mike Nelson, Britain's Deadliest Secret Agent", while "The Bootneck Boy" was about a kid who joins the Marines (instead of a kid who joins the RFC). *Battle's* lingo tended to be tougher (almost every strip had someone saying "Blimey!", for years a forbidden word in comics), as did its strips. "Rat Pack" starred Britain's Toughest Criminals. Kabul "The Turk" Hasan, Ron

Weasel, Ian "Scarface" Rogan break jail to become Commandos: "My knife says I stay alive, friend!" "*Uuuuh!*" War Libraries, pocket-sized 64-page comic-books telling one long story, began in September 1958 with "Fight Back to Dunkirk", No.1 of *War Picture Library*. Produced for a higher age-group than the comic weeklies, teenagers and up, these books can be considered the first successful attempt to raise the age-level of comics in Britain. *Air Ace Picture Library* took off in January 1960 (No.1 "Target Top Secret"), and *War at Sea Picture Library* in February 1962 (No.1 "Devil's Cargo"). Thomson's still-running *Commando* started in July 1961 (No.1 "Walk or Die"), but the oddest has to be the tall oblong *Giant War Picture Library* (No.1 "The Red Devils") which was issued in batches of four titles a month from June 1964.

"Of Danger We Don't Care – We're Blackhawks!"

"Like a huge steamroller the Nazi war machine crushes all of Europe. One day a new name appears on the horizon, a name that strikes terror in the hearts of men ... Blackhawk! Like an angel of vengeance Blackhawk and his men swoop down out of nowhere, their guns belching death and on their lips the dreaded song of the Blackhawks:

"Over land, over sea,
We fight to make men free,
Of danger we don't care –
We're Blackhawks!"

In America the comic-books went to war long before the nation itself did, and of all the heroes thrown up by the crisis, none have lasted longer than the black-clad "Blackhawk". Born in *Military Comics* No.1 in August 1941, four months before Pearl Harbor was bombed, Blackhawk was the guise of a Polish pilot who formed a secret squadron based on a private island equipped with disappearing forts and a revolving zeppelin shed. The Blackhawks: Chuck, the Yankee wireless whiz; Hendrickson the Dutch

weapons wizard; Olaf the Swedish gymnast; Stanislaus the powerful Pole; André the Parisian playboy; Chop-Chop the cheery Chinese cook ever ready with his chopper to make hamburger of the Huns. Drawn by Charles Cuidera, Will Eisner's original concept changed several times during Blackhawk's lengthy career (as well as *Military*, later *Modern Comics*, he has starred in over 250 issues of his own title), notably changing him from a Pole to a true-blue son of Uncle Sam.

Military Comics as originally designed by Eisner came in two parts, the front 32 pages being the "Army Section" (Stories of Military Action on Land) and the second half being the "Navy Section" (Stories of Naval and Air Action on the Sea). Backing up Blackhawk in part one were "Loops and Banks of the Red Dragon Squadron", "Archie Atkins, Desert Scout", and a science-fiction secret weapon, "The Blue Tracer", as magical as any of Fred Guardineer's conjuring heroes: "Spreading its telescopic wings and retracting its wheels, the million horse-power engine starts the

propeller, the Steel Monster leaps into the air!" ... "Gee, look at us go!" The second section featured "Death Patrol", a kind of B-movie Blackhawk bunch. Del Van Dine, millionaire playboy, flies a mob of hijackers to England and sets up a freelance Foreign Legion of the Air. The squadron, as created by the cartoony pen of Jack Cole, was a remarkable forecast of *The Dirty Dozen*: Hank the cattle rustler, Slick Ward the con man, Peewee the forger, Gramps the pickpocket and Butch O'Keefe, safe-cracker! Cole's idea of an RAF "colonel's" speech was equally cartoony: "Good 'eavens! 'Ow did you ever do h'it?"

Group action seems to have been a favourite theme of comic-book warfare. The first was the patriotic trio who made their fighting debut in the equally patriotically titled *All-American Comics* No.1, April 1939. "Red White and Blue" featured Red Dugan of the Marines, Whitey Smith of the Army, and Blooey Blue of the Navy: their nicknames were the first contribution to comics of William Gaines, the 16-year old son of Max, the pioneering publisher. More will be heard of young Bill. Red, Whitey and Blooey, for some months a pre-war team, operated undercover for G2, the Government agency that sought out spies. But the most popular team of

the war years was undoubtedly "The Boy Commandos", a youthful group which must have been ace in reader-identification. This gang of four organized by Captain Rip Carter, was a global variation on the East Side Kids of Monogram movies: doiby-hatted Brooklyn ("We'll fix dose babies!"), Pierre Chavard from France ("Ma foi!"), Jan Haasen from Holland ("Ve vill catch dem!"), and Alfy Twidgett from London ("A bit balmy h'if ye asts me!"). Created by another great comic-book team, Joe Simon and Jack Kirby, they made their debut in *Detective Comics* No.64 (June 1942), and by winter were starring in their own *Boy Commandos* title, which ran into 1949. Fighting teams returned in the Sixties with *Sgt Fury and his Howling Commandos* (1963), *Captain Savage and his Leatherneck Raiders* (1968) and *Combat Kelly and the Deadly Dozen* (1972).

War Comics was actually the first all-war comic-book in America. Dell published No.1 in March 1940, and between the fictional heroics of "Scoop Mason, War Correspondent" and "Greg Gilday and the Martians"(!), a number of factual features were introduced, including the story of the German sea raider, *Graf Spee*. Once America was in the war, Dell enlarged this idea to produce the all-

factual comic-book, *War Heroes* (July 1942) and changed the title of *War Comics* to the more serious sounding *War Stories*. But perhaps the most fascinating of all the wartime comic-books was *War Victory Comics* (1942), published by the US Treasury Department for the promotion of War Bonds and Stamps. Virtually every comic artist in America contributed a special adventure of his characters, from both newspapers ("Li'l Abner", "Blondie", "Joe Palooka") and comic-books ("Green Hornet", "Superman"). And it only cost 5 cents a copy!

The new boom in war comics during the Fifties created dozens of titles and one classic. This was *Frontline Combat*, published by William Gaines' remarkable EC Comics outfit, under the editorship of the even more remarkable Harvey Kurtzman. A brilliant cartoonist and parodist, he was also able to turn his pen to writing and drawing some extremely serious war strips, the classic of a classic series being the Special Iwo Jima Issue of *Frontline Combat* (No.7, July 1952). Within Kurtzman's impressionistic cover were four features, "Iwo Jima" drawn by Wallace Wood, "The Landing" by Bill Elder, "The Caves" by John Severin, and "Mopping Up" by Jack Davis.

War Comics *No.2* © *May 1940 Dell Publishing*
War Victory Comics *No.1* © *Summer 1942 US Treasury/ Family Comics*
Military Comics *No.1* © *August 1941 (facsimile) Comic Magazines/ Quality. Drawn by Will Eisner*
Devil Dogs Comics *No.1* © *1942 Street and Smith*
Boy Commandos *No.1* © *September 1973 (1942 reissue) National Periodicals. Drawn by Jack Kirby*
G. I. Joe *No.24* © *August 1953 Ziff-Davis*

D-Day *No.1* © *August 1965 Charlton Comics. Drawn by Masulli and Mastrosero*
Marine War Heroes *No.13* © *April 1966 Charlton Comics. Drawn by Ernie Bache*
Frontline Combat *No.7* © *July 1952 EC Comics. Drawn by Harvey Kurtzman*
Combat Kelly and the Deadly Dozen *No.1* © *June 1972 Marvel Comics. Drawn by John Severin*
Sgt Fury and his Howling Commandos Annual *No.1* © *1965 Marvel Comics.*
Capt Savage and his Leatherneck Raiders *No.1* © *January 1968 Marvel Comics*

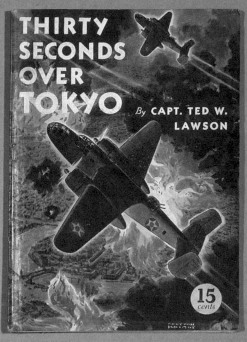

The Comics Keep 'em Flying!

War in the air was already an everyday experience for the All American Aircrew who staffed Fiction House's *Wings Comics*: Captain Wings, Suicide Smith, The Skull Squad, Clipper Kirk, not forgetting Jane Martin and Greasemonkey Griffin. When the States entered the war, the *Wings* team had beaten them to it. And they were not alone. In September 1940, rival pulp-publishers Street and Smith put out a comic-book version of their story magazine, *Bill Barnes America's Air Ace*. As early as July 1941 General Barnes was urging his young readers to "join my US Air Warden Cadets and Defend Your Country! You will be trained to spot and report airplanes exactly as many of the legionnaires and other organizations are doing right now!" For their handsome badge and

Full Instructions on How to Proceed, readers were urged to send General Bill five cents and a promise to "faithfully perform all duties required of me in learning how best to defend our country." In the same issue Bill flies a bomber to England, is awarded the Victoria Cross and an apple pie, and promises to be back next issue "when his Death-Defying, Hair-Raising, Danger-Disdaining Adventures will Thrill You to the Marrow!"

Captain Flight, Master of the Sky, was given his own comic-book title in 1944, but his back-up characters remained firmly on the ground: "Professor X, Crime Doctor" and "Dash the Avenger". *Skyrocket Comics* (1944) was a similar concoction, with only the lead strip airborne. Lieutenant Ted Howard invents the

Skyrocket, a plane which can speed at 750 miles per hour for over 4,000 miles, thus enabling him to "cast caution to the winds in a daring raid on Hirohito's Heathen Homeland!" The Lieut's back-up strips included "Doctor Vampire" and "Inspector Pratt". *Spitfire Comics*, with its Battle of Britain cover, was as fake as its issue number (No.132 was actually No.1!). The title strip, "Spitfire Sanders", turned out to be about a glamorous American secret agent! Much more honest was *The American Air Forces*, a combination of comic and photogravure magazine. The lead strip was the first comic-book interpretation of the Invasion of Europe on 6 June 1944, as drawn by Charles Quinlan. Also of unusual interest was an article, "Fliers of the Future", in

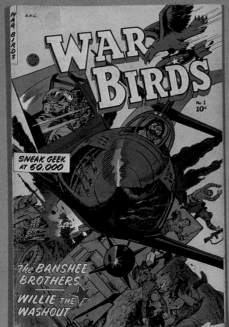

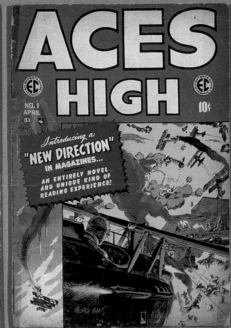

the gravure section. It was by-lined Major Zack Mosley, Florida Wing Commander, with nary a mention of his "Smilin' Jack" strip. And in 1943 the McKay Co published a strip version of the Book of the Month Club Best-seller, *Thirty Seconds Over Tokyo*, Captain Ted Considine's account of how he bombed Japan on 18 April 1942.

The Fifties revival of interest in aerial warfare brought a new hero to comics, *Captain Steve Savage and his Jet Fighters* (1950). In No.10, Mort Lawrence drew a three-chapter Korean story called "Operation Destruction", in which he used an unusual effect for the explosions. He simply left all such panels uncoloured, so that they stood out starkly against the rest of the page. Fiction House entered the new fray with *War Birds* (1952), finding room among the Korean war heroes for a finely drawn

flashback feature about the Battle of Britain. Charlton Comics cornered the war comic field with many titles, including the 1956 *Fightin' Air Force*, the 1958 *US Air Force*, and the exceptional 1968 *War Wings*. They even issued a war comic for the girls, *Sue and Sally Smith, Flying Nurses* (1963). But the only comic-book to concentrate on the truly heroic days of wartime flying, the string and woodwork brigade of 1914-1918, was an EC "New Direction" title, *Aces High*. Although it only lasted five issues, its standards of art and writing flew as high as its name.

Bill Barnes America's Air Ace Comics No.4 © September 1941 *Street and Smith. Drawn by Jack Binder*
The American Air Forces No.1 © 1944 Flying Cadet Publishing
Skyrocket Comics No.1 © 1944 *Harry Chesler Features*

Spitfire Comics No.132 (No.1) © 1944 Malverne Herald
Captain Flight Comics No.1 © March 1944 Four Star Publications
Thirty Seconds Over Tokyo © 1943 David McKay. Drawn by Clayton Knight

War Birds No.1 © 1952 Fiction House
Fightin' Air Force No.11 © March 1958 Charlton Comics. Drawn by Maurice Whitman
Captain Steve Savage No.10 © October 1955 Avon Periodicals. *Drawn by Everett Raymond Kinstler*
War Wings No.1 © October 1968 Charlton Comics
Aces High No.1 © April 1955 EC Comics. Drawn by George Evans
Sue and Sally Smith Flying Nurses No.48 (No.1) © Charlton Comics. *Drawn by Dick Giordano*

Sad Sack and his Funny Friends

The funny side of war soon found its way into the American comic-books, providing patriotic chuckles for those not impressed with superheroics. *Joker Comics* No.16, a random specimen from June 1944, has "Tessie the Typist" emulating the heroine of the pop song, "Rosie the Riveter", by signing on at the Ajax Aviation Co while boyfriend Skidsy, as per the cover cartoon, signs on with Uncle Sam. "Star and Tar", merry matelots on leave, settle the hash of a Fifth Columnist ("I'm gonna make sausage meat outta you, Adolph!") and remind readers, "Every time you buy a War Bond you Slap a Jap!" An oddball pair, "Rolly and Solly", also put paid to a suspicious person who makes remarks like "Down mit you, you little slimy, rotten, dirty, dumbkopf, American swine!"

GIs proved to be mass devourers of comic-books. Circulations soared, and Harry A. Chesler initiated a pocket-sized series of service-oriented comic-books designed to tuck into uniform pockets. *First Class Male* (1942) alternated pages of strips with funny letters from "Bill O. Lading" to his various girl friends, while *Riggin' Bill* did the same thing for the Navy: "Waves of Laughter for the Boys in Blue".

But the real star of service strips came from the ranks in action. "The Sad Sack" was created by George Baker for the Army's own weekly magazine, *Yank*. Baker had been an animator with the Walt Disney Studio, and although his scratchy pen-work on the Sack seemed a world away from cute li'l cartoon critters, his strips were pure pantomimes, GI gems of visual humour. From 1944 the Bell Syndicate began to distribute Baker's Sack to home-town papers, and when the artist was duly discharged from the Army he began to draw a weekly strip about his character, also duly discharged. For a while Sack coasted along on his popularity with ex-servicemen, but his mishaps in "civvy street" were never quite as hilarious as they had been under fire. But a new career was nigh. In 1949 Harvey Publications tried him out in his own comic-book, *Sad Sack Comics*, giving him the catchline, "Loved by Millions!" The body of the book consisted of reprinted Sunday strips, but each issue had a brand-new cover cartoon drawn by Baker himself, an unusual added attraction. The comic, a steady success, slowly switched to all-new material. Although not by Baker, and although betraying Baker's visual purity in favour of standardized dialogue balloons, the new-style comics had much greater appeal for youngsters. To Baker's original regiment (Sergeant Circle, General Rockjaw) were added Sadie Sack the ugly WAC, Muttsy the Talking Dog, and even a Little Sad Sack! And from the original comic-book there came a parade of spin-offs, including one which must surely have surprised any old GI still subscribing: *Sad Sack Navy Gobs 'n' Gals* (1972).

The only post-war army cartoon to catch the public fancy is "Beetle Bailey". A Classic stumblebum soldier, Beetle made his newspaper debut on 3 September 1950, rose (but never from the ranks) to become the second most popular comic strip in the States, and put a tentative big foot into comic-books in May 1953. Created by Mort Walker (who, it may be recalled, won a dollar in the *Tip Top Comics* cartoon contest in February 1938), Beetle is supported by General Halftrack, Lieutenant Flap, and the only one of the awkward squad to get his own comic-book, *Sarge Snorkle*. Mort Walker, one of the few cartoonists to care about his characters, supervises his comic-book operation from a concrete castle in Connecticut, the world's only Museum of Cartoon Art.

First Class Male *No.1* © *1942*
Remington-Morse/Chesler
Riggin' Bill *No.3* © *1942 Remington-*
Morse/Chesler
Private Bill *No.6* © *1943 William*
Wise/Chesler
Joker Comics *No.16* © *June 1944*
Marvel Comics
Canteen Kate *No.2* © *August 1952*
St John. Drawn by Matt Baker
Beetle Bailey *No.1* (OS 469) © *May*
1953 Dell. Drawn by Mort Walker
Sarge Snorkel *No.10* © *September*
1975 Charlton Comics/King Features

Sad Sack and the Sarge *No.1*
© *September 1957 Harvey*
Publications. Drawn by George Baker
Sad Sack's Funny Friends *No.27*
© *May 1960 Harvey Publications.*
Drawn by George Baker
Sad Sack Laugh Special *No.1*
© *1958 Harvey Publications. Drawn*
by George Baker
Sad Sack's Army Life *No.1* (Harvey
Hits *No.17*) © *February 1959*
Harvey Publications. Drawn by
George Baker

Sad Sack USA *No.1* © *November*
1972 Harvey Publications
Sad Sack With Sarge and Sadie *No.1*
© *September 1972 Harvey*
Publications. Drawn by George Baker
Sad Sack's Muttsy the Talking Dog
No.1 (Harvey Hits *No.74*) ©
November 1963 Harvey Publications.
Drawn by George Baker
Sad Sack Navy Gobs 'n' Gals *No.2*
© *October 1972 Harvey Publications*
Little Sad Sack *No.5* (Harvey Hits
No.83) © *August 1964 Harvey*
Publications. Drawn by George Baker

ATOMIC COMICS

"On August 5 1945 a single bomb from a single B-29 devastated the Japanese city of Hiroshima – and with its detonation the world entered a new era: the Atomic Age!" A quote, not from the *Encyclopedia Britannica*, but from Rudy Palais' "The Bomb That Won The War", lead feature in No.1 of *Science Comics* dated January 1946. And with it, comics entered the Atomic Age, too, although *The Comic Book Price Guide* lists a one-shot title, *Atomic Bomb*, with the highly suspect date of 1942. This was more likely a Canadian re-covering of an older American comic-book, as was No.1 of *Atomic Comics*, dated January 1946. In England, *The Atomic Age Comic* (1947) featured "Atomic Tommy the Bullet Proof Crime Smasher", drawn by veteran creator of "Rob the Rover" Walter Booth. "Tommy's electronic jacket radiates a form of atomic energy which deflects bullets and gives him the strength and agility of ten men." The first American atomic superhero was presumably "The Atom", a supporting star of *All-American Comics* from October 1940, although the creators, Flinton and O'Connor, failed to explain the mystery of Al Pratt's super-strength, or his choice of name.

The mushroom cloud ushered in a new crowd of superheroes, beginning with Barry Dale, scientist working at the Atomic Institute, who discovers he is radio-active. "Evidently my body is so geared as a result of working with radium and uranium that it can explode atoms and give me atomic strength!" Swifter than thought Barry becomes *Atoman* (February 1946), nicely drawn by Bob Kane's ex-assistant on *Batman*, Jerry Robinson. The same month brought *The Atomic Thunderbolt* from Norton and Peterson. Professor Josiah Rhonne, "leading scientist of the atom bomb project", pulls the wrong switch and transmutes Willy the Wharf Rat into the invincible, indestructible Thunderbolt. A revived interest in atomics during 1965 brought two new nuclear heroes, Captain Atom, who soon took over the title of *Strange Suspense Stories*, and *Nukla*. Captain Atom was Captain Adam, "Air Force career man, physics prodigy at eight, chemist and ballistics genius" who, accidentally trapped in an Atlas missile, sur-

vives the explosion. "At the instant of fission Captain Adam was not flesh, bone and blood at all. The dessicated molecular skeleton was intact, but a change never known to man had taken place." Adam had become Atom. Nukla was formerly Matthew Gibbs, U-2 pilot whose mind survived atomic disintegration with the power to direct atomic explosions at will. The threat of nuclear war inspired several titles. *Commander Battle and the Atomic Sub* (America's Secret Weapon) found a good deal of trouble on the sea bed when men from Mercury occupied the ruins of Atlantis. But more trouble was in store for those who bought the comic: it was designed in "The Great New Process of Truevision", an attempt at two-dimensional 3-D that made it nigh on impossible to read! *Atom-Age Combat* was a frightener from February 1958, predicting the progress of the Third World War between the US and "another country". As a clue, their officers wear button-up collars, monocles, and say things like "A good joke, is it not?" A better joke, perhaps, were the funny animal comics sparked off by the nuclear age, from Al Fago's *Atomic Mouse* (1953) to Hanna-Barbera's animated *Atom Ant* (1966).

Science Comics No.1 © January 1946 Humor Publications. Drawn by Rudy Palais
Atoman No.1 © February 1946 Ken Crossen. Drawn by Jerry Robinson
Atomic Comics No.1 © January 1946 Daniels Publications. Drawn by Thomson
The Atomic Age Comic © 1947 Burn and Co. Drawn by Walter Booth
The Atomic Thunderbolt No.1 © February 1946 Regor Co. Drawn by Larry Norton
Strange Suspense Stories No.75 © June 1965 Charlton Comics. Drawn by Steve Ditko

Commander Battle and the Atomic Sub No.1 © July 1954 Titan/ACG
Atom-Agc Combat No.1 © February 1958 St John Corp
Atomic Mouse No.3 © July 1953 Capitol Stories. Drawn by Al Fago
Atomic Rabbit No.11 © March 1958 Charlton Comics. Drawn by Maurice Whitman
Atom the Cat No.12 © August 1958 Charlton Comics. Drawn by Pat Masulli
Atom Ant No.1 © October 1965 Hanna-Barbera/Gold Key

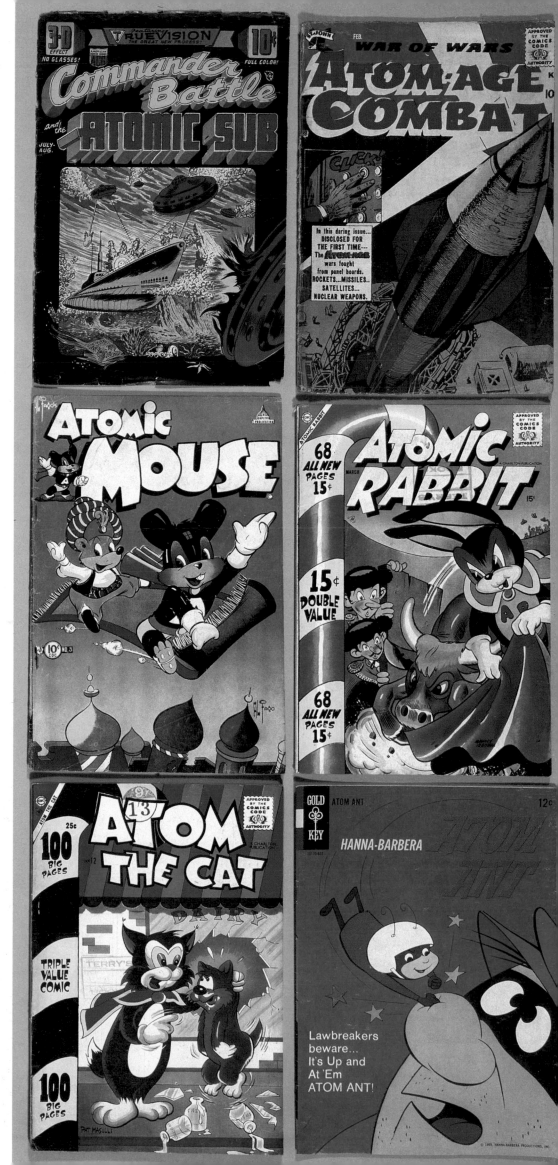

THE COMIC-BOOK CRAZE:
Comics with your Comics

By the Forties the craze for comic-books reached such a pitch in the United States that newspaper publishers, worried about their huge broadsheet comic supplements, cast a quizzical eye at the soar-away success of the 10-cent comic-book. Remembering, perhaps, that with *Famous Funnies* their own Sunday strips had been father to the comic-book, they were more than merely interested when comic-book artist Will Eisner came to them with his idea for a newspaper supplement in comic-book format. He showed them how a double-page spread of their broadsheet could be so printed that, when detached, folded and cut by the eager young reader, it turned into a neat, 16-page comic-book. It was an asset that Eisner and his staff were comic-book men from the word go and had never worked in the style and format of the syndicated Sunday page artists. The Eisner comic-book supplement looked just like a regular comic-book as sold on the newsstands. It was tried, and found immediate success with the comic-book-crazed kids. Furthermore, in his own personal comic-book, Eisner developed his art and writing beyond the limits imposed by the regular publishers, evolving a new maturity and sophistication suited to

his new audience. In its 12-year run, the weekly *Spirit Section* scaled the summit of American comic-book art. "The Spirit", a masked detective, was backed with other comic-book-style strips: "Lady Luck" by Chuck Mazoujian, "Mr Mystic" by Bob Powell, and later "Clifford", the first comic strip by Jules Feiffer.

The *Spirit* comic-book began on 6 February 1940; by April the *Chicago Sunday Tribune* had introduced its own pull-out and cut-up *Comic Book Magazine*. The main contents were partly regular Sunday pages cut in half, six panels to a page, rather like the old, original reprint comic-books; some extremely ancient reprints such as Frank King's "Bobby Make-Believe" from 1915; and a photo-serial with speech balloons adapted from Republic's film, *Drums of Fu Manchu*. By 1942 the *Comic Book* section was running specially drawn serials like "Fighting With Daniel Boone" by C. C. Cooper, "Vesta West and her Horse, Traveler" by Ray Bailey and "Adventures of Hy Score" by George Merkle. The *Philadelphia Sunday Bulletin* produced its own pull-out comic-book called *Fun Book*. Local cartoonist Bil Keane was the mainstay with his "Silly Philly" strip. Other papers carried Gilberton's *Classic*

Comics as a foldover comic supplement, an idea echoed recently by *Family Radio and TV*, which gives away *King Classics* as a comic-book. In Canada the *Toronto Sunday Sun* includes a 16-page comic-book which sports covers drawn by its young readers. But the first newspaper to include a proper comic-book complete with a quality paper cover was the *Columbus Dispatch*. Working with Stan Lee at Marvel Comics they gave away the 20-page *Special Edition: Spider-Man vs The Hulk* in 1979.

Special Edition: Spider-Man vs The Hulk © *1979 Marvel Comics Group/ Columbus Dispatch*
Sunday Sun Comics No.50 © *26 October 1960 Toronto Sunday Sun*
Lawrence of Arabia No.7 © *27 July 1981 Family Radio and TV*

Comic Book Magazine © *28 April 1940 Chicago Sunday Tribune*
Comic Book Magazine © *6 December 1942 Los Angeles Sunday Times*
Fun Book © *11 January 1948 Philadelphia Sunday Bulletin. Drawn by Bil Keane*
The Spirit Section © *19 January 1947 Will Eisner/Philadelphia Record. Drawn by Will Eisner*

GIVEAWAY COMICS: "A Daisy for Christmas!"

GULF FUNNY WEEKLY

PUBLISHED ONCE A WEEK—*FREE* AT ALL GULF STATIONS

THE UNCOVERED WAGON   By Stan Schendel

The American comic-book was born out of the commercial connection, and even as Max Gaines was packaging his *Famous Funnies* for the newsstands, he was putting together another comic-book for the giveaway trade. This was a compilation of Sunday strips by Percy L. Crosby, and under the title *Skippy's Own Book of Comics* it was boosted on the "Skippy" radio programme during 1934. The only way children could get a copy was to persuade Mom to buy them a tube of Phillips Dental Magnesia! The Skippy book was a regular 52-page comic-book, the first to concentrate on a single cartoon character. But it was not the first giveaway comic. This honour is held by a remarkable and little-known tabloid issued by Gulf Oil and called, reasonably enough, *Gulf Funny Weekly* (the first four editions being entitled *Gulf Comic Weekly*). Yes — weekly; and virtually the only weekly, certainly the only successful weekly, comic ever published in America. It ran without a break from May 1933 to May 1941, a grand total of 422 issues. And, more importantly, it was not a reprint comic but consisted entirely of original strips drawn specially for it. Although the adventures often centred on cars, oil, petrol, and related matters, there was no distasteful plugging of the sponsor's product, and the long-running "Uncovered Wagon" by Stan Schendel, "Curly and the Kids" by Victor, and "Smileage" by Svess, were fun in their own right. In 1935 Gulf changed their radio show comedians from Will Rogers and Irvin S. Cobb to Phil Baker and Bottle the Butler. They were featured on the front of the *Funny Weekly* in a strip by Schendel, the first American radio stars in the comics. Reflecting the popularity of the mid-Thirties adventure strips, Gulf introduced their own aviator in 1937, "Wings Winfair and his Round the World Flight". Originally drawn by Lyndell, the serial was taken over by Fred Meagher from 1938. On 10 February 1939 the comic was reduced to comic-book size, but remained only four pages.

In the pre-war period promotional comics were mainly of the reprint kind. *Gilmore Cub*, the only one to try the full broadsheet format, was a monthly eight-pager from the Gilmore Oil Co of Los Angeles. Mostly reprints of John Hix's "Strange As It Seems" pages via the McNaught Syndicate, it also included a special centre-spread of circus cut-outs. *Butterfly Comics*, an eight-page comic-book from Butterfly Bread, was a miscellany of strips from *Popular Comics*, plus "Red Magic", a novelty feature by A. W. Nugent, the "Funland" man. *Daisy Comics* was the first flirtation from Daisy Air Rifles, who would use comic-books as a main advertising medium for many years. Santa Claus introduced No.1 (December 1936 — Daisy's Golden Jubilee Year) with a "Howdy Kids!", then went on to describe "this swell little

book" as "a brand new idea, and I sure hope you get some real fun out of it." In its 36 pocket-sized pages were reprints from *Famous Funnies* ("Hairbreadth Harry", "Seaweed Sam", "Buck Rogers"), plus Santa's concluding advice: "Get a Daisy for Christmas".

Gulf Funny Weekly No.5 © *June 1933 Gulf Refining Co. Drawn by Stan Schendel*

Gilmore Cub No.1 © *April 1935 Gilmore Oil Co. Drawn by John Hix*
Butterfly Comics No.1 © *1936 Butterfly Bread. Drawn by Bill Holman*
Daisy Comics No.1 © *December 1936 Daisy Manufacturing Co*
Gulf Funny Weekly No.392 © *25 October 1940 Gulf Oil Corporation. Drawn by Victor*

A Whiz with your Wheaties!'

In the Forties kids got a Whiz with their Wheaties. Not just the usual charge from a bowl of the well-known "Breakfast of Champions", but a *Whiz Comics*, a special 32-page reduced-size edition of the popular Fawcett comic-book starring "Captain Marvel", "Ibis the Invincible" and full supporting cast. The special issue came sticky-taped to two packages of Wheaties, which made it tough to remove and mint copies impossible to obtain, a curse for any collector. More handsomely presented were the earlier *Little Orphan Annie Comics* issued by Quaker Puffed Wheat, the "Vitamin Rain Breakfast Food". Not only were the reprint strips backed up with new "Adventures of Captain Sparks", Commander of the Secret Guard; you could get an Official Insignia Cap just like his, or a Mysterious Whistle ("blows three ways"), or even a Mysto-Snapper Membership Badge ("sends secret telegraph signals") through the comic. Of course, you needed a few extra boxtops, too.

The longest run of any giveaway comic-book began in 1946 with the *Boys and Girls March of Comics*. No.1, a reprint of a "Goldilocks" strip, was a regular 32-page comic-book, given away free by the Sears Roebuck stores. The series, reprinting Dell Comics such as *Popeye*, *Donald Duck* and others, travelled through several changes of format: half-size, oblong, and currently pocket-sized. Produced by KK Publications (founded by Kay Kamen, the man who merchandized Mickey Mouse), *March of Comics* was the brainchild of Sig Feuchtwanger. It was the same Sig who, in 1947, packaged a neat set of four 16-page reprint comic-books for Popped Wheat: *Dick Tracy*, *Little Orphan Annie*, *Smilin' Jack* and *Terry and the Pirates*. Comic-book heroes now well outnumber newspaper strip characters in giveaways. Superman, following on a 1954 giveaway for Kelloggs, has recently reappeared in several super-bly produced original comic-books for Radio Shack, beginning with "The Computers that Saved Metropolis", co-starring the TRS-80 Computer Whiz Kids and the "insidious master of villainy", Major Disaster. The Marvel Comics heroes may also be found in well presented giveaways: *The Amazing Spider-Man* "Origin Edition" came free with any size "All" ("the Detergent with Bleach, Borax and Brighteners!") during 1979, while *Captain America and the Campbell Kids* made an unlikely team-up in 1980, on behalf of the popular soups. At the junior end of the market, Harvey Comics produced *Tastee-Freez Comics* in 1957, adding the advertising characters of Tee and Eff to "Casper the Friendly Ghost" and his chums. As Tee and Eff put it, "Have Mom serve super, duper, doubly delicious Doozys!" The message was less icky in Harvey's 1976 tie-up with American Airlines, providing inflight entertain-

ment with their *Astro Comics*: Casper the Ghost flew again.

In recent years more advertisers have preferred to create their own comic-book characters than adapt existing heroes. It sounds contradictory to begin with *Buster Brown Comics*, but trade mark apart, the famous shoe company had long since evolved away from Richard Outcault's original character of the early years. Instead their comic-book starred "Smilin' Ed" and his radio pals, Mr Traveller the Explorer, Alkali Pete the Old Westerner, Jim Nazium the Athlete, and, of course, Squeekie the Mouse, Midnight the Cat, and Froggy the Gremlin. The comic ran from 1945 to 1960, after which Buster Brown Shoes tied up with the *March of Comics* series. *Jo-Joy Comics* also started in 1945, a well-produced Christmas series for the W. T. Grant Stores. "Popsicle Pete" started as a sponsored strip in No.13 of *All-American Comics* (1940), and made it into his own *Popsicle Pete Fun Book* in 1947, where he showed ice-cream addicts how to form a swing band with the aid of bags from Popsicles, Fudgsicles, Chocsicles and Creamsicles. You swapped them for musical instruments: 100 bags for a Saxophone Kazoo, 200 for an enamelled drum: "Amuse your family and neighbors!"

The Adventures of Peter Wheat began in 1948, drawn by the delightful brush of Walt Kelly: it was a comic given away by bakeries. Equally well drawn, but in a very different mode, was Bob Powell's original superhero, *Major Inapak the Space Ace* (1951). Inapak, "the best chocolate drink in the world" (according to Major Inapak) contained the New Wonder Vitamin, Crystalline B12, which no doubt was a help in following the instruction to "punch out on perforated lines".

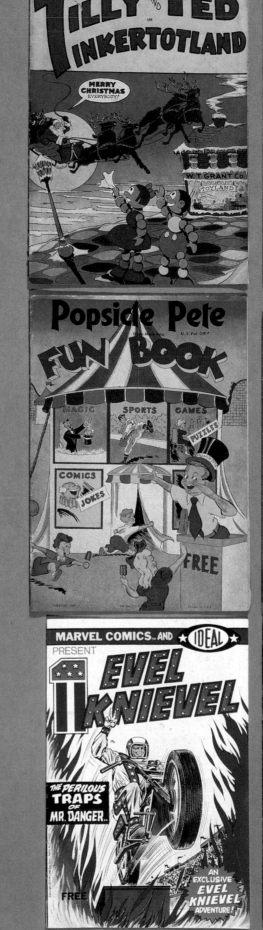

"We are the Ovaltineys!"

Strictly speaking, the first British comic to be produced for promotional purposes was not a giveaway. *Fun Fare* cost one penny, but was only sold by the Lancashire and Yorkshire Dairies. The price was fair enough, as the eight-page, red-and-black comic, forecasting in format the many wartime one-shots to come, was 99 per cent entertainment. The commercial message was well hidden in a strip entitled "Monica the Merry Milkmaid", an early effort of Basil Reynolds. The comic was packaged by the Fleet Street agency of Adams and Fidler, whose studio produced the *Daily Express* comic and other supplements.

The sales message was heavily emphasised in *Ovaltiney's Own Comic*. The big competition was to count the number of times the word Ovaltine appeared in it: the winner received a bar of Ovaltine Chocolate! *Ovaltiney's Own* was the most successful giveaway comic of them all. It came tucked inside every copy of *Rattler, Dazzler* and *Chuckler*, three weekly comics published by Target of Bath, so its circulation was considerable. In addition it was plugged every Sunday on the Ovaltiney's programme on Radio Luxembourg, and a further tie-in was its front-page adventures of "Elsie, Winnie and Johnnie", who were heard on the programme as the "imaginary family" of impressionist Harry Hemsley. The only trouble with the Ovaltiney comic was its artwork,

which being supplied by Target Publications' regulars, was not of the highest order. However, this did not stop the comic from clocking up a record run of 128 weekly editions from 26 October 1935 to 2 April 1938. The best of the pre-war giveaway comics was *Happy Families*, issued by Birds Custard. Four editions were produced, the last two blossoming from red and black into full colour. Ben Somers was the main artist, very good with complete adventure strips like "White Chief of the Bangui", but unfortunately saddled with having to draw a front page based on the traditional "Happy Families" playing card characters, which was a current Birds Custard advertising gimmick. The ugly Victorian designs were a decided turn-off to the youngsters of 1938. The comic, designed by the G. S. Royds agency, was unique in that each issue featured a famous "guest star" from a newspaper strip. No.1 has "Bobby Bear" of the *Daily Herald* in a special page by Rick Elmes.

Commercial comics were slow to make a post-war comeback, one of the first being the small but colourful *Scotty Comic*, given away in stationery shops with Scotch Tape during 1963. Next came the best, an excellently produced 16-page photogravure comic called *Wonder Weekly* (1968). It cost sixpence and was only obtainable at Esso Garages, but ran for a year before being cancelled. Many top art-

ists contributed, including George Parlett, and as with all professional British comics, there were Grand Free Gifts with the first two issues: an "Instant Fix Power Zoom Racecar", and a "Wonder Boy Gun", a variation on the classic cardboard banger. The comic was supposedly edited by the current Esso trademark, "R-r-r-roaringly yours, Tiger", but was actually edited by Roberta Leigh, the lady who gave you television's "Torchy the Battery Boy".

Tesco, the supermarket chain, tried their own comic in 1969. *Fun 'n' Games* cost sevenpence and came with a free chocolate Milky Bar, but its 24 pages of commercialized characters proved too much for the price ("Mr Quorange in the Land of Quosh", "Albert and Sidney the Kennomeat Men"). Advertising characters were acceptable to children as long as they didn't have to pay for them, hence little oblong comics of *Klondike Pete* were okay as long as they came free inside a packet of "Golden Nuggets". A variation on the giveaway was the comic published by KP, the snack division of United Biscuits. In exchange for some empty crisp bags you got a copy of the 24-page epic adventure of Steve Crisp, a boy who, imbued with Psika-Forces by aliens from Harmon, develops super-powers. Designing himself a super suit he muses, "A couple of initials for luck. How about KP? I'm the Crisp with the punch, they're the crisps with a crunch!" Thus was born *Captain Krunch* (1977). The following year brought several attractive giveaways, *The Fizzer* from Corona fizzy drinks, *The Muncher* from Wimpy hamburgers, and one of the most delightful of all, *The Menu*. This colourful comic was exactly that, a menu designed like an eight-page Beano. So many copies disappeared from the Rock Garden Restaurant in Covent Garden that the proprietor had to slap on a 50 pence charge.

Ovaltiney's Own Comic *No.1* © *26 October 1935 Target/Wander. Drawn by Louis Diamond*
Happy Families *No.1* © *1938 Alfred Bird/G. S. Royds. Drawn by Ben Somers*

Fun Fare *No.1* © *1934 Lancashire and Yorkshire Dairies. Drawn by Wasdale Brown*
Fun 'n' Games *No.1* © *25 October 1969 Tesco/Arly*
Wonder Weekly *No.1* © *5 July 1968*

Esso Petroleum/Plant News
Princess of Asgaard © *1971 Danish Bacon*
Orange Hand © *1974 Orange Hand*
Captain Krunch © *1977 KP Foods. Drawn by Alf Saparito*

The Muncher *No.1* © *1978 Wimpy/ Trent Press. Drawn by Graham Allen*
The Fizzer *No.1* © *1978 Corona*
The Menu *No.1* © *1 April 1978 Rock Garden Restaurant*

COMMERCIAL COMICS:
Sunny Jim and Sons

*"High o'er the fence,
O'er the fence leaps Sunny Jim,
Force is the food,
It is the food that raises him!"*

One of the first (and still remembered) jingles in British commercial radio was the song of Sunny Jim, broadcast over Radio Luxembourg through the Thirties. The character, toppered and periwigged, still appears on the boxes of Force Wheat Flakes just as he did

on the front page of *Funny Pips* No.1, dated 12 September 1903, making him the oldest, as well as the first, commercial cartoon character. Jim's adventures as a strip hero as drawn by "Yorick" (Ralph Hodgson) lasted only the 16 issues of the comic, but his name and fame seem eternal. Commercial characters were not admitted to the sacred pages of British comics, and it was left to the enterprise of Mick Anglo to produce the first sponsored comic actually to be sold in the shops, rather than given away. This was *Pioneer Western* (1950) which led off with a United States Ranger who bore the curious name of "Timpo Tim", not so curious when you read the introductory panel: "Re-enact his adventures with the lifelike models made by Timpo Toys." The rest of the strips tied in, too: "Mystery on the Farm" ("The Timpo range of model farm animals will make you a model farmer"), "Kamba the Jungle Boy" ("All animals shown are taken from lifelike Timpo Toys"), even "Buffalo Bill". It was not until 1983 that a major publisher, IPC, formed a liaison with a toy manufacturer to commercialize *Battle* into *Battle Action Force*.

In the USA, comic-books have been tying-in with commercial products since D. S. Publications issued No.1 of *Elsie the Cow Comics* in 1949. This ungainly lady was adapted from the advertising campaign for Borden's Milk, appearing in plug-less adventures with her husband Elmer and her calves, Beulah and Beauregard. Less commercial, more civic-minded, was Dell's use of *Smokey Bear*, the furry symbol of the US Department of Agriculture's Forest Fire Prevention Campaign. Smokey, a real orphan bear cub saved from the flames by Judy Bell, starred in several comic-books from 1955. Less civic-minded, more commercial was *Ronald McDonald* (1970), a Charlton Comic based on the clown who endorses "Big Mac" and the other delights of McDonald's hamburger heavens. Ronald's surprise guest star was "Professor Phumble", no great surprise to those who noticed the cartoonist's signature: Bill Yates drew both.

Several comic-books sprang from

musical sources. *Bozo the Capitol Clown*, heard on the children's records issued by that company, appeared in several Dell comics from 1950. This was also the year of *Rudolph the Red-Nosed Reindeer*, a seasonable hit for Gene Autry and destined to be an annual comic-book hit for DC Comics. The following year the top kiddie-disc was *Frosty the Snowman*, which became Dell's annual answer to DC's Rudolph. The popular and hilarious Fifties gimmick of speeded-up voices brought fame to a non-existent singing group called "The Chipmunks". Named Alvin, Simon and Theodore the trio made their Dell comic debut as *The Three Chipmunks* (1959). The toy tie-in returned when Mattel's best-selling Barbie Doll was turned into a Dell comic in 1962. Having conquered the pre-teen market with dolls and their fitted dresses, Mattel turned their attention to the boys. The result was *Hot Wheels*, which DC duly adapted into a comic-book in 1970. In the Eighties Marvel Comics tied in with Ideal Toys to produce *Team America* (1982), while DC joined Atari Inc for a comic starring "the strangest SF heroes of all". Not so strangely, it was called *Atari Force* (1984).

Elsie the Cow Comics *No.1*
© *October 1949 DS Publications*
Pioneer Western Comic *No.1*
© *1950 Wyndham House. Drawn by Mick Anglo*
Smokey Bear *No.2* © *May 1970 Gold Key*

Rudolph the Red-Nosed Reindeer *No.3* © *December 1952 National Comics/R. L. May*
Bozo the Capitol Clown *No.5* © *April 1952 Dell Publishing/Capitol*
Frosty the Snowman *No.2* © *November 1952 Dell/Hill and Range*
Ronald McDonald *No.3* © *January 1971 Charlton/McDonald Systems. Drawn by Bill Yates*
The Three Chipmunks *No.1042 (No.1)* © *October 1959 Dell Publishing/Monarch Music*
Barbie and Ken *No.3* © *May 1963 Dell Publishing/Mattel Inc*
Team America *No.1* © *June 1982 Marvel Comics/Ideal Toy Corp. Drawn by Bob Layton*
Hot Wheels *No.1* © *April 1970 National Periodicals/Mattel Inc. Drawn by Alex Toth, Dick Giordano*
Atari Force *No.1* © *January 1984 DC Comics/Atari Inc. Drawn by Garcia Lopez*

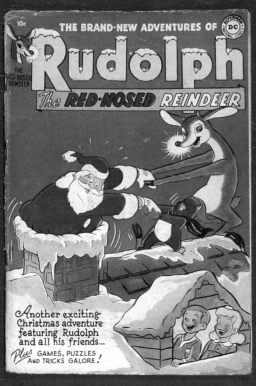

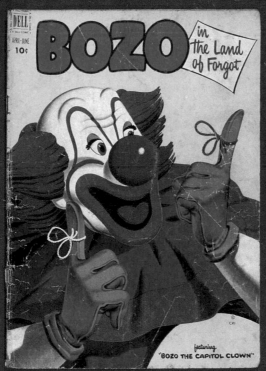

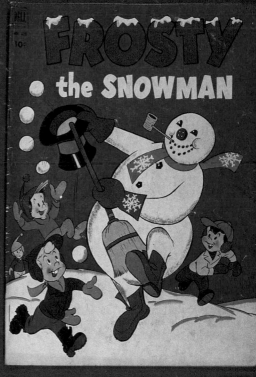

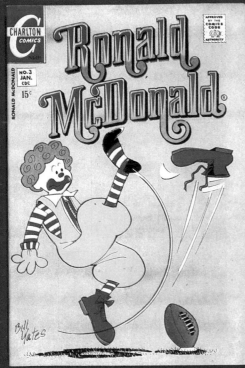

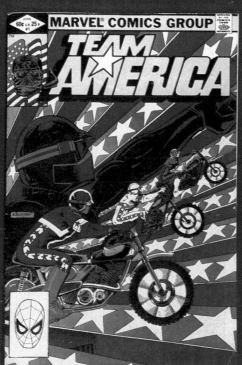

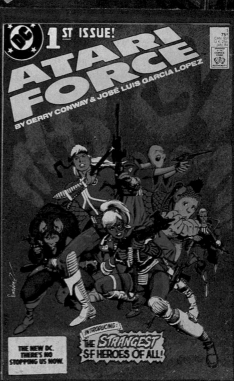

PROMOCOMICS: Nick O'Teen, Hijacker of Health!

Promotional comics designed to illustrate ideas and concepts rather than commercial products are rare birds in Britain, a curiosity for a country so steeped in strips. The earliest seems to be a series sponsored by the Royal Society for the Prevention of Accidents. Their first effort, *Safety Light*, published in the late Thirties, was a rather pallid black-and-green booklet. Quite unlike the average comic of the period in both design and format, ROSPA had made the mistake still common among promotional comics today. They had not commissioned comic artists and writers to produce it. When they returned to the comic concept after the war, they

made sure they did not make the same mistake again. *Traffic Light* (1946) was edited for them by John L. Bott, the experienced Amalgamated Press editor who had created *Happy Days*, and printed in their familiar four-colour style by the AP, too. Bott used one of his favourite artists to draw the front page, "In Silly Billy Land" – Fred Robinson, who had drawn "Crazy Castle" for *Happy Days*. Later ROSPA comics were less ambitious: *The Happy Highway* (1947), *The Traffic Roundabout* (1950), *The Friendly Beacon* (1951) and others were all drawn by Bob Wilkin, a neat but uninspired artist. There were also some independent road safety comics, such as

the funny-looking *Safety Fun* (1946) by Bob Mortimer, published by the Cambridge Accident Prevention Council, and *Careful Nippers* (1950), a tabloid comic drawn and published by Brian White, featuring his popular pre-war strip hero from the Daily Mail, "The Nipper".

National Savings, always keen to inspire schoolchildren in the morality of saving, not spending, their pocket money, introduced *Moneybox* to post-war classrooms. It carried the catchline "Here's Fun and Interest for Young Savers" and featured the adventures of "Bond and Stamps the Helpful Tramps". Brightly printed in colour, the comic failed as a comic because once again it was not designed by comic men. When National Savings returned to the promocomic idea in 1981, they made no such error. *Money Fun*, featuring their popular advertising character, "Melvin Moneyspider", was edited and drawn by experienced artists, including Basil Reynolds (from *Mickey Mouse Weekly*) and Jim Baikie. It also chanced to include the last published strip to be drawn by Wally Robertson, who had begun drawing for comics in 1913!

Religious ideas have been introduced into a few comic publications: the Salvation Army's long-established *Young Soldier* has lately increased its strip cartoon content, and Christian Publicity put out *Plus*, "The Extra Special Paper". An intriguing item for collectors is *The Young Warrior*, a monthly comic issued by the Worldwide Evangelization Crusade. For some years the front-page strip "William the Warrior" was drawn by the *Beano's* own Dudley D. Watkins. He drew the feature free as part of his contribution to Christianity. Also "based on Christian ethics to meet the need of today's children" is *Hotshot*, "The Picture Paper with a Purpose". Its purpose is that of the Band of Hope, to persuade its young readers to swear off strong drink. Another health crusade is carried out by the Health Education Council, who use the American character Superman in their comic campaign. In eight pages of full-colour pictures an English artist pits the American superhero against the evil Hijacker of Health, Nick O'Teen. Political comics arc scldom tried, perhaps because the parties consider comics to be the concern of kiddies. The first was *Form*, a photogravure 12-pager published by the Conservative Party in 1959. The next created much more of a stir when it was published in 1981. *The Stormer*, "Britain's Only Nationalist Comic", featured a front page villain called "Billy the Yid the Kosher Cowboy". At least the comic was honest enough to carry the motto: "H. M. Government Health Department Warning: This Publication Contravenes the Race Act!" It was published by the National Front.

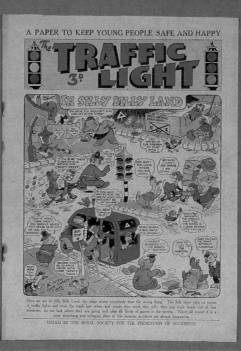

CLASSIC COMICS: "Chock Full of Exciting, Chilling, Thrilling Adventure!"

October 1941, and the Gilberton Company of New York launched the first title in their *Classic Comics* series, *The Three Musketeers*. Editor Albert Raymond penned a few suitable words of introduction: "Unforgettable, unmatched and unsurpassed is each of the *Classic Comics* titles, stories by the world's immortal authors, each portraying his favorite hero and heroine so characteristically and faithfully reproduced in *Classic Comics*. Read and thrill to the exploits, adventure, romance, excitement that these great writers have created; you'll long remember the enjoyment and pleasure each book will give you."

To depict in 62 four-colour comic-

book pages Alexandre Dumas' masterpiece of 1844, Editor Raymond chose Malcolm Kildale, artist of 1939's unlikeliest superhero, "Speed Centaur". This selection of the second-rate was to be a hallmark of *Classic Comics* artwork for many years, and makes suspect the oft-expressed good intentions of the Gilberton Company: "Each page chock full of exciting, chilling, thrilling adventure!" Particularly crude in execution were Stanley Maxwell's slaphappy brushwork on *Robinson Crusoe* (No.10), Louis Zansky's awkward panelling of *Don Quixote* (No.11), and Allen Simon's utterly repulsive *Hunchback of Notre Dame* (No.18). *Classic Comics* became *Classics Illustrated* with issue No.35, *The Last Days of Pompeii*, published March 1947. This was Gilberton's first attempt at an upmarket shift. The second came in March 1951 when No.81, *The Odyssey*, was the first to be issued with a painted cover. One by one, as they came up for reprinting, the back issues had their crude linework covers replaced by newly painted pictures.

Gilberton's 28-year run and 169 titles was a record nowhere near matched by their emulators. In 1942 Dell started a *Famous Stories* series with Robert Louis Stevenson's *Treasure Island* as depicted by Robert Bugg. It was superior to *Classic Comics* in every way, yet after No.2, *Tom Sawyer*, the series closed. Dell had better luck later when in 1948 they initiated a long run of illustrated Zane Grey novels beginning with *Spirit of the Border*. In 1944 the David McKay Company issued six editions of *The American Library*, compilations of King Features daily strips adapted

from current best-sellers. *Ideal (A Classic Comic)* was a Timely Publication launched in 1948 with *Antony and Cleopatra*: inside the strip was entitled "All for the Love of a Woman!" Timely's ideals were decidedly unclassical; No.2 was called *The Corpses of Dr Sarcotti*. *World's Greatest Stories* No.1 (1949) was *Alice in Wonderland*; No.2 was *Pinocchio*; there was no No.3. *Fast Fiction* (1949) was a series which went in the other direction. After four issues it changed its snappy title and slogan ("World famous action thrillers streamlined by *Fast Fiction*: Tops in reading pleasure because they're edited for action!") for the heavier heading, *Stories by Famous Authors Illustrated*: "A Treasury of Celebrated Literature". Neither gambit did Seaboard Publishers any good: after 13 numbers they folded. For the record, No.1 was *The Scarlet Pimpernel* and No.13 *Scaramouche*.

In recent times *King Classics* (1977) have published English language editions of the Spanish-originated comic-books; No.1 was *A Connecticut Yankee in King Arthur's Court*. Marvel Comics also started a run of *Marvel Classics*, beginning with *Dr Jekyll and Mr Hyde* (1976). This was actually a comic-book enlargement of a pocket-sized series called *Pendulum Illustrated Classics*, put out three years earlier in 1973. Last, but definitely least, Fox Features. They published a pair of highly spurious classics in 1950, *Samson and Delilah*, neatly timed to look like an official adaptation of the Victor Mature/Hedy Lamarr biblical epic, and *The Black Tarantula*, a horror comic disguised as a literary adaptation complete with the fraudulent label, "One dollar, now ten cents"!

Classic Comics No.1 © October 1941 Gilberton. Drawn by Malcolm Kildale
King Classics No.1 © 1977 Editorial Bruguera/King Features

Zane Grey's Spirit of the Border No.197 (No.1) © September 1948 Dell Publishing
Famous Stories No.1 © 1942 Dell Publishing. Drawn by Robert Bugg
World's Greatest Stories No.1 © January 1949 Jubilee Publications

Fast Fiction No.4 © January 1950 Seaboard. Drawn by Jim Lavery
American Library No.4 © 1944 David McKay Co/King Features
Stories by Famous Authors Illustrated No.3 © December 1949 Seaboard. Drawn by Henry Kiefer
Ideal (a Classical Comic) No.1 © July 1948 Timely Comics
A Feature Presentation No.5 (No.1) © April 1950 Fox Features
A Spectacular Feature No.11 (No.1) © April 1950 Fox Features

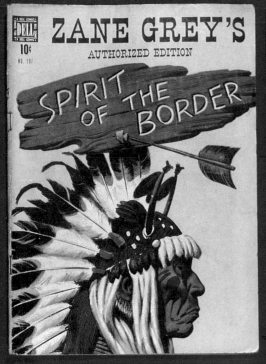

ZANE GREY'S
AUTHORIZED EDITION

SPIRIT OF THE BORDER

DELL
10¢

Famous Stories

NUMBER ONE
10¢

THE COMPLETE STORY OF
Treasure Island
BY ROBERT LOUIS STEVENSON

CAN. EDITION

Further Adventures of Lewis Carroll's
ALICE
in Wonderland
THROUGH the LOOKING-GLASS

WORLD'S GREATEST STORIES Nº 1

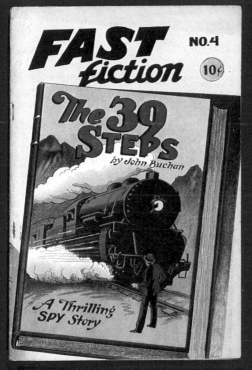

FAST fiction NO.4
10¢

The 39 STEPS
by John Buchan

A Thrilling Spy Story

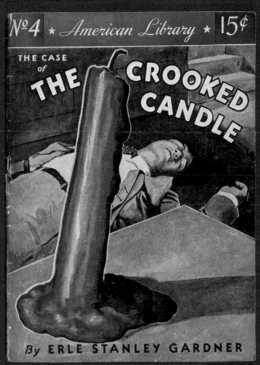

Nº 4 ★ American Library ★ 15¢

THE CASE of
THE CROOKED CANDLE

BY ERLE STANLEY GARDNER

A TREASURY OF CELEBRATED LITERATURE
NO. 3

STORIES BY Famous
AUTHORS Illustrated

SHE
SHE H. RIDER HAGGARD

10¢

IDEAL
A CLASSICAL COMIC
ANTONY AND **CLEOPATRA**
10¢ K

JULY NO. 1

IF *MARK ANTONY* WOULD RATHER EMBRACE *CLEOPATRA* THAN LEAD HIS TROOPS IN BATTLE, IT IS TIME FOR THEM TO FEEL MY DAGGER'S STING!

A FEATURE PRESENTATION

APR.
now 10¢

the BLACK TARANTULA

A SPECTACULAR FEATURE

SAMSON and **DELILAH**

APR. 10¢

CLASSICS ILLUSTRATED: British Style

By the time Gilberton's *Classic Comics* reached Britain, they were well into the upper end of the market. The title had changed to *Classics Illustrated* and the covers had switched from bold linework to soft-edged paintings. When the importation of American comic-books was stopped, Strato Publications began a well-produced British edition series with the necessary full-colour printing done in Dublin. For reasons of their own, they rearranged the publication order beginning with a new No.1, *Huckleberry Finn*, in October 1951. By 1960 the publication had passed to the distributors, Thorpe and Porter, whose successful schedule required more titles than Gilberton were currently producing. Acting under license they contracted a British studio to produce a sequence of brand new *Classics Illustrated* beginning with a revised version of No.84, *The Gold Bug* by Edgar Allan Poe. This was followed by a list of 12 completely new classics, starting at No.143 with Daniel Defoe's obscure *Sail With The Devil*, subtitled "Captain Singleton's Adventures". The artist was Norman Light and the studio and colour production (the litho printing, done in Sweden, required hand painting) was by Mick Anglo, the man who gave you

Marvelman! The classics chosen for picturization included several epics (*The Aeneid, The Argonauts*), some fantasies (*The Canterville Ghost, The Queen of Spades*), a very feminine *Through the Looking-Glass* by Jennifer Robertson, and perhaps the only cartoony *Classics Illustrated* ever, an *Adventures of Baron Munchausen* by your author. The final number reached by the British Editions was 164, although original *Classics* were continued on the continent in multi-language editions.

The first British comic-books actually to emulate the *Classics Illustrated* format were published by Philipp Marx under his Amex imprint. The series title was *A Classic in Pictures*, the subtitle "The World's Greatest Stories Illustrated". The format followed Gilberton's exactly, save that the 48 inside pages were in two colours (red and black) rather than four. No.1, published in 1949, was a well illustrated but unsigned picture version of Charles Dickens' *Oliver Twist*. Marx always issued his comics in pairs, and No.1 was accompanied by the second of his *Classics* titles, Sir Walter Scott's *Ivanhoe*, with rousing artwork by A. Philpott. Some years later all twelve of Marx's *Classics* were reissued. It would be churlish to suspect Mr Marx of sharp practice, but

the series was given a new running title, *Famous Stories in Pictures*, new and redesigned cover paintings, and a new imprint, Bairns Books, one of Marx's several subsidiaries. They looked like completely new publications, especially as the colour was dropped from the inside pages.

More in British comic tradition, although owing inspiration to the *Classics* by Gilberton, was the *Picture-Show* series put out through Woolworths by Juvenile Productions. The stories of *Robin Hood* and *Robinson Crusoe* were told in colourful picture strips drawn very much in the style of the nursery comics of the Thirties. Much more action-packed were the pocket-sized *Thriller Comics*, 68-page booklets which reprinted classic serials that had appeared earlier in the weekly *Knockout Comic*. No.1, published in partnership with No.2 in November 1951, was *The Three Musketeers*, an Eric R. Parker serial from 1946. The companion book was *Dick Turpin*, serialized by Derek Eyles in 1948. Later the classical aspect was lost and the series changed title to *Thriller Picture Library*.

Look and Learn, an educational weekly, included picture serials from the classics, and several of these were later reissued in comic-book format by the juvenile publisher, Franklin Watts. A new, simplified, large letter text was added by a Ms Betty Root, billed a little confusingly as Lecturer at the Institute of Reading in the University of Reading. *King Solomon's Mines* and its companion titles bore the message: "Picture Classics are suitable for children of all ages and anyone who enjoys a good read." There was certainly a good read to be had in Oval Projects' picture strip edition of *Macbeth* (1982): William Shakespeare's play, unlike Gilberton's *Classic* condensations, was, proclaimed the cover, "the entire text, unabridged and unexpurgated". Critics were anything but unanimous: "The comic-book *Macbeth* is a step forward" (Clive James, *The Observer*); "The Bard in comic format? O Gods, give us a break!" (Jack Kroll, *Newsweek*); "My favourite bit is the witches!" (Desmond Proctor age 15).

Picture-Show of Robinson Crusoe
© *Juvenile Productions*
King Solomon's Mines © *Franklin Watts/IPC*
The Canterville Ghost © *Thorpe and Porter*

Through the Looking Glass
© *Thorpe and Porter. Drawn by Jennifer Robertson*
Adventures of Baron Munchausen
© *Thorpe and Porter. Drawn by Denis Gifford*
Oliver Twist © *1949 Amex*

Ivanhoe © *1949 Amex. Drawn by A. Philpott*
Westward Ho! © *1949 Amex. Drawn by Colin Merritt*
Treasure Island © *Bairns Books*
Ivanhoe © *Bairns Books*
Henry V © *Bairns Books*

TRUE COMICS: "A Thousand Times More Thrilling!"

"Truth is Stranger and a Thousand Times More Thrilling than Fiction!" proclaimed the bannerline under the title of *True Picture Magazine*. Unfortunately it was a thousand times less saleable: even a swift title shift to the more commercial *True Comics* failed to save the steady decline of this subsidiary of Parents Magazine Press. After absorbing one by one its collapsing companion comics (*Calling All Boys/ Tex Granger, Calling All Kids, Jack Armstrong*), *True* became a mail-order only title and disappeared. But for a while it rode high on the comic-book boom (No.1 was dated April 1941), promoted through Parents' Magazine as a quality non-fiction comic suitable for the children of caring homes: "*True Comics* will introduce you to men and women who have made history by their courage, brilliance and perseverance." George J. Hecht, publisher, listed a glossy panel of Senior Advisory Editors assisting Harold C. Field, editor: Karl S. Bernardt, Professor of Psychology at Toronto University; George H. Gallup, Director of the Institute of Public Opinion; Rev Frederick G. Hochwalt of the Catholic Welfare Conference; David S. Muzzey, Professor Emeritus of History at Columbia University, and others. There was also a panel of Junior Advisory Editors, five of whom were credited as Movie Stars (Gloria Jean, Roddy McDowall, Shirley Temple, Virginia Weidler and Darryl Hickman) and one as Eddie's Daughter (Janet Cantor)! They were later joined by Joel Kupperman, Quiz Kid.

Five months later publisher Hecht personally introduced No.1 of *True's* companion magazine, *Real Heroes*, a document of some historic interest. He begins: "There are now being published some 75 'comic' magazines, a large number of which feature stories of supermen of one kind or another. Many of these stories tell how fictional characters overcome difficulties by superhuman or impossible means. While recognizing that there is a demand for such fanciful stories, we believe there is also a demand for magazines in which all of the colored picture stories are completely true. We are counting on your help in spreading the news that there is a new magazine, not about impossible supermen, but about *Real Heroes*." Hecht's Senior Advisory Editors now included Hendrik Willem Van Loon, author of *The Story of Mankind*. *Real Heroes* ran to 16 issues, not many, but 12 better than its immediate imitator, *World Famous Heroes*. Street and Smith's "cover job", *Trail Blazers*, also ran to four issues before switching to superheroics as *Red Dragon*. Other true titles included *Real Life Comics* (1941), which mixed past and present personalities (Robert Louis Stevenson and Clark Gable in No.33), and *Real Fact Comics* (1946) which followed the same formula (H. G. Wells and Lon Chaney in No.3).

Max Gaines and his EC (for Educational Comics) augmented his successful *Picture Stories from the Bible* with further Picture Stories: *American History* (1945), *World History* (1947) and *Science* (1947). The latter topic lent itself to strip illustration, and stimulated *Marvels of Science* (1946), the first of many comics to bear the imprint of Charlton Publications, *Future World* (1946), and the Canadian *Science Comics* (1951). Their preoccupation with the future almost puts these titles into the science-fiction category.

The oddest of all the factual comics was *Picture News*, an attempt to produce a comic-book newspaper. Editor Leigh Danenberg addressed "Boys and Girls, Mothers and Dads" in No.1, datelined 1 January 1946: "*Picture News* looks the same as other books, but with appearance and method of presentation the likeness ends. *Picture News* reports the news with its endless appeal and its prophecy of things to come, in action and speaking and color pictures. Now *Picture News* for the first time uses this new medium of action pictures and color and dialogue to make life real on the printed page. Here is why, in presenting the news, we outdo all others. Our artists in their minds' eye can see what the camera cannot photograph, and thus picture scenes and characters and action with skilful accuracy plus human understanding. Action pictures with color and

dialogue is picture-writing for the age of television and atomic energy." The courageous but doomed experiment lasted nine issues, collectable today only for its curiosity value – and its pages of cartoon comment on current events by the veteran newspaper humorist, Milt Gross.

Picture Stories From American History *No.1 © 1945 Educational Comics. Drawn by Allen Simon* Picture Stories From World History

No.1 © Spring 1947 Educational Comics. Drawn by Allen Simon Picture Stories From Science *No.1 © Spring 1947 Educational Comics. Drawn by Allen Simon*

True Comics *No.47 © March 1946 Parents' Magazine* Real Heroes *No.1 © September 1941 Parents' Magazine* Real Fact Comics *No.3 © July 1946 Detective Comics. Drawn by Dick Sprang*

World Famous Heroes Magazine *No.1 © October 1911 Comic Corp.* Trail Blazers Picture Stories *No.3 © July 1942 Street and Smith* Picture News *No.1 © January 1946 Lafayette Street Corp.* Marvels of Science *No.1 © March 1946 Charlton Publications* Future World Comics *No.1 © Summer 1946 George Dougherty. Drawn by Allen Ulmer* Science Comics *No.1 © March 1951 Export Enterprises (Canada)*

COMICS TO DO YOU GOOD

"Since the comic strip is the language of many millions of boys and girls in America, why not let God speak to them in their own tongue?" The self-answering question was posed by Dr Francis C. Stifler, Editorial Secretary of the American Bible Society and Conductor of Bible Periods over the National Broadcasting Company Network. He was also on the Editorial Advisory Council of ten religious authorities who each wrote enthusiastic introductions for the world's first comic strip Bible. Issued in quarterly parts, *Picture Stories from the Bible* began in Fall 1942, and on completion was reissued in bound volumes as Old and New Testament Editions. It was another first for the man who created the American comic-book, M. C. Gaines, and he used his knowledge of the comics world in promoting this daring venture. Each issue was bannerlined "For the First Time in Colored Continuity!" and the colourful advertisements scattered through companion comic-books were also eye-catching: "You will Thrill with the Daring and Exciting Stories of Daniel, Solomon, Samson, Joshua and David!" His covers were considered a shade too exciting, however, and No.2, captioned "David defeats the Philistines by Slaying and Beheading Goliath!", was replaced in reissue by four small panels of slightly less exhilarating scenes, such as "Joseph Welcomes His Father". Gaines ranged through religion for his Advisory Council, enlisting Dr William Ward

Ayer of the Calvary Baptist Church, Dr Alexander M. Dushkin of the Jewish Educational Committee, Dr J. Quinter Miller of the Federal Council of the Churches of Christ in America, Rabbi Ahron Opher of the Synagogue Council, Raimundo de Ovies, Dean of the Cathedral of St Philip, and Frank S. Mead, author of *See These Banners Go*. His choice of scriptwriter and artist was less inspired: Montgomery Mulford did his best to combine words from the Protestant King James Bible, the Catholic Douay Bible, and the Jewish Publication Society version, while Don Cameron just drew. Gaines formed a new company to publish his bible books, calling it Educational Comics, known by it initials as EC. In a few years EC would come to represent a very different kind of comic.

The first religious body to use comic strip format for their own purposes was the Catechetical Guild of St Paul, Minnesota. Their *Timeless Topix No.1* was published in November 1942 and thence ten times a year, July and August being excluded as the comic was sold only in schools. Originally a 16-page, 5-cent comic (possibly the first to be printed in smooth full-colour litho), *Topix* shortened its title to become a standard 52-page comic-book from October 1946. This was the year when two further religious comics came on to the market, *Catholic Comics* in June and *Treasure Chest* in December. *Sunday Pix*, published by David C. Cook in

Illinois, is an American curiosity. An eight-page colour weekly, it is closer to the British traditional comic than any other US publication. It was sold through Sunday Schools at 5 cents a copy, and the indicia includes the strange claim that *Sunday Pix* was registered with the Post Office on 29 March 1902, yet Volume 1 Number 1, illustrated here, is dated 1 May 1949!

Billy Graham, the international evangelist, added comics to his all-media campaigning in 1951, publishing *The Story of Naaman the Leper* "as portrayed by Cliff Barrows, Music Director-Narrator". Closer to regular comics are the publications of Fleming H. Revell, whose Spire Christian Comics are advertised with the traditional "POW!". Spire's titles ("Bold! Colorful! Exciting! Action-packed!") include strip adaptations of the books *God's Smuggler* and *The Cross and the Switchblade*, pop-oriented comics like *The Gospel Blimp* and a run of titles starring the eternal teenager, Archie: *Archie's Clean Slate*, *Archie's Family Album*, and *Archie's One Way* ("Archie's Exciting Exploits as an Active, Witnessing Christian!"). And in recent times Marvel Comics have added to their superhero line with *Francis, Brother of the Universe* (1980) and *The Life of Pope John Paul*.

Timeless Topix *No.2 Vol.2* © *October 1943 Catechetical Guild* Sunday Pix *No.1* © *1 May 1949* *David C. Cook Co. Drawn by Ames*

Picture Stories From The Bible © *December 1943 Educational Comics. Drawn by Don Cameron* Tales From The Great Book *No.1* © *February 1955 Famous Funnies. Drawn by John Lehti* Catholic Comics *No.5* © *October 1946 Catholic Publications* Francis Brother of the Universe *No.1* © *1980 Marvel Comics. Drawn by John Buscema* The Crusaders *No.1* © *1974 Chick Publications. Drawn by Jack T. Chick* Billy Graham Presents Naaman the Leper *No.1* © *1951 Grason Co. Drawn by Norman Hamilton* The Cross and the Switchblade *No.1* © *1972 Spire Christian Comics. Drawn by Al Hartley* God's Smuggler *No.1* © *1972 Spire Christian Comics. Drawn by Al Hartley* Archie's Love Scene *No.1* © *1973 Archie Enterprises/Spire Christian Comics. Drawn by Al Hartley*

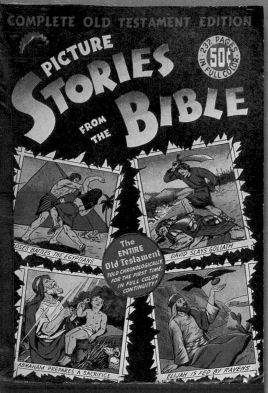

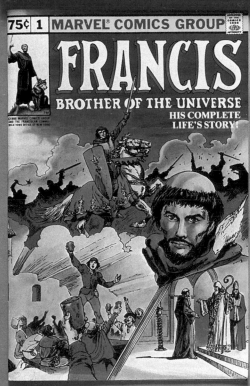

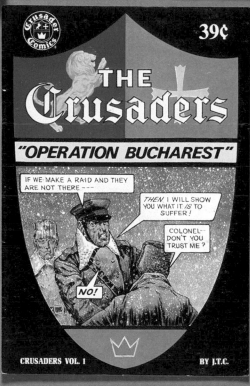

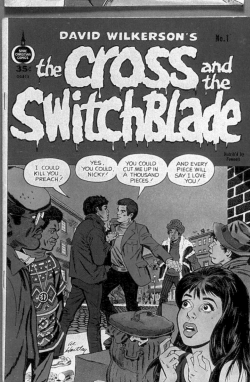

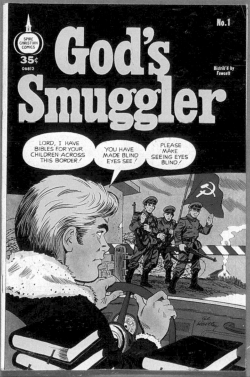

EDUCATIONA COMICS: Dagwood Splits the Atom!

The use of comic-books in the fields of education and information was an obvious step in the American tradition of "If you can't lick 'em, join 'em!" Max Gaines, the pioneer publisher, was the first to enlist educational authorities in the endorsement of his comic-books, to soothe worried parents and teachers, and promote acceptability of the booming field. The first Editorial Advisory Board of the Superman DC Comic Magazine Group consisted of Josette Frank, staff adviser of the Children's Book Committee of the Child Study Association of America; Dr William Moulton Marston of the American Psychological Association; Dr C. Bowie Millican of the Department of English Literature, New York University; Ruth Eastwood Perl, Ph D, of the American Psychological Association; Dr W. W. D. Sones, Director of Curriculum Study, University of Pittsburgh; Dr Robert Thorndike, an educational psychologist from Columbia University; and Lieutenant Commander Gene Tunney of the US Naval Reserve and one-time World Heavyweight boxing champion. With so many education experts involved in comic-books, it could not be long before comic-books began working directly for education.

Dagwood Splits the Atom was produced in 1949 by King Features Syndicate, distributor of most of the top newspaper strips. Although only Chic Young's clumsy husband of the "Blondie" strip is starred in the title, the comic included all of King's favourite characters, Popeye and Olive Oyl, Jiggs and Maggie, and even Toots and Casper. Mandrake the Magician acted as the conjuring instructor. The narrative was prepared by Lieutenant General Leslie R. Groves, the retired head of the organization which had developed the atomic bomb, and doctors John Dunning and Louis Heil. The book was drawn by Joe Musial, star cartoonist of the King Features "bullpen" from 1932, who drew covers for *King*

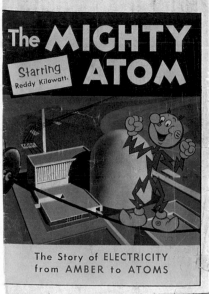

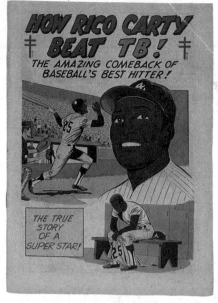

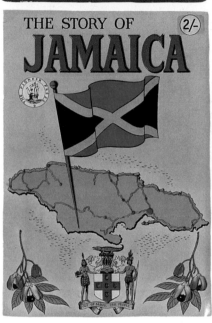

Comics and later took over The Katzenjammer Kids. The success of the comic, one of the first to use strip technique for education, led to a follow-up for the New York State Department of Mental Hygiene starring Blondie, which won Joe a Citation from the US Congress. Soon King's Education Division, proudly proclaiming themselves as "Originators of Comics for Education", was a full-time section producing specialized comic-books currently catalogued in ten divisions. The *Comics Math Library* has "Hagar the Horrible" explaining perimeters, the *Comics Reading Library* has eight titles including *Tim Tyler's Luck*, the *Career Awareness Program* presents 15 books about Popeye trying jobs ranging from Agri-Business to Fine Arts, there are 24 *King Classics Libraries*, and a *Spanish-English Program* with *Popeye el Marino* and Blondie and Dagwood renamed *Lorenzo y Pepita!*

Walt Disney Productions entered the educational field in 1978 with two *Mickey Mouse and Goofy* comic-

books, exploring energy conservation. Other familiar comic-strip faces from the newspapers include Al Capp's hillbilly hero in *Li'l Abner Joins the Navy*, a recruiting promotion, and *Li'l Abner and the Creatures from Drop-Outer Space*, an attempt to interest schoolleavers in the Job Corps. Joe Palooka, Ham Fisher's boxing "champeen", starred in *It's All in The Family*, a 16-page promotion for the American Way of Family Life, and Bill Holman's "foo fireman" *Smokey Stover* was an obvious choice for the National Fire Prevention Protection Association with his "hot tips". One of the most fascinating of these special comic-books is *It's Fun To Stay Alive* (1948), a road safety promotion of the National Automobile Dealers Association. Inside a crude cover was a bright, litho-coloured array of specially-drawn road-safety strips featuring "Henry", "Bruce Gentry", "Abbie an' Slats", and "Bugs Bunny".

Dagwood Splits the Atom © 1949 *King Features. Drawn by Joe Musial*

Mickey Mouse and Goofy Explore Energy © *1976 Walt Disney/ Educational Media Co*
Popeye the Sailor and Health Careers *No.1* © *1972 King Features. Drawn by George Wildman*
Li'l Abner Joins the Navy © *1950 Toby Press. Drawn by Al Capp*
Smokey Stover © *1953 Feature Publications. Drawn by Bill Holman*
It's All in the Family © *1944 Armed Forces Information Division. Drawn by Ham Fisher*

It's Fun to Stay Alive © *1948 National Automobile Dealers*
The Mighty Atom © *1959 Reddy Kilowatt/Electrical Utilities*
How Rico Carty Beat TB © *1971 National Tuberculosis Association*
The Story of Jamaica © *1963 Pioneer Press (Jamaica)*
Consumer Comix © *1975 Wisconsin Department of Justice. Drawn by Peter Loft and Denis Kitchen*
The Amazing Spiderman © *1976 Marvel/Planned Parenthood. Drawn by Ross Andru*

CRIME COMICS

"Mr Crime" was the fanged spectre in a top hat who drifted through a Forties comic-book, hosting and commenting upon the action with remarks like "Heh! Heh! Atta boy, killer! Give it to 'em! Live up to your name of Cop-Hater Crowley! Heh, heh, heh!" The comic-book was called *Crime Does Not Pay* (June 1942) and Mr Crime might well have been the appellation of its creator, editor and illustrator, Charles Biro. For, with the introduction of the world's first comic-book to concentrate on crime, Biro set rolling the trend that would virtually end comic-books as we knew them. For the snowballing success of *Crime Does Not Pay* brought about not only a Biro-produced companion, *Crime and*

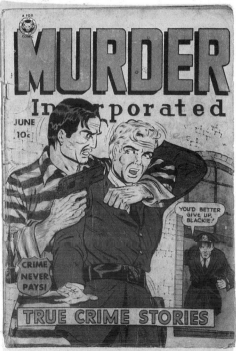

Punishment (April 1948), but a blood-thirsty host of imitators from editors and publishers less honourable than Biro and his partner, Lev Gleason. But although Biro's intentions were doubtless sincere – his stories were usually based on fact, and always pointed the title moral – his methods showed little regard for youthful susceptibilities or standards of taste.

Flicking through an average issue of the comic the eye recoils at such crudely cartooned strips as "Kill Crazy Keast" ("You bugheaded bloodhounds, come and get me! Ha-ha!"), "Landru the Terrible" ("Ugh, what a stench! Smells like human flesh!"), "Twin Idols of Evil" ("The dirty blighter! He's shooting himself! Blast the devil, the law should have had the pleasure!"), and "The Case of the White Eyed Butcher" ("Ah, what a beautiful thing a corpse is! Ha, ha, ha!"). These and more fill the November 1944 issue, which includes a house ad for Biro's other comic, *Daredevil*: "Don't miss the year's biggest surprise! Witness the most horrible torture instrument of all time in use – the Double Iron Boot!" Hard to believe that Biro's first strip, drawn for Harry Chesler's *Star Comics* in 1936, was a chucklesome fantasy called "Gooby Land"! Even harder to believe is Biro's old studio buddy from the same comics writing and drawing a crime comic so horrific that it would relegate *Crime Does Not Pay* to the nursery! Jack Cole, whose "Back Home in the Ozarks" was one of the first truly wacky strips, and whose "Plastic Man" was the most way-out superhero ever, turned his graphic talents to the vilest violence ever committed to comic-books. *True Crime Comics* (May 1947) lured young readers with its front cover offer of $100 reward for James Kent ("He's a Crook! He's a Killer! He's an Escaped Convict!"), then shattered them with "Murder, Morphine and Me! The True Confessions of a Dope Smuggler by Mary Kennedy." This flashback narrative begins with a crazed addict jabbing blonde Mary in the eyeball with a hypodermic, continues with a montage of the human dregs she acts as "hostess" to ("Sweetsh lil gal inna worl!"), and goes rapidly downgutter from there. There is no light relief. "Demons Dance on Galloway Moor"

is Cole's furiously-paced depiction of the Sawney Bean cannibal clan, but even he is outdone by the artist who followed on with "Boston's Bloody Gang War". This is the one which shocked the world when Dr Fredric Wertham used it as pictorial evidence in his classic study, *Seduction of the Innocent*. Two bound men are being dragged face-down behind a speeding car. "A couple more miles oughtta do the trick!" "It better! These ***!! gravel roads are tough on the tires!" "But you gotta admit, there's nothing like 'em for erasing faces!" "Superb! Even Big Phil will admire this job, if he lives long enough to identify the meat!"

But before the commercial conscience of the comic publishing world could be touched by the angry blare of publicity, almost everybody had a go at crime comics. Marvel turned *Wacky Duck* into *Justice Comics*, *Willie* into *Crime Cases*, *Cindy* into *Crime Can't Win*, and *Sports Action* into *Crime Must Lose*. Fox turned *My Desire* into *Murder Incorporated*, *Star Presentations* into *Spectacular Stories* (dragging in an unauthorized Sherlock Holmes as narrator), and initiated a notorious title, *Crimes By Women*. EC started *War Against Crime*, turned *International Comics* into *Crime Patrol*, and topped them all with *Crime Suspenstories*. More responsible, but still pretty tough, was Joe Simon and Jack Kirby's *Justice Traps the Guilty*.

It all ended in a United States Senate hearing, by which time crime comics had had their day and were being superseded by something even worse: horror comics. Charles Biro, the man who began it all, tried to advance comic-books out of the children's market and into an area that was acceptable to adults. He coined the term "Illustories" and enlarged his page-size to match that of *Life* magazine. No.1 of *Tops* was published in 1949; it was discontinued after No.2. Biro returned to his first field, nursery fantasy, and in the guise of cheerful "Uncle Charlie" launched *Uncle Charlie's Fables* (1952). It didn't mean much, and in 1962 he left comics to become a graphics artist at NBC television. Ten years later he died.

Spectacular Stories Magazine *No.1*
© *July 1950 Fox Features*
Murder Incorporated *No.1*
© *June 1950 Fox Features*

Crime Does Not Pay *No.36*
© *November 1944 Comic House.*
Drawn by Charles Biro
True Crime Comics *No.1 (No.2)*
© *May 1947 Magazine Village.*
Drawn by Jack Cole
Crime Patrol *No.1 (No.7)* © *Summer*

1948 EC. Drawn by Johnny Craig
Crime Mysteries *No.1* © *May 1952*
Ribage
Crimefighters *No.1* © *April 1948*
Marvel Comics
Down With Crime *No.1*
© *November1951 Fawcett Pubs.*

Wanted Comics *No.33* © *January*
1951 Toytown. Drawn by Mort
Lawrence
Crime Suspenstories *No.1* © *October*
1950 EC. Drawn by Johnny Craig
Fugitives from Justice *No.5*
© *St. John*

HORROR COMICS:
The Classic Monsters

Frankenstein: Classics Illustrated
No.16 © *August 1943 Gilberton Co.
Drawn by Robert Hayward Webb*

The first 100 per cent all-horror comic-books came from *Classic Comics*. Among the many "Masterpieces of Literature from the Pens of the World's Greatest Authors" as adapted into comic format by the Gilberton Company, there were several of a nature which normally librarians would tend not to allow into junior school hands. However Gilberton, undeterred by any finer sensibility than whether or not the literary work was out of copyright, cheerfully issued *Dr Jekyll and Mr Hyde* in August 1943; it was No.13 on his publication schedule. Robert Louis Stevenson's prose, as' adapted by Evelyn Goodman, was classic in the wrong way. Dr Jekyll, dressed as a toreador at a party ("To life! To laughter! To a gay evening!"), makes a new discovery: "Your eyes are blue, Lorraine. Very blue. Have they always been that way?" Bad enough to doctor the story but far worse was the visualization by Arnold L. Hicks. The double-page spread it takes to change the good Jekyll into his evil half Hyde is more than enough to upset a young mind, without the later close-up of his boot crushing a bird. Pages are devoted to Hyde creeping up on Lorraine, choking her with his claws, bearing her off, and when she rejects him ("An ugly man like me needs a beautiful wife!"), attempting to club her to death with his knobkerrie. Ms Goodman's scenario owed more to the 1932 Paramount film version than to Stevenson's novella, and the cinema is a clear influence on Gilberton's choice of classics. One by one they parallel the great Hollywood horror films, almost down to their original running order: *The Hunchback of Notre Dame* (1923, remade 1939), *Dracula* (1930), *Frankenstein* (1931), *Murders in the Rue Morgue* (1931), *Dr Jekyll and Mr Hyde* (1932), *The Invisible Man* (1933). To be fair, Gilberton did not publish a Dracula comic (despite strong rumours to the contrary). The title was first used for a Spanish fantasy comic in 1971, which featured the fabulous vampire on the cover painting only.

Classic Comics No.18, published in March 1944, was *The Hunchback of Notre Dame*. Once again Evelyn Goodman did her stuff, this time with Victor Hugo's immortal prose: "As the wheel turns, Quasimodo quivers under his bonds, the whip-lashes dig into his flesh, and soon blood streaks down his back." "Oh ...Oh!" Allen Simon's artistic interpretation was so raw in its graphic violence, so slapdash in its half-page portraits of the ugly hunchback, that for the 1949 reprint eight pages of it had to be deleted. Even this was not enough to satisfy those very comic-book critics whom Gilberton had set out to please with his originally noble project, and in 1960 a completely new, sanitized edition was picturized by George Evans and Reed Crandall.

It was inevitable that the immortal monster of Mary Wollstonecraft Shelley's *Frankenstein* should be turned into a *Classic Comic*, and No.26, as interpreted by Robert Hayward Webb and Ann Brewster, was published in time for Christmas 1945. Webb and Brewster, a team more at home with Fiction House heroes, replaced *Classics'* earlier crudity with comic-book competence, and although their Monster bore more than a passing resemblance to Boris Karloff's movie interpretation, their 43-page condensation was closer to the original novel than any of the many *Frankenstein* films. Or, indeed, any of the many *Frankenstein* comic-books, which have ranged through Dick Briefer's burlesque, which began quite seriously as "The New Adventures of Frankenstein" in *Prize Comics* No.7 (December 1940) before turning funny and graduating to his own *Frankenstein Comics* five years later, to Dell's totally silly conversion of the Monster into a superhero in 1946.

The *Classic Comics* version of Edgar Allan Poe's "Murders in the Rue Morgue" was thankfully not expanded, as the Universal movie had been, to suit the macabre personality of Bela Lugosi. The artist, Arnold L. Hicks, was mercifully restrained for once, although the uncredited scriptwriter was less so with Poe's prose: "There is only one logical solution. A monster ape! *A Killer Ape!*" The strip formed part of a trilogy, *3 Famous Mysteries* (No.21, July 1944); the other two were Louis Zansky's "The Sign of Four" from Conan Doyle, and a particularly horrible visualization of Guy de Maupassant's "The Flayed Hand". Drawn by Allen Simon, of course. A follow-up to this successful book was *Classics* No.40, *Mysteries by Edgar Allan Poe*, beginning with August Froelich's "black bloody page in history when murder, terror and treachery ran rampant in the streets", "The Pit and the Pendulum". H. C. Kiefer, the cover artist, then tackled "The Adventures of Hans Pfall", spoiling the whimsy of space travel by balloon with grisly close-ups of the high-flying Dutch hero as he cries "I'm bleeding from my nose and ears! *Ug!*" and "Quickly taking my penknife, I cut a vein!" Following this light relief came Harley M. Griffiths' "Fall of the House of Usher" in low-key greens and purples.

The last of the horror classics to receive comic *Classics* treatment was H. G. Wells' Victorian science-fiction story, *The Invisible Man* (No.153). By November 1959, when this was issued, the horror comics scandals were over and the clean, crisp artwork of Norman Nodel is testimony to the success of the campaign. It is superior (oddly enough) to *Superior Stories* No.1, which had been the first comic-book version of the Wells novella, published four years before. Pete Morisi's drawings suited the comic's label, "For Adults and Children". Much more exciting were those of Dino Castrillo and Rudy Mesina, who drew the 1977 version for *Marvel Classics Comics* No.25. Curiously, while all three comic-books strove to suggest an English atmosphere, each fell down badly, even ludicrously, in their depiction of the British policeman's uniform.

Frankenstein: Marvel Classics Comics No.20 © 1977 Marvel Comics. Drawn by Dino Castrillo
Frankenstein No.1 © 1945 Crestwood. Drawn by Dick Briefer
Frankenstein No.2 © September 1966 Dell Publishing
The Invisible Man: Classics Illustrated No.153 © November 1959 Gilberton Co. Drawn by Biggs
The Invisible Man: Superior Stories No.1 © May 1955 Nesbit Publishers
The Invisible Man: Marvel Classics Comics No.25 © 1977 Marvel Comics. Drawn by Dino Castrillo
Dr Jekyll and Mr Hyde: Classic Comics No.13 © August 1943 Gilberton. Drawn by Arnold L. Hicks
Dr Jekyll and Mr Hyde: Star Presentations No.3 (No.1) © May 1950 Fox. Drawn by Wallace Wood
Dr Jekyll and Mr Hyde: Supernatural Thrillers No.4 © June 1973. Drawn by Win Mortimer

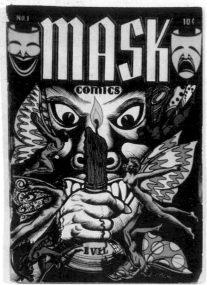  

  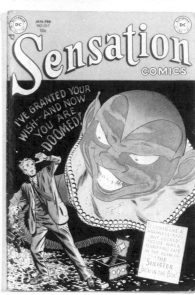

Bandwagon to Hell

American comic-books had always had a touch of the horrors right from the start. *New Fun* No.1, back in February 1935, had set its science-fiction hero, "Don Drake on the Planet Saro", against gigantic ants, and right on the front cover of No.3 Don encountered an alien with six legs, 11 tentacles and innumerable teeth. In No.6 (October) "Dr Occult the Ghost Detective" met a Dracula derivative known as the Vampire Master. Doc's lovely assistant, the aptly but oddly named Rose Psychic, shot the fiend full of silver bullets and he vanished "in a terrific burst of dazzling brilliance!" "Speak to me, Rose!" gasped Doc, bending over her, his eyes mere slits as he tried not to look down her low-cut nightie. "Oh, Doctor Occult!" sighed Rose, 'That was no ordinary vampire!'

But he was the first comic-book vampire, and the men responsible, scarce more than boys in fact, signed themselves Leger and Rueths. Rear-

range those names a little, add a letter here and there, and you come up with Siegel and Shuster, otherwise Jerome and Joseph or Jerry and Joe, the writer and artist who, in a year or so, would create the character who would take comic-books leaping into a dazzling future – Superman. Meanwhile, in the newly renamed *More Fun Comics*, their Dr Occult would pursue his ghost-detecting at serialized length, ridding the normal world of such abnormal monstrosities as Methuselah the Ancient One, a Werewolf, and Koth from the Supernatural World. Doc would also put paid to the Spectral Killer, a spirited survivor of the electric chair. *Funny Picture Stories*, the strangely named original adventure strip comic-book, published a six-page horror strip in its No.2 (December 1936). "The Monster Man" was written and drawn by Arthur Pinajian, who described his story thus: "Here Dick Kent stacks his life against the death mania of a mad-

man." The unjolly green-faced giant who kidnapped Dick's chum Gloria turned out to be the henchman of mad Dr Jacob Van Ridder. "That's Rafah, a Mongolian I picked up in the Far East. Because I saved his life he has become my devoted servant and has followed me to the four corners of the world!" At the climax "the Monster appears like a grim ghost but the law arrives and Kent hears the blast of a copper's gun, like thunder!" The first horror comic arrived in December 1943. *Suspense Comics*, advertised as "The Most Unusual Comic in the World", followed the radio tradition established by *The Shadow* and *The Man in Black*: it had a mysterious know-all narrator, "The Grey Mask". Radio-style hosting would become a horror comic trademark with EC's terrible trio, The Crypt Keeper, the Vault Keeper and the Old Witch. *Suspense* No.4 includes "The Devil to Pay" ("You can't kill my daughter, you fiends! How much blood can you spill?"), "Invitation to Horror" ("Is it true that a maniac is a maniac regardless of his position in society?"), and "Adventure into Yesterday" ("Merci-

182

ful Dieu! I am as a boy of twelve!!"). *Mask Comics* (February 1945) was milder in content despite a marvellously evil cover by L. B. Cole. The first really successful horror comic came from the American Comics Group, *Adventures into the Unknown*. It began in Fall 1948 and ran to August 1967, a long run for any kind of title, 174 issues. Its success was perhaps due to its relatively clean art style, never going overboard into the gruesome gothic that would bring the genre into disrepute. Even the serialized "Spirit of Frankenstein" was an interesting extension of the original story.

Black Magic (October 1950) was another quality comic-book designed and edited by the partnership of Joe Simon and Jack Kirby. Their "True Amazing Accounts of the Strangest Stories Ever Told" lasted for 49 issues. Marvel Comics were into the field early, developing their radio-based *Suspense Comics* (1949) into a horror comic, and similarly adapting *Marvel Mystery Comics* out of the superhero style and into *Marvel Tales* (August 1949), presenting "The

Strangest Stories Ever Told". It worked, so *Captain America* became *Captain America's Weird Tales* from No.74 (1950): how the mighty fall. (But Cap would return!) As the trend to terror grew, Marvel introduced no fewer than eleven horror titles. Harvey converted their superheroine *Black Cat* to *Black Cat Mystery*, and added *Witches Tales*. Ace put out *Beyond* and *Web of Mystery*, Avon revived *Eerie*, which they had tried as a one-shot back in January 1947, Fawcett started seven, from *Worlds of Fear* (1952) to *Strange Stories from Another World*. ACG added a companion for *Adventures into the Unknown*, entitled *Forbidden Worlds*; another long run – 145 issues. Even DC Comics climbed aboard the bandwagon with *House of Mystery*, which holds the record run of any horror comic. Starting in December 1951 it is still running today, "conforming to the Comics Code" since No.36 (April 1955). Its immediate success did what many a super-villain failed to do; it defeated Wonder Woman. Her original title, *Sensation Comics*, was turned into a horror comic from No.107 (January 1952).

Mask Comics *No.1* © *February 1945 Rural Home. Drawn by L. B. Cole*
Suspense Comics *No.4* © *June 1944 Et-Es-Go*
Adventures Into the Unknown *No.11* © *June 1950 American Comics Group*
Black Magic *No.1* © *October 1950 Headline. Drawn by Jack Kirby*
Blue Bolt Weird Tales *No.119 (No.1)* © *June 1953 Star Publications. Drawn by L. B. Cole*
Sensation Comics *No.107* © *January 1952 National Comics. Drawn by Alex Toth*

Worlds Beyond *No.1* © *November 1951 Fawcett Publications*
Beware Terror Tales *No.1* © *May 1952 Fawcett Publications*
Unknown World *No.1* © *June 1952 Fawcett Publications*
Monster *No.1* © *1953 Fiction House*
The Thing *No.1* © *1952 Charlton Comics. Drawn by Tyler and Forgione*
The Tormented *No.1* © *July 1954 Sterling Comics*

"Suspenstories We Dare You to Read!"

Out of the Night *No.1* © *February 1952 American Comics Group*
Witches Tales *No.1* © *January 1951 Harvey Publications*
Witchcraft *No.1* © *March 1952 Avon Periodicals*

"The chief contribution of American literature is horror" wrote Paul Buhle in the special Surrealism Issue of *Cultural Correspondence* (Fall 1979). If comic-books can be considered literature, then Buhl's statement will be considered by many comics connoisseurs to hold true. Certainly if Superman represents the original, pure comic-book hero, then the Vault Keeper, the Crypt Keeper and the Old Witch are the darker side of the dime. For a while, in the Fifties, evil triumphed over good to such an extent that even the superheroes succumbed. But the rising tide of illustrated evil reached unspeakable peaks as publishers, editors, artists and writers sought to outdo one another in their greed for sales, and what had begun as the most creative era in comic-books crashed in nationwide, even global, shockwaves that brought the entire industry tumbling down.

The beginning and the end of the billion-dollar comic-book industry belong to two men, a father and son named Gaines. M. C. (for Max Charles), having given the kids of the world *Famous Funnies* for their laughs and *Picture Stories From The Bible* for their sins, was happily running his little EC (for Educational Comics) line when, in 1947, he was suddenly killed in a motorboat accident. His son, William, inherited EC, keeping the logo but changing its meaning: EC now stood for Entertaining Comics. *International Comics* (1947), initiated by Max as a laudable attempt to arouse young Americans into taking note of the world outside, became *International Crime Patrol*, then *Crime Patrol* starring "Captain Crime", an attempt to cash in on the best-selling *Crime Does Not Pay*. In the December 1949 issue the horror began. Al Feldstein, a writer/artist whose main contribution to the medium had been a line in tightly-sweatered teenagers, contributed a strip called "The Crypt of Terror". Feldstein, a great fan of radio thrillers, modelled his story, "Return From the Grave", on *Inner Sanctum* and similar shows. He had his tale told by a sinister narrator, a straggly-haired cadaver called "The Crypt Keeper". The same month, in a companion comic-book called *War Against Crime*, out of "The Vault of Horror" came a hooded terror called "The Vault Keeper", telling a tale entitled "Buried Alive". The man who signed it was the same Al Feldstein. At the end of each strip appeared an appeal: "If you like this type of story, won't you write and tell me? Thank you." The response must have been extraordinary, for in April 1950 *Crime Patrol* changed its name to *The Crypt of Terror*, *War Against Crime* turned into *The Vault of Horror*, and *Gunfighter*, EC's one and only western title, had headed for the last roundup and became *The Haunt of Fear*. For a change, this one was run by a hostess, a cackling crone called "The Old Witch". Her artist/writer remained the same: Al Feldstein.

All three comics carried the same splash on their covers: "Introducing a New Trend in Magazines – Illustrated Suspenstories We Dare You To Read!" It was a dare many kids were eager to take up and there, of course, lay the rub. Children were the traditional target audience of the comic-book trade, and while Gaines, Feldstein and Co were clearly trying to upgrade their product, their New Trend titles were being bought and read by children. Parents and teachers began to react and, from them, the retailers and distributors. Gaines granted them a quick point, and after only three issues *The Crypt of Terror* changed its name to *Tales From the Crypt* (October 1950). It was his one and only concession. Four years later he was called before a Senate Sub-Committee where the Democratic Senator for Tennessee, Estes Kefauver, held up the current number of *Shock Suspenstories*, a title Gaines had introduced in 1952. "This", said the Senator, "seems to be a man with a bloody axe holding a woman's head up, which has been severed from her body. Do you think that's in good taste?" "Yes, sir," said Gaines "I do, for the cover of a horror comic. A cover in bad taste might be defined as holding the head a little higher so that the blood could be seen dripping from it." Gaines had already submitted to censorship when the cover of *Vault of Horror* No.32 (August 1953) had the meat-cleaver removed from a walking corpse's head. But even EC's covers dared not depict some of the horrors lurking within. The bottom was really scraped in *Haunt of Fear* No.19 (May 1953) with the story "Foul Play". A losing baseball team takes its revenge on one of their players by dismembering him and using his parts for a final, moonlit game. His leg becomes the bat, his head the ball, his hands the catcher's mitts, his scalp the brush, his torso a chest protector, his heart the home plate. The Crypt Keeper concluded what he was pleased to call his "fungo-fable", "See the long strings of pulpy intestines that mark the base lines. See the two lungs and the liver that indicate the bases, the stomach rosin-bag, and all the other pieces of equipment that once was Central City's star pitcher, Herbie Satten." The words are stomach-turning enough without the lovingly detailed full-colour illustrations by Jack Davis.

Following the US Senate investigation, and the establishment of the Comics Code Authority in 1954, Gaines editorialized, somewhat tongue in cheek, that the anti-horror comics lobby was a dirty Communist plot, then threw in the blood-stained towel. He cancelled all his titles, tried a "New Direction" series that failed to catch on and quit comic-books for adult magazines. What the father had begun, the son had just about finished.

The Vault of Horror *No.12 (No.1)*
© *April 1950 EC Comics. Drawn by Johnny Craig*
The Crypt of Terror *No.17 (No.1)*
© *April 1950 EC Comics. Drawn by Johnny Craig*
The Haunt of Fear *No.15 (No.1)*
© *May 1950 EC Comics. Drawn by Johnny Craig*
Tales From the Crypt *No.20 (No.1)*
© *October 1950 EC Comics. Drawn by Johnny Craig*
The Vault of Horror *No.32*
© *August 1953 EC Comics. Drawn by Johnny Craig*
Shock Suspenstories *No.12 (EC reprint No.3)* © *1953/1973 EC Comics. Drawn by Al Feldstein*

Out of the Nursery, Into the Crypt

British juvenile publishing has always had one foot in the grave. Buried deep in its Victorian past are those weekly works which earned the label of "Penny Dreadfuls". Their heroes were villians – *Varney the Vampire, Sweeney Todd the Demon Barber of Fleet Street* – and although their dark deeds were told in black massed text, their front pages were illustrated with horrific highlights lovingly over-engraved. Alfred Harmsworth, idealistic publisher of the period, founded his *Halfpenny Marvel* (1893) to combat the evil, only to have his occasionally bloodthirsty weekly branded a "Ha'penny Dreadfuller"! Nevertheless it was Harmsworth's Amalgamated Press which developed the classic form of British children's comic, and the nursery tradition was still flying high in the Thirties. A horror strip would have been unthinkable; even comic snakes were taboo!

Thrill Comics (1940) changed all that. With 36 pages of unrelieved action for threepence, Gerald G. Swan's very British imitation of an American comic-book offered "Voyage to the Moon" with Buck Preston, flying crocodiles, and a race of hairy, walking hippos, as drawn by William McCail. "Polo the Jungle Bred" starred a lion-raised Tarzan-type stabbing a bear with a spike and finding a white man encased in crystal. "The Bat", a superhero saviour of concentration camp victims, crept head-first down castle walls like Dracula revived. "The Iron Warrior" was a robot with a built-in hatchet who cleft an outsize alligator and pulled the head off a gigantic eagle. Even the artwork of William A. Ward, who drew the last three strips, almost matched the horror of his script, despite his being more at home drawing Donald Duck for *Mickey Mouse Weekly*! Ward also supplied Swan's *Slick Fun* with "Master of Sin", hunchback and crime king, and followed up with a serial called "Horror Island", the first genuine British horror strip. Its heroes, two submariners, were on a murderous mission from the start, seeking some legendary Spanish vampires who lurked within a lagoon within an iceberg. "Two creatures, survivors of some awful primeval curse, crouched in the shadows of their crumbling time-worn tomb, their eyes flaming redly in their hideous faces" were eventually destroyed, a few issues later, by the traditional silver bullets. Despite its title, *Thrill Comics* usually had a funny cover. An exception was 1942's Special Spring Number, which had a moody red, yellow and green portrait of Ward's "Krakos the Egyptian".

By the time the American Horror Comics began to creep across the ocean, Gerald G. Swan had converted his American-style comic-books to traditional British format. There was nothing to prepare the young readers' minds for what was about to hit them. From 1946 the comic-books began to return to the corner newsagents' shops. Insufficient in number to interest the major distributors, they once again became the sideline of the small men, arriving as ballast and dumped in bundles of an assorted gross. Actual titles and types were of no interest to anyone except the overgrown kids who remembered them from 1939, or the fast-growing breed of young comic fans for whom the 52-page books of full-colour funnies were a brand new experience. Not that many of them were funnies any more: for every *Giggle Comics* or *Ha-Ha Comics*, there were a dozen super-heroes, and even the adventure titles showed signs of a new trend towards crime, fantasy and horror. One memorable cover featured a grisly head impaled on a spike, while a British Beefeater gasped in a block-lettered balloon, "Cripes! It's a bleedin' 'ead!" Worse was to come.

The first public shot was fired in the *Sunday Dispatch* in 1949. In a leading article called "Comics that take Horror into the Nursery" the Honorary Secretary of the Society for Christian Publicity wrote: "Morals of little girls in plaits and boys with marbles bulging in their pockets are being corrupted by a torrent of indecent coloured magazines that are flooding bookstalls and newsagents. Not mere thrillers as we used to know them, these are evil and dangerous – graphic coloured illustrations of modern city vice and crime." In the course of a long article the Hon Sec illustrated his argument with some ill-chosen examples of mainly British comics of the day, detailing somewhat lasciviously R. Beaumont's not very well drawn heroine of "The Golden Scarab" on the front of *Comet*, and Dennis M. Reader's equally scrappy "Cat Girl" from Swan's *Topical Funnies*. He is also heavy-handed with a cover of *Sexton Blake Library*, not realizing that the pre-war detective hero had graduated to the adult market, and fails to appreciate the burlesque quality of Al Capp's "Fearless Fosdick", not understanding the comic overkill is a parody of "Dick Tracy". The Hon Sec concludes, "I shall not feel I have done my duty as a parson and father of children until I have seen on the market a genuinely popular children's comic." A year later and his duty was done: the Hon Sec was the Reverend Marcus Morris, and he created *Eagle*.

After 1950, when importing American comics was once again banned (this time because of a dollar crisis), British publishers began to reprint them direct from proofs or matrixes. It was these black-and-white editions of the EC horror comics and

their imitators that brought about the public outcry that led to the *Children and Young Persons (Harmful Publications) Act* of 1955. Horror comics disappeared, but although the Bill was renewed in 1965, a glance at many of today's British comics suggests that it may have lost its teeth.

Thrill Comics Special Spring Number © *April 1942 Gerald G. Swan. Drawn by William A. Ward*

Legend Horror Classics *No.1* © *1975 Legend. Drawn by Kevin O'Neill*
Strange Stories *No.1* © *Spencer*

Black Magic Comics *No.1* (*British Edition*) © *1952 Thorpe and Porter*
Comics to Hold You Spellbound *No.1* (*British Edition*) © *1951 Thorpe and Porter*
Eerie Comics *No.1* (*British Edition*) © *1951 Thorpe and Porter*

Ghostly Weird Stories *No.1* (*British Edition*) © *1953 Arnold Book Co*
Startling Terror Tales *No.1* (*British Edition*) © *1953 Arnold Book Co*
Tales from the Crypt *No.2* (*British Edition*) © *1954 Arnold Book Co*
Spellbound Magazine *No.1* © *1952 Cartoon Art Productions*
The Bat Magazine *No.2* © *1952 Cartoon Art Productions*
Suspense Magazine *No.1* © *1952 Cartoon Art Productions*

A World of Horror!

The fascination of the horror comic spread out from EC like some global plague, an affectionate infection that continues to erupt in faraway comics with strange sounding names. In Japan, the violently explicit pocket-sized comic-books stained with tears of blood wept over torn-out tongues, have titles like *The Headless Female Ghost*, *Even a Ghost Is Afraid*, and *The Little Drunken Fairy*. Why the weeping of blood should be such a comic-book cliché is unclear, unless it is the result of some compulsory eye operation which renders all Japanese comic-book characters out of Oriental ovals into Occidental Os. Once hastily past the colourful covers, the comics adopt the European tradition of black-and-white interiors: just as well with the plots they tell, although their artists' crude way with decapitations and physical combustions is closer to simple cartooning than the EC school of loving elaboration.

German horror comics go to opposite extremes. Every page, usually 32, is printed in colours so bright that they effectively lighten even the darkest of their strip stories. However, just like the Japanese comics, the German covers are much more exciting (and better drawn) than their contents. The longest-running title appears to be *Gespenster Geschichten* (*Ghost Stories*): No.429, published 1982, leads off with a nine-page tale whose title needs no translation: "Das Spuk-Haus von London"! The British capital has always been obsessively spooky to the Germans, who continue to adore the fogbound mysteries of Sherlock Holmes and to make major movies out of the dated tales by Edgar Wallace. Bastei-Verlag of Bergisch-Gladbach publish four weekly horror comics in all, the other titles being *Geister Geschichten* (which also translates as *Ghost Stories*), *Spuk Geschichten* (which, according to my *Deutsch-English Dictionary*, also translates as *Ghost Stories*), and *Vanessa die Freundin der Geister* (*Vanessa the Girl Friend of Ghosts*). The latter comic is designed for ghost-loving girls and is decidedly milder in its hauntings than

its bloodthirstier companions. Between the two extremes comes the Swedish comic-book *Mystiska Tvaan* (1971). The heroes are two young boys living in Stockholm who get mixed up in mysteries. The artist, Rolf Gohs, is also a photographer, and he uses his own photographs to make the milieu realistic. He also uses the lack of expensive interior colour to create pages filled with dense black shadows, rather in the manner of the old monochrome horror films of the Thirties which, for many, are superior in mood to the modern technicolor blood of Hammer Films. Spanish comics have their percentage of horror titles, but mostly in the adult area. However, one popular children's comic, *Mortadelo*, the solo comic named for Francisco Ibanez's hilarious series, "Mortadelo y Filemon, Agencia de Informacion", put out a Horror Special (or "Especial Horreur") in 1977, mixing a few slightly macabre adventure strips with some less macabre comic ones. One Spanish horror comic which needs no English translation is entitled *Horror Comics*, thus proving that the term coined back in the Fifties has become part of the international language of the Eighties.

Vanessa
Die Freundin der Geister

Nr. 33 · DM 1,90

BASTEI

Im Schloß der Ruhelosen
und andere unheimliche Geschichten

Österreich S 15/Belgien F 42/Frankreich F 6,-/Italien L 1300/Luxemburg F 42/Niederlande f 2.40/Spanien P 110/Schweiz Fr 2,-

Nr. 429 · DM 1,80

GESPENSTER
GESCHICHTEN

BASTEI-COMIC

Zusätzlich
Ein geheimnisvolles Abenteuer
von Hansrudi Wäscher

**Das Spuk-Haus
von London**
und vier weitere
unheimliche Geschichten

Österreich S 14/Belgien F 39/Frankreich F 5,-/Italien L 1200/Luxemburg F 39/Niederlande f 2.25/Spanien P 90/Schweiz Fr 1,90

Geister
GESCHICHTEN

BASTEI

Nr. 70 · DM 1,90

EXTRA STARK!

**Aufstand
der Dämonen**
Eine große Geschichte um Manos,
den Dämonenjäger

Österreich S 14/Belgien F 39/Frankreich F 5,70/Italien L 1200/Luxemburg F 39/Niederlande f 2.25/Spanien P 90/Schweiz Fr 1,90

Spuk
GESCHICHTEN

BASTEI

Nr. 141
DM 1,80

Österreich S 14
Schweiz Fr 1,90
Belgien F 24
Frankreich F 5
Italien L 1000
Luxemburg F 34
Niederlande f 2.25
Spanien P 35

**Die Nacht auf
dem Höllenriff**
und andere Gruselstories

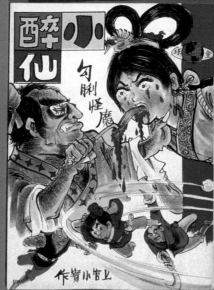

COMIC HORRORS:
Frankie Stein and Friends

Dick Briefer, fresh out of the Art Students League, celebrated his 21st birthday by having his first strip published in No.1 of *Wow! What a Magazine*. It was July 1936, and *Wow* was the first comic-book to be packaged by Sam Iger. Being early days in the new industry, Iger let his cartoonists have their head, and was quite unconcerned when Briefer turned in his contribution for No.3, a crude but vigorous strip adaptation of "The Hunchback of Notre Dame". It was the first classic horror in comic-books but was not the reason *Wow* folded with the next issue: publisher John Henle's money ran out. When Iger and his cartoonist partner Will Eisner set up Universal Phoenix Features to supply material for *Wags*, the export-only comic, Briefer was signed on to start his Hunchback all over again. Beginning with the 23 April 1937 issue of the weekly *Wags*, Briefer's atmospheric serial became the first horror strip to be seen in Britain. (*Wags* was never distributed in the States). Briefer, evidently a horror film obsessive, went on to create "The New Adventures of Frankenstein", an updated adaptation of the Shelley classic, for *Prize Comics*. The series, still obviously trademarked by Dick's rapid brushwork, although he sought to hide himself behind the penname "Frank N. Stein", began in No.7 (December 1940). After four years of pretty horrific adventures (and definitely horrific drawings) the character suddenly switched to comedy. As Briefer's ideas got wilder and wackier, his art got looser. The "new" Frankenstein was so successful that he was awarded his own comic-book from the Summer of 1945. Briefer's inspiration was obviously *The Bride of Frankenstein* (1935), James Whale's somewhat satirical sequel to the Shelley story, mixed with the monstrous cartoons of Charles Addams in the *New Yorker*. But it was Briefer's version that inspired the first British attempt at a comic horror, "Krankenstein the Monster Funster" in *Crash Comics* (1947), a craven confession I have made elsewhere (see *Frankenstein File*, NEL 1977). Curiously, the American comic Fran-

kenstein returned to horror in a 1952 revival, while the British comic Frankenstein stayed strictly for laughs. Northern cartoonist Ken Reid created "Frankie Stein" for *Wham!* (20 June 1964), a double-page epic that got so out of hand that the publishers, Odhams, refused to print at least one episode. Frankie was later revived in funnier form by Robert Nixon: on his first day at school, Professor Cuthbert Cube's monstrous creation bounces off a trampoline, crashes flat-head first through the headmaster's study, and brings down the clocktower! The comic was No.1 of *Shiver and Shake* (10 March 1973), Britain's first horror comic (with the accent on the comic). The strips included "The Duke's Spook", "Scream Inn" ("We're Only Here For The Fear!"), a very Victorian affair by Bryan Walker, "Soggy the Sea Monster", and "Sweeney Toddler", a beastly brat. There was also a monster-packed parody of a TV soap opera called "Horrornation Street", and Ken Reid was given his head with a back-page colour pin-up, "Creepy Creations". No.1 was "The One-Eyed Wonk of Wigan"! But it was Frankie Stein who proved the great favourite and he continues to be frightfully funny in *Whoopee* and his own annual *Summer Special*.

The first American comic-book to make fun of fear was *Spooky Mysteries*, a 1946 creation of Jason Comic Art. "Mr Spooky", "Super Snooper the Hound for Clues", "Barney Bungle" and the rest were fun, but ahead of

their time. Much more successful was *Tales Calculated to Drive You Bats*, an Archie Publication which came along in November 1961, well in the wake of the horror comic scare. The burlesques by Orlando Busino ("Hugo the Werewolf" "Tut-Tut the Mummy") and the mock ads for "Ogre, the Only Deodorant made especially for Monsters", were so cartoony they could only have been calculated to drive you to smile. Most of the other funny monster comics owed their origins to television. *The Munsters* (1964) was adapted from the marvellous television series based on the old Universal Pictures creations, with tall Fred Gwynne as Herman Munster and Yvonne De Carlo as the vampiric Lily. *The Addams Family*, based on the Charles Addams cartoons, seems only to have been a comic-book based on the Hanna-Barbera animated version of 1974, rather than the live-action series of ten years earlier. *Mr and Mrs J. Evil Scientist* and *Frankenstein Jr* were also Hanna-Barbera cartoon series, while *Milton the Monster* came from the rival studio of Hal Seeger. *The Little Monsters* ('Orrible Orvie and Awful Annie, offspring of Demonica and Mildew Monster) and *Melvin Monster* (drawn by John Stanley of the *Little Lulu* comics) were both original creations for comic-books, although their styling owed a lot to televisual inspiration.

Whoopee Frankie Stein Summer Special *No.1* © *May 1977 IPC Magazines. Drawn by Robert Nixon*
Monster Fun Comic *No.1* © *14 June 1975 IPC Magazines. Drawn by Robert Nixon*
Spooky Mysteries *No.1* © *1946 Your Guide. Drawn by Jason*

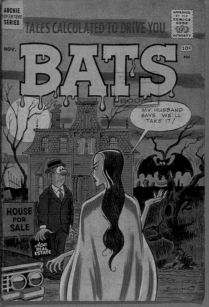

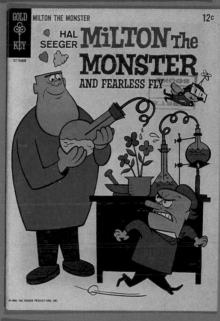
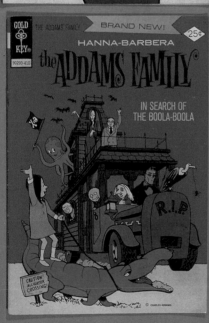
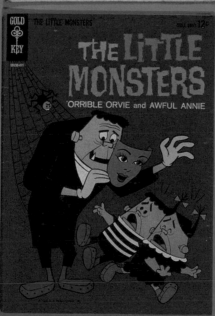

Tales Calculated to Drive You Bats
No.1 © November 1961 Archie
Publications. Drawn by Busino
The Munsters *No.1 © October 1964*
Gold Key/Kayro-Vue
Frankenstein Jr and the Impossibles
No.1 © October 1966 Gold Key/

Hanna-Barbera
Mr and Mrs J. Evil Scientist *No.1*
© November 1963 Gold Key/Hanna-
Barbera
Milton the Monster *No.1*
© February 1966 Gold Key/Hal
Seeger

The Addams Family *No.1*
© October 1971 Gold Key/Hanna-
Barbera
The Little Monsters *No.1 © August*
1964 Gold Key
Melvin Monster *No.8 © May 1967*
Dell. Drawn by John Stanley

TEENAGE COMICS:
"The Mirth of a Nation!"

They billed him as "The Mirth of a Nation" and "America's Top Teenager", but across the top of *Archie Comics* No.21 in July 1946 they blazed a third headline: "This printing is over 1,306,000 magazines"! From his birth as a back-up feature in *Pep Comics* No.22 dated December 1941, Archie had become the top selling comic-book in America. In his honour, his publishers, MLJ Magazines, even changed their name to Archie Comic

Publications Inc. And with many titles still selling today, Archie stands alongside Superman and Batman as the third longest-lived comic-book hero with an unbroken run of 43 years – and he's still not a day over sixteen!

America invented teenagers around the turn of the Thirties, a concept crystallized in the movies by Judy Garland and Mickey Rooney at MGM and Donald O'Connor and Peggy Ryan at Universal. It was natural for comic-books to reflect their cinematic popularity, but even John L. Goldwater, editor of *Pep* and the "J" in MLJ, could hardly have anticipated the extent to which the character he created would catch on. Archie Andrews, the freckle-faced carrot-top of Riverdale High, first bared his gap-toothed grin on the cover of No.36 of *Pep Comics* and, from No.41, he became a fixture. *Pep's* star super-heroes, the Shield and the Hangman, had met their match. In No.49 Archie delivered a second body-blow: his strip moved to the front of the comic-book. The third and fatal punch came in No.66 (March 1948). Not only was there no Shield strip, there was perhaps the world's first Bad News and Good News Message. The Shield G-Man Club was no more: "Turn in your identification card, gang, and we will mail you in return an Archie Club button!" The teenage revolution had won. Every strip starred a teenager, from Archie's pal Jughead, to Archie's gals, Betty and Veronica, down to Katy Keene the Pin-Up Queen.

Black Hood, another MLJ super-hero, met with a worse fate. Even his comic-book title was stripped from him: *Black Hood Comics* was transmogrified into *Laugh Comics* at No.20 (Fall 1946). The star, of course, was Archie, plus Betty and Veronica, Katy Keene and a new girl, Suzie. Archie's own title, called *Archie Comics* of course, started in Winter 1942, and is still running. Soon other spin-offs appeared, built around Archie and his pals. Jughead Jones, the droopy-eyed dimwit in the beanie, starred in a string of titles beginning with *Archie's Pal Jughead* (1949). Betty Cooper and Veronica Lodge, the

blonde and brunette rivals for Archie's favours, made their debut in their own *Archie's Girls Betty and Veronica* (1950). There was even a comic-book series for *Archie's Rival Reggie* (1950), and another illustrating the adventures of Archie as a small boy.

Bob Montana is the cartoonist credited with the visual creation of Archie, and it was he who drew the newspaper continuity when King Features syndicated a daily strip of Archie from 1947. Other artists who helped turn out the incredible number of Archie comics included Bill Vigoda, and Bob Bolling for the pre-teens.

One thing which has kept Archie ahead of the comic crowd is his publisher's ever-ready eye for the current craze. At the time of the *Man From Uncle* TV series, Archie became the Man From Riverdale. When superheroes made a comeback, Archie turned into Pureheart the Powerful. Not to be outdone, Jughead became Captain Hero, Betty switched to Superteen, and Reggie the rival to arch-enemy, Evilheart!

Pep Comics *No.66* © *March 1948 Archie Publications. Drawn by Al Fagaly*
Laugh Comics *No.26 (No.7)* © *April 1948 Archie Publications. Drawn by Al Fagaly*

Archie Comics *No.26* © *May 1947 Archie Publications. Drawn by Al Fagaly*
Archie at Riverdale High *No.10* © *September 1973 Archie Enterprises*
Little Archie in Animal Land *No.17 (No.2)* © *Winter 1957 Archie Publications. Drawn by Bob Bolling*
Archie's Girls Betty & Veronica *No. 10* © *Fall 1953 Archie Publications*
Archie's Pal Jughead Annual *No.5* © *1957 Archie Publications*
Reggie's Wise Guy Jokes *No.27* © *October 1973 Archie Publications*
Archie's Madhouse *No.1* © *September 1959 Archie Publications*
Archie as Pureheart the Powerful *No.1* © *September 1966 Radio Comics*
Life With Archie *No.56* © *December 1966 Archie Publications*

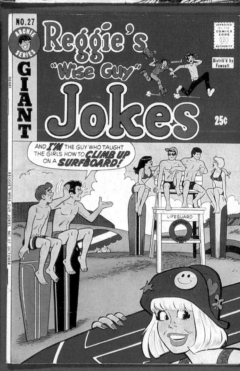

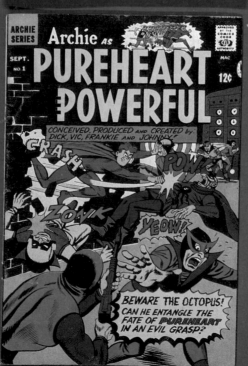

Harold Teen and Destiny's Tots

Harold Teen *No.209 (No.2)*
© January *1949 Dell Publishing Co*
Henry Aldrich *No.3* © *October 1950*
Dell Publishing Co
Andy Hardy *No.480 (No.3)*
© *July 1953 Dell Publishing Co*
Buzzy *No.15* © *September 1947*
National Comics . Drawn by George
Storm
Dudley *No.2* © *January 1950*
Feature Publications. Boody Rogers
Patches *No.5* © *November 1946*
Taffy Publications/Orbit

A Date With Judy *No.1* © *October*
1947 National Comics
Ginger *No.8* © *Winter 1953 Archie*
Comics. Drawn by Harry Lucey
Junior Miss *No.29* © *1948 Timely*
Comics/Marvel
All Teen Comics *No.20 (No.1)*
© *January 1947 Marvel Comics*
Junior Hopp Comics *No.2*
© *April 1952 SPM Publications*
Slick Chick Comics *No.2*
© *1947 Leader Enterprises*
The Kilroys *No.1* © *June 1947*
B and I Publishing
Hi-Jinx *No.1* © *July 1947 B and I*
Publishing. Drawn by Jack Bradbury
Prez *No.1* © *September 1973*
National Periodicals. Drawn by Simon
and Grandetti

If Archie was "America's Typical Teenager" of the comic-books, then certainly the holder of that title in the newspaper strips was "Harold Teen". Carl Ed (pronounced "Eed"), his creator, prided himself on keeping up with the current "slanguage". From the Twenties (Harold's strip started in the *Chicago Tribune* on 4 May 1919) to the Fifties (it only ended with Ed's death in 1959) the strip was a living lexicon to teenage talk. In the Twenties, Harold's "queen" or "sheba" was Lillums Lovewell. In the Thirties, she was his "snazzy li'l heartbeat" and he was her "precious li'l sweet cake": like all good comic heroes, Harold was slow to mature. Much of the woo was pitched around the Sugar Bowl café', run by Pop Jenks, noted for his notices. "Oil Up the Tonsils – Gedunk!", "Sprink Is Here – Gedunk!" and "Ersters Rah! Rah! Rah! in Stoo!" is a random selection. Harold's half-pint rival was Shadow Smart ("I'm small but I'm wiry – I'm a mite but I'm mighty"), known to Pop Jenks as Destiny's Tot.

The teenage radio rage, "Henry Aldrich", immortalized in the movies by Jimmy Lydon ("Hen-ree!" "Coming, mother!"), was a late arrival in comic-books, as was "Andy Hardy", played in the films by Mickey Rooney. Dell put them into their comic-book line in the Fifties. But in the Forties it was the Archie influence that caused teenage comics to break out like acne. DC Comics introduced "Buzzy" in *All Funny Comics* (1943), and pushed him into his own comic-book a year later, complete with Archie-type headline, "America's Favorite Teenager!" Buzzy Brown, bane of Cupcake High, drove a jalopy that had more slogans per inch than Pop Jenk's Sugar Bowl: "Runs On Rhythm", "Bucket of Bolts", and, when parked, "Do Not Disturb". Buzzy was drawn by George Storm, one of the originators of the American adventure strip. Another veteran from the early comic-books was Boody Rogers, who drew the doings of Dudley. This lad was given to cursing in

verse: "Hot yam from Alabam!" he would cry; "Gee from Kankakee!" and even "Holy sox from Fort Knox!"

Bobby-soxers – the name given to teenage girls – came into their own when DC Comics adapted the popular radio series, *A Date With Judy*, as a comic-book. In introducing No.1 Judy Foster wrote, "The dream man with the crew cut is Oogie", adding with innocence, "That brunette with the bangs is Tootsie, my bosom enemy". The feminine curve, outlawed in British comics, was quite the opposite in America. The teenage trend overlapped into other genres: *Hi-Jinx* had hep cats that really were – cats, that is. It was subtitled, *Teenage Animal Funnies*! The ultimate teenage comic was the 1973 *Prez*: "First Teen President of the USA", quite a way from *The Kellys*: "The Most Popular Mag for a Guy and his Drag". But 1973 was a long way from 1950!

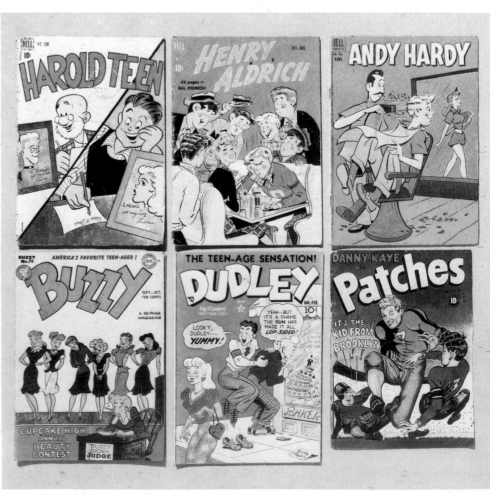

194

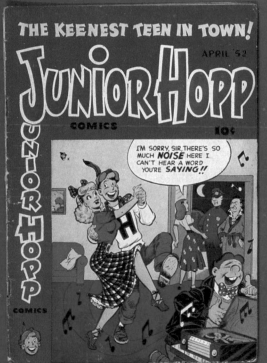

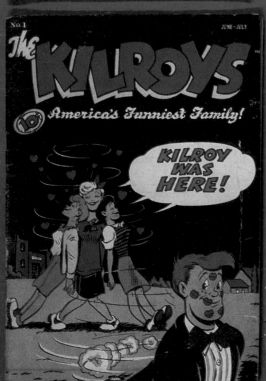

Pop Go the Comics!

When pop music burst on the teen scene, what more natch than that comics should dig a little of that jive, get in the groove, Jackson, and shoot the funnies to me, bunnies! It was in March 1948 that No.1 of *Juke Box Comics* cut its first rug, packed with pictorial biographies of hit parade favourites. Atlas tried a different tack with their *World's Greatest Songs*, turning the lyrics into comic strips. "Young at Heart", Frank Sinatra's current hit, was the only pop. The rest were "traditional", thus avoiding copyright fees: "Frankie and Johnnie" drawn by Al Hartley, "Abdullah Bulbul Amir" by Dave Berg and, would you believe, "The Star Spangled Banner" by John Forte.

Pop stars entered into comics with *Pat Boone* in 1959, a DC comic which broke from traditional imagery by having artist Bob Oksner delete all his frame-lines. Pat Boone wrote his own personal editorial, beginning "Hi all" and signing off "Always your boy". For a later teenage era, Charlton Comics put out their *David Cassidy* from March 1972, drawn by S. Gumen. Copyright was acknowledged to Columbia Pictures, but it is doubtful whether John, Paul, George and Ringo got any of the 25-cent admission price to Charlton's *Summer Love*. Although featured on the cover, the story "The Beatles Saved My Romance" is, frankly, a catch-quarter. The Beatles appear only in one panel of the 62-panel strip, and then only as pictures outside a cinema. How did the Beatles save Patti's romance? "Aren't they married? If they can do it, so can we!"

Harvey Pop Comics began in 1968 with psychedelic adventures of a group called The Cowsills: "It's the ultragrooviest pop art ever!" By the time the publisher got around to issuing No.2, The Cowsills had moved on to other pastures to be replaced by Bunny, Queen of the In Crowd, with her Rock Happening. It never happened again. *Marvel Première* celebrated its 50th edition with the comic-book debut of the outrageous Alice Cooper. It proved to be his farewell appearance too, as far as comic-books go.

Rock Comics broke rules all along the way. It was tabloid, only 8 of its 28 pages were in colour, and its artwork was over the top. Axe McCord so rocks the classics that Beethoven bursts from his grave to seek revenge as Captain Feedback the Malevolent Maestro! The heroes of *Loops*, a rock 'n'roll comic from California, were

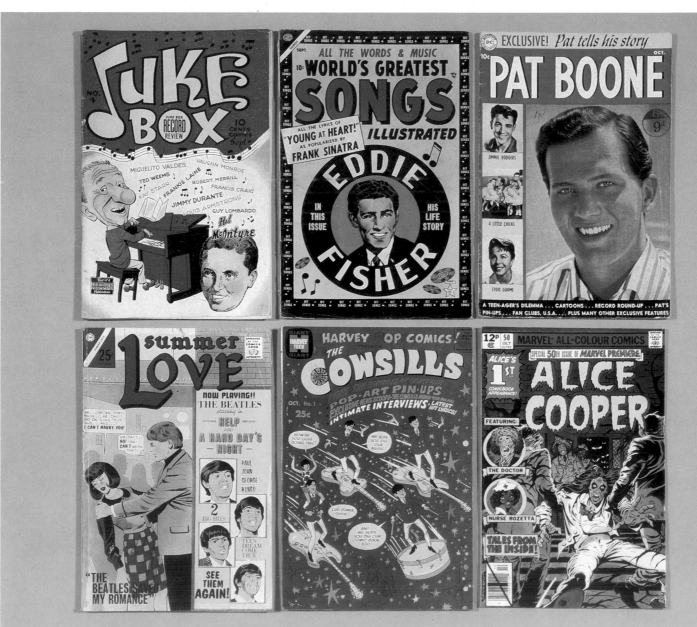

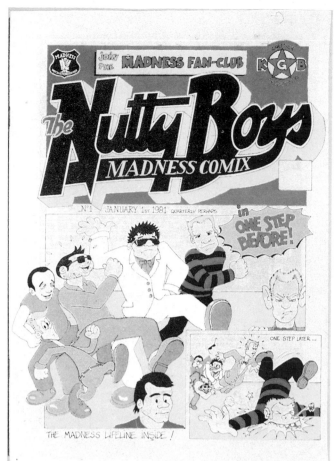

deejays Steve Dahl and Gary Meier in their unending battle with Discoman. The British pop group, Madness, publish their own comic-book, *The Nutty Boys*. The comic is as funny as they are, if you dig me, Jackson . . .

Juke Box *No.4* © *September 1948 Famous Funnies Inc*
World's Greatest Songs *No.1* © *September 1954 Atlas Comics*
Pat Boone *No.1* © *October 1959 National Comics*
Summer Love *No.47 (No.2)* © *October 1966 Charlton Comics*
Harvey Pop Comics *No.1* © *October 1968 Harvey Publications*
Marvel Première *No.50* © *October 1979 Marvel Comics*

Loops *No.1* © *July 1980 Rock Comix. Drawn by Thom Enriquez*
The Nutty Boys Madness Comix *No.1* © *January 1981 Madness Information Service. Drawn by Blum and Mitchell*
Rock Comics *No.1* © *July 1979 Landgraphics. Drawn by Neal Adams*

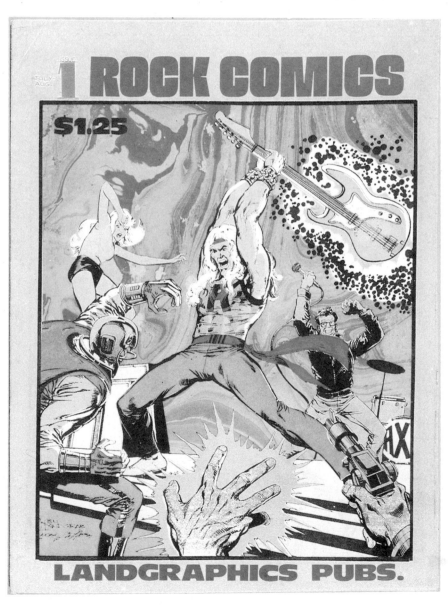

GIRLS' COMICS:
From Bécassine to Bunty

While the rest of the world published comics on the unisex principle, their contents including an occasional heroine ("Susie Sunshine and her Pet Poms" in *Rainbow*; "Keyhole Kate" in *Dandy*), the French quietly invented the first comic designed specifically for girls. *La Semaine de Suzette* was the title, Maurice Languereau was the publisher and the year was 1905. His heroine was Bécassine, whose full-colour misadventures were spread in a serial across the centre pages. A moon-faced scatterbrain, Bécassine was guilty of clumsy but well-intentioned blunders which quickly made her a favourite with the comic's readers. Soon the artist, Jean Pierre Pinchon,

found his strips bound into annual albums. The first book of Bécassine appeared in 1913: thirty more were to follow. Thus the moony maidservant may be said to have mothered the whole French tradition of reprint comic albums.

A British comic for girls was tried in the Twenties, No.1 of *The Playbox* appearing on 14 February 1925, complete with a "Lovely Free Balloon". Front page stars were "The Hippo Girls", who came as a surprise to those who read the *Rainbow*. They turned out to be the twin sisters of Tiger Tim and the Bruin Boys, and must have been just as big a surprise to them. The boys had been larking about in

comics for 21 years without so much as a mention of such siblings as Tiger Tilly, Gertie Giraffe and Olive Ostrich! Inside the comic there were "Fun and Frolics in Fairyland" presided over by Old Mother Hubbard, "Peggie and her Piggies" and a serial strip, "Little Betty, the Tale of a Lonely Little Girl". The Editress was none other than Mrs Hippo herself! The experiment proved a failure, and by 1927 "The Chummy Boys" had taken over the cover to help turn *Playbox* into a regular comic for both boys and girls. The Italians had considerably more success with *Primarosa*, launched as "The Journal for Little Girls" in 1933. Incredibly, all the strips in it were British, selected from several Amalgamated Press comics for their feminist content. "Susie Sunshine and her Pet Poms" became "Liliana e i suoi Volpini"!

The first American comic-book for girls was published by the Parents' Institute. *Calling All Girls* No.1 (September 1941) was half four-colour comic, half photogravure magazine, an attractive formula devised by Executive Editor Frances Ullman. But the most fascinating reading in the whole comic is the listing, as Junior Advisory Editors, of Gloria Jean, Shirley Temple, Virginia Weidler, Jane Withers, and the Moylan Sisters. For younger girls, the Parents' Institute introduced *Polly Pigtails* (January 1946) and, for older girls, *Sweet Sixteen* (August 1946).

British publishers tried girls again in the Fifties, and launched *School Friend*, reviving a long-defunct title of a prewar story-paper. No.1 (20 May 1950) was a sell-out, and the weekly ran for 16 years, mainly on the popularity of its front page serial, "The Silent Three at St Kit's", drawn by one of the few women strip artists, Evelyn Flinders. *Girl* (2 November 1951) was brought out as a companion to the best-selling *Eagle*, a boys' comic. It failed to make the grade until the high-flying front page adventures of "Kitty Hawk and her All Girl Crew" were grounded in favour of the more traditional boarding-school larks of "Wendy and Jinx". Both were drawn by Ray Bailey, so he had no complaint. The longest running girls' comic is *Bunty*, which began on 18 January 1958, and regularly re-runs the boarding school capers of "The Four Marys". When it comes to comics, girls, it seems, are traditionalists to a man.

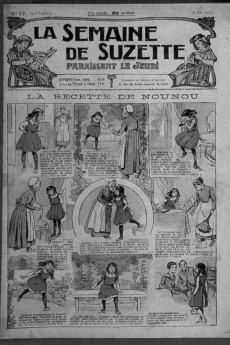

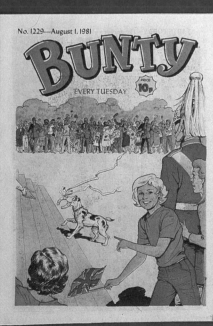

The Playbox *No.1* © *14 February 1925 A.P. Drawn by Herbert Foxwell*

Primarosa *No.3* © *2 July 1933 Marzorati. Drawn by Roy Wilson*

Girl *No.1* © *2 November 1951 Hulton Press. Drawn by Ray Bailey*

Sweet Sixteen *No.7* © *July 1947 Parents' Institute*

Calling All Girls *No.21* © *September 1943 Parents' Institute*

Polly Pigtails *No.19* © *August 1947 Parents' Institute*

Lily *No.481* © *22 February 1971 Editorial Bruguera (Spain)*

Sissi *No.220* © *15 June 1964 Editorial Bruguera (Spain)*

Tina *No.11* © *18 March 1977 Oberon (Holland)*

La Semaine de Suzette *No.17 Vol.14* © *30 May 1918 Gautier (France)*

Bunty *No.1229* © *1 August 1981 D. C. Thomson (Royal Wedding)*

Judy *No.1097* © *17 January 1981 D. C. Thomson (21st Birthday)*

ROMANCE COMICS: "How Far Should a Girl Go?"

"How far should a girl go?" asked the headline on *Young Love* No. 56. As far as the nearest news stand where, for 30 years from the forties to the Seventies, romance comics purveyed their four-coloured heartaches at 10 cents a time. Then they were best-sellers; today they are gone and only the most dedicated of collectors trouble to seek them out. Yet romance comics raised the standards of the industry by creating a new market, the first truly adult market for comics, aimed at the maturing female. More, they published generally the best artwork in the business. Its characters were human and realistic, the very antithesis of the superhero. Curiously, romance comics were created by a team of artists who had been responsible for one of the super-est superheroes of them all, Captain America!

Joe Simon and Jack Kirby, back in harness after Jack's war service, created the first romance comic-book for eccentric publisher Bernarr MacFadden's Hillman Periodicals, and No.1 of *My Date* duly appeared in July 1947. After four issues it folded and Simon and Kirby moved to the Prize Comics Group. Given the chance to create several titles, they put up the idea for *Young Romance*. This time they hit the jackpot. No.1 was dated September 1947, and it was still running in 1963 when the Prize people sold out to National/DC. *Young Romance* continued without a hiccup and finally closed in November 1975 at No.208, after achieving a longer run than any of its many rivals. Simon-Kirby's success brought virtually all the other comic-book publishers – Fawcett Publications in particular – into the new field. "The curtain is drawn aside on the intimate drama of real-life romances in these picture-love-story magazines that thrill and captivate," said Fawcett's advertisement introducing *Exciting Romances*, *Sweetheart Diary*, *Romantic Western*, *Life Story*, *Sweethearts* and *Cowboy*

Love. It appeared in *True Stories of Romance*. Notice that the word "comics", with its juvenile and superhero connotations, never appeared in these Fawcett titles. Another trademark, taken over from their line of Western film star comic-books, was the use of colour photographs for their covers.

Romance comics may be graded through the age-groups at which they are aimed. Beginning with the first blush of adolescence, *Going Steady* asked "Is Sal Mineo looking for a steady?", while *Hi-School Romance Datebook* was more sensational with "I

a sinking heart I realise that Hargood Thorpe's play means more to him than I do!" For girls brought up on the old Bernarr MacFadden pulp-appeal of the word "True", there was *True Sweetheart Secrets* and *True Tales of Love*. ("I was reaching for the stars and nothing else would do"). For the happily affianced there was *Sweethearts*, *Heart Throbs* and Charlton's *I Love You*: ("I silently thanked the Almighty for having helped me find such a love in Allan's arms!"). And for the happily married – well, Charlton had them covered too, with no fewer than four comics: *Just Married*, *Brides in Love*, *Secrets of Young Brides*, and *Secrets of Love and Marriage*: ("Even though I was a teacher, I had yet to have my Lesson In Love!"). And after marriage? Well, no publisher ever dared issue anything called *Divorce Comics*, but the shadier side of life after the altar was illustrated by DC's *Secret Hearts*, ACG's *Confessions of the Lovelorn* and *My Secret Life*: "It was the secretiveness of our romance that lent it charm, like the taste of Forbidden Fruit!" From Charlton, of course.

Romance comics overlapped into other genres, too. There was *Cowgirl Romances* from Fiction House, their answer to Fawcett's *Cowboy Love*, *True War Romances* from Quality Comics, and any number of hospital comics from Charlton, from *The Young Doctors* to *The Three Nurses*. The lead story in No.23 of *Nurse Betsy Crane* was entitled "Labour of Love". A new dimension was added to romance comics with No.1 of *3-D Love*: only the scripts remained flat.

Lovers' Lane *No.1* © *October 1949 Lev Gleason Publications. Drawn by Charles Biro*
All For Love *No.1* © *April 1957 Feature Publications*
My Love *No.1* © *July 1949 Marvel Comics*
True Sweetheart Secrets *No.1* © *May 1950 Fawcett Publications*

Cowboy Love *No.3* © *September 1949 Fawcett Publications*
Cowgirl Romances *No.5* © *1951 Fiction House*
True War Romances *No.13* © *February 1954 Comic Magazines/ Quality*
3-D Love *No.1* © *December 1953 Stereographic Publications*

Tried to Elope" ("Love can be so deep at fifteen"). There was also *High School Confidential Diary*: "I had seen him in the library. Something in my heart called out Take Me!" This was a Charlton Comic, published by specialists in the romance field. Theirs were *Teenage Love*, *Teen Confessions* and *Teenage Confidential Confessions* ("He was a man. I was sixteen, frightened, confused. I was a woman too soon!").

After graduation, girls were offered *Girls' Love* and *Girls' Romances* from DC, *My Love* from Marvel and *Career Girl Romances* from Charlton: "With

FANTASTIC COMICS: From Slumberland to Wonderland

The comic strip is the perfect medium for fantasy. As with animation, anything can happen in a drawing; the artist's imagination is the only limit. And yet in the hundred and more year history of strip cartooning, only one artist has used his drawing-board to pin down in pictures his free-ranging fantasy. That man was Winsor McCay, a painter of circus posters who was born in 1869, and who became a comic-strip artist with "Tales of the Jungle Imps" in 1903. The following year he began his first journey into the subconscious mind with "Dreams of a Rarebit Fiend". For three years McCay's characters suffered wild nightmares after eating a supper of toasted cheese. What made McCay's fantasies so fascinating was his totally realistic way of illustrating them, a technique which he was to apply to his next fantasy series in full colour, and so perfectly that it was recognized as an instant classic, perhaps the first in comic-strip art.

"Little Nemo in Slumberland" began on 15 October 1905, in the way it would always begin and always end: with a little boy in his night-shirt falling asleep and waking up in the morning. The odd thing about Little Nemo's dreams was that they happened in continuity, narrating a serialized epic in the world of Slumberland, and that they featured the same recurring characters. There was the cigar-puffing, green-faced Flip, Impy the laughing cannibal, tall-toppered Doctor Pill in his pince-nez, King Morpheus and his little daughter, the Princess, and Slivers the dog.

The adventures, often featuring the most eye-boggling perspectives and size contrasts, continued to 1911, when McCay left the *New York Herald* for more money with William Randolph Hearst. He was not allowed to take his title with him, so Little Nemo and Co continued their adventures "In The Land of Wonderful Dreams". Years later McCay's son, a much lesser talent, revived Little Nemo and Impy for Harry Chesler's comic-book, *Star Comics* (1937), but the magic had gone. The only Sunday strip to touch McCay's creativity was "The Kind-Der-Kids", a freewheeling serial drawn by Lyonel Feininger for the *Chicago Tribune* from 29 April 1906. It ran 31 weeks.

In Britain surprisingly little of the classic *Alice in Wonderland* nonsense has found its way into the comics. Fantasy seems to be generally confined to the talking animals of the Tiger Tim type. But one comic well rooted in whimsy was *Sparks*, al-

though, when it started on 21 March 1914, it was just another ha'penny paper like all the others. After a war-time collapse, publisher James Henderson revived it on 3 May 1919 as a three-ha'penny coloured comic, his first venture in the nursery style pioneered by his ex-employee Alfred Harmsworth's *Rainbow*. The first issue, numbered 277, featured on the front "The Adventures of Ken and Katie" who, with Pussy Snowball, wandered into familiar fairy-stories every week, quite without the aid of Little Nemo's dreams. The back page, however, told a different tale. "Dennis in Dreamland" was a total rip-off, from the top-hatted, pince-nezed Mr Sandman, via a black-faced clown companion, to a regular end-panel of nightgowned Dennis falling out of bed. Nevertheless, artist Louis Briault managed some nice moments, such as Mr Sandman's amazing invention, the Submarautoplane. Other fantasy strips in *Sparks* were "Peter and Peggy in Toyland", "Polly and Pat in Picture Book Land" (by Walter Booth, soon to create the adventure strip with "Rob the Rover"), and "Merry Malcolm and Happy Harriet and their Magic Toys". It would be 20 years before another fantasy comic was launched: *Magic* came from D. C. Thomson on 22 July 1939. Within its 24 pages there was "Peter Piper, Picking People Out of Pickles" with his magic Pipes of Pan, "Uncle Dan the Magic Man", and "The Tickler Twins in Wonderland": Mick and Trixie drink shrink-juice, follow a white rabbit down his hole, and rid King Boz's realm of a fiery dragon.

Dreaming returned to American Sunday supplements on 12 January 1947, when Neil O'Keeffe began drawing "Dick's Adventures in Dreamland". There was no fantasy within Dick's dreams, however; they were all historically accurate adventures. The comic-books produced a few good fantasies, such as Howard Post's "Alex in Wonderland" in *Wonderland Comics* (1945). Λ fast-talking Macaw pops out of a boy's comic-book and flashes him into a wise-cracking Wonderland. Post later drew the superior and thoroughly delightful "Jimmy and his Magic Book" for *More Fun Comics*, and later still the amusing newspaper strip "Dropouts". *Toyland Comics* (1947) was an unusual title to come from the guts-and-girlies publisher Fiction House, but it was scripted and drawn with all that com-

pany's care and attention to detail. Unfortunately this meant that the witch, Old Dame Spiteful, was a shade more scary than many a little mind could cope with. But the most consistently successful fantasies in kiddies' comic-books have been those created by the Harveys, Alfred, Leon and Bob. Their series about " Stumbo the Giant" and his fairyland playmates have given comic-books a world of their own.

San Francisco Examiner Comic Section © *6 April 1913. Drawn by Winsor McCay*
Sparks *No.1 (No.277)* © *3 May 1919 James Henderson*
The Magic Comic *No.1 (facsimile)*
© *22 July 1938 DC Thomson. Drawn by Harry Banger*
Wonderland Comics *No.1*
© *Summer 1945 Feature Publications. Drawn by Howard Post*
Toyland Comics *No.1* © *January 1947 Fiction House. Drawn by Bob Lubbers*
Adventures in Wonderland *No.1* © *April 1955 Lev Gleason. Drawn by Bill Walton*
Uncle Charlie's Fables *No.1* © *January 1952 Lev Gleason. Drawn by Charles Biro*
Dick's Adventures *No.1 (OS 245)* © *September 1949 Dell/King Features. Drawn by Neil O'Keeffe*
Stumbo Tinytown *No.1* © *August 1963 Harvey Comics*

FRIENDLY GHOSTS AND GOOD LITTLE WITCHES

A psychic phenomenon well worth ten cents worth of any psychologist's spare time would be the extraordinary longevity and continuing popularity of "Casper the Friendly Ghost". What is it about this cute'n'cuddly little sheeted spectre that has made him a best-seller among comic-books for no less than 35 years and a lucky 13 different titles? Casper's career began in a small way in a short story for children written by Mr Seymour Reitt. Famous Studios, the animation subsidiary of Paramount Pictures, bought the tale and had it adapted by Bill Turner and the old Felix the Cat creator, Otto Messmer. Directed by Isador Sparber, *The Friendly Ghost* went on

release in November 1945 as a suitable short for Halloween. The story of a little ghost in search of friendship who finally wins the favour of a family by frightening away the wicked landlord won enough approval from *Noveltoon* series fans for Famous to commission a couple more cartoons, the first of which enjoyed the punning title of *There's Good Boos Tonight* (1948). Again response was unexpectedly enthusiastic, so in 1950 Paramount began releasing a regular series of Casper cartoons, which did wonders for the new comic-book which had been launched a few months earlier (September 1949) by Archer St John. After seven issues the comic was taken over

by Harvey Publications, who inexplicably switched the title from *Casper the Friendly Ghost* to *The Friendly Ghost Casper* (August 1958). Editor Leon Harvey also dropped the miscellaneous supporting characters St John had been using in favour of an all-spooky book. In came "Wendy the Good Little Witch", a cute kiddy who had three green-faced Wicked Witches to trouble her, just as Casper had "The Ghostly Trio". There was also "Nightmare", a galloping ghost, and "Spooky the Tuff Little Ghost" from Brooklyn, with his goil Poil. Clearly the Harvey boys had hit a lucky streak, for not only did Casper increase his quota of comic-book titles (*Casper's Ghostland* in 1958, *Casper's Space Ship* in 1972, *Casper's TV Showtime* in 1979), but all his supporting cast got their own titles, too (*Wendy the Good Little Witch* in 1960, *Nightmare and Casper* in 1963). Another Harvey character in a similar supernatural vein is *Hot Stuff the Little Devil*, whose comic-book began in October 1957 and doubled up in 1962 with *Devil Kids*. Hot Stuff is decidedly more devilish than Casper.

The first rival comic-book to cash in on Casper's creepy capers was *Homer the Happy Ghost* (1955), drawn by Dan De Carlo and published by Atlas. Homer had a remarkably similar crowd to Casper's in support – "Zelda the Scatterbrained Witch", "Dugan the Dead End Ghost", "Melvin the Mixed-up Ghost" – but nobody seemed to mind, and Homer had a reprint revival 14 years later. *Spunky the Smiling Spook*, a wandering wraith looking for a home to haunt, was a 1957 series masterminded by Sam Iger, and in the same year *Timmy the Timid Ghost* came from Pat Masulli at Charlton.

Timmy had the usual kind of cast: "Maxie the Tough Li'l Ghost", "Gus the Goofy Li'l Ghost" and "Wilma the Witch". *Li'l Ghost* ("He's So Cute") wound up the spirited sequence in 1958, backed by "Tuffy the Tough Li'l Ghost" and "Donald the Dense Li'l Ghost". The publisher was Archer St John, who had started the whole thing with the original *Casper* ten years before.

One of the first funny ghosts to scare up the laughs in British comics was drawn by Reg Parlett, "Harry's Haunted House" in *Whizzer and Chips* (1969). Reg had a finger (or five) in the spooky comic *Shiver and Shake* (1973): he drew a spectre called "The Hand".

Shiver and Shake *No.1* © *10 March*
1973 IPC. Drawn by Mike Lacey
Casper the Friendly Ghost *No.2*
© *February 1950 St John Publishing*
Casper and the Ghostly Trio *No.1*
© *November 1972 Harvey Comics*
Spooky Spooktown *No.1*

© *September 1961 Harvey Comics*
Li'l Ghost *No.1* © *February 1958*
St John. Drawn by Al Fago
Spunky *No.3* © *January 1958 Four*
Star Comics
Timmy the Timid Ghost *No.12*
© *October 1958 Charlton Comics.*

Homer the Happy Ghost *No.1*
© *November 1969 (1957) Marvel*
Comics. Drawn by Dan De Carlo
Wendy the Good Little Witch *No.1*
© *August 1960 Harvey Publications*
Hot Stuff the Little Devil *No.15*
© *September 1959 Harvey.*

205

THE FIRST SPACEMEN:
Buck, Flash and Brick

"Good night!" exclaimed Buck Rogers as a uniformed girl fell out of the sky at his feet. "A hundred yard jump! And a girl soldier, too! Holy cats! Who can she be?" She was Wilma Deering wearing her inertron flying-belt, and it was the 25th century. As Buck remarked in episode three, "I had difficulty in convincing the girl I had slept for five hundred years." No difficulty in convincing the readers, though, especially the young, open-minded, air-minded, science-minded boys of the 20th century. They took America's first comic-strip spaceman to their hearts and let their minds soar into the skies as brave Earthmen – and Earthgirls – battled Killer Kane and the invading Mongols, fighting disintegrator rays with rocket-pistols and giving the world a new word: "Zap!"

The 25th Century had dawned on 7 January 1929, as far as comic-strip readers were concerned, but in fact it dated back to August 1928. That was when Philip Nowlan's novella, *Armageddon 2419 AD*, was published in the pioneering science-fiction magazine, *Amazing Stories*. John F. Dille of the John F. Dille Co read it, thought it would be great stuff for his strip syndicate, and commissioned Nowlan to script it. There was only one stricture: change the hero's name from Anthony to the cowboy cognomen, Buck. Staffer Dick Calkins, an

air-minded artist who liked to sign himself "Lt.", was assigned the illustration. No great shakes by any standard, his decorative, even antiquated, drawings, so totally outmoded today, still have a quaint charm, and must have had great impact half a century ago. There was much more excitement in store once Buck was awarded his big Sunday page from 30 March 1930. Firstly, it featured a completely separate serial starring Wilma Deering's kid brother Buddy and the young Princess Allura of Mars; secondly it featured a much better artist. Although they continued to be signed Dick Calkins, the highly designed pages were clearly by a more professional pen. The first of Buck's quality ghost-artists was Russell Keaton (later the creator of "Flyin' Jenny"), followed by Rick Yager, who was to draw the page for 25 years. It was Yager who drew the memorable serial, "The Great Martian Invasion of Earth", in which the reformed space-pirate, Black Barney, helped Buddy and Allura best the Tigermen ("Arrgh!").

On 7 January 1934, aboard an East-bound transcontinental plane, Flash Gordon, "Yale graduate and world-renowned polo player", met Dale Arden, passenger. Suddenly a flaming meteor tore loose from a strange planet which was rushing towards Earth, sheared off a wing, and the pair

parachuted into the garden of dishevelled, wild-eyed Dr Zarkov. Within seconds the trio were aboard Zarkov's rocket-ship bound for Mongo, Ming the Merciless, red Monkeymen, Prince Thun of the Lion Men, Tsak the Terror of the Tunnel, giant Droks, Kala King of the Shark Men, the great crab-clawed Gocko, the tentacled Octosak, and a catalogue of extra-terrestial oddities that keep Flash busy to this day. At first Alex Raymond's artwork was fairly unadventurous, superior of course to Calkins' but suffering from apprenticeship to more hidebound comic strips such as "Tillie the Toiler", "Blondie", and "Tim Tyler's Luck". But soon it flowered, and many a great Sunday page stands tribute to the art of the man many consider the finest ever to grace the comics. Comic-book reprints do the strip little justice: *King Comics* (1936) not only condensed the full pages to suit their small format, they crudely relettered Raymond's distinctively neat style. Britain fared better, for the science-minded boys' paper, *Modern Wonder*, ran Flash as a back-page serial, fully coloured in glorious photogravure. (Buck Rogers had to make do with a two-colour red and black job in *Everybody's Weekly*.)

Brick Bradford, the third pre-war spaceman, started as a Sunday page in November 1934 (although his daily strip adventures had begun on 21 August 1933). Written by William Ritt, drawn by Clarence Gray, Brick was an all-purpose science-fiction adventurer, breezily travelling to other planets, to the centre of our own, or into the atom world within a copper coin. Dr Timak's Time Top was another useful device with which Brick cheerfully explored the past and the future, along with his faithful companions, Kalla Kopak and Bucko O'Brien. Brick failed to make the transatlantic trip to Britain, however, although he turned up all over pre-war Europe.

Buck Rogers *No.1* © *July 1964 Gold Key/National Newspapers*
Flash Gordon *No.1* © *October 1950 Harvey Comics/King Features*
Brick Bradford *No.5* © *July 1948 Best Books/King Features*

Hurrah *No.93* © *14 March 1937 Editions Mondiales (France). Drawn by Clarence Gray*
L'Avventura *No.38* © *2 October 1947 Crucilla/King Features (Italy). Drawn by Austin Briggs*
Leyendas *No.133* © *1945 Americana/King Features (Spain). Drawn by Alex Raymond*

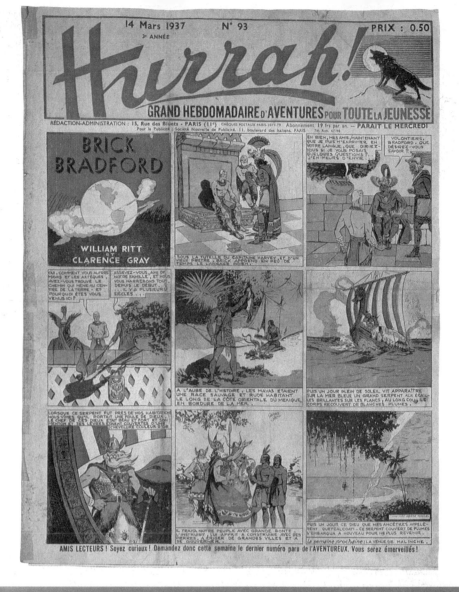

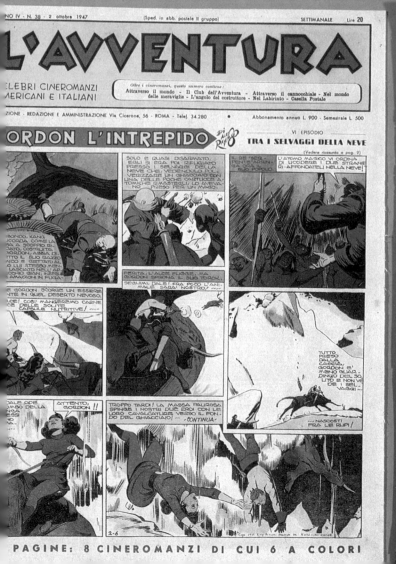

SCIENCE FICTION COMICS: "The Universe of the Future"

Science fiction, a form that would make even the superheroes shove over, had its place in comic-books from the very beginning. Indeed, in *New Fun* No.1 (February 1935) it had two places, and both of them drawn by Clemens Gretter. The first, "Don Drake on the Planet Saro", sent its titular hero and his bosom companion, Betty, to a new planet by balloon: "Whew! We've been tumbling about for hours!" says Betty. The planet is inhabited by Midget Men, and, as shown in full colour when Don was promoted to the cover of No.3, by Many-armed Beasts. Clem's second serial was "2023 Super Police", which sent Rex, his girlfriend Joan, and a comic-relief cab-driver on a stratosphere mission in Professor Shanley's stratoplane-submarine,

known as the "Hi-Lo". Under the sea in episode three Rex encounters a Many-Armed Beast. Life on Planet Saro in 1935 and under the sea in 2023 seemed strangely similar. Whether "Dan Hastings", futuristic hero of Harry Chesler's *Star Comics* (February 1937), also met a Many-Armed Beast, is uncertain but likely: Dan had the same writer and artist as Don and Rex, Kenneth Fitch and Clemens Gretter. Fitch, destined to remain a comic-book writer for the rest of his days, was a creative chap, especially when it came to naming names. His planet of Mexady was ruled by a Mexadian called Galada Eutopas, in cahoots with a scientist called Kurp Ursulis.

The first science-fiction comic-book arrived in August 1938, bearing the slightly contradictory title of *Amazing Mystery Funnies*. Joe Hardie wrote the editorial: "Your Uncle Joe has felt for a long time that many, many boys and girls and grown-ups too would welcome a comics magazine devoted to amazing and mystery stories. Therefore, after gathering together the bestest of the best material for this type of magazine, we present it herein for your approval." Purchasers who disapproved, having discovered that everything in the comic except the cover was reprinted from back numbers of *Funny Picture Stories* and other Uncle Joe publications, were doubltless advised to re-read that editorial before claiming a 10 cent refund. Uncle Joe's use of the word "gather" was, no doubt, well advised. The cover by Bill Everett was, however, prophetic of better things to come. From No.2 he drew "Skyrocket Steele" – "It's a honey!" wrote Uncle Joe. "You'll get a great kick following the fantastic adventures of people living in the year X (about 2500 AD) – you'll be thrilled by their rocket-ships that travel through space from planet to planet, their strange weapons, and their unusual civilization." No.3 added another new serial, "Dirk the Demon – 24th Century Archaeologist". This was also by Everett and was a curiosity about a future Baron's son, his pals and their skycycles. "Air Sub DX" – "a deadly

weapon of war if in the wrong hands" – arrived in No.7, manned by Professor Gray, Tim and Rita, and drawn by Carl Burgos. Later the back-up reprints were joined by a good and rare one from the newspapers, "Don Dixon and the Hidden Empire". This serial by Carl Pfeufer was a close swipe of Flash Gordon, right down to Wanda as Don's "Dale" and Dr Lugoff as his "Dr Zarkov"; even the underworld city of Pharia was ruled by a Ming-like Karth.

Planet Comics was cut from better stuff; its parent pulp was *Planet Stories*, and its publisher Fiction House. Even its headline was a variation on its grown-up partner: *Planet Stories* was "Strange Adventures on Other Worlds – The Universe of Future Centuries"; *Planet Comics* was "Weird Adventures on Other Worlds – The Universe of the Future". The lead strip had a title that not only told all, it set the formula for the 73 editions to come: "Flint Baker and the One-Eyed Monster Men of Mars". Originally drawn by the cartoony creator of "Frankenstein", Dick Briefer, Fletcher "Flint" Baker hastily completed a rocket-ship, a legacy from his scientist father, and shot off to Mars in the company of Harry Parker, murderer by shovel of his locomotive fireman, Phil Godwin, murderer by pistol of his sister's gangster groom, and Cliff Grant, murderer of a mesmerist who had forced him to steal. Oh yes, and Mimi Wilson, girl reporter of the *New York Globe*. Another *Planet Comics* hero was "Auro – Lord of Jupiter", a 21st century orphan raised by a sabre-toothed tiger. The boy becomes something of a superman up there, as "the tremendous gravitational force of this planet slowly turns his earthly muscles to steel." Then there was "The Red Comet, Mystery Man of Space", who had the ability to grow larger or smaller, according to how he set the dial on his intra-atomic space-adjuster. Later in the run came "Crash Barker and his Zoom Sled" (his sidekick was called Wheel Barrow!), "Cosmo Corrigan", "Norge Benson", "Star Pirate", and finally, and so typical of Fiction House, "Gale Allen and her Girl Squadron". She was quickly

followed by "Mysta of the Moon", "Futura", and the long-legged Lyssa of "Lost World". The *Planet Comics* pin-ups had arrived.

Certainly more serious, definitely less sexy, and decidedly more boring was *Superworld Comics*. It was also thoroughly disappointing, considering it was edited and published by the very man who had invented, if not the form, then certainly the term, "science fiction". This was Hugo Gernsback, but pace-making as his *Amazing Stories* magazine may have been in

April 1926, his comic-book left a lot to be desired in April 1940. Even Frank R. Paul, Gernsback's top fantasy artist, proved to be hopeless at strip-cartoon technique: his "Mitey Powers Battles Martians on the Moon" looks about as silly as its title.

The rest of *Superworld's* heroes were not much brighter: "Hip Knox the Super Hypnotist". The exception was the last strip you would expect to find in a futuristic comic, reprints from Winsor McCay's "Little Nemo" of 1910!

Planet Comics *No.1* (*British Edition*) © *Locker/Fiction House*
Miracle Comics *No.4* © *March 1941 Hillman/Harry Chesler*

Amazing Mystery Funnies *No.1* © *August 1938 Centaur Publications. Drawn by Bill Everett*
Superworld Comics *No.1* © *April 1940 Komos. Drawn by Frank Paul*
Science Comics *No.1* © *February 1940 Fox Features. Drawn by Lou Fine*
Weird Comics *No.1* © *April 1940 Fox Features. Drawn by Lou Fine*

SF With EC

"We at EC are proudest of our Science Fiction." Such was the boast of publisher William M. Gaines and editor Albert B. Feldstein, and it was justified, if only because there was little to be proud of in their other titles, *Vault of Horror* and *Haunt of Fear*. There was a lacing of horror comics style about the early issues of *Weird Fantasy* and *Weird Science*, both laun-

ched with the others in the "New Trend" month of May 1950; but as the comics developed and explored new areas of imagination they matured into adult classics of their kind. Unfortunately their market appeal shrank in proportion, and soon the two comics merged into one, *Weird Science Fantasy* (March 1954), at an increased price of 15 cents. This sky-high hike put off more buyers than expected and from August 1955 the title changed again. As *Incredible Science Fiction* it lasted only four more issues, even at

the old price of 10 cents, proving either that America was not ready for an adult comic-book, or that truly pride goeth before a fall. But during the tangled run (complicated by the fact that *Weird Science* was originally called *Saddle Romances*, and *Weird Fantasy* switched from *A Moon, A Girl, Romance*) the EC SF comics published many well-drawn, well-written strips, including a host of Ray Bradbury stories which they cheerfully swiped, and, when caught at it by their comic-loving author, just as cheerfully paid for!

Comics had been adapting science-fiction novels back in the Thirties (and quite legally!). Bill Gaines' father, Max, started it, as he had started so many things in the comic world, by introducing a strip version of Carl H. Claudy's *The Mystery Men of Mars*, the first of that author's juvenile series, "Adventures in the Unknown", in No.1 of his *All-American Comics* (April 1939). This concerned two college students, Alan "the brains" and Ted "the brawn", who took a trip in Professor Lutyens' anti-gravity spaceship, "The Wanderer", and "fell upwards" to Mars. Edgar Rice Burroughs' science-fiction novels were second only in popularity to his Tarzan series. His *At the Earth's Core*, written in 1914 around the "hollow earth" theory popular at the time, came into comics in 1940 as "Dave Innes of Pellucidar". The serial started in No.2 of *Hi-Spot Comics* and was drawn by the author's youngest son, John Coleman Burroughs. ERB's first published story, *Under the Moons of Mars* (1912), transported Earthman John Carter to the planet, which its multi-coloured inhabitants called "Barsoom". John Coleman Burroughs turned it into a newspaper strip in 1941, and a comic-book adaptation began in 1952, drawn by Jesse Marsh, Dell's Tarzan comic artist since 1946. Marvel Comics recently revived ERB's original spaceman in typical Marvel Comics fashion. Gil Kane and Dave Cockrum drew *John Carter, Warlord of Mars* (June 1977) as interpreted by writer Marv Wolfman: "We won't be adapting the novels. Instead, we'll be building on Burroughs' work in a way never before dreamed possible." Except, perhaps, by those who had seen Roy Thomas's Marvel version of H. G. Wells' *War of the Worlds* in *Amazing Adventures* (May 1973), which starred "a crimson-haired demon named Killraven"!

DC Comics turned to the cinema for their lead adaptation when they launched their first science-fiction comic-book, *Strange Adventures*, in August 1950. Appropriately they chose *Destination Moon*, the George Pal dramatised documentary that began the whole boom in science-fiction cinema. *Strange Adventures* was such a success that DC introduced a second SF title, *Mystery in Space*, in April 1951. Both comics were edited by Whitney Ellsworth, whose crudely cartooned "Little Linda" was on the cover of *More Fun* back in 1935. Surprisingly for an ex-artist, Ellsworth gave bylines to his authors, not his artists, although certain stylists like the young Frank Frazetta stood out.

Avon Fantasy Classics, a series of comic-books put out by a paperback publisher, were complete adaptations of novels, such as Wallace Wood's picturization of Ralph Milne Farley's *An Earthman on Venus*. Wood, an excellent artist in true comic-book tradition, also drew an Avon original, *Flying Saucers* (1950), a sensationalized documentary, and created a new hero for Avon in Rod Hathaway, *Space Detective* (1951). Ziff-Davis, publisher of the SF pulp magazine *Amazing Stories*, converted it into a comic-book as *Amazing Adventures* (1950), and then introduced their own regular hero, Brett Crockett in *Space Busters* (1952). The early Fifties were thick with sci-fi comics, most of them opera in the Thirties tradition of Buck, Flash and Brick. There were the usual conversions, too, as publishers rushed aboard the space-wagon, but none seems more appropriate to its time than *Cowboy Western Comics*, which Charlton quickly switched to *Space Western Comics*.

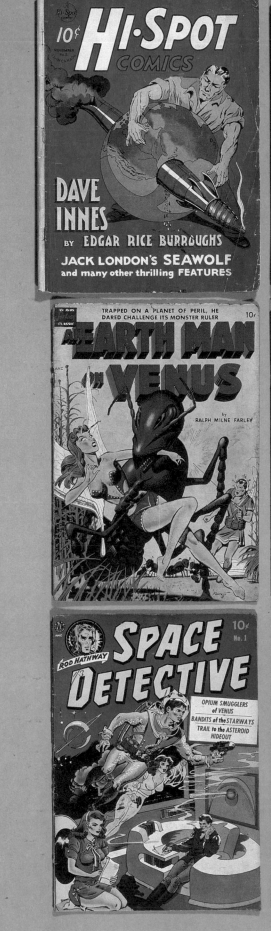
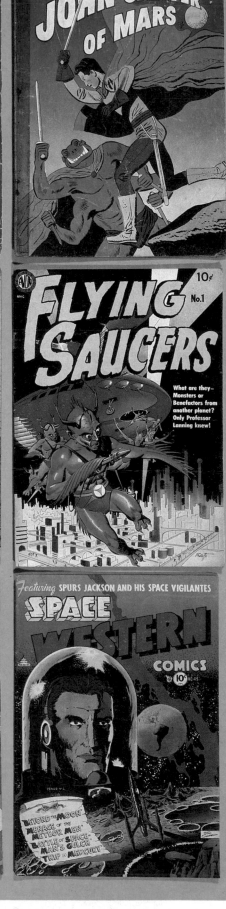

Weird Science *No.12 (No.1)* © *May 1950 EC Comics. Drawn by Albert Feldstein*
Weird Fantasy *No.13 (No.1)* © *May 1950 EC Comics. Drawn by Albert Feldstein*
Weird Science-Fantasy *No.23 (No.1)* © *March 1954 EC Comics. Drawn by Wallace Wood*
Incredible Science Fiction *No.30 (No.1)* © *August 1955 EC Comics. Drawn by Jack Davis*
Strange Adventures *No.1* © *August 1950 National Comics*
Mystery in Space *No.1* © *April 1951 National Comics*

Hi-Spot Comics *No.2* © *November 1940 Hawley. Drawn by John Coleman Burroughs*
John Carter of Mars *No.1 (OS 375)* © *February 1952 Dell. Drawn by Jesse Marsh*
An Earthman on Venus © *1951 Avon. Drawn by Gene Fawcette*

Flying Saucers *No.1* © *Avon Periodicals. Drawn by Gene Fawcette*
Space Detective *No.1* © *July 1951 Avon. Drawn by Wallace Wood*
Space Western Comics *No.43* © *April 1953 Charlton Comics. Drawn by Stan Campbell*

DAN DARE, Pilot of the Future

Dan Dare, the definitive British spaceman, proud bearer of the OUN (Order of the United Nations) for his leadership of the Venusian Expedition of 1996, and the subtitle "Pilot of the Future", was born on the front page of *Eagle* No.1 on 14 April 1950. Dan was fathered by Frank Hampson, a Mancunian illustrator who had never drawn a strip before, and Marcus Morris, a cleric who, enraged by the importation of American horror and crime comics, determined to create a wholesome weekly for British children. Together they designed *Eagle* (christened by Mrs Hampson from the design of a church lectern) and its heroes, notably Dan Dare (from "Dare to be a Daniel"), Padre of the Future. When they hawked their dummy comic around London publishers, it was taken up by Hulton Press, whose only contact with juvenilia had been the sensational *Boys Magazine* back in the Twenties. By 1950 Hulton's were a major force in magazine publishing, producing the

photo-weekly *Picture Post*, the monthly pocket mag for men *Lilliput*, and *The Farmer's Weekly*. *Eagle* would become their first comic, and Edward Hulton awarded it a budget worthy of any other major magazine. In return, Morris retained full editorial authority, Hampson became art editor, and all overt religious propaganda was dropped in favour of a commercial, but Christian, policy. The resulting comic, launched on a wave of promotion unknown in Britain, quickly reached a weekly circulation of a million copies. By any standards, *Eagle* was outstanding; by the contemporary standards of the rest of the day's comics, still suffering from post-war austerity and lack of inspiration, *Eagle* was a knockout. Its 20-page tabloid colour-gravure format did as much to stagger the boys of the Fifties as *Mickey Mouse Weekly* had the kids of the Thirties. There was the radio favourite "PC49", an exciting western, "Seth and Shorty, Cowboys", a back-page religious strip called "The Great Adventurer", also by Hampson; but the star turn was the two-page serial of Dan Dare.

Dan, jut-jawed, jagged-eyebrowed, bestrode *Eagle* like a colossus, as Frank Hampson's artwork improved week by week. He was the first to apply studio techniques to strip illustration, building models for his spaceships and futuristic cities so that they should appear correct from every angle, photographing life-models in specially-made uniforms for his comic-strip cast, researching current space technology to build on for his predictions. For scientifically-minded boys, the Fifties was the Space Age, and Dan Dare its symbolic pioneer.

Dan, and *Eagle*, rocketed to worldwide fame, as Frank Hampson was later surprised to discover when he was the guest at the 1975 International Comics Festival in Lucca, Italy. Among the thousands of antique comics for sale there were copies of *Il Giorno dei Ragazzi* starring "Dan Dare, Pilota del Futuro", *Plavi Vjesnik* from Zagreb starring "Den Deri, Pilot Buducnosti", and *Falken* from Stockholm starring "Dan Djarv, Framtidspilot". Although Dan Dare had long since been grounded in Britain (*Eagle* ended at No.991 on 26 April 1969), and a disillusioned Hampson had withdrawn from comics to work as a graphics technician in a college, both Dan and Frank were known and appreciated. So much so that the International Jury of the Lucca festival presented the forgotten Frank with their top Yellow Kid Award!

Dan Dare came out of temporary retirement on 26 February 1977 to star in No.1 of the new, all-science fiction comic, *2000 AD*. But this much-boosted "new" Dare was not the old Dan: he wore a crewcut, used bad language ("My God!" might conceivably have reflected the Rev Morris's original intent, but what of "Drokk it!"), and had barely a trace of his famous eyebrow. The artwork of Bellardinelli, colourful and violent, was later toned down by Dave Gibbons, but Hampson hated this vulgarization of his creation. Dan was soon dropped, but once again made a comeback, on 27 March 1982, in a revival of his old comic *Eagle*. This was much closer in spirit to Hampson's original, thanks to the loving artwork of Gerry Embleton (Ron's talented brother). Although Hampson, neglected, remains in the wilderness, his hero, like all the great ones of fiction, has a life of his own.

Eagle *No.1* © *14 April 1950 Hulton Press. Drawn by Frank Hampson*
Eagle *No.8* © *9 July 1953 Advertiser Newspapers (Australia). Drawn by Frank Hampson*
Falken *No.1* © *12 January 1955 (Stockholm). Drawn by Frank Hampson*
Plavi Vjesnik *No.437* © *7 November 1963 (Zagreb). Drawn by Frank Hampson*
Il Giorno dei Ragazzi *No.35* © *11 October 1962 (Italy)*

Daredevils of the Stratosphere

A decade before Dan Dare took the air, "Crash Carew – Daredevil of the Stratosphere" roared through red-tinted space on the two-colour front page of *Comic Adventures* (1942), an independent fourpenny comic that managed to appear three times a year during the blacked-out Forties. Crash's artist was Nat Brand, the Scot who invented the first British super-hero, "Derickson Dene, Super-Inventor", back in the pre-war *Pilot*. Much influenced by Alex Raymond (and why not?), Brand was Britain's best adventure strip artist of his day, handling "Dandy McQueen of the Royal Mounted", "Halcon, Lord of the Crater Land", and "Bentley Price, Detective", with equal Raymondesque expertise. Crash was partnered in his stratospheric daredeviltry by Billy, his boy assistant; "Swift Morgan" had more luck: his artist, Denis McLoughlin, gave him a well-drawn, well-endowed young lady called Silver, a pin-up in the best *Planet Comics* tradition. Swift Morgan travelled in time and space, but, like Crash Carew, only in two-tone colour, although his publisher, Boardman (of *Okay* fame), used costlier photogravure.

The sci-fi boom of the Fifties, boosted by American B-movies and comic-books, was soon noted by the minor British comic-book publishers, and Scion of Kensington High Street was quick to blast-off with No.1 of *Space Hero*: "Amazing Stories of the Future" (1951). Norman Light drew the two main strips, "Galactic Patrol" featuring Brad Kane, who had neither a boy buddy nor a pin-up girl, but a Mexican navigator named Carlos Lopez; and "Commander Wade Kirkman", who had a whole squadron of Space Commandos. Light later drew and published his own SF comic, *Spaceman* (1953), "the Comic of the Future". This spotlighted "Captain Future" and his Star Rovers Patrol, Slim Williams, Tubby Saunders, Sunset Biggs and Jock Hart, who all joined in to sing the song of the Star Rovers: "For it's always good weather, When good Spacemen get together!". Also featured was "Bill Merrill of the Scientific Investigation Bureau", drawn by young Ron Embleton, returned from the wars.

"Captain Valiant", Ace of the Interplanetary Police Patrol arrived in *Space Comics* (1953) complete with super-slogan, "Forward to the Future". The first Hon Mem of the IPP was named as Tex Ritter, a slightly unexpected choice. Vic Valiant's war against the Reussis was illustrated by Mick Anglo, who equipped his hero with such useful items as a Space Stiletto, Radar Goggles, Videoscope Helmet, Midget Self-propelling Bombs, Anti-radio-activity Shield, Contra-gravity Boots, and Service Tie. Vic was to the comic-book crowd what Dan Dare was to the higher class of *Eagle* reader, and although *Space Comics*' success pushed Anglo into creating and running several similar series (*Pete Mangan of the Space Patrol, Space Commander Kerry, Space Commando Comics*), none of them came near to Captain Valiant in length of run; he even went weekly for a while, an achievement matched only by Mick's *Marvelman*.

Among the "proper comics", the first attempt at an all science-fiction series was *Rocket*, launched on 21 April 1956 as "The First Space Age Weekly". Modelled closely on *Eagle*, this 16-page tabloid, eight of them in full colour, blasted off with a variation of Dan Dare in "Captain Falcon", and a pale shadow of Frank Hampson in artist Frank Black. Ley Kenyon, aqua-lung expert from Jacques Cousteau's underwater team, actually wrote and drew the back-page serial, "Professor Jack Ransom Discovers the Seabed Citadel", and another great name acted as editor, the legless Battle of Britain pilot, Douglas Bader. In his

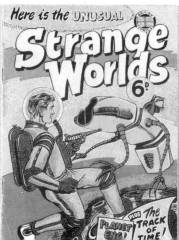

opening editorial, Bader wrote "The new Elizabethan Age has found horizons wider than the first Elizabethans envisaged. The depths below our sea and the space round our planet form the immediate horizons which man is straining to cross." Perhaps 16 pages of SF was too much for the New Elizabethans to take, or perhaps there were too many American spacemen (Flash Gordon, Brick Bradford and Johnny Hazard were all on call) for it lasted only 32 weeks.

It would be 21 years before another all-SF weekly comic was tried, during which time the Space Age had dawned in reality and imaginative fiction was overshadowed by the actuality of Man on the Moon. Then suddenly SF made a comeback in 2000 AD, datelined 26 February 1977 as "Tomorrow's Comic Today!" The comic, complete with free plastic Space Spinner, presented 32 pages illustrating "a future thrilling, amazing, frightening, wilder than your wildest imaginings – a future you will be living in!" Whether children would actually enjoy living in it is another matter, for as depicted by Tharg's team of artists (Tharg is the extraterrestrial editor given to greeting his Earthlets with "Splundig Vur Thrigg!") the future is a world of unrelieved violence. "Harlem Heroes" are the sportsmen of tomorrow playing Aeroball, the Most Dangerous Game ("Uuuulgh!"); "Flesh – Man fights prehistoric monster in a ferocious struggle for food" ("Aieee!"; "Invasion – A man called Savage takes on the Asian invaders who destroyed his home, his family, his country!" ("Aaaah!"); "MACH1 – Not so much a secret agent, more a secret weapon" was John Probe, activated by Compu-Puncture Hyperpower ("Aaaargh!"). Plus the "new" Dan Dare ("Drokk it!"). Readers were invited to "experience future shock again next week" in Prog.2. They were not disappointed; added to the roster was "Judge Dredd", grim-faced avenger of Mega-City One, licensed to dispense instant justice in the form of six varieties of death from his "lawgiver" gun. It says a lot for the comic and its readers that Judge Dredd quickly topped the revamped Dan Dare in the popularity polls, rose to supplementary newspaper strip stardom in the *Daily Star*, and became the first British comic hero to invade America in his own comic-book (No.1 November 1983). As some kind of misguided

tribute, the publisher branded this enterprise "Eagle Comics".

Swift Morgan *No.1* © *1948 Boardman. Drawn by Denis McLoughlin*
Space Comics/Captain Valiant *No.50 (No.1)* © *May 1953 Arnold Book Co. Drawn by Mick Anglo*
Space Commander Kerry *No.50 (No.1)* © *August 1953 L. Miller. Drawn by Mick Anglo*
Space Commando Comics *No.50 (No.1)* © *September 1953 L. Miller. Drawn by Mick Anglo*
Strange Worlds *No.14* © *1953 Man's World. Drawn by Sydney Jordan*

Super-Sonic *No.13 (No.1)* © *December 1953 Sports Cartoons*
Spaceman *No.7* © *1953 Gould-Light. Drawn by Norman Light*
Space Ace *No.1* © *August 1960 Atlas*

Rocket *No.1* © *21 April 1956 News of the World. Drawn by Frank Black*
Judge Dredd *No.1* © *November 1983 Eagle Comics. Drawn by Brian Bolland*
2000 AD *No.1* © *26 February 1977 IPC Magazines*
Strijd Om Trigie (Trigan Empire) © *1973 Uitgeverij/IPC (Holland). Drawn by Don Lawrence*

SPORT IN THE COMICS:
The Great Race

Roy Race, better known as "Roy of the Rovers", is unique in the history of British comic heroes. Kicking off as the cover star of *Tiger* No.1, he has held that position since 11 September 1954. Twenty-two years later he branched out into No.1 of his own weekly comic, suitably entitled *Roy of the Rovers* (25 September 1976), an event he celebrated with a phone-in ("Dial 01 261 6272 – Roy is waiting for your call!"). And he was the first character in British comics to fall in love, get married and raise a family. All of which would be remarkable in any case, but even more in Race's case; for Roy is a sportsman, the footballing manager of Melchester Rovers – and historically sport and strips seldom if ever mix.

The field is littered with the corpses of sporting comics. The first ever, a disaster called *Sports Fun* launched on 11 February 1922 by the editor and staff of *Film Fun*, lasted a luckless 13 weeks. Even a major revamp into a colourful story paper failed to extend the title's life beyond another 29. It seemed from the whistle that sports and strips were fated not to appeal, even when the mighty Tom Webster, the original British sports cartoonist of the *Daily Mail*, was hired to draw the covers. Webster, who originated the frameless narrative technique so swiftly beloved by sports cartoonists, sold millions of copies of his annual reprint books, but did little to help the fast-falling circulation of *Sports Fun*. The interior strips were, frankly, weird: "My Funniest Experience on the Field by Fanny Walden, the Famous Tottenham Hotspur and English International Wing Forward" had little appeal, it seems, even drawn by the *Film Fun* star artist, Billy Wakefield. Likewise "What I'd Like to Do to the Referee When We Win by Stanley Fazackerly, Everton" – no matter how cleverly caricatured by Alexander Akerbladh. From *Sports Fun* on, sporty characters were relegated to filler strips, such as Harry Banger's fat "Alfie the All-Round Sport" in *New Funnies* (1940). The only other serious strip truly to catch the imagination was the illustrated version of "The Truth About Wilson", a long-running serial of an imm-

ortal athlete. This began as a story in the wartime *Wizard* and was revived as a strip in the 1964 *Hornet*.

In America the most successful sporting strip of all time is "Joe Palooka", a tow-headed simpleton who became "champeen" of the world. Created by Ham Fisher in 1928, by the Forties the reprint *Joe Palooka Comics* was selling over a million copies a month. This was less to do with Fisher's talent as an artist than his talent at hiring great assistants: his first had been Al Capp, who would go on to create "Li'l Abner". Fisher was, like Joe's manager Knobby Walsh, a great promoter, and wrote in his editorial, in No.6 of the comic-book, of his meeting with President Truman. "With all the dignity I could command I said, 'Mr President, it is a great honor and privilege to meet you.'

And, boy, he sure floored me with his answer. 'Glad to meet you, Ham,' he said. 'Say, does Joe catch the so-and-so he's chasing?' 'Mr President, you read my strip!' I gasped. 'Never miss it,' he replied.'"

Street and Smith, the pulp publishers, were first in the comic-book field with an all-sports title which they called *Sport Comics* (1940). They opened with the life in pictures of baseball star Lou Gehrig, and shortly changed their title to *True Sport Picture Stories*. The comic had a centre section of 16 pages in sepia photogravure, making it half a magazine. A similar format was introduced into *Sport Stars* (1946), a four-issue flop from the Parents' Institute, publishers of *True Comics*. A comic of the same title was introduced by Marvel Comics in 1949, but changed its name to the snappier *Sports Action* from the second issue. The editorial policy of "true life" strips remained the same. Evidently sensing some kind of trend in the air, Star Publications changed the title of their popular *Dick Cole* (1948) to *Sport Thrills* from No.11. It was the kiss of death: four more issues and the baseball king was counted out. Charlton Comics had a try in 1955 when they revived one of the oldest boys' heroes in American fiction as a comic-book. After surviving half a century on the printed page, *Frank Merriwell at Yale* lasted four months as a comic. Even the experienced DC found the sporting life a short one: *All-American Sports* published in October 1967 failed to survive to No.2.

One great sporting craze of the Fifties did finally make it into the comics in a big way. It began with Fawcett's *Hot Rod Comics*, a fairly technical affair starring "Clint Curtis" by Bob Powell. The same month, November 1951, saw Charlton issuing No.1 of *Hot Rods and Racing Cars*, again a combination of fact and fiction. The winner was clear: Fawcett's title ran seven issues, Charlton's a whopping 120. No wonder Charlton entered another seven titles in the race: *Teenage Hotrodders* (1963), *Drag Strip Hotrodders* (1963), *Top Eliminator* (1967), *Hot Rod Racers* (1967), *World of Wheels* (1967), *Drag'n'Wheels* (1968), and the comic combination *Surf'n'Wheels* (1969). The hot rod comics are now gone with the hot rods themselves, and the current champ of the sporting comics is an all-rounder from Germany, *Sport-Billy* (1979).

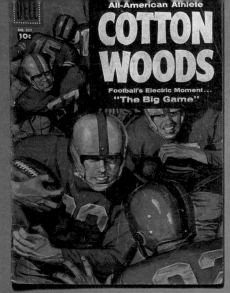

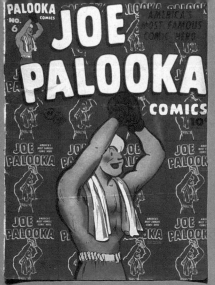

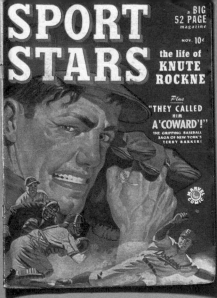

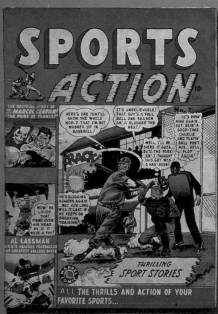

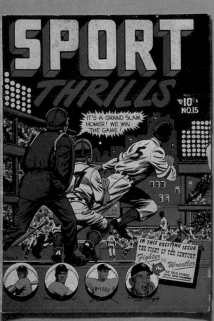

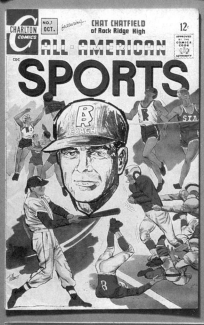

Sports Fun *No.1* © *11 February 1922 Amalgamated Press. Drawn by Tom Webster*
Roy of the Rovers *No.1* © *25 September 1976 IPC Magazines*
Joe Palooka Comics *No.6* © *September 1946 Harvey Comics. Drawn by Ham Fisher*
Cotton Woods *No.837 (No.1)*

© *September 1957 Dell Publishing.*
Sport Stars *No.1* © *November 1949 Marvel Comics*
Sports Action *No.7* © *1950 (Canadian Edition) Bell/Marvel*
Sport Thrills *No.15* © *November 1951 Star. Drawn by L. B. Cole*
All-American Sports *No.1* © *October 1967 Charlton Comics.*

Drawn by Anthony Tallarico
Frank Merriwell at Yale *No.1* © *June 1955 Charlton Comics. Drawn by Dick Giordano*
Hot Rod Comics *No.1* © *November 1951 Fawcett Publications. Drawn by Bob Powell*
Sport-Billy *No.59* © *1982 Bastei-Verlag (Germany)*

LOCAL COMICS:
Oor Wullie and his Pals

"Oor Wullie" (Our Willie to the Sassenachs and other non-subscribers to Scotland's *Sunday Post*) is the longest-running comic strip hero in the D.C. Thomson publishing empire. He was born in Dundee on 8 March 1936 and is still going strong, never shifted from his pride of place on the front of the *Fun Section*, the pull-out and fold-over comic supplement tucked inside the *Sunday Post*. Oor Wullie's motto, "Oor Wullie, Your Wullie, A'body's Wullie", aptly

described the universality of his nature, as if Dudley D. Watkins' delightful, dungareed drawings were not enough. To capture more of his flavour, the following verse from one of the many *Oor Wullie Annuals* (first published 1940), should be sung to the tune of "Comin' Thro' the Rye":

"Gin a body meet a laddie,
Fower an' a half feet high,
Towsy-heided, rosy-cheekit,
Mischief in his eye,
Patchit breeks an' bulgin' pockets,

Fu' of spirit forbye,
Then like as no' ye've met Oor Wullie,
Scotland's wee fly guy."

Wullie begins and ends every adventure as he did his first, sitting on an upturned bucket. Between these obligatory prologues and epilogues he wends his way between house, school, and shed, wherein lives his wee moose Jeemy. Other pals include Fat Boab, Soapy Soutar, Wee Eck and, in the adult world, PC Murdoch. Wullie, a delight though he is, does not travel well, his local accent as delineated in his speech balloons being almost impenetrable. The same may be said for "The Broons" (The Browns), a family strip that also shares the *Fun Section*. The cast has remained the same for 48

years: Paw and Maw Broon and their massed offsprings Maggie and Hen, Daphne and Joe, Horace, the Twins, and the Broon Bairn. The *Fun Section*, originally eight pages, reduced to four since the war, used to sport a single panel commotion between Jock McDade and his gang and PC Flannelfeet, set in Auchentogle and drawn by Chick Gordon. He specialized in these "Casey Court"-type cartoons, drawing "The Cheery Chinks" in *Rover* for many pre-war years. But if *Sunday Post* fun is incoherent to the English, what then of *Sradag* (1960), a broadsheet comic entirely in the Gaelic?

Other unreadable comics published in the British Isles (unreadable to the English residents, anyway) include another Gaelic comic. This is *Tir Na Nos* (1947), issued in Ireland as a supplement to *Our Boys*, a Catholic paper that is itself content to be printed in English. Some strips are local in contents, others English reprints: "Miceal Moncai" is actually Alan Fraser's "Mickey the Monk" from *Comic Capers*! The patriotic Welsh have a number of comics and children's magazines in the local language. The oldest is *Hwyl*! which has been running since 1949, mostly drawn by Ivor Owen. *Sboncyn (The Grasshopper)* is a more recent monthly, a colourful comic begun in May 1980 which has developed a style of its own, quite different from British traditional. Its purpose is primarily to entertain, whereas *Cymraeg* (1956), *Bore Da* (1966) and *Deryn* (1980) are magazines with a mission, to encourage the young Welsh to learn their own language.

BLACK COMICS:
From Poor Li'l Mose to Black Goliath

The Negro as a butt for slapstick appeared in comic strips from the earliest years. In Europe, fun was made of the ignorant African native, and in America the Southern Negro was treated in much the same way. In 1894 Frank Wilkinson was drawing the weekly happenings in "Comic Cuts Colony" for that paper, while its companion ran "Chips Colony" from 1895. "Chowgli the Black Boy" was another well-drawn *Chips* strip beginning in 1899, and a heartily laughing Negro was almost a trade-mark of the early coloured editions of British comics, with the caption "Dis am coloured and no mistake!" (*Comic Cuts Christmas Number* 1896). Their American counterparts, the Sunday supplements, frequently featured Negro characters. James Swinnerton, originator of the American "funny animals", also had a way with black families, see his "When Fahder Came Back: A Thanksgiving Day Incident", that filled the front page of the *New York Journal* comic on 25 November 1900. Inside Carl Anderson draws the tribulations of a coloured cook in "Kinetoscope Showing Alice Serving the Turkey". And in the *New York Herald*, Richard Outcault ran the weekly adventures of "Poor Li'l Mose" (1901) before devising his white caucasian mischief-maker, "Buster Brown".

American comic strips, reflecting the popular stage and screen of the period, classed Negroes as "frightened darkies", shoeshine boys, railway porters, and water-melon stealers. As to kiddy characters, the "plantation piccaninny" was still the image by the Forties: *New Funnies* (1942) ran a series based on Walter Lantz's animated cartoons starring "Li'l Eightball", and not much better could be said for Bumbazine, Walt Kelly's coloured kidlet in his early "Albert and Pogo" strips in *Animal Comics* (1942). The first all-Negro comic-book seems to have been *Clean Fun*, a two-colour one-shot from the Specialty Book Co of Columbus, Ohio. Billed as "Something entirely new and vastly different in a comic book; Inspirational as well as Entertaining", the strips starring "Shoogafoots Jones", signed McDaniel, were

footnoted with "short, pithy, inspirational epigrams taken from the book *Stray Thoughts* by Crump J. Strickland." Sample stray thought: "Don't waste your time trying to figure out why a black hen lays a white egg. You better get the egg!" The first comic-book for Negroes in regular format was *All-Negro Comics*, published in 1947. Because of its expected minority sales, the price was high at 15 cents. Fawcett Publications were the first commercial comic-book publishers to make a try for the Negro dime. *Jackie*

Robinson (May 1949) starred the famous baseball player in factual and fictional strips — "Jackie Robinson Battles the Teenage Terror!" Fawcett followed up with *Joe Louis Comics* and *Negro Romance*, both 1950. *Golden Legacy* (1966) was published by Negroes for Negroes, and followed the *Classics Illustrated* technique in its strip illustration of "The Birth of Haiti".

Negro heroes cast in the comic-book mould began with *Lobo* in 1965. A black cowboy in the aftermath of the

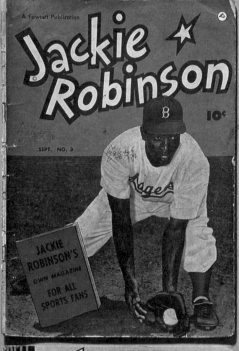

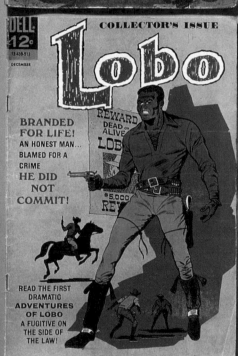

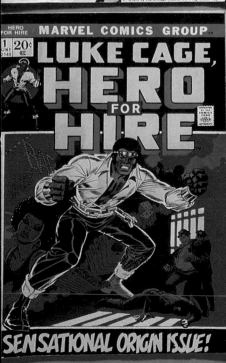

Civil War, Lobo's career was short (two issues), but whether due to poor circulation or poorer artwork is not known. *Friday Foster* was the first black heroine in newspaper strips, drawn by Spanish artist Jore Longaron for the *Chicago Tribune* Syndicate from 18 January 1970. Friday is the sophisticated assistant to fashion photographer Shawn North, and also made it into her own Dell comic-book in 1972. Marvel Comics created their first black comic-book around Luke Cage, star of *Hero For Hire* (June 1972). Lucas, a violent loner in Seagate Prison, finds it easy to bust out once Doc Burstein gives him a bio-chemical overdose in his experimental lab. A superhero is born, but one given to a different turn of phrase from C. Kent or B. Batson: "You freakin' mealymouth!" Marvel followed with *Black Goliath* (February 1976), real name Bill Foster, buddy of Yellowjacket and several other superpeople.

The Australian Aborigine has figured in a number of indigenous comics, but few so endearingly as the little black star of George Needham's 1940s *Bosun and Choclit Funnies*. Choclit's editorial letters addressed to "Dear Massas" are a little hard to take. *Mo and Jo* "de gr-reat de-tac-tifs" are from New Zealand. *Pop*, "Nigeria's Own Picture Paper for Children", is full of local flavour, but in fact edited and drawn in England. More authentic is *Sauna Ya Dawo*, a bilingual comic from Zaria.

Mo and Jo © 1945 (*New Zealand*)
The Bosun and Choclit Funnies *No.57* © *Elmsdale Publications* (*Australia*). *Drawn by George Needham*
Little Leopards Become Big Leopards © *Africa Christian Press*
Pop *No.1* © *1975 Pikin Publications* (*Nigeria*)
Clean Fun *No.1* © *1944 Specialty Books. Drawn by McDaniel*
Sauna Ya Dawo © *1974 Northern Nigerian Publishing Co*

Golden Legacy *No.1* © *1966 Fitzgerald Co. Drawn by Leo Carty*
Jackie Robinson *No.3* © *September 1950 Fawcett Publications*
Friday Foster *No.1* © *October 1972 Dell/Chicago Tribune*
Lobo *No.1* © *December 1965 Dell*
Hero for Hire *No.1* © *June 1972 Marvel. Drawn by George Tuska*
Black Goliath *No.1* © *February 1976 Marvel. Drawn by George Tuska*

RADIO COMICS:
"Wired for High-Tension!"

"Listen, Folks!" was the title Stanley Gooch gave his Editor's Chat in No.1 of *Radio Fun*, the world's first wireless comic, published 15 October 1938. "When I spoke to Flanagan and Allen, Sandy Powell, Big-Hearted Arthur Askey, and Ethel Revnell and Gracie West, and suggested they should appear personally in *Radio Fun* and entertain you every week, they were all tickled to the topknot with the idea. 'Just leave it to us, Mr Editor!' they chorussed, 'We'll make your readers titter till their tonsils ache!'" And they did, and their broadcasting successors did too, for many years. Indeed it was not until 1961 that *Radio Fun* finally succumbed to the television age, after a grand total of 1167 issues. When it started in 1938, British radio broadcasting was at the peak of its Golden Age, and although the early issues showed a certain trepidation about its chosen subject matter – it gave its prime page-one position to Roy Wilson's hayseed horse, "George the Jolly Gee-Gee", and supported the radio stars with the likes of Clark Gable and "Stymie and his Magic Wishbone" – *Radio Fun* soon settled down into a well-drawn galaxy of wireless stars. The 1939 war soon cut it down from 28 pages to 16, but its popularity only increased, for those dark years were the bright ones for radio, the only entertainment for many an evacuee.

In America, there was no comic-book devoted to broadcasting stars as *Movie Comics* had been to those of the cinema. The first strip series in the comic-books to have a radio origin was "Gang Busters", which *Popular Comics* introduced in 1938 with the credit line, "Based on Phillips H. Lord's Famous Radio Feature". In the same year a *Gang Busters* comic was introduced into David McKay's *Feature Book* series, but it was not until December 1947 that a real *Gang Busters* comic got going. It was published by DC Comics and "Based on the Smash Radio Hit" heard on the ABC Network, and the artwork by Dan Barry and Carmine Infantino made sure that the comic's essentially crime-oriented content concentrated on action rather than brutality. *The Green Hornet* ("He hunts the biggest of all game, public enemies that even the G-Men cannot reach") came to radio in 1938 and to comic-books in 1940, making a long-running success in both and doing the whole thing again in television. The Hornet in reality was playboy publisher Britt Reid, whose secret identity was known only to Kato, his Oriental houseboy; and to millions of readers of the comic-book, of course. What was less well known was that Britt Reid was actually the great grand nephew of the Lone Ranger! They also shared the same father, radio writer Fran Striker. A similar sort of superhero of the airwaves was *Captain Midnight*, alias Captain Albright, soldier-inventor and leader of the Secret Squadron. Again, this secret was shared by those millions of young listeners who mailed in the required label from a tin of Ovaltine! Or who planked down their ten cents for a copy of Fawcett's comic-book version. This began in September 1942, with Captain M(idnight) being introduced by another, equally famous Captain M(arvel).

Not really a superhero, but certainly super and definitely heroic, was *Jack Armstrong the All-American Boy*. Sponsored by Wheaties ("Breakfast of Champions"), this clean-limbed lad had been broadcasting since 1933, and came into comics with his own *Adventure Magazine*, by courtesy of the Parents Institute, 14 years later. Jack led off his Message to the Boys of America with his All-American Motto: "To keep myself straight and strong and clean, in mind as well as in body!" His other All-American Motto, to always eat Wheaties, was refreshingly absent. Cantering in a hot second to Tom Mix in the radio rodeo came *Bobby Benson's B-Bar-B Riders*. The cowboy kid was 12 years old when, astride his golden palamino, Amigo, he first yelled "B-Bar-Beeeeee!" over the airways back in 1932. And when Bob Powell drew him for his comic-book in 1950, he hadn't aged a bit! The original mystery man of American radio was "The Shadow", who narrated suspense stories on behalf of Blue Coal from 1930. Street and Smith, the pulp publishers, put him into his own magazine in April 1931, and in March 1940 adapted him into his own monthly *Shadow Comics*. The crime-cracking adventures of Lamont Cranston, wealthy playboy with the power to cloud men's minds, was vividly depicted by Bob Powell, who cleverly used the blue separation to indicate Cranston in his secret self, the cloaked and invisible Shadow. Less active a host to broadcast mysteries, one who invited listeners "to join me on another journey into the realm of the strange and terrifying" on the Mutual Network from 1943, was *The Mysterious Traveler*. Bob Powell, who seemed to cut a corner in radio comics, drew him for Transworld from 1948. The following year Marvel Comics moved into radio with *Casey, Crime Photographer* and *Suspense*, both from the Columbia Broadcasting System. *Suspense* ("Dangerous Adventure-Mysteries wired for High Tension!"), hosted since 1942 by the sinister Man in Black, included among its strip-adaptors – Bob Powell.

Children's programming came into the comic-books, too. EC adapted the fantasy *Land of the Lost* in 1946, using one of the few lady artists in comics, Olive Bailey. *Let's Pretend*, another whimsical series, was drawn as a 1950 comic-book by Chad Grothkopf, the "Hoppy the Marvel Bunny" man. *Silly Pilly*, hero of Frank Luther's Maltex Program ("This hot brown cereal is so delicious it does its own coaxing!"), starred in his own comic-book in 1950, followed in 1951 by *Sparkie*, "America's Beloved Radio Pixie", complete with his disappearing dog, curiously called Bunny. Among the comedy shows doubling up as comic-books were the domestic squabbles of *Fibber McGee and Molly* (1949), *The Adventures of Ozzie and Harriet* (1949), and *My Friend Irma* (1950), which all had one thing in common: none of them were drawn by Bob Powell.

Radio Fun *No.64* © *30 December 1939 Amalgamated Press. Drawn by Reg Parlett*
Green Hornet Comics *No.1* © *December 1940 Helnit. Drawn by Bert Whitman*
Captain Midnight *No.1 (facsimile)* © *September 1942 Fawcett Publications*

Gang Busters *No.4* © *June 1948 National Comics*
Shadow Comics *No.101* © *August 1949 Street and Smith. Drawn by Bob Powell*
Suspense *No.1* © *December 1949 Marvel Comics*
Mysterious Traveler Comics *No. 1* © *November 1948 Transworld*

Publications. Drawn by Bob Powell
Adventures of Ozzie and Harriet *No. 4* © *April 1950 National Comics*
My Friend Irma *No.6* © *December 1950 Marvel Comics. Drawn by Dan de Carlo*
Land of the Lost Comics *No.8* © *November 1947 Entertaining Comics. Drawn by Olive Bailey*

STARRING THE STARS

"Stars of Stage, Screen and Radio", the old showbiz catchphrase, might have been coined for the comic-books. The first stage personality to star in a comic was Dan Leno, "The Queen's Jester" – Queen Victoria's, that is. *Dan Leno's Comic Journal*, with the Music Hall star drawn in strips by Tom Browne, began on 26 February 1898. Thirty years later, the first American comic-book built around a star made its debut: *Charlie McCarthy in Comics*, a 36-page tabloid, "presented" by the ventriloquist Edgar Bergen. "Our Gang", Hal Roach's long-running "Little Rascals" of two-reel movies, first appeared as a weekly comic strip in the British *Dandy* (4 December 1937), in which their inventive adventures were illustrated by Dudley D. Watkins.

The American comic-book, *Our Gang* (rather inaccurately bannerlined "First Time in Comics") began in September 1942, with the very different artwork of Walt Kelly.

Among the supporting characters were two who eventually took over the comic from Spanky, Buckwheat and Co – the cartoon animals, Tom and Jerry. *Super Magic Comics* (May 1941) featured "The Astounding Adventures of the Mysterious Blackstone". This fabulous stage personality later starred in his own *Blackstone Master Magician Comics*, where he was billed

as "The Only Living Comic Book Character". There is no record of Our Gang bringing suit.

The late Forties brought a rush of comedians into comics: *Abbott and Costello Comics* No.1 was a complete adaptation of the Universal movie, *The Wistful Widow of Wagon Gap*, cartooned by the veteran C. M. Payne of "S'Matter Pop" fame. He was so old he signed himself "Pop". *The Three Stooges* No.1 was also adapted direct from the knockabout trio's Columbia two-reelers. Norman Maurer drew Larry, Curly and Moe in *Uncivil Warriors* and *Hoi Polloi*, then married Moe's daughter and wound up as a film producer reviving the comedians' screen career in a series of full-length features! Dramatic film stars also found themselves starring in comic-books: Alan Ladd and Dick Powell (both 1949), Sabu and Frank Buck (both 1950) and serial star Buster Crabbe (1954), who was billed as "The All-American Hero". In the space of only 32 pages, Buster found himself in today's jungles, yesterday's West and tomorrow's Outer Space.

CINEMA AND COMICS

Comics in America had flirted with films from the first years. Whitman published a one-shot based on *Police Car 17*, a Tim McCoy B-movie, as early as 1934. Once the monthly comic-book had been established, Dell's *The Comics* began running strip adaptations of Tex Ritter movies. Norman Fallon drew *The Mystery of the Hooded Horsemen* in No.7 (April 1938), followed by *Frontier Town* in No.9. By December, Tex had switched to *Popular Comics* No.35 for *Starlight Over Texas*. Other Monogram Pictures followed, including *Mr Wong Detective*, starring Boris Karloff as the oriental sleuth (*Popular Comics* 39).

The first American comic-book to devote itself entirely to the cinema was *Movie Comics*, "64 pages of Natural Colors" first published in April 1939. "Here it is, boys and girls", wrote C. Elbert, the Editor, "The newest idea in Comics and Movie Books, a combination of both which we believe you will like very much." Not enough of the boys and girls did, apparently, for the enterprise folded with No.6. This may be due to the rather messy presentation of the films, advertised as being "Printed in the New Natural-Color Photo Process." This turned out to be a combination of coarse half-tone blocks, tinted with the usual dotted primaries and embellished with extremely crude hand-lettering. However, one claim of Editor Elbert's has come true: "*Movie Comics* will also serve as a permanent record of the pictures you have enjoyed, which you can refer to again and again, with pleasure and entertainment."

If you can find them, and if you can afford them, *Movie Comics* do just that. The first issue alone features strip adaptations of *Gunga Din* (Cary Grant), *The Great Man Votes* (John Barrymore), *Fisherman's Wharf* (Bobby Breen), *Scouts to the Rescue* (Jackie Cooper), and, most surprising of all for a children's comic, *Son of Frankenstein* (Boris Karloff and Bela Lugosi). Subsequent editions featured John Wayne in *Stagecoach* (No.2), Bing Crosby in *East Side of Heaven* (No.3), Gene Autry in *Blue Montana Skies* (No.4), Louis Hayward in *The Man in the Iron Mask* (No.5) and Laurel and Hardy in *A Chump at Oxford* (No.6).

The next link between comic-books and the cinema came in December 1946, when Fiction House launched No.1 of their *Movie Comics* ("World Premiere of Hollywood Highlights"). Learning from the prewar mistake of converting film stills to strip panels, editor J. F. Byrne had his team of artists transmogrify films into pure comic strip format. Bob Lubbers, the company's brilliant adventure artist with an eye for the ladies ("Firehair", "Senorita Rio", "Camilla"), was given the cover and lead story, Paramount's *Big Town*, and had no problems. It starred B-movie lovelies Hillary Brooke and Veda Ann Borg. Back-up strips were all original material posed against a Hollywood background: "Johnny Danger of the Screenland Patrol" and "Mitzi of the Movies". But, once again, the formula was wrong and the comic-book only ran for four issues. Famous Funnies Inc had better luck with their *Movie Love*. Aimed at teenage girls, it successfully mixed film adaptations with pictorial biographies of current box-office idols. No.1 was published in February 1950, and the title sustained 22 bimonthly issues

A different approach was tried with *Fawcett Movie Comics*, which began in 1949 with a George Montgomery western, *Dakota Lil*. This time the entire comic-book concentrated on one single movie, told in 32 pages of drawings. The Fawcett formula worked and soon a companion book was launched, *Motion Picture Comics*. The first, numbered 101, appeared in 1950 and was devoted to *The Vanishing Westerner*, a Republic B-Western starring Monte Hale, who was already featured in his own regular comic-book for Fawcett. The two Fawcett film titles concentrated on Westerns, and especi-

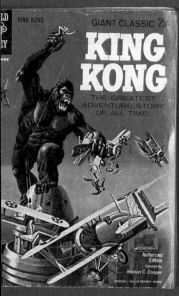
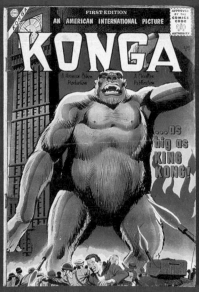

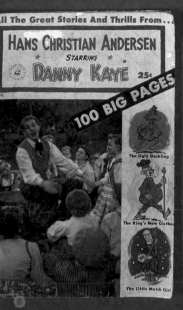

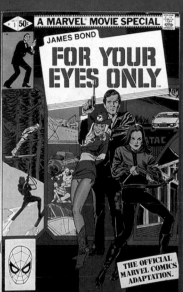

ally those starring cowboys, who also had their own Fawcett comic-books: Rocky Lane, Lash La Rue, and Hale. However, it is the Fawcett titles' occasional flirtation with science-fiction films of the Fifties that makes them more interesting to collectors. Among them were *Destination Moon* and *The Man From Planet X*. DC Comics set out to match their rival's movie comics with *Feature Films*, launched in March 1950, but even Bob Hope in *Fancy Pants* failed to extend the series beyond four. *Movie Thrillers* did even less well, running to only one issue despite a fine interpretation of *Rope of Sand* by Ogden Whitney (creator of "Skyman").

Most of the film comics since the Sixties have been one-shots, occasionally linked by a series title, such as Dell's *Movie Classics*. But with the blockbuster science-fiction films of the

Seventies, including *Star Wars* (1977), comic-book adaptations have been extended into long-running original comics in their own right. This concept first occurred to Charlton Comics, when the success they had with their adaptation of *Konga* (1960) spun off into a run of 23 issues, not to mention *The Return of Konga* and *Konga's Revenge*.

Movie Comics *No.1* © *April 1939 Picture Comics*
Feature Films *No.1* © *March 1950 National Comics/Paramount*
Movie Comics *No.1* © *December 1946 Fiction House. Drawn by Bob Lubbers*
Movie Love *No.11* © *October 1951 Famous Funnies*
Movie Thrillers *No.1* © *1949 Magazine Enterprises/Paramount*
Motion Picture Comics *No.102*

© *January 1951 Fawcett Publications*
Fawcett Movie Comic *No.8*
© *December 1950 Fawcett Publications*

King Kong Giant Classic © *1968 Gold Key/Western/Merian Cooper*
Konga *No.1* © *1960 Charlton Comics. Drawn by Steve Ditko*
Reptilicus *No.1* © *August 1961 Charlton Comics. Drawn by Rocco Mastroserio*
Destination Moon © *1950 Fawcett Publications/George Pal*
Hans Christian Andersen © *1953 Ziff-Davis/Samuel Goldwyn*
The Three Stooges in Orbit © *1962 Gold Key/Normandy*
James Bond *No.1* © *October 1981 Comics/Eon. Chaykin and Coletta*
Star Wars Weekly *No.1* © *8 February 1978 Marvel Comics/ Twentieth Century-Fox. Drawn by Howard Chaykin*

227

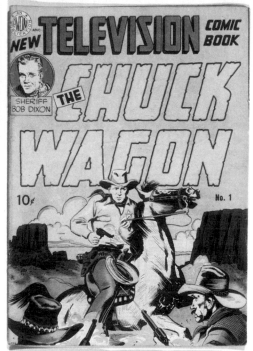

TV COMICS: "And AW-A-A-Y We Go!"

Television comics began, appropriately enough, with *Television Comics* in February 1950. The only trouble with this Standard publication was that it had absolutely no connection with genuine television! Its star, "Willy Nilly the Wonder Puppet" and his pals, Wendy and Bobo the Chimp, were all created for the comic-book by Vincent Fago. Little readers must have gone spare trying to tune in to the non-existent programme. The first telly-connection proper was Avon's *Sheriff Bob Dixon's Chuck Wagon* in October 1950, proudly bannered "New Television Comic Book". Sheriff Bob rode the square-screen range for the Columbia Broadcasting System, and greeted his "Comic Book Posse" with his two rules:

1: Always be a loyal, clean, upstanding American and be proud of it.

2: When you are sure you are right, fight for it; when you know you are wrong, admit it.

The folks over at Standard could have done with a dose of Dixon's law. Cowboys were great staples of Fifties television, bringing a breath of open air to the small screen in the darkened corner. Dell Comics, who would soon devote almost their entire range of Four-Color One-Shots to television series, put a first foot into the stirrup with *Sergeant Preston of the Yukon* (OS 344, August 1951); *Annie Oakley*, *Davy Crockett* and the more adult *Gunsmoke* soon followed the trail. Charlton Comics converted two of their titles to cope with the TV cowboys, *Six Gun Heroes* emphasized *The Adventures of Kit Carson* starring Bill Williams (March 1958), and the same month *Cowboy Western* turned into *Wild Bill Hickok and Jingles*, with a cover emphasizing comedy sidekick Andy Devine over a baffling back view of star Guy Madison.

Children's shows came into comics quite early, with two rival circus series. First in the field was *Super Circus*, a "Big 52-page Comic Carnival" published by Cross Comics in January 1951. All the television stars were featured: Mary Hartline the daredevil blonde, Claude Kirchner the ring-master, and the two clowns, Cliffy and Scampy. Toby Press followed with *The Big Top*, which starred the Boy Acrobat, Ringmaster Jack and Laffy the Clown in a well-drawn version of the CBS-TV series. An adventure series much enjoyed by children was *Ramar of the Jungle*, in which Jon Hall played the White Witch Doctor of the Upper Congo. The Charlton comic-book actually looked more exciting than the TV series, wherein Ramar had to grapple more with grainy back-projection than with real animals.

Television's early comedy stars also appeared in their own comic-books. The first in both media was Milton Berle, whose *Uncle Milty Comics* (December 1950) was advertised as "America's greatest TV comic becomes the nation's favorite comic-book character". Berle, brought up in burlesque, had a phenomenal memory for gags, and this was brought out in the comic-book story, "The Old Jokes' Home". The comic also serialized Berle's biography as a strip. By the time Lucille Ball broke into comics with her *I Love Lucy* (1953), and *Jackie Gleason* did the same (1955), the fat man's catchphrase sym-bolized the permanancy of the link that had been forged between comic-books and television: "And aw-a-a-y we go!" The last of television's "golden age" comedians, Phil Silvers, marched into DC comics with his *Ser-geant Bilko* (1957), left-wheeling off a separate series for his dishevelled stooge, *Private Doberman* (1958).

Family situation comedies came to comics in 1954 with *My Little Margie*, starring Gale Storm. Charlton had a runaway success with this series, quickly spinning off two more comics, *My Little Margie's Boyfriends* (1955) and *My Little Margie's Fashions* (1959). Another teen-appeal TV show was *The Many Loves of Dobie Gillis* (1960), a DC comic which took care to capture the likeness of star Dwayne Hickman. Of a different style, but still catching clever likenesses, was the more recent *Partridge Family* comic-book drawn by Don Sherwood. The problem of lifelike representation in comic strips is seen by many afficionados as stifling to the freedom of the cartoonist. Certainly the main-line insistence on photographic covers for television and film comic-books makes for boredom in bulk, although they may prove unrivalled souvenirs of bygone stars in the years to come.

Television Comics *No.8* © *November 1950 Standard Comics. Drawn by Vincent Fago*
Sheriff Bob Dixon's Chuck Wagon *No.1* © *November 1950 Avon/CBS. Drawn by Everett Kinstler*
Six Gun Heroes/Kit Carson *No.45* © *March 1958 Charlton Comics*
Cowboy Western/Wild Bill Hickok *No.67* © *March 1958 Charlton Comics. Drawn by Maurice Whitman*
Super Circus *No.1* © *January 1951 Cross Publications*
The Big Top *No.1* © *1951 Toby/CBS*

Uncle Milty *No.2* © *February 1951 Cross Publications*
Jackie Gleason *No.1* © *September 1955 St John*
The Lucy Show *No.1* © *June 1963 Gold Key/Desilu*
Sergeant Bilko *No.2* © *August 1957 National Comics/CBS*
Ramar of the Jungle *No.4* © *April 1956 Charlton Comics. Drawn by Maurice Whitman*
The Many Loves of Dobie Gillis *No.1* © *June 1960 National Comics/TCF*

"We Want Muffin the Mule!"

Television, considered by many in the comics profession to be the cause of shrinking circulations, was not an enemy back in the Fifties. It was seen as a new source of inspiration, a shot in the arm akin to the cinema and the radio. In Britain the Amalgamated Press was caught napping: the old firm that had brought new excitement to the comics in the Twenties with *Film Fun* and the Thirties with *Radio Fun* was beaten to the television post by an absolute outsider, the *News of the World*! This veteran Sunday newspaper (motto, "All Human Life Is There") silently set up a juvenile publishing division and launched No.1 of their *TV Comic* on 9 November 1951. Running to eight pages, all in full colour photogravure (making it a British first), it was supposedly edited by "Jennifer", the smiling little girl who hostessed children's television on the BBC (then the only TV network in the country); the real editor was an old-time cartoonist, Blos Lewis. *TV Comic* concentrated on those characters made familiar through the 5 pm to 6 pm children's slot, many of them puppets. There was Annette Mills (film star John's sister) with her "Muffin the Mule", a separate strip for grumpy "Peregrine the Penguin", and another for "Prudence Kitten". Francis Coudrill, today a noted painter, was then almost as famous as a ventriloquist. His cowboy puppet, "Hank", was an old-timer who rode his toothy hoss, Silver King, in pursuit of villainous Mexican Pete. The only living human in *TV Comic* was Richard Hearne, who appeared as his funny old man, the eccentric "Mr Pastry". *TV Comic* remained rooted in the junior end of television for many years, introducing such now nostalgic bygones as "Mr Turnip" and "Sooty" in 1954. They began upping the age-level in 1961 when the Hanna-Barbera cartoon "Huckleberry Hound" arrived, followed by the first strip versions of Gerry Anderson's "Supercar" and "Fireball XL5". "Dr Who" signed on in 1965.

When the thoroughly pipped AP entered the television scene, it was with *TV Fun*, well in the tradition. No.1 (19 September 1953) proves the endurance of comedian "Big-Hearted Arthur Askey": he was on the front page of *Radio Fun* in 1938, and here he was on the front page of *TV Fun* in 1953. Stanley Gooch, editor of both comics, followed his instinct and selected for his strips personalities who appealed to young televiewers but who were in no way linked with "children's television". A wise man, Gooch, and a great editor: he knew that his young readers preferred programmes their parents enjoyed, not just those which bore the label, "for children". So the stars of *TV Fun* were not those of *TV Comic*: they were Jack Warner, "Popular Star of Stage, Screen and Radio", Professor Jimmy Edwards "The Pride of St Caper's", and Diana Decker "The Cutie Queen of the TV Screen". One sentimental touch: Roy Wilson, who had drawn "George the Jolly Gee-Gee" for the original front of *Radio Fun*, now redrew him as "Hoofer the Tee-Vee Gee-Gee"! Although more stars were added to the bill later, the comic never quite hit the target, and from 5 September 1959 it shifted gear completely, turning into a romantic comic for girls by simply changing one letter of its title: *TV Fan*!

At the comic-book end of the British market, L. Miller, the reprint king, was persuaded to try something new and British. *TV Heroes*, a 32-page monthly, boasted "Your Favourite TV Stars and others in Action!" in bold type, but in tiny type printed this intriguing disclaimer: "The publishers wish to make it clear that there is no connection between this magazine and the transmission of any television programme." The fact that *TV Heroes* starred "Robin Hood", "Daniel Boone", "The Last of the Mohicans", "Wyatt Earp", "Sir Lancelot", "Annie Oakley" and "William Tell", all characters who were also the titles of television programmes, was, you see, sheer coincidence! Mick Anglo, who edited and later reissued *TV Heroes* as a "new" comic-book called *TV Features* (1960), atoned by editing an excellent television comic called *TV Tornado* (1967). But this, too, could not escape the Anglo touch: the much boosted comic heroes on the cover (Superman, Batman, and The Man From UNCLE) were inside, all right, but as stories, not strips.

British animated cartoons made for television have been few and far between, more through lack of finance than lack of talent. Most of them have been of the "limited animation" variety, made cheaply, but with artistic integrity, for children's television. In recent times, however, two well-animated series have made it, both as successful cartoons and into the comics, and both have been good-humoured burlesques of the super-hero genre. *Superted*, created by Mike Young originally for Welsh language television, appears in *Pippin*, and *Danger Mouse*, by Brian Cosgrove and Mark Hall, runs in *Look-In*.

TV Comic *No.1* © *9 November 1951 News of the World. Drawn by Neville Main*
TV Fun *No.1* © *19 September 1953 AP. Drawn by Arthur Martin*
TV Tornado *No.1* © *14 January 1967 City. Drawn by Mick Anglo*
TV Action *No.1 (No.59)* © *1 April 1972 Polystyle. Gerald Haylock*
Pippin *No.890* © *14 October 1983 Polystyle*
Look-in *No.10/82* © *6 March 1982 Independent Television*

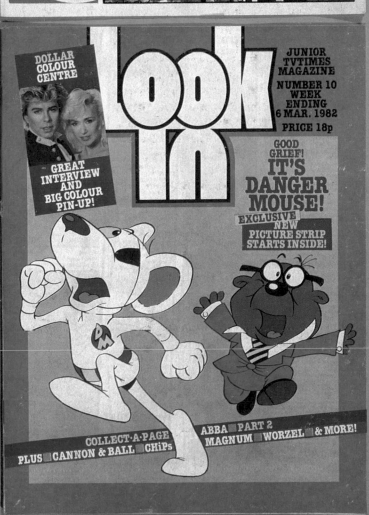

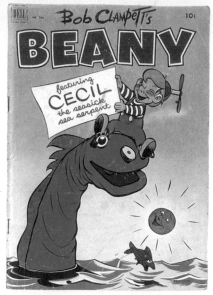

Saturday Spectaculars

"Preeee-senting the most Sensational Cartoon Action Extravaganza ever to leap at you from your Titanic TV Screen! Kick off your weekend with mind-staggering Adventure, Action and uproarious Comedy, all in Colossal Color!" If the preamble introducing No.1 of *America's Best TV Comics* (1967) has a Marvel Comics flavour, small wonder: that comic-book company packaged the 68-page special for the ABC that figured largely in the title, the American Broadcasting Company. Designed to boost ABC's Saturday morning spectacular (9.00 am *Casper the Friendly Ghost*; 9.30 *The Fantastic Four*; 10.00 *The Amazing Spider-Man*; 10.30 *Journey to the Center of the Earth*; 11.00 *King Kong*; 11.30 *George of the Jungle*; 12.00 *The Beatles*) the comic-book was unique in its mixture of strips, several of which normally appeared under rival trademarks. Even the ads were for new TV series, including an uncomfortable half-page

promoting Marvel's rival *Batman*! By 1967 American children's television had grown out of the hand-puppet stage into weekend chunks of cartoons, three hours at a stretch.

Bob Smith's *Howdy Doody* (1949) was one of the first television puppets to make it into the comic-books, a carrot-topped cowpoke equipped with the usual goofy sidekick so traditional to all western heroes, Dilly Dally. There was also a regulation supporting cast: crusty Mr Bluster, a clown called Clarabell, and an odd-looking bird called Flub-a-Dub. There was no attempt to keep any puppety qualities; the characters were treated as straight cartoon heroes. "The Great Foodini", star of a Monday-through-Friday series on CBS television, *Lucky Pup*, proved luckier than the title character and appeared in his own comic-book from 1950. Foodini, a fork-bearded magician (his name is a pun on that of Houdini), was given speech and movement by Morey Bunin, and face and

form by his wife, Hope. *Time For Beany* was such a successful puppet series that it not only made it to the comics, but was later turned into a fully animated cartoon show. *Beany* (1952) had a lot going for him behind the screen: he was created by Bob Clampett, one of the great men of animation. Clampett has been in cartoon films since 1931, and made many of the best ever Warner Brothers shorts including *Porky in Wackyland*, *Falling Hare* (with Bugs Bunny), and *Horton Hatches the Egg* from a Dr Seuss book. One of the least attractive puppets on television must have been *Life With Snarky Parker* (1950), at least if the Fox comic-book version is anything to go by.

One of the first animated cartoon series made for American television, and the first to make it into his own comic-book, was *Crusader Rabbit* (1956). Inspired by the superhero syndrome, this little white bunny was unique in that he spurned the usual

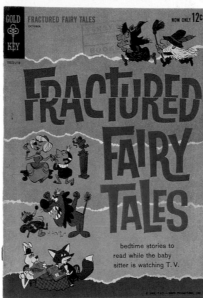

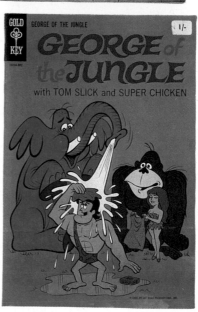

cloak and costume, but not the comical sidekick, in this case a stripey tiger called Rags. An even funnier kind of superhero was *Tom Terrific* (1957): "Attention, all evil-doers everywhere! Now hear this! Tom Terrific and Mighty Manfred the Wonder Dog are on the lookout! So beware!" Billed as "the World's Greatest All-around Full-time Hero", tiny Tom and tired Manfred were the first TV cartoons to be produced by the famous old-time animation company, Terrytoons. Paul Terry had sold out to CBS Television, and Gene Deitch, hot from the innovative UPA, was now in charge. Tom wore a funnel on his head, a magic hat that could turn him into anything, a power he found useful in combating his mortal enemy, Crabby "Rotten to the Core" Appleton. Terrytoons soon packaged many a TV series with their old cinema releases plus "Deputy Dawg", and a new run for *New Terrytoons Comics* began in 1960.

Limited animation technique, so essential for economic television production, did not necessarily equate with limited imagination. Jay Ward

proved this when he joined with Bill Scott, another ex-UPA talent, to produce *Rocky and his Friends* (1960). This series starred Rocket J. Squirrel, (Rocky for short), a fearless flying squirrel from Frostbite Falls, assisted by the usual, but unusual, idiot, Bullwinkle Moose. Their eternal foes were Boris Badenov, master of spies and disguise, and pallid Natasha Fatale. Supporting shorts included *Fractured Fairy Tales* and *Dudley Do-Right* of the Mounties, both of which won their own comic-books. The series was so popular with older children, thanks to its high standard of gaggery, both verbal and visual, that it was awarded an adult-time rerun as *The Bullwinkle Show*. Ward and Scott later produced another fun-filled series that made all age-groups chortle, *George of the Jungle* (1968). This sendup of *Tarzan of the Apes* was backed with "Tom Slick" ("Yay!") and "Super Chicken", whose alter ego was millionaire playboy Henry Cabot Henhouse III. Henry's "cry in the sky", a strangled cluck, was not heard in England until 1983, when the new *Good Morning Britain* show ran these old Jay Ward

cartoons with some success.

Howdy Doody *No.7* © *March 1951 Dell/Robert Smith*
Foodini *No.2* © *May 1950 Continental/Bunin*
Beany *No.1 (OS 368)* © *January 1952 Dell/Bob Clampett. Drawn by Jack Bradbury*
Crusader Rabbit *No.1 (OS 735)* © *October 1956 Dell/Classic Enterprises*
America's Best TV Comics © *1967 ABC/Marvel*
King Leonardo *No.1 (OS 1241)* © *November 1961 Dell/Leonardo*

Tom Terrific *No.1* © *Summer 1957 Pines/Terrytoons*
New Terrytoons *No.1* © *June 1960 Dell/Terrytoons*
Underdog *No.1* © *July 1970 Charlton Comics/Leonardo. Drawn by Frank Johnson*
Rocky and His Friends *No.3 (OS 1166)* © *March 1961 Dell/Ward*
Fractured Fairy Tales *No.1* © *October 1962 Gold Key/Ward*
George of the Jungle *No.1* © *November 1968 Gold Key/Ward*

Hanna-Barbera: "Smarter than the Average Comics"

The action-packed, never-ending cat-and-mouse chase that was "Tom and Jerry", roaring through over 100 films in 25 years and winning seven Academy Awards, seems a long way from the ambling, drawling slopoke that is "Huckleberry Hound". Yet Tom and Jerry and Huck and Yogi come from Bill and Joe, the same Hanna and Barbera. Only the screen size has changed, from widescreen cinema to square-eyed television, and with it has gone forever the full flowing luxury of old-time animation. William Hanna and Joseph Barbera, veteran partners from the Thirties and earlier, were the first to rationalize expensive animation, once the pride of all the major studios, into a production-line system able to cope with the weekly, sometimes daily, demands of TV. Their Hollywood fun-factory is highly systematized, with the cartoon staff busy as bees in their cubby-holes. (Being cartoonists they personalize the cubicles with inspirational pin-ups: it was a patriotic thrill to discover one with a very British Bonzo!) Part of the system is to produce the comic-books and strips which run around the world in company with the cartoons: there is hardly a spot on the globe whose kids don't watch Hanna-Barbera productions and read Hanna-Barbera comics.

After MGM closed their animation studios, Tom and Jerry went chasing along in perpetual re-runs; Bill and Joe were less lucky. Their first series for television, and the first to be issued as a comic-book, was *Ruff and Reddy* (1958), dog and cat pals who set the H-B formula for TV, one large (Ruff the dog), one small (Reddy the kitten), forever talking. Using radio techniques as inspiration, Hanna-Barbera transferred most of their jokes from expensive visuals to inexpensive verbals. Then came "Yogi Bear" (big) and Boo-Boo (small), dwellers in Jellystone Park. (Yogi's name is an All-American pun on Yogi Berra, a baseball champ.) These hungry bears were a single segment of the first half-hour television cartoon series, *The Huckleberry Hound Show*. Huck, the drawling dawg, had no adventures of his own, but acted as a cartoon master-of-ceremonies. Also in the show was "Pixie, Dixie and Mr Jinks", a cat-and-mouse formula that avoided any suspicion of swiping from their earlier cartoons by doubling the mouse quota. Huck, as voiced by Daws Butler, became so popular that the first regular Hanna-Barbera comic was built around him. *Huckleberry Hound Weekly*, produced especially for Britain, arrived on 7 October 1961. Its colourful tabloid format was designed to rival the long-running Walt Disney *Mickey Mouse Weekly*. Soon *Yogi Bear's Own Weekly* came out as a companion (27 October 1962), and 10 years later a renaissance on television prompted a new weekly comic, *Yogi and His Toy* (26 February 1972). This was unique in British comics history: every single issue, and there were 35 of them, carried a Free Gift (the first was a pack of four crayons plus stencils)!

The first TV cartoon series created specifically for an adult audience instead of children was *The Flintstones* (1960): a comic-book series and a newspaper strip began the following year. Unusual in that the programmes told a single situation comedy story instead of several short segments, the characters of Fred and Wilma Flintstone and their neighbours Barney and Betty Rubble got their laughs by transplanting modern language and behaviour to stone-age Bedrock.

There have been more Hanna-Barbera series and characters than can possibly be catalogued here, from the cowboy horse *Quick Draw McGraw* (1959) to the space age *Jetsons* (1963), from *Top Cat* (1961), known for years in Britain as *Boss Cat* (the BBC refused to give free advertising to a cat food), to *Scooby Doo Where Are You* (1970). And, funnies apart, there are also the adventure cartoons, from *Jonny Quest* (1964) to *Super TV Heroes* (1967), a comic-book type crowd including "The Herculoids" and "The Mighty Mightor". The total production boggles the mind; one can only echo Fred Flintstone – "Yabba-dabba-doo!"

Ruff and Reddy *No. OS 1038* © *October 1959 Dell Publishing/ Hanna-Barbera*
Snagglepuss *No.1* © *October 1962 Gold Key/Hanna-Barbera*
The Flintstones Bigger and Boulder *No.1* © *November 1962 Gold Key/ Hanna-Barbera*
The Jetsons © *Strexel (Singapore)/ Hanna-Barbera*
Top Cat *No.6* © *April 1963 Gold Key/Hanna-Barbera*
Wacky Races *No.1* © *May 1969 Gold Key/Hanna Barbera*
Jonny Quest *No.1* © *September 1964 Gold Key/Hanna-Barbera*
Space Ghost *No.1* © *December 1966 Gold Key/Hanna-Barbera*

Huckleberry Hound Weekly *No.1*
© *7 October 1961 City Magazines*
(GB)/Hanna-Barbera
Yogi and His Toy *No.1*
© *26 February 1972 Williams*
(GB)/Hanna-Barbera

Skubbidu *No.5* © *1974 Williams*
(Oslo)/Hanna-Barbera
Kremenkov Zabavnik *No.37*
© *7 June 1972 Graficki Zavod*
(Beograd)/Hanna-Barbera

Braccobaldo Festival *No.3* © *1977*
Flash (Milan)/Hanna-Barbera

The Where and When of Dr Who

The heroes of British science-fiction television have proved a constant headache to artists endeavouring to adapt them for the comics. One lot are all puppets, the other a single hero with an ever-changing face. The puppets came along first, all creations of the same man, bald, benign Gerry Anderson, mild-mannered assistant from Gainsborough Studios who slid into children's television in 1961 with a terrible attempt at a western called *Four Feather Falls*. Puppet cowboys proved anything but quick on the draw, so the next year he developed a science-fiction series called *Supercar*. This land/sea/air vehicle in the good old tradition worked fine, but hero Mike Mercury, inventor Professor Popkiss, and even Mitch the Monkey looked thoroughly artificial. Anderson's third series, *Fireball XL5* (1962), had much the same faults: a super spaceship, but Steve Zodiac and Space Doctor Venus were hardly more serious than their comic-relief crew, Robert the Robot and Professor Matthew Matic. The strip cartoonists had a hard time making their pictures look exciting. In *TV Comic* Neville Main didn't really try, but the American comic-book versions made up for the dreary interiors with exciting covers. But in 1964 came a new series, *Stingray*: things were about to change for the better.

TV Century 21 No.1 was published on 23 January 2065 (dated 100 years ahead, much to the confusion of comic collectors). It was a handsome full-colour photogravure tabloid in *Eagle* style, but its 20 pages were devoted to television heroes, most of them belonging to Gerry Anderson. The comic did, too, for it was licensed by his AP Films to City Magazines. For the first time top artists worked on the Anderson puppets, producing painted art second only to Frank Hampson's Dan Dare work. There was Ronald Turner, Mike Noble, Eric Eden (a Hampson assistant); and soon Frank Bellamy, another *Eagle* graduate, joined to illustrate *Thunderbirds*. This

was Anderson's latest series, made with higher budgets and to a double running time of 50 minutes. Soon *TV21* (as it came to be called) lost a spare rib and gave birth to *Lady Penelope* (22 January 1966). This was designed as a comic for girls, with Frank Langford drawing milady's full-colour centre-spread serial. Anderson's next TV series, and therefore next comic, was *Joe 90* (18 January 1969). Joseph McClaine, a nine-year-old schoolboy and adopted son of Professor Mac, doubled as a special agent for WIN (the World Intelligence Network). The series had exciting hardware, but perhaps nine-year-old schoolboys do not interest nine-year-old schoolboys: the comic

folded after 34 weeks. An Anderson series which failed to get a comic of its own was *Captain Scarlet and the Mysterons* (1967); it had to make do with a couple of pages in *TV Tornado*.

Dr Who is the longest-running series of any kind, never mind science-fiction, on British television. It began on November 1963 and shows no sign of coming to a conclusion. The problem with any long-running success is how to maintain continuity of character (since it's not made by Gerry Anderson, real humans are employed). BBC television came up with a brilliant solution: as the tale is a fantasy, anyway, simply change the leading actor from time to time, and make this physical switch part of the plot.

Thus William Hartnell, who played the eccentric Time Lord in the beginning, changed into Patrick Troughton, who changed into Jon Pertwee, who changed into Tom Baker, and so on ad infinitum. This proved to be amazingly acceptable to the viewing millions, but tough potatoes for the artists who drew Who strips

The Dr Who artists have changed about as frequently as Who himself, and perhaps more so. He has also tardissed around from comic to comic, and even country to country. Neville Main was the first to draw the doctor for *TV Comic* (1965), while the doctor's classic enemies, the Daleks, spun off on their own to the back page of *TV Century 21*, a colourful serial by Ron Turner. In 1972 both Dr Who and the Daleks turned up in *TV Action*, drawn

by Gerry Haylock. Finally, on 17 October 1979, former comic fan Dez Skinn, who had rocketed to the top of Marvel-UK, launched *Doctor Who Weekly*. It was these black-and-white strips, drawn by the excellent Dave Gibbons, that were reprinted in full colour in America (*Marvel Premiere No.57*, December 1980). Thus Doctor Who's Tardis accomplished something British comic artists had dreamed of for years.

T.V. Century 21 *No.1* © *23 January 1965 City/AP Films*
Lady Penelope *No.1* © *22 January 1966 City/AP Films*
Joe 90 *No.1* © *18 January 1969 City/Century 21*
Doctor Who Weekly *No.1* © *17 October 1979 Marvel Comics*

Supercar *No.2* © *February 1963 Gold Key/ITC*
Steve Zodiac *No.1* © *October 1963 Gold Key/ITC*
Dr Who and the Daleks © *1976 Dell/British Lion/BBC*
Marvel Premiere: Doctor Who *No.57* © *December 1960 Marvel Comics. Drawn by Joe Sinott*
Space 1999 *No.1* © *November 1975 Charlton/ATV. Drawn by Joe Staton*
Star Trek *No.1* © *July 1967 Gold Key/Desilu*
The Six Million Dollar Man *No.1* © *June 1976 Charlton/Universal. Drawn by Joe Staton*
The Bionic Woman *No.1* © *October 1977 Charlton/Universal.*

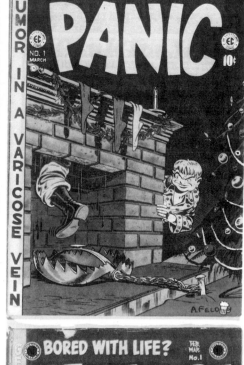

MAD COMICS: "Humor in a Jugular Vein!"

The famous face of Alfred E. Neumann, the "What Me Worry?" Kid whose gap-toothed grin beams from the covers of *Mad Magazine*, has perplexed students of that phenomenon of international publishing since he first lurked in the background of that grown-up magazine's teenage parent, *Mad Comics*. Some see a likeness to the jug-eared baldy who became the symbol of early American comics, "The Yellow Kid". Others see Alfred as the alter-ego of the smiling, shiny, slimline satirist who created *Mad* out of the wholecloth of his warped mind back in October 1952, in Room 706 (Dept. 1), 225 Lafayette Street, New York City, the home of Educational Comics Inc (EC). In his first ever editorial, "Mad Mumblings", Kurtzman describes his new concept: "We were tired of the war, ragged from the science-fiction, weary of the horror. Then it hit us! Why not do a complete about-face? A change of pace! A comic book! Not a serious comic book ... but a *comic* comic book! Not a floppity rabbit, giggly girl, anarchist teenage type comic book ... but a comic mag based on the short story type of wild adventures that you seem to like so well."

No.1 of *Tales Calculated to Drive You Mad*, soon to be subtitled "Humor in a Jugular Vein", was a totally new idea: a comic-book that made fun of comic-books! To this point in strip history, only once had this kind of thing happened before, when Al Capp burlesqued Chester Gould's "Dick Tracy" as "Fearless Fosdick", a strip within his own strip, "Li'l Abner". Kurtzman's first issue lampooned four familiar types of comic-book story. The lead strip, "Hoohah!", drawn by Jack Davis, was a spooky horror strip filled with massively over-lettered sound effects ("*Kapoka Kapoka Kafonk!*" ... "*Squeeeeeeaawk!*" ... "*Eeee Heee Heee Clumpity Clump!*"). Then came the Science Fiction Department with "Blobs!", drawn by Wally Wood with more weird sound effects ("*Pokkita Queeek!*" ... "*Kaphud Bdoom!*"). The Crime Dept presented "Ganefs!", a gangster spoof by Bill Elder with one climactic "*Phud!*", and meanwhile, back at the ranch, the Western Dept wound up with "Varmint!", drawn by John Severin. Laconic cowboy Textron Quickdraw returned to Yucca Pucca Gulch (stomping ground of Kurtzman's old hero, "Potshot Pete") but could hardly be seen for the sound effects: "*Yahoo!*"..."*Plonkaplink!*"... "*Bludabl-blam!*"

"Hey, look!" cried Kurtzman, using the title of his pioneering zany page in the old Marvel Comics days, as reader response poured in. The EC audience, a notch above the grade school crowd, dug his send-ups. To fill a bi-monthly book, Kurtzman had to look beyond self-parody. First it was other publishers' comic-books: "Superduperman" (Wally Wood drew him with a Good Housekeeping Seal of Approval on his chest) had a knockdown fight to the finish with his rival, "Captain Marbles". Bill Elder drew typical teenager "Starchie" as more typical of teenagers: an acne-studded, chain-smoking, sex-mad blackmailer! It was Elder who developed a marvellous line in imitation, making "Gasoline Valley" an amazing lookalike for Frank King's

newspaper strip, the first in which the characters actually grew older, as in real life. In Kurtzman's version, Skizziks grows older in every panel, from doorstep baby to shrivelled old man. Then it was television's turn, as Kurtzman burlesqued the popular Jack Webb as "Dragged Net" ("*Domm-da-dom-domm!*"). Cartoon films came in for it with "Mickey Rodent", movies with "Frank N. Stein", advertising with "The Rubber Bubble Kids". The media world was Kurtzman's oyster, with or without Potrzebie. There was only one snag: all the other ferschlugginer publishers started to put out *Mad* imitations. With a scornful cry of "Hoo-Ha!" Kurtzman's publisher, Bill Gaines, answered back the only way he knew how: he put out an imitation, too! Gaines' favourite editor/writer, the faithful Al Feldstein, was given the job, and *Panic* No.1, "Humor in a Varicose Vein", arrived in February 1954 with "My Gun Is the Jury", a Mickey Spillane spoof by Jack Davis, and a TV satire, "This Is Your Strife" by Joe Orlando. Not bad stuff, certainly better than most of the copy-jobs, but when compared with the parent publication, the genius of

Kurtzman as creator/editor/writer/designer shines forth like a ferschlugginer beacon. All the more so when his Mad work is weighed with his exceptional, totally serious, war comics.

Mad *No.1* © *October 1952 EC Comics. Drawn by Harvey Kurtzman* Panic *No.1* © *March 1954 EC Comics. Drawn by Al Feldstein* Flip *No.1* © *April 1954 Illustrated Humor* Get Lost *No.1* © *February 1954 Mikeross. Drawn by Andru and Esposito* Wild *No.1* © *February 1954 Atlas Comics. Drawn by Joe Maneely* Riot *No.1* © *April 1954 Atlas Comics*

Eh! *No.1* © *December 1953 Charlton Comics. Drawn by Don Ayers* Yak Yak *No.1 (OS 1186)* © *1961 Dell Publishing. Drawn by Jack Davis* Brand Echh *No.1* © *August 1967 Marvel Comics. Drawn by Jack Kirby* Crazy *No.1* © *February 1973 Marvel Comics. Drawn by Tom Sutton* Arrgh! *No.1* © *December 1974 Marvel Comics. Drawn by Tom Sutton* Plop! *No.1* © *October 1973 National Periodicals. Drawn by Basil Wolverton*

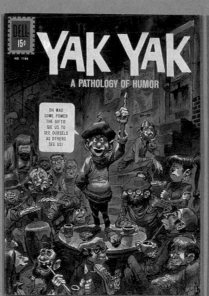

SWORD AND SORCERY: "By Crom!"

"Before man could read or write, he had his legends! and no legends were more thrilling, more colourful, more filled with fantasy and high adventure, than the legends of Asgard, Home of the Gods – birthplace of the Mighty Thor!" With these words ("Written with Passion by Stan Lee, Drawn with Pageantry by Jack Kirby, Inked with Power by Vince Colletta, Lettered with Pride by Artie Simek"), Marvel Comics launched their "Tales of Asgard – Home of the Mighty Norse Gods", and began a new comic-book cult, Sword and Sorcery. The term is attributed to the novelist Fritz Lieber, who coined it in 1960 to define that sub-genre of science-fantasy where near-naked mortals wield their blood-stained weapons against the forces of evil, set in a misty, distant land in a distant, misty age. "The Mighty Thor" began as a supporting strip in *Journey Into Mystery* No.83 (August 1962), and in the beginning was your run-of-the-Marvel superhero: weak Dr Don Blake whacks his walking-stick and turns into the legendary God of Thunder (the walking-stick turned into his hammer!). Soon Dr Don faded away, and from No.126 (March 1966), *Journey Into Mystery* turned into a comic-book called *Thor*.

The Sword and Sorcery scene was set in October 1970, when Marvel published No.1 of *Conan the Barbarian*: "Come with us to the Hyborian Age! Back to the dark centuries which sprawl between the sinking of Atlantis and the dawn of recorded time, to the days when the now-forgotten land of Aquilonia was the mightiest of na-tions, and a man's life was worth no more than the strength of his sword-arm!" From the pages of the late Robert E. Howard's series of stories, which began with "The Phoenix on the Sword" in *Weird Tales* (1932), Barry Smith, a new talent from Eng-land, created an exciting if violent comic-book combining the muscular vigour of Jack Kirby with a decorative overlay of his own. The scripts were by Roy Thomas, a former comic fan whose first published work was a sort of sword-and-sorcery adventure of Charlton's *Son of Vulcan* (January 1966). His dialogue style hadn't chan-ged a bit: "Now, merciless Kong, be careful for your safety, for you have aroused the wrath of one whose powers come from the Gods of Mount Olympus!" (1966); "You'll call forth

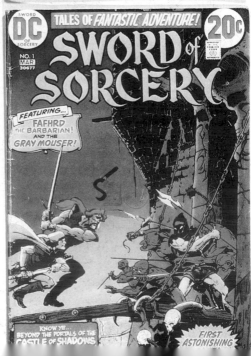

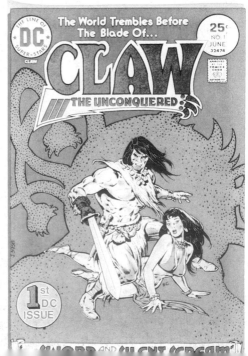

no more fiends from beyond, not while there is yet breath in Conan's body and strength in Conan's arm! Death to the harbingers of Hell!"

DC Comics woke up in 1973 and, cunningly contacting the writer who coined the label, brought out No.1 of *Sword of Sorcery*, adapting Fritz Leiber's story series, started in 1934, of "Fafhrd and the Gray Mouser". This beloved pair of wandering, sword-swinging rogues was drawn by Howard Chaykin in a way that made you wish Burt Lancaster and Nick Cravat could have filmed them. The many comic-books in the S and S genre that have followed the blood-stains down the years have all been distinguished by their high-quality artwork and low-quality dialogue. Even *Red Sonja* ("She-Devil with a Sword") finds time to cry "A single stroke will disarm you and give the slither-things the meal they darkly crave!" as she dispatches a demi-man down into the untold depths. Sergio Aragones hits the right tone in his *Groo the Wanderer* (1982): "My rump is killing me. God, how I hate horses!"

Tales of Asgard *No.1* © *October 1968 Marvel Comics. By Jack Kirby*
Conan the Barbarian *No.1* © *October 1970 Marvel Comics. Drawn by Barry Smith*
Kull the Conqueror *No.1* © *June 1971 Marvel Comics. By Ross Andru*
Sword of Sorcery *No.1* © *March 1973 National Periodicals. Drawn by Howard Chaykin*
Claw the Unconquered *No.1* © *June 1975 National Periodicals. Drawn by Ernie Chua*
Arak Son of Thunder *No.1* © *September 1981 DC Comics. Drawn by Ernie Colon*

Hercules *No.1* © *October 1967 Charlton Comics. By Sam Gillman*
Hercules Unbound *No.1* © *November 1975 National Periodicals. Drawn by Garcia Lopez*
Wulf the Barbarian *No.1* © *February 1975 Atlas Comics. Drawn by Larry Hama*
The Barbarians/Iron Jaw *No.1* © *June 1975 Atlas Comics. Drawn by Pablo Marcos*
Marvel Feature/Red Sonja *No.1* © *November 1975 Marvel Comics. Drawn by Dick Giordano*
Groo the Wanderer *No.1* © *December 1982 Pacific Comics. Drawn by Sergio Aragones*

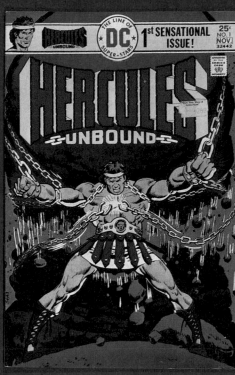

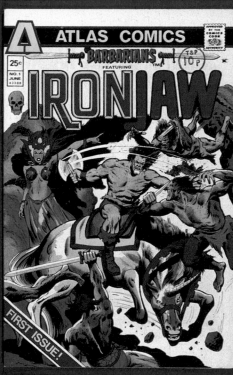

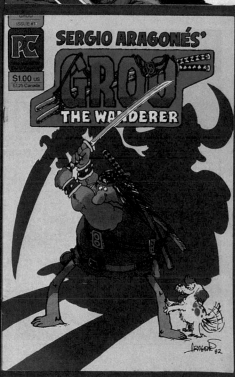

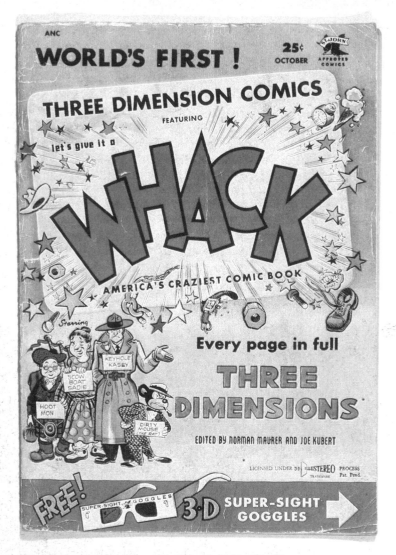

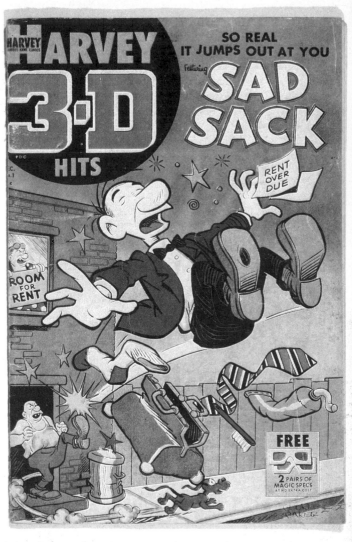

STEREOCOMICS:
"They Jump Right Out of the Page!"

"Hey, kids!" cried the cover of *3D Funny Movies* No.1, "3 Dimensional Comics are 3 Times as Funny!" They were also nearly three times the price (25 cents) and certainly three times the eye-strain. A brilliant advancement of comic strip technique, 3D comic-books followed in the sensational wake of Arch Oboler's pioneering stereo-scopic feature film, *Bwana Devil* (1952). Oboler, an ex-radio writer of mystery series, made millions with his skilfully sold 3D B-movie. Nobody minded wearing the vital polaroid spectacles necessary to experience the much-boosted "A Lover in Your Arms – a Lion in Your Lap!" The comic-books that cashed in on the cinema craze fell back on the century-old anaglyph system, which had been patented by Ducros du Hauron as far back as 1858. By reading the comics through double-coloured cardboard and celluloid "Magic Specs", left eye red, right eye green, the double-

printed strips that looked like an off-register blur came together and "jumped right out of the page!"

3D comics were the brainchild of Joe Kubert, one of the great men of American comic-books. At the age of 13 the Brooklyn boy's obvious talent and keenness convinced publisher Harry A. Chesler to give him a menial job in his art studio. Three years later Joe had soaked up so much know-how that he was a sought-after stylist among the superhero comics: his take-over of "Hawkman" in 1944 is a watershed. Serving with the Army in Germany in 1951 Joe first saw red/green 3D photographs in a movie magazine. He was immediately inspired to adapt the system to comics, and on his demobilization set up a studio to supply complete comic-books for the St John Publishing Company. His partner in the venture was another top comic-book artist, Norman Maurer, who not only drew

The Three Stooges comic but married Moe's daughter. Movie-mad Maurer (later to realize his ambition and produce new Three Stooges films), fully aware of the imminent 3D boom about to burst via *Bwana Devil*, was excited by Joe's desire to make a 3D comic. His brother, Leonard, was of scientific bent, and together they worked out the ways and means of adding the third dimension to a till-now two-dimensional art form. Using several layers of transparent acetate sheets for the drawings, so that they could be shifted to the left for the first (red) photographing, then to the right for the second (grccn), the partners did dummy runs with Kubert's prehistoric hero, "Tor", and Maurer's beloved Three Stooges. They showed the results to Archer St John, and the publisher was more than impressed. He handed them the finished artwork for a *Mighty Mouse Comics* and asked them to convert it to 3D. The September issue of *Three Dimension Comics No.1 Starring Mighty Mouse* went on sale on 3 July 1953. Kids went wild and despite the high 25 cent price snapped up 1,250,000 copies! The excited St John ordered all his titles to be converted to 3D, and the American Stereographic Corporation (Kubert and Maurer) and the Illustereo Process were in business.

In October came Illustereo editions of Kubert's *Tor* and Maurer's *Three Stooges*, plus No.1 of *Let's Give It a Whack*, a stereoscopic rip-off of EC's *Mad*. In this brilliant effort Joe and Norm not only satirise several types of contemporary comic-book (*Ghastly Dee-fective Comics*; *Tales of the Wooly West*; *Animated Horror Comics* starring Dirty Mouse the Rat), they poke fun at their own invention. "The 3-D-T's" tells the story behind the stereo craze, with artists crying "We're going blind! 72 hours without food or rest! (gasp!) It's inhuman!", and callous Kubert replying, "Hah! Who said comic artists were human?" Many a true word is spoken in jest, but Kubert has surely atoned for any such attitude. Last year near New York I found him the genial dean of his own school for budding comic artists.

Whack! No.1 © October 1953 St John Publishing. Drawn by Norman Maurer

Harvey 3-D Hits (Sad Sack) *No.1 © January 1954 Harvey Publications. Drawn by George Baker*

Funny 3D *No.1 © December 1953 Harvey Publications (British Edition)* 3-D Dolly *No.1 © December 1953 Harvey Publications (British Edition)* Captain 3-D *No.1 © December 1953 Harvey Publications (British Edition). Drawn by Jack Kirby* Adventures in 3-D *No.1 © November 1953 Harvey Publications (British Edition). Drawn by Bob Powell* True 3-D *No.1 © December 1953 Harvey Publications (British Edition)*

"Thru Space! Thru Time! And into the Third Dimension!"

No sooner was the soar-away success of the *Mighty Mouse* 3-D comic-book obvious than the biggest men in the comic-book business set their best technical minds to analysing the anaglyphs. It was Jack Adler of DC Comics who engineered a special edition of *Superman* rushed out by September 1953. The large-sized comic-book's subtitle, "In Startling 3-D Lifelike Action!", was the only clumsy thing about it, although afficionados of stereoscopy point out that the artwork has only four levels of depth. This scarcely bothered the kids, and sales were such that a similar book of *Batman*, subtitled just as clumsily "Adventures in Amazing 3-D Action", was dashed out for December. These proved to be the only DC 3-Ds, although they reprinted *Batman* in 1966 with added photographs of the actors in the television series.

The Harvey brothers (Alfred, president; Leon, editor; Robert, business manager) were next in the field with their *Adventures in 3-D* (November 1953). They addressed their bespectacled readers thus: "After many years of research and experiment, we now bring you the most startling magazine produced in three-dimensional illustration by our own exclusive process. The results produce a sensational True-Life depth never before accomplished in story illustration." A footnote to the indicia read, "The three-dimensional effects in this magazine are manufactured under an exclusive process, patent pending by Harvey Publications." The Harveys were making sure they weren't going to hear from the American Stereographic Corporation's solicitor, although it might have been tricky to prove that "many years of research" claim when the *Mighty Mouse* 3D comic had only been out for two months. Harvey also confronted parental fears of eye damage by printing an "Important Statement" signed by Bertram King and Stanley Sobel, Visual Consultants. It read in part:

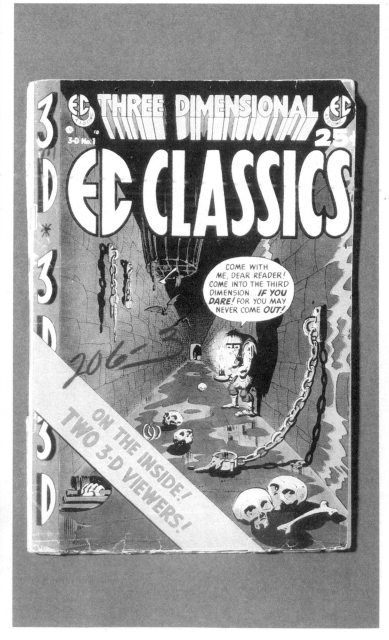

"Reading these new 3-D comic magazines is similar to the eye-training exercises used in doctors' offices for years. The added interest of absorbing stories and action-packed pictures will make eye-training a lot of fun for thousands." Subscribers to "Harvey Famous Name Comics" got through plenty of eye-training fun in the next month or so: titles ranged through *True 3-D*, *Funny 3-D*, *3-D Hits*, *3-D Dolly*, and the first fully dimensional superhero, *Captain 3-D*. "Thru Space! Thru Time! And into the Third Dimension!" leaped Captain 3-D, thanks to young Danny Davis and his Magic Specs. Thanks also to the hard-edged artwork of Jack Kirby, at the top of his creative comic-book form. The Harvey 3-D comics, to be fair, differed from the Kubert-Maurer comics in that they used the new Craftint system for tinting backgrounds.

In December 1953 Fiction House joined in the 3-D game with the funny animal book, *3-D Circus*, an unlikely religious item entitled *The First Christmas*, and their best-selling *Sheena the Jungle Queen*, outstanding in every way. The same month Star Publications issued 3-D editions of their *Jungle Thrills* and *Indian Warriors*, and a shoal of one-shots from other publishers included *Felix the Cat*, *3-D Love*, *Animal Fun*, *Jet Pup*, *Noodnick* and *The Space Kat-Ets*. Harvey even put out a 3-D edition of the earliest comic kids of them all, *The Katzenjammer Kids* (No.26, January 1954), but it stands as a sign of the time: only one story was in stereo. In less than six months the 3-D boom was over. The last big one came from EC Comics. William Gaines issued *Three Dimensional EC Classics* in the Spring of '54. To do so he had sought out one Freeman H. Owens, who in 1936 had patented his "Method for Drawing and Photographing Stereoscopic Pictures in Relief", bought the rights, and slapped an infringement suit on all the other 3-D comic publishers. It did him little good, and his second special, *Three Dimensional Tales from the Crypt*, was his last. It sold nowhere near its print run of 300,000 copies.

The US 3-D bubble had burst. In Britain, there had been locally printed editions of the Harvey titles, double-priced at a shilling by the United Anglo-American Book Company, who issued them in their "Streamline American Comics" series. But nobody, artist or publisher, experimented with stereoscopics for thirty long years. Then, on 26 February 1983, David Hunt Editor announced: "It's another *Eagle* first as you Leap into the Amazing World of 3-D!" Evidently Hunt reckoned, and probably correctly, that none of his ten-year old readers remembered the stereocomics of 1953. Inside *Eagle* there were four pages printed in the familiar red/green, plus a pair of Magic Specs manufactured by Karran Products of Lightwater, Surrey. Only two of the pages were drawn, a strip called "Gil Hazzard Codename Scorpio". Cam Kennedy's cars came crashing out of page one, but the second page made little use of the gimmick, being confined to talking heads. *Look-In's* answer to *Eagle* five weeks later was a disappointment: a scattering of photographs and no artwork at all. But the cover, showing ET looking directly out through the taped-on 3-D specs, was an eyeful!

ADULT COMICS: "Trapped in a World They Never Made!"

Comics began as illustrated entertainment for adults: Ally Sloper brought rowdy good humour to *Punch*-style satire, then Weary Willie and Tired Tim broadened into burlesque. The impish pranks of the Katzenjammer Kids made an immediate appeal to children, and as the 20th century grew older, comics grew younger. It was not until America went to war in the Forties that comic-books found a new, more adult market in the GIs and added pin-up pretties to their pictures and explicit violence to their stories. Charles Biro ran into parent/teacher trouble when he tried to upgrade comic-books with *Crime Does Not Pay*, and so developed the first comics magazine aimed at the adult audience, *Tops*, in 1949. It failed, as did his hope to upgrade the word "comics" into "illustories". After the horror comics scandals had led to the introduction of the Comics Code, William Gaines at EC launched his first attempt at an adult-oriented comic-book, a 68-page black-and-white magazine entitled *Shock Illustrated* (October 1955). In his

editorial introduction Albert Feldstein explained aims: "*Shock Illustrated* is the first of a new series of magazines to present a novel and revolutionary development in the art of story-telling. We at EC call this new form of adult entertainment 'Picto-Fiction', a careful combination of two arts, the art of writing and the art of illustration." *Shock*, followed by *Crime Illustrated* and *Confessions Illustrated*, lasted for only three editions. Clearly adults were about as interested in Picto-Fiction as they were in Illustories.

In 1964 came *Creepy* – and success: a new publisher, James Warren, had entered the magazine field and boldly declared his first effort as "Comics to Give You the Creeps!" Evidently the bad word was not as off-putting to adults as had been suspected. *Creepy* was modelled closely on the EC horror comics of the Fifties, but without the brightness of the usual four colours; the artists developed a line and grey-tint technique which was both striking and, somehow, grown-up. So although Jack Davis, Joe Orlando, Reed

Crandall, George Evans, Frank Frazetta, Al Williamson and the rest were all ex-comic-book artists of great repute, it was in the pages of Warren's *Creepy*, soon to be joined by *Eerie* (1966), *Blazing Combat* (1965), and the glamorous monstress *Vampirella* (1969), that some of their best artwork ever was to be found. Craving to get a crack at this new style of comic-book where inhibitions and restrictions could be abandoned, some artists set up their own publications. Gil Kane, who had drawn just about every adventure hero from Hopalong Cassidy to The Incredible Hulk, created *His Name Is Savage* (1968) as a 41-page illustrated novel, while the old innovator Jack Kirby produced two adult strip magazines, *Spirit World* and *In The Days of the Mob* (1971). Jack was definitely neither "Jolly" nor "Jumpin'" on these occasions.

Marvel Comics was the first of the major comic-book publishers to enter this new field, and in July 1968 Stan Lee wrote and produced No.1 of *The Spectacular Spider-Man*. It took John

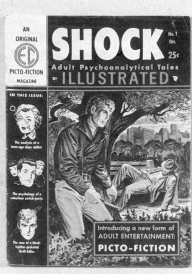

Romita and a staff of 15 artists, letterers and researchers to execute this 52-page "Super Spidey Spectacular". Marvel soon became pace-setters in the adult area, with titles embracing horror (*Haunt of Horror*, 1974; *Legion of Monsters*, 1975; *Tomb of Dracula*, 1979), science-fiction (*Unknown Worlds*, 1975), rock music (*Kiss*, 1977) and superheroes (*The Rampaging Hulk*, 1977). Strip adaptations of movies followed in the series *Marvel Super Special* (No.18: *Raiders of the Lost Ark*, 1981), a title which brought full colour into this previously monochrome field. Marvel also pioneered humour in the adult comics with *Comix Book* (1974), which brought the Underground into the Overground, and *Howard the Duck* (1979), an offbeat strip about a funny animal "trapped in a world he never made": the human world! The French adult comic, *Metal Hurlant*, arrived in America as *Heavy Metal* (1977), put out by the folks who bring you *National Lampoon*. Marvel, inspired, answered this European invasion with *Epic Illustrated* (1980), which stands as the all-time reply to the scornful statement that "comics are kids' stuff".

Shock Illustrated No.*1* © *October 1955 EC*
Crime Illustrated *No.1* © *December*
Blazing Combat *No.1* © *October 1965 Warren Publishing. Drawn by Frank Frazetta*
1955 EC. Drawn by Joe Orlando
Creepy *No.1* © *1964 Warren Publishing. Drawn by Jack Davis*
Eerie *No.1* (*No.2*) © *March 1966 Warren Publishing. Drawn by Frank Frazetta*
Vampirella *No.1* © *September 1969 Warren Publishing. Drawn by Frank Frazetta*

His Name Is Savage *No.1* © *June 1968 Adventure House. Drawn by Gil Kane*
Spirit World *No.1* © *1971 Hampshire. Drawn by Jack Kirby*
Comix Book *No.1* © *1974 Marvel Comics. Drawn by Peter Poplaski*
Howard the Duck *No.1* © *October 1979 Marvel Comics. Drawn by Gary Hallgren*
Epic Illustrated *No.1* © *Spring 1980 Marvel Comics. Drawn by Frank Frazetta*
Heavy Metal *No.1* © *April 1977 HM Communications. Drawn by Nicollet*

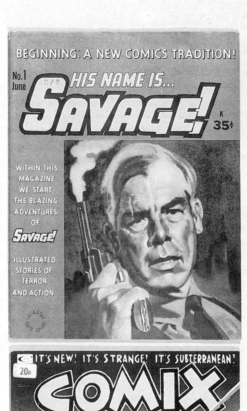

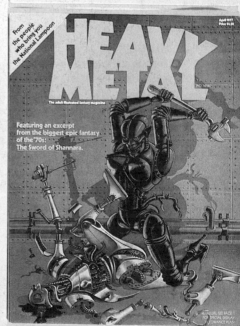

UNDERGROUND COMICS: "Keep on Truckin'!"

"Mr Sketchum is at it again!" announced the cartooned editorial of *Zap Comix* in 1968 (comic-book buyers already knew there was something odd about this one: the number one was numbered "0"!). "Audacious! Irreverent! Provocative! You bet!" Mr Sketchum the comic artist was the pen-name and persona of R. Crumb, whose mysterious initial eventually turned out to stand for nothing more exotic than Robert. *Zap Comix* looked much like any other comic-book at first glance, but turned out to be just black and white inside and five times the usual price. There were other differences, too, as San Franscisco comics fans discovered when they bought this product of their local Apex Novelty Co. Although the strips looked pretty funny (they were drawn in a throwback style resembling a cross between Fred Schwab and Dick Ryan), there was a meaning in them more grown-up than anything ever seen in comic-books before. R. Crumb was using the comic-book format to say something personal about the world, commenting with burlesque and outspoken frankness upon the contemporary human condition as he saw it and experienced it. The cartoonist soon dropped the Mr Sketchum alias and began to star himself in his strips. "Me, Myself and I presents The Many Faces of R. Crumb, (He's Cute and Clever!!), an Inside Look at the Complex Personality of the Great Me!!!" shows the "long-suffering artist-saint" and "the gregarious clowner and all-around funny fellow" in many moods, from "out-of-it dull-witted fool" to "wasted degenerate". In other words, as a very human being.

Crumb, a former designer with the American Greetings Card Co (he drew the sophisticated "Hi-Brow" series), had contributed to Harvey Kurtzman's *Help!* and created the first genuinely adult funny animal, "Fritz the Cat", for *Cavalier*, a man's mag. In other words, he was a fully rounded professional. In the free-and-easy air of San Francisco in the Sixties, it was an obvious step for Crumb to use his artistic talents to express himself in comics, as others were using the new "free press" newspapers to express themselves in writing. As more issues of *Zap Comix* were compiled, Crumb created new cartoon characters of all kinds, such as "Bobo Bolinsky", "Angelfood McSpade" ("She's sock-a-delic, she's all heart – and th' rest o' me aint bad, either!"), and the little bearded Zenist, "Mr Natural".

Zap Comix, with its promised package of "52 action-packed pages of Gags, Jokes and Kozmic Trooths", became the first American Underground comic, produced by and for the independently minded minority who rejected the mass-produced media of the majority. Other cartoonists came flocking in, each with his own attitude. All they had in common was a love for the comic-book form and a desire to break down taboos. In Texas, Gilbert Shelton created "Wonder Wart-Hog", the Hog of Steel who was really Philbert Desenex, reporter. This randy burlesque of Superman graduated from Shelton's University mag to Kurtzman's *Help*, and after that overground monthly's collapse, into the comix (as the underground variety was now permanently labelled). Shelton's best heroes are not burlesques, but a trio of drug-culture

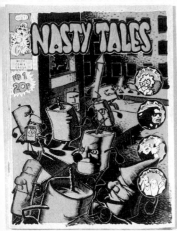

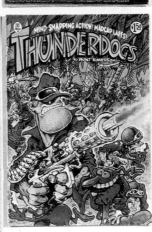

supported the underground by drawing his long-term hero, The Spirit, for No.3 of *Snarf* (1972). This led to Will joining forces with publisher/cartoonist Denis Kitchen for a successful relaunch of *The Spirit*.

British underground comix began by reprinting, then went on to imitate the Americans. *Nasty Tales* (1971) achieved the desired notoriety when it was prosecuted for obscenity, but collapsed after a "not guilty" verdict. A completely unique comic ensued, however: *The Trials of Nasty Tales* (1973), in which all the cartoonists drew their interpretation of the case. Two major talents have emerged from the British underground, Bryan Talbot with his fantastic adventures of "Chester P. Hackenbush, Psychedelic Alchemist" in *Brainstorm Comix* (1975), and Hunt Emerson, whose Krazy Kat inspiration and Birmingham humour won him the honour of being the first British cartoonist to draw a complete comic for American publication, *Thunderdogs* (1981).

Mr Natural *No.1* © *August 1970 Apex Novelties. Drawn by R. Crumb*
Zap Comix *No.3* © *1968 Apex Novelties. Drawn by S. Clay Wilson*
The Best of Wonder Wart-Hog *No.1* © *1963/1973 Rip Off Press. Drawn by Gilbert Shelton*
The Fabulous Furry Freak Brothers *No.1* © *1971 Rip Off Press. Drawn by Gilbert Shelton*
It Ain't Me Babe *No.1* © *July 1970 Last Gasp. Drawn by Trina Robbins*
Junkwaffel *No.1* © *1971 Print Mint. Drawn by Vaughn Bodé*
Dan O'Neill's Comics and Stories *No.1* © *January 1948 Company and Sons. Drawn by Dan O'Neill*
Bijou Funnies *No.8* © *1973 Krupp Comic Works/Kitchen Sink. Drawn by Harvey Kurtzman*
Snarf *No.3* © *November 1972 Kitchen Sink. Drawn by Will Eisner*

Nasty Tales *No.1* © *April 1971 Meep/Bloom*
The Trials of Nasty Tales © *1973 H. Bunch*
Ogoth and Ugly Boot *No.1* © *1973 Cozmic Comics/H. Bunch. Drawn by Chris Welch*
Near Myths *No.1* © *September 1978 Galaxy Media. Drawn by Graham Manley*
Brain Storm Comix *No.1* © *1975 Alchemy Publications. Drawn by Bryan Talbot*
Thunderdogs *No.1* © *1981 Rip Off Press. Drawn by Hunt Emerson*

revolutionaries, Frankling, Fat Freddy and Phineas, known collectively as "The Fabulous Furry Freak Brothers" (not forgetting Fat Freddy's Cat who appears in his own sub-strip like Mutt and Jeff's subsidiary hero, Cicero's Cat). The first underground artist to truly shock even some of the underground, so outrageous were his images, was S. Clay Wilson, a Kansas cartoonist whose "Captain Pissgums and his Pervert Pirates" (*Zap* No.3) put into pictures what the classic *Good Ship Venus* hardly dared sing about.

Underground comix quickly spread, and, like the crime and horror comics which they often parodied, found themselves in trouble. Prosecutions led to an "Adults Only" label, and their sales points were limited to the kind of shop children seldom frequented. This was just as well, for many of the comix were lampoons or extreme versions of famous overground titles, and at an innocent glance could have been mistaken for them. For example, EC horror comics were a popular inspiration, with Rick Griffin's *Tales From The Tube* (1973), Rick Veitch's *Two-Fisted Zombies* (1973), Richard Corben's full colour *Weird Fantasies* (1972), and *Air Pirates Funnies* (1971) by Dan O'Neill and friends, which brought a copyright suit from Disney Productions for its use, or mis-use, of Mickey Mouse. Traditional genres, as well as characters, were considered fair game: Bill Griffith's *Young Lust Comics* (1971) and Jerry Lane's *Middle Class Fantasies* (1973) satirised familiar forms, while Bobby London's *Dirty Duck Book* (1971) was inspired by George Herriman's old Krazy Kat. The Women's Lib movement found underground comix a new way of illustrating their aims, and some excellent women artists emerged with *It Ain't Me Babe* (1970), which led to the regular *Wimmen's Comix* (1972). *Gay Comix* (1980) expressed the other side of the coin.

The American underground owes a great deal to Harvey Kurtzman, the *Mad* man. He originated the phrase when the October 1954 issue of *Mad* ran a feature entitled "Comics Go Underground", and after moving on to *Help*, gave space to R. Crumb and other new-trend cartoonists. A sort of patron saint, Kurtzman drew the cover for a full-colour edition of *Tales Calculated to Sell You Bijou Funnies* (1973), while another much admired overground artist, Will Eisner, also

THE COMIC WORLD:
The Laughter Goes Round and Round

Comics began with only one purpose, to make their readers laugh. Today, despite the advent of adventure, violence, fantasy, sex, politics, and personal artistic statements, it is the funny comics that are still the world's best-sellers, from the British *Beano* to the Dutch *Donald Duck*. It is the funny characters who live longest ("The Katzenjammer Kids" were born 1897), travel farthest ("Bristow", the London office clerk, turns up in Africa with a dot-tinted face), reach the largest audience ("Peanuts" appears in hundreds of newspapers and comic-books around the world).

The international exchange in comics began early in the century when Moses Koenigsberg formed King Features Syndicate and began touting William Randolph's Hearst's daily and Sunday strips at home, and then abroad. The Katzenjammers and others began appearing in the British *Big Budget* in 1902. The flourishing British comic industry, developing independently of America's, found little room for Yankee strips, and they were not popular with the young readers. Their style clashed with the more conservative and more detailed native artwork. British strips were more acceptable throughout Europe. By the Thirties there were French, Spanish and Italian editions of *Rainbow* as *Jumbo*, and its animal hero, Tiger Tim, as Tigre Tino, etc. But before the decade ended, American strips from King Features had ousted the British funsters. After the *Eagle* revolution of the Fifties British strips became popular again, and both comic and newspaper characters pop up in comics around the world. The unlikeliest traveller is undoubtedly "Andy Capp", the chauvinistic layabout who was invented by Reg Smythe for the Northern edition of the *Daily Mirror* in 1957, and who seems to have hit an international nerve. American characters remain supreme, however, and you can find Popeye, who strolled casually into the "Thimble Theatre" strip on 17 January 1929, in Israel, Denmark (as "Skipper Skræk") and, possibly pirated, in Japan.

Most countries have their own comic heroes, some of whom travel.

Others remain national favourites, raising local laughter for many years, all unknown to the outside world. One such is "91 Karlsson", a simple country bumpkin doing his required stint in the Swedish Army. *91 An* (*Number 91*), as his comic-book is called, began his military service back in 1932, and is still waiting for his discharge! No.91's term of silly soldiering has run longer than the life of his creator: Rudolf Petersson died in 1970, but cartoonist Nils Egerbrandt soldiers on. An army comic which has travelled is *Sergeant Bottleneck*, an Italian series reprinted in Australia. Australia, in its turn, gave the world a thoroughly delightful kid strip in "Ginger Meggs". Jimmy Bancks, a slapstick stylist, first drew Ginge (or just plain "Ginger" as he was syndicated in America) for the Sydney *Sunday Sun* on 13 November 1921. Bancks died back in 1952, but his Ginge goes rushing on like a red-headed whirlwind.

The Canadian comic-book boom of the war years brought forth *The Funny Comics* (1942), which was soon taken over by its hero, "Dizzy Don". Drawn by a Toronto entertainer called Manny Easson, each page was a gag ("I'll give you ten dollars to let me paint you." "Don't be silly, how would I get the paint off afterwards?") As a gagster, Dizzy was about as good as Manny was an artist. A later Canadian comic was *Knockout* (1974), an Ontario enterprise in British style by emigrant Terry Fletcher, who drew a crude but funny-looking "Sheerluck Holmes and Dr Wotnot".

Marten Toonder is the Dutch cartoonist who created the popular "Tom Poes" back in 1938. As "Tom Puss" the strips were reprinted in the British magazine, *Leader*, and with colour cartoon books the cuddly little kitten soon became a post-war favourite. Tom's regular comic-book began in Holland in November 1947, and Toonder's delightful designs are currently reprinted in Germany and elsewhere. The excellent full-colour printing techniques available to German comics also do justice to their reprints of the French strip, "Asterix". This half-pint hero of Ancient Gaul was created as a serial for the Parisian comic weekly, *Pilote*. His adventures, written by René Goscinny and drawn by Albert Uderzo, were soon gathered into albums, and in this format have been translated into several different languages, despite the problems of pun-packed dialogue. And so the laughter not only goes on and on; it goes round and round.

Super Cata Plasma *No.4* © *1979 Bruguera (Spain). Drawn by Schmidt* New and Old *No.134* © *1980 (China)* 91: AN *No.12* © *1972 Semic (Finland). Drawn by Nils Egerbrandt* Popeye *No.60* © *(Israel) King Williams (Italy). Drawn by T. Pagot* Calimero *No.1* © *November 1972* Tuffa Viktor *(Andy Capp)* © *1968 Williams (Norway). Drawn by Reg Smythe*

Ginger Meggs *No.14* © *1937 Associated Newspapers (Australia). Drawn by James Bancks* Asterix der Gallier *No.1* © *1961 Dargaud/Ehapa (Germany). Drawn by Albert Uderzo* Sergeant Bottleneck *No.6* © *1955 Apache Comics (Australia). Drawn by Guido Scala* Funny Comics *No.1* © *1942 Bell (Canada). Drawn by Manny Easson*

Fix und Foxi *No.23* © *Kauka Verlag (Germany). Drawn by Rolf Kaukas* Tom Puss *No.1* © *1983 Carlsen (Germany). Drawn by Marten Toonder* Cucurucho y Tios Rius *No.11* © *1975 Editorial Posada (Mexico). Drawn by Fernando Llera* Knockout *No.1* © *January 1974 Knockout (Canada). Drawn by Terry Fletcher*

INDEX